CANNIBALISM AND THE COMMON LAW

The family portrait in oils of Tom Dudley, painted by an unknown artist in New South Wales, possibly on Dudley's twentieth wedding anniversary in 1897. Original in the possession of a descendant, by whose permission it is reproduced.

Matching family portrait of Phillipa Dudley.

CANNIBALISM AND THE COMMON LAW

The Story of the Tragic Last Voyage of the *Mignonette* and the Strange Legal Proceedings to Which It Gave Rise

A.W. Brian Simpson

The University of Chicago Press
Chicago and London

A. W. BRIAN SIMPSON is professor of law at the University of Chicago and at the University of Kent, Canterbury. Among his many publications are *Introduction to the History of the Land Law* and *A History of the Common Law of Contract*. He is also an avid maritime buff and, as preparation for writing this book, signed on as a sailor on a square rigger.

The University of Chicago Press, Chicago 60637
The University of Chicago Press, Ltd., London

Printed in the United States of America

91 90 89 88 87 86 85 84 5 4 3 2

Library of Congress Cataloging in Publication Data

Simpson, A. W. B. (Alfred William Brian)
Cannibalism and the common law.

Bibliography: p.
Includes index.
1. Dudley, Tom. 2. Stephens, Edwin. 3. Mignonette (Boat) 4. Trials (Murder)—England—London. 5. Cannibalism. I. Title.
KD372.D83S57 1984 345.42'02523 83-5071
ISBN 0-226-75942-3 344.2052523

You Landsmen and you seamen bold,
Attention give to me
While I a tragedy unfold
Upon the briney sea.

—"Ballad of the *Sea Horse*"

Contents

Preface

Leading cases are the very stuff of which the common law is made, and no leading case in the common law is better known than that of *Regina v. Dudley and Stephens.* It was decided in 1884 by a court of the Queen's Bench Division, sitting in the lord chief justice's court in the Royal Courts of Justice in London. In it, two profoundly respectable seamen, Captain Tom Dudley and Mate Edwin Stephens, lately of the yacht *Mignonette,* were sentenced to death for the murder of their shipmate, Ordinary Seaman Richard Parker, after a bench of five judges had ruled that one must not kill one's shipmates in order to eat them, however hungry one might be. This ruling, as we shall see, may have satisfied some public need in Victorian times but at first sight seems curiously irrelevant to any problem likely to be encountered in contemporary Britain. Nevertheless, as a legal precedent on the law of homicide, it is still used not infrequently in the courts—while writing this book, I was in the courtroom where the case was decided when Lord Justice Lawton, presiding over the Court of Appeal, Criminal Division, cited *Regina v. Dudley and Stephens* as illustrating the proper role of strict law and royal mercy; the context was a case involving killing under extreme provocation. So the case remains very much alive, and this is true wherever the common law system exists.

"The Case of the *Mignonette*," as it was popularly called at the time, attracted worldwide interest in 1884, and lawyers and law students have been arguing about it ever since. Today, all over the common law world, the decision possesses a pre-eminent status as the case used to introduce students both to the peculiarities of legal reasoning and to the practical and ethical problems with which law is ultimately concerned. From a professional standpoint, it was and is a central authority on what is called "the defense of necessity," and the facts of the case raise in dramatic form the problem of reconciling the instinct for survival with a moral code that respects the sanctity of human life. If circumstances make it "necessary" for one person to kill another in order to survive, does the law permit such an act?

Although the legal and moral issues involved in the case have generated a very considerable legal literature, real understanding of the decision has hitherto been limited, for those who have commented on the case have known in the main only as much of the story of the *Mignonette* as is encapsulated in the law reports. Donald McCormick's *Blood on the Sea,* published in 1962, is the only book on the case, and was never included in the British Trials series; he made public a considerable amount of background information about the story and the individuals concerned but did not set out to relate the story (which he imaginatively elaborated) to legal and maritime history generally. The isolation of a leading case from its historical context may be acceptable for certain legal purposes, but an exploration of the strange world of survival cannibalism and its conflict with Victorian parlor morality and the common law will, I hope, make it clear that no real understanding of the story of the yacht *Mignonette* and the leading case to which its loss at sea gave rise is really possible without journeying well outside orthodox legal sources. Indirectly, perhaps, this study may also illuminate some wider issues of legal theory; but I have confined myself to telling the story of a great tragedy of the sea and of the strange legal proceedings to which it gave rise. The book is not at all concerned to consider the technical status of the legal defense of necessity, except insofar as this is essential to that story: such a matter is exhaustively considered in professional legal works. Since this study is not intended as a law book or designed primarily for professional scholars, I have not encumbered the pages with footnotes. But all statements in the text are based on historical sources (to which the bibliography is a guide). Except where clearly indicated, no events, conversations, or thoughts have been invented: of course there are matters of judgment involved in the use of the evidence.

A very large number of people and institutions have helped me most generously by answering my many inquiries: I hope I have not inadvertently missed anyone in the listed acknowledgments. The Nuffield Trust gave me special assistance with a research grant that enabled me to pursue my inquiries much more thoroughly than would have been possible otherwise. For the facilities afforded me, I am also greately indebted to the Social Sciences Faculty of the University of Kent and the Law School of the University of Chicago (where an interim account of the research was published as the William W. Crosskey Lecture in Legal History in February 1980). For work on typing the text, I am indebted to Liz Cable, Valerie Heap, Shirley Woodward, and in particular Joan Denning, who not only typed the first and very messy draft but criticized it in detail and dealt with not much fewer than 400 letters of inquiry. Finally, I am grateful to Captain Mike Kichenside and the owners, officers, and crew of the brigantine *Eye of the Wind,* who enabled me to secure some first-hand, if somewhat remote, experience of the world of the old sailing ships, now sadly almost lost. Any nautical errors in this text are certainly not their fault.

Acknowledgments

Transcripts of Crown copyright records in the Public Record Office appear by permission of the Controllers of Her Majesty's Stationery Office; references are given in the bibliographical notes.

I am grateful to the following persons and organizations for permission to quote material used in this book:

The British Library for the ballads "Richard Parker and the Ship Mignonette," "The Loss of the Betsey," "The Female Cabin Boy," and "The New York Trader," quoted on pages 253, 100, 292, and 106.

The Cornwall County Record Office for ballads concerning the *Brig George* (DDX 106/29) and the *Essex* (DDX 106/32) quoted on pages 117, 141, 313, and 316.

The Curators of the Bodleian Library for the ballad "The Terrible Tale of the Sea" (John Johnson Collection), quoted on page 254.

The Devon County Record Office (DRO 997Z/Z18) for the fragmentary ballad "A Ship in Dreadful Stormy Weather," quoted on page 100.

The Hon. Mrs. Crispin Gascoigne for material from the Harcourt MSS, quoted in chapter 9.

Mr. James N. Healy for the ballad "The Sorrowful Fate of O'Brien," reprinted on page 142, from *Ballads and Songs of the Sea,* edited by James N. Healy and published by the Mercies Press, Bridge Street, Cork, Ireland.

The incorporated Council of Law Reporting for England and Wales for the text of the special verdict and explanatory note reproduced as appendixes A and B.

The National Library of Ireland, for the ballad "The Sorrowful Loss of Life . . . On Board the Francis Spritt," reproduced in appendix C.

Material in chapter 7 first appeared in the author's article, "Regina v. Archer and Muller (1875): The Leading Case That Never Was," *Oxford Journal of Legal Studies* 2 (1982): 181–96.

1
Sergeant Laverty Makes an Arrest

As I wuz a-walkin' down Arwenack Street
Gimme way, hey, blow the man down,
A saucy policeman I happened to meet,
Gimme some time to blow the man down.

—Traditional Chanty

Although history has no beginning and, what is sometimes forgotten, no end, stories are different. That of the yacht *Mignonette* and her crew—Dudley, Stephens, Brooks, and Parker—originated in Falmouth on Saturday, September 6, 1884. For a drama of the sea there could be no more appropriate location. Today Falmouth has become a tourist town, with the sad and unattractive features that inevitably follow. In 1884 it was a real seaport, and most of its 11,000 inhabitants lived directly or indirectly off the sea. The town lies on the Western side of a magnificent natural harbor, rivaled only in England and Wales by the Milford Haven estuary in Pembrokeshire; and Falmouth Roads could be entered without difficulty by any ship afloat in the nineteenth century at virtually any state of tide or weather. The entrance is more than a mile wide, and the only obstacle is the prominent Black Rock in mid-channel. Sailors are capable of hitting anything, and it was there, by some monumental incompetence, that the *White Ship* carrying William, son of King Henry I, was wrecked in 1120, taking prince, courtiers, and treasure to the bottom, where presumably they all still lie. But as far as I know, no ship of any importance has hit it since, and as long as a ship avoids the Manacles

Reef to the west (and many have not), the approach to the anchorage is as fair as it could be.

Falmouth's rise from merely local to international importance began in the seventeenth century. In 1688 it became a packet boat port: from Falmouth small, fast, armed sailing vessels of around 200 tons' burden carried mails and passengers around the world. Packet boats operated under government contract, and the selection of Falmouth depended on its other principal asset, a location at the entrance to the English Channel. As a starting point this was ideal, for in the days of sail the passage through the channel from the east was uncertain and hazardous, as the prevailing winds are westerly. In 1863 Brunel's Great Western Railway was linked to Falmouth, reducing the time required to travel to London; but by then, as an ocean passenger terminus, it was in decline. The post office contracts had been lost in 1852, and Southampton had begun to develop as an ocean terminus. But because it lay further to the west, Falmouth nevertheless continued to prosper, and no similar safe anchorage for Atlantic vessels exists on the north coast of France. So Falmouth, like Cork in Ireland, functioned as a port of call for foreign-going trading vessels, the first and last link with the newly developed international telegraph system; and Atlantic ships were repaired and provisioned there. In the late nineteenth century, some 20 or more ocean vessels called there each week for orders from cargo agents or owners; and, after bad weather in the Atlantic, the anchorage would be crowded with vessels sheltering or seeking repair. Even after the dominance of the great sailing barques had ended, Falmouth long retained its importance. So the inhabitants of the town knew more or less all there was to know of the perils of the sea and the customs of those who had their business in the deep waters.

On Friday, September 5, 1884, somewhere well to the west of the Lizard, a Falmouth resident named Gustavus Lowry Collins was cruising in Pilot Boat 13, seeking work. He was a first-class Trinity House pilot, and it was the practice for Falmouth pilots to meet vessels entering the channel well out at sea, sometimes as far west as the Scillies. At some point on that day, Collins hailed a German sailing barque, the *Moctezuma,* which hove to and took him on board. The *Moctezuma,* under the command of Captain P. H. Simonsen, was bound for Hamburg. Normally she would not have entered an English port but needed to do so because she had on board three English sailors who, as castaways, had been rescued 38 days earlier in the South Atlantic. Pilotage was compulsory—and Pilot Collins was therefore engaged to advise the captain as he brought the *Moctezuma* in and boarded her as she lay hove to. After the yards had been squared away and the *Moctezuma* was again sailing up channel, Captain Simonsen invited the pilot into his cabin, no doubt for the traditional drink. One of the castaways followed them in. He was a very short man with reddish hair and beard, and he spoke with a broad Essex accent. He introduced himself as Tom Dudley, former captain of the British-registered yacht *Mignonette* (which he probably pronounced "Mighenette" with a hard "g"). He started to tell how she had been lost in a storm on a voyage to Sydney, New South Wales, and of the terrible sufferings of the survivors, adrift for 24 days in an open boat. Collins inquired how many had survived. "I asked him how many there were in the boat. He said 'four.' I asked him what had become of the other one. He had previously told me three had been picked up." Some vague suspicion may well have prompted this inquiry, for a Falmouth pilot would know of the expedients traditionally used to prolong life in such circumstances. Tom Dudley was quite willing to explain. The fourth man, he explained without embarrassment, had been killed and eaten. Telling the story in court, later Collins was to say, "I asked Dudley who killed him. He said, 'I did.' " As if this candor were not sufficient, Tom Dudley also described the killing in some detail. It must have been obvious that Captain Simonsen already knew what had happened. The pilot's reaction to all this is not recorded; for reasons that will appear, he may not have been particularly surprised, and whatever other conversation took place is not recorded. He did not speak to the other two survivors; not possessing Dudley's status as a ship's master, they would not, of course, have entered the captain's cabin but have remained forward, in the accommodation appropriate to men of subordinate rank.

On the morning of Saturday, September 6, the *Moctezuma* entered Carrick Roads; there was a strong southwesterly wind blowing. The *Moctezuma* probably rounded up and anchored on Falmouth Bank off Trefusis Point, lying about a mile away from the town. It was not the normal practice, when a vessel called at Falmouth, for the crew to be allowed ashore to encounter the temptations of drunkenness, brawling, desertion, and the risk of venereal disease. Ships were a sort of prison; local services were brought to them by watermen in bumboats. Through them, or perhaps through the pilot (whose home at 10 Norfolk Road lay a short distance from the center of the town), the story of the *Mignonette* and her three cannibals circulated rapidly through Falmouth. William Hodges, a licensed waterman, brought them and Captain Simonsen ashore, and quite a crowd gathered to see them. The crowd included a seven-year-old boy, Alfred Rose, who watched them land at Barracks Opie Quay. Some 87 years later in 1971, at the age of 94, he was interviewed by a journalist, Patrick Marnham, and recalled the occasion; by then he must have been the last man alive who saw the three men land.

The other two castaways were Edwin Stephens, who had been mate of the *Mignonette,* and Edmund Brooks—usually known as "Ned" or "Neddy." The three landed early in the morning, and went at first to the Sailors' Home. All were weak and could walk only with difficulty. At the Home, which was looked after by a Captain José, they received refreshments and might have expected, if necessary, to be accommodated. Their arrival had been witnessed by the customs office, and a customs officer had a word with them. There was at the time a cholera scare, about which the mayor of Falmouth was particularly concerned, and thus considerable vigilance surrounded the arrival of a foreign vessel that might be carrying the disease. They were also observed by James Laverty, a sergeant of the Falmouth Harbour Police Force; this was a force quite distinct from the borough police force, or the local branch of the county police, under Inspector George Pappin. Captain Simonsen may well have visited the shipping agents in Arwenack Street, Messrs G. C. Fox, as Robert Fox of the well-known Quaker family was the German vice-consul at the port. Captain Dudley, like a good captain, set about the care of his crew, drawing money from a bank so that they could inform their families by telegram of their safe arrival. At 9:00 A.M. he himself telegraphed his wife, Phillipa, at their home in 1 Myrtle Road, Sutton, in Surrey: "Mignonette foundered, July 5th; 1200 miles from the Cape. In boat twenty-four days; suffering fearful. Am well now." At about 11:00 A.M. all three men, together with Captain Simonsen, went to the customs house. There in the Long Room they met a prosperous local pluralist, Robert Gandy Cheesman, shipping master, superintendent of the Mercantile Marine Office, collector of customs for the West Cornwall District, and receiver of wrecks. To judge from his large and somewhat flamboyant house, he did rather well out of these various offices. Indeed, one cannot but derive the impression that Robert Cheesman may have been a man who, though punctilious as to forms and procedures, had an eye to the main chance and a tolerant approach to the traditional Cornish practice of smuggling. Among the surviving correspondence (which deals with such bizarre administrative matters as the supply of tins of diarrhea powder to outdoor staff), there is his letter of July, optimistically if implausibly reporting all quiet on the smuggling front: "I beg to report no runs have been effected or attempted . . . I am not aware of any organisation existing in the locality for carrying out an illicit trade." But, if he and his men may not always have been overenthusiastic at rummaging (to use the technical term), they knew the correct procedures. And so, when Dudley said to him, "We are come to make our statements with reference to the loss of our vessel, the *Mignonette*. . . ," the appropriate forms were at hand. The collector was too important to handle this directly himself and passed them to Samuel John Louttit Tresidder, his chief clerk, who set about taking their depositions.

In thus volunteering to give an account of the loss of the *Mignonette*, the three men were merely conforming to the scheme for regulating merchant shipping governed by the Merchant Shipping Act of 1854 and an amending act of 1876. As shipping master Mr. Cheesman was empowered to "make inquiry respecting such loss, abandonment, damage, or casualty." He possessed the powers conferred by the act upon specially appointed inspectors employed by the Board of Trade (the responsible government ministry) to supervise merchant shipping—he could summon people before him, require the production of documents, administer oaths, or require formal declarations as to the truth of what he was told. So if they had not come voluntarily, the sailors could have been and no doubt would have been compelled to appear.

These obligatory statements reporting losses at sea were not intended to provide material for the criminal prosecution of sailors; indeed, given the general principle accepted in English criminal procedure—that no one must be made to incriminate himself—such an idea would have been regarded as quite improper when the system was established. Their primary function was to advance the policy of increasing safety at sea. This task was entrusted to the Board of Trade and exercised through its Marine Department, first established in 1850, which had to collect basic information about maritime casualties—the name of the ship, what cargo it carried, where it was lost, and so forth. Incidentally, other administrative needs were also served by the system, including the recording of deaths at sea. A standard form was used to record all the information obtained; after signature, these forms were dispatched to the Board of Trade in London, which could, at its discretion, decide to hold a formal wreck inquiry into the casualty. Official inquiries into wrecks had been recommended by a select committee of the House of Commons back in 1836. This recommendation was first implemented for steamships by legislation in 1846 and later extended to sailing vessels in 1850. An inquiry could lead to the loss of a master's or mate's certificate of competence, but this penal element was regretted by the Board of Trade. Formal wreck inquiries were not held as a matter of course. Most losses at sea were not formally investigated at all; and where there were no passengers lost, it was the usual practice not to hold such an investigation. Cargo owners and seamen were expected to look after themselves; but passengers, it was thought, required paternalistic care. The *Mignonette* carried neither passengers nor cargo, and the loss of so small a vessel with so little loss of life among the crew was in itself a trivial incident, certainly not worth formal investigation.

Dudley's and Stephens's depositions survive in the original. Dudley records details of the yacht; her crew of four; including the boy, Richard Parker; and her voyage. He attributes her loss laconically in the space provided to "stress of weather"; this was and still is a standard category, like "pilot error" in air crashes. He also states candidly that, after the vessel foundered, "on the twentieth day the lad Richard Parker was very weak through drinking salt water. Deponent, with the assistance of the Mate Stephens, killed him to sustain the existence of those remaining, they being all agreed the act was absolutely necessary. . . ." Dudley continues to explain that all three survivors lived thereafter off Richard Parker's dead body. Stephens's deposition was equally to the point: "On the twentieth day, Deponent agreed with the Master that it was absolutely necessary that one should be sacrificed to save the rest, and the Master selected Richard Parker boy as being the weakest. Deponent agreed to this and the Master accordingly killed the lad. . . ." Richard Parker's death certificate, based on these statements, records the cause of death as simply "killed." Behind these two depositions must lie a definite decision by Dudley and Stephens to tell the full truth. Some months later, Dudley's wife, in a letter that survives in the Public Record Office, recorded that her husband told his story "not paliating [*sic*] a *single circumstance* tho' entreated never to divulge it [italics in original]." The delay in going to the customs house may have been the result of these entreaties—last-minute arguments as to the wisdom of such candor. But there is no direct evidence of this, nor is it possible to tell whether one or both of Dudley's companions wished the matter concealed. By the time they landed, the gossip in Falmouth may have persuaded Stephens and Brooks of the futility of any concealment, for once the pilot knew the story, all Falmouth would learn of it within a matter of hours.

Ned Brooks also made a sworn statement, though somewhat later. When he did so, neither Dudley nor Stephens was in the Long Room. His deposition appears to exist no longer, and it is consequently impossible to be sure of its contents; there is no satisfactory indirect evidence from newspapers or other sources. The principal file on the case—that of the treasury solicitor—has been lost, probably through bombing in World War II. Brooks's deposition would surely have been in the file.

While Dudley and Stephens were making their depositions, the vigilant Sergeant Laverty was hovering about in the customs house. He had seen all three men earlier and had spoken to Brooks, who gave him their names. Probably he had already heard gossip about the killing of young Richard Parker and, like a conscientious officer, was keeping his eyes and ears open. After Dudley made his statement, there was some conversation between Mr. Cheesman and Dudley—Cheesman was apparently present all the time the deposition was being taken, out of curiosity only and not (as he was to insist later) in any of his three official capacities. He asked Dudley to elaborate: "How did you kill the boy?" Dudley then gave him a long account of the events leading up to the killing, and this culminated in an animated description of how the job was done. He demonstrated how the boy was lying in the bottom of the boat, and how he thrust a penknife into Parker's throat. He even produced the knife itself, with its two-inch-long blade. This was all too much for Sergeant Laverty, who with studied courtesy asked Dudley "to be kind enough to give it to me." Dudley did so and then made an unfortunate remark. He said he did not want to lose it, as he would want it as a keepsake; he apparently wanted to preserve a memento of a remarkable experience. The sergeant assured him that he could have the knife again "on some future occasion" and then left the customs house for the town clerk's office, with the intention of securing a warrant for the arrest of the three men.

After Laverty left, Dudley produced a considerably longer and fuller handwritten account of the whole affair and gave this to Mr. Cheesman for transmission to the Board of Trade. This document, entitled "Account of foundering Migenette 33 tons" also survives and describes the killing of Parker. It ends, "I think I have given most of the particulars of the sad affair. I remain yours faithfully Thos Dudley Master Late 'Migenette.' " Dudley had written this account while on board the *Moctezuma,* probably intending it as a letter of explanation to the yacht's owner, to whom he would expect to report on the loss of the vessel.

Later Mr. Cheesman tried hard to give the impression that he had at no point supposed himself to be involved in any possible criminal investigation or proceedings. But these protestations were disingenuous and for local consumption only. In truth, he had realized at once that the business could not be simply regarded as completed once the statements were signed and the three men allowed to go home, much less allowed to leave on *his* authority. He must have known that, where there appeared to have been a death by violence, under Section 269 of the Merchant Shipping Act he had a legal obligation to report to the Board of Trade and take steps to bring those involved to justice. But the sailors certainly did expect to be allowed to leave for home, and at 12:00 M. Dudley telegraphed his wife: "Am here, and as well as can be expected; hope to be enabled to finish work and leave for home tonight." Mr. Cheesman was also using the telegraph service and (as was his invariable practice), cautiously seeking instructions from London. At 2:50 P.M., possibly after some behind-the-scenes discussion with Sergeant Laverty, he cabled both the Marine Department of the Board of Trade and the registrar general of shipping in Basinghall Street in London:

> Survivors wreck of Yacht *Mignonette* of Southampton brought here by German Barque *Moctezuma* after having been in open boat for twenty four days with only two one-pound tins of turnips no water Richard Parker boy killed on twentieth day by Thomas Dudley who holds mates certificate to sustain survivors lives boy was killed twenty fifth July . . . should the survivors be detained for enquiries please telegraph if I must apply to police.

To this the registrar general replied at 3:15 P.M. that the survivors should be detained, but he added, "You will no doubt receive instructions from the Board of Trade." The Board of Trade officials had at first considered informing the police but then changed their minds and telegraphed that no action should be taken; a letter was, however, at once dispatched by messenger to the Home Office. This passed the situation to that institution, as the office of state concerned with matters of law and order.

Down at Falmouth, Mr. Cheesman became increasingly anxious, for by 3:20 P.M. he had heard nothing from the Board of Trade. He telegraphed again for instructions. "Please reply to my telegram respecting Mignonette as soon as possible as the master and crew are anxious to leave Falmouth." Shortly afterward, the unhappy man received wholly inconsistent instructions—from Basinghall Street to detain the men, from the Board of Trade to take no action. From the Home Office, virtually closed for the weekend, nothing was forthcoming.

Meanwhile the good sergeant had obviously also run into local difficulty in obtaining his warrants; the discussions must also have involved one Superintendent Bourne, the officer commanding Falmouth's own borough police force of three constables. The task had already consumed some four hours—a delay not explicable by the short distances involved; clearly, there was no great enthusiasm for issuing the warrants. Eventually, however, they were issued on the signature of the mayor of Falmouth, Mr. Henry Liddicoat. Henry Liddicoat was also *ex officio* chairman of the borough justices of the peace and ran a grocery and wine merchant's business conveniently close to the customs house at 4 Market Strand. What went on behind the scenes among the mayor, the superintendent of police, and the shipping master we shall never know. But some hint of the arguments involved is probably to be found in a leader in one of the local papers, *Lake's Falmouth Packet and Cornwall Advertiser,* on September 13. The writer would almost certainly have talked to the mayor about the matter:

> Were the local authorities justified in causing Dudley, Stephens and Brooks to be apprehended? We consider they were. Some people have even gone so far as to take exception to this, the almost universal opinion. But they have no ground to stand on. Here are three men who arrive at Falmouth with an open confession of having killed a fellow human being. This story was therefore certain to obtain a wide publicity, and when the nation became aware that these men with such a terrible tale of the shedding of human blood, were at large in the country, without a searching investigation having been made with their case, a universal cry of condemnation would assuredly have gone forth against the Mayor of Falmouth for allowing them to escape.

Such, by 1884, was already the power of the press. So it was that late in the afternoon the three men were arrested, and Tom Dudley was allowed to send yet another telegram to his wife, his last for the day: "Shall not be able to come home tonight until things are settled here." The three men were then lodged together in a room in the police station at 33 Market Street.

All three were quite astonished at being arrested, Tom Dudley in particular. There is no reason to doubt that this astonishment was entirely genuine. Sergeant Laverty was later to say in court, "When I arrested him Captain Dudley seemed greatly surprised that he was to be made a prisoner" and added that "he seemed to show a great deal of excitement." Today, of course, anyone in the same position would be equally astonished *not* to be arrested; furthermore, today there would surely be no hesitation whatsoever in arresting men who confessed to such a killing. Most surprising of all is the frank way in which Dudley and Stephens both volunteered what had happened—what precisely Brooks admitted is, as we have seen, not known. Dudley indeed went beyond mere frankness; he seems to have shown a positive enthusiasm for revealing all, adding to his statutory deposition a quite unnecessarily long letter to the Board of Trade, reinforced by a reenactment of the killing in the very presence of an officer of the law. He even wanted to preserve a memento of the occasion. An account of the matter published in the *Spectator* a week later emphasized particularly the strange features of Dudley's behavior:

> He did not, be it understood, make a "confession" as one who has committed a crime and was full of remorse, but simply narrated, with the straightforward truthfulness with which a sailor usually describes any noteworthy incident of a voyage. He had, apparently, no idea whatsoever that he was liable to any legal proceedings, and when arrested expressed nothing but astonishment. . . .

Later, in November, a leader in the *Standard* made the same point:

> The most remarkable feature, in some respects, of the whole case is the extraordinary candour of the three men when they were landed in an English port. Without, apparently, the slightest misgivings as to the manner in which their tale would be received, or the faintest sense of having done anything the law could punish, they told their story, in all its revolting detail, to the Collector of Customs at Falmouth, and afterwards embodied it in statutory declarations.

Clearly some fundamental barrier of incomprehension existed between the captain and crew of the *Mignonette,* men of the sea; and Sergeant James Laverty, the local representative of the common law of England. On land, at least, honesty did not appear to be the best policy.

2
The *Mignonette* Goes Foreign

"Good morning Shipping Master." "Good morning Jack" says he,
Haul away me bully boys
We've all got to go.
And have you got a fine ship for to carry me over the sea?
Fare thee well me bully boys
We've all got to go.

—Traditional Chanty

The *Mignonette*'s only ocean voyage began on Monday, May 5, when the yacht put out to sea from the village of Tollesbury in Essex. Situated at the head of a maze of creeks between the estuaries of the Colne and Blackwater Rivers, this village, previously dependent on agriculture and oyster dredging, came to be a nationally known yachting center in the late nineteenth century. Tom Dudley himself was a yachtsman, as his father was, and so too were Ned Brooks and young Richard Parker. The tragedy of the *Mignonette* was therefore essentially a yachting tragedy and was so conceived at the time; to locate its background we must therefore move back into the strange lost world of Victorian yachting.

A yacht is primarily any vessel built or used for recreational purposes, in contrast to one employed commercially to carry cargo or passengers; in England, yachts in this sense originated in the seventeenth century. There is, however, another and older conception of a yacht as a vessel of state, serving not simply to provide pleasure but to display high status through ostentatious and ritualized expression of wealth and grandeur. As such, yachts must be large, expensive, and in one sense useless; their economic function is not to be an asset but a liability. Some yachts of state still exist, but with the decline of royalty and the rise of envy, there are few left. But even today many private yachts do not serve a simple recreational function as racing or cruising vessels; they are also symbols of the owner's wealth, courage, or success. The egalitarian cant adopted by contemporary apologists of yachting tends today to play down this function of yacht ownership, just as it encourages an emphasis on the widespread ownership of relatively inexpensive sailing dinghies. In the nineteenth century, less apologetic attitudes toward prosperity existed, and in Victorian and Edwardian times yachting was conspicuously and without embarrassment associated with flamboyant displays of personal wealth.

Yachting had also become associated with another mechanism for marking differences in social prestige—membership in an exclusive club—it being the function of such clubs to heighten the pleasures of membership to the few by denying it to the many. The earliest yacht club in Britain was founded in 1720, the Cork Water Club. It became the Royal Cork Yacht Club and began as an exclusive dining club associated with an organization of yacht owners. This operated under an "admiral" and conducted mock war games and flotilla cruises. Races for wagers must have always been conducted in response to private challenges, but it was considerably later that the formal organization of such races came to be viewed as a principal function of a yacht club. Even in the late nineteenth century, individual clubs did not organize races at all frequently; one race meeting a year seems to have been not unusual. The timing of such regattas enabled racing enthusiasts to move from regatta to regatta around the coast. Cowes's week in August, traceable back to a race organized by the Royal Yacht Club in 1826, soon became the principal annual function and by the late nineteenth century had developed into an orgy of vulgar self-advertisement.

By 1884 there existed some 58 British yacht clubs, and similar clubs exited elsewhere in British dominions—for example, in Gibraltar (founded 1829) and Sydney (The Royal Sydney Yacht Squadron, founded in 1862). Some few English yacht clubs date back to the late eighteenth century; the Cumberland Fleet, direct ancestor of the Royal Thames, was founded in 1775. But it was in the nineteenth century, with the increase in middle-class wealth, that yacht clubs increased dramatically in number. The association between royalty and yachting, fostered by Queen Victoria and Prince Albert (and continued in this century, particularly by George V) reinforced the social prestige of the sport. To belong to the Royal Yacht Squadron was to have arrived indeed; however, lesser mortals could still be very proud of membership in less exalted clubs and could hold membership status in many clubs. With the rise in the popularity of yachting among the relatively wealthy, there developed a literature of yachting—periodicals such as the *Field* and *Hunt's Yachting Magazine,* started in 1852, recorded the exploits of the racing yachts, albeit with boring repetitiousness. The scale of the sport is indicated by the fact that the 1884 edition of *Hunt's Yacht List* enumerates some 3,219 sailing yachts and, if one includes steam yachts, more than 4,000 vessels in total. These were not small sailing dinghies but very substantial craft. Included, for example, were 395 schooners, some rated at well over 100 tons under the system known as "Thames measurement." Also included were many smaller yachts, but no racing dinghies; they had yet to be invented. Yachts, in 1884, were *real* yachts.

The building, fitting out, provisioning, sailing, and maintaining of this large fleet provided considerable employment, much of it seasonal in character. Some owners skippered their own vessels and either sailed them alone or with amateur help; they were called "Corinthians," and a special club was founded to cater to such owner skippers. But many yachts were sailed by professional crews with professional captains. They were hired annually for the season between March and September when yachts were kept in commission, spending the rest of the year in other employment—often as fishermen or on home trade vessels. In comparison with the tough and precarious life of the merchant sailor, even in the summer months, that of a yachtsman was comfortable, more secure, and, by the standards of the times, reasonably well remunerated. A captain (or "sailing master," as he was called) on an undistinguished yacht would receive significantly more than a seaman; William Cooper, who as "Vanderdecken" wrote the standard yachting textbooks of the period, suggested that in 1873 a top-grade sailing master might be paid £100–£150 for a season and be retained for the whole year. Comparison with rates of pay in ocean-going sailing vessels is difficult, since there existed very considerable variations between different ports and different voyages, but the comparable average monthly rate for first mates on all sailing vessels was only £5.8s., and the seamen's weekly rates for all coasting vessels were £1.19s.7d. to £1.6s.4d. Higher pay may not have been the main attraction; regularity of employment and the fact that yachting, in contrast to work on commercial vessels, was positively enjoyable, may have been the principal factors. In the main yachts did not go to sea in bad conditions; the huge over-canvased yachts of the period were essentially adapted to provide exciting sailing in light winds. Conditions were therefore good, in comparision with those suffered by fishermen and deep-sea sailors, and free clothing and other perquisites also came the way of the crew from a generous owner. Relatively few yachts were regularly raced, and they formed an aristocracy. They moved from regatta to regatta, starting the season in May at Harwich and ending the season at Dartmouth. To become a captain or crew member of a successful racing yacht was highly prestigious and could also be very profitable, for prize money appears to have been shared at least in part by the crew; very considerable sums of prize money were available—in the 1869 season, for example, £6,723 in all was distributed.

Yachtsmen, particularly sailing masters, were a special type of gentleman's gentleman, with whom there existed the typical master-servant relationship. In part this involved an easy familiarity and almost friendship: in part the professionals were treated as if they did not exist. Thus in the pages of *Hunt's Yachting Magazine* or the *Field* they are hardly mentioned, except in occasional pieces, such as one in 1883 on their management, in which the author proceeds ungenerously from this principle: "The natural tendency of all persons who are paid for their services, at so much per week, month or year, is to save themselves all the trouble they can." Numerous contemporary accounts caution the yacht owner against the risk of slovenly or even fraudulent conduct by unreliable yacht hands. One survivor from this lost world, Budge Frost of Tollesbury, has redressed the balance by telling me that in his experience all his yachting employers appeared to be more or less insane.

In addition to crews, large numbers of shipwrights, riggers, sail makers, and chandlers lived off yachting; and much effort and ingenuity went into serving the needs of their patrons. Goy of London, operating from 2 Praed Street, provided appropriate clothing for the crews, hierarchically graded. Captain's suits cost from 84s. to 100s., mate's from 68s. to 90s., while trousers and guernseys for hands could be had for as little as 20s. a set. Embroidering the yacht's name on the guernsey cost 1s.6d. extra. John Redfern & Sons of Cowes provided bed linen, appropriately graded into three categories—for owner's berths, for captain's and steward's, and for "forecastle hands." The latter did not receive sheets but slept under Witney blankets and were prudently supplied with Strong Towels. The Yachtsman's Brand of Very Old Scotch Whisky could be delivered on board at 44s. per dozen bottles, and Balkwill and Elliot of Plymouth provided the finest soda water to go with it at 2s. per dozen bottles. Cool drinks could be secured by purchasing Ash's Patent Piston Freezing Machine and Hand Wine Cooler for £4, and community singing could be organized on the larger yachts with the aid of Chappell's New Yacht Pianos, at prices ranging from 15 to 250 guineas. Less agreeable aspects of life afloat could be combated with Schweitzer's Anti-dyspeptic Cocatina and an extraordinary precursor of the modern blue-flush toilet, marketed by the London Patent Automatic Disinfection Company. This, it was claimed, "effectively neutralises and destroys all foul gases," particularly if charged with the celebrated Perfumed Anti-zymotic Crystals. The extravagant air of this enviable world is peculiarly well caught by a letter sent in 1885 to *Hunt's Yachting Magazine* by "Enquirer." He wondered if his costs for a 20-week season were about right. Modestly he explained that he did not run a *large* yacht: merely a "snug little yawl" of 80 tons. On it he employed a crew of nine—captain, mate, five seamen, a steward, and a cook; the bill for the season came to just under £1,000, and this was apparently quite reasonable; a normal figure was about £12 a ton. In 1885, £1,000 was not a small sum of money.

The *Mignonette* herself had been built in 1867 at Brightlingsea in Essex; she was launched on August 12 and would have cost between £770 and £930. Her builder was either Robert, Albert, or Edwin Aldhous, probably Edwin, though Robert is named on her registration certificate. There were a number of members of this family engaged in boat building, the business having been started by one James Aldhous back in the 1830s. The 1882 edition of *Kelly's Directory* lists a partnership of Aldhous and Rushbrook in business on Waterside as ship builders (this would be Edwin); Albert Aldhous as a yacht, gig, and boat builder; and Robert simply as a builder. The three brothers probably worked as an informal partnership. Later accounts tend to refer simply to "Aldhous" yachts, some of which may still exist from this period—*Dusmarie,* an 1884 yawl (originally *Daisy*), still does but has been very extensively rebuilt in modern times. Aldhous yachts were well known in the racing world, and the great craft tradition associated with the family came to be dispersed only when the yard, run from 1914 as a limited company, closed in 1962.

However, *Mignonette* was not primarily built for racing but, rather, as a cruiser and fishing boat; by the late 1860s the Aldhous family had largely moved out of the precarious business of building racing boats. She was registered at London (No. 56845) on September 16, 1867, as 52 feet in length; 12 4/10 feet in beam; and 7 feet, 5 inches deep. Her net tonnage (an artificial assessment of usable space) was 19.43 tons, and tonnage by Thames measurement was 31, though Tom Dudley always seems to have thought her tonnage was 33.

In spite of fairly exhaustive searches, I have been unable to locate a photograph of her or of *Peregrine,* a very similar but slightly smaller yacht built by one of the Aldhous family in 1873. Three drawings of the *Mignonette*—two by Dudley and one based on drawings by Stephens—do, however, survive; I also possess a very indistinct photograph of a half-model of her hull. Dudley's drawings were made while he was on the *Moctezuma* and survive in the Public Records; Stephens's were used by the artist employed by the *Illustrated London News,* which covered the story. The model of the hull has a curious history. An article published in 1922 by "G.E.C." in the *Mariner's Mirror* records that the Buckingham Arms Hotel in Great Missenden possessed a model of the *Mignonette*'s dinghy, made for the trial of the men, and its brass crutches (i.e., oarlocks), on which the corpse of Richard Parker had, it was said, been dismembered. This hotel is now a bank; however, a photograph of the lounge has been traced, and enlargement of a portion of this clearly shows a model not of the dinghy but of the *Mignonette* herself. Mr. E. H. Payne, who once worked in the hotel, recalls the grim detail that the crutches were indeed deeply scored, as by a knife. The model may have been a builder's model or, more probably, an incompleted model made on the *Moctezuma.* The licensee of the hotel in 1922 was Amy Marshall Brown, then married to a London accountant; her maiden name was Harrison, and she had formerly been a Mrs. White. How these relics came into her possession is obscure, but "G.E.C." recorded in the *Mariner's Mirror* in 1922 that her father had been a sea captain who befriended Dudley; local tradition claims that her father was Captain William Harrison of the *Great Eastern.* The date of his death makes this impossible; more probably the father or relative was Henry John Newman Harrison (born in Reigate in 1849); a master mariner, he had commanded union line ships, including the *Anglian* and *Asiatic,* on which Stephens had served, and the link may have been through him and not Dudley. The contents of the hotel were dispersed in a sale in 1927, and the relics that I have attempted to trace appear now to be lost.

From these and from a description by one of her owners, it is possible to form a reasonably clear picture of the *Mignonette*. She was originally rigged as a yawl, carrying, in addition to her mainmast, a very small mizzenmast set right aft almost on the taffrail. This technically made her a yawl, but she was essentially a cutter. She carried a very large spread of canvas, and with her topmast set up, her rig rose some 60 feet above her deck. At the very top flew her flag, divided vertically into white and red, with white nearer the mast. She was very strongly constructed, with timbers typical of a 40-tonner; Aldhous yachts had a reputation for heavy construction. In addition to 16 tons of internal lead ballast, she carried two or three tons externally on the keel. In consequence she was a very stiff boat—that is, one with a high initial resistance to heeling—and fast. Her lines were modeled on those of a particularly fast smack, the *Fashion,* and she was the typical size of an Essex fishing smack. Her sails were by Lapthorn, the well-known sail makers; they had been made in 1879. She carried a small and very light dinghy (or "punt," as it was then called). It was clinker built of quarter-inch mahogany, 13 feet long, four feet in beam, and a mere 20 inches in depth; I possess a photograph of it. It was built in 1880 by Albert Aldhous. An account published in Sydney in 1884 claimed that after her original construction she had been modified, an original square transom stern being converted into an elliptical counter stern, built up on her original structure. This is compatible with the evidence that *Mignonette* was modeled on a fishing smack and indeed used for fishing by her original owner. Her original registration particulars describe her stern as "square," while Dudley's 1884 drawings show her with a counter stern.

The *Mignonette* had originally been built for Phillip Patmore of Cricksea in Essex, but he sold her on November 1, 1870, and purchased in her place a rather smaller cutter, *Willow Wren,* 48 feet long and rated at 30 tons; she was very much older, having been built in 1813, and he continued to sail her as a Corinthian with a crew of three for many years, certainly as late as 1887. *Mignonette*'s new owner was Thomas Hall, a gentleman of private means and a lawyer of 6 Barnard's Inn; and he was probably responsible for altering her appearance to correspond to contemporary fashions in racing vessels. He belonged to various clubs—the Royal Albert, the New Thames, The Junior Thames, and the Royal Welsh. In his ownership, *Mignonette* had a professional skipper, one Captain Thomas Coppin of Brightlingsea, and a crew of three. She raced most years in the annual ocean race of the New Thames Club, but with limited success. On June 16, 1875, she came third in 6 hours, 53 minutes; next year, on June 6, she came last, so far behind as not to be timed. In 1879 she did not race at all, but in 1879 on June 30 she was third on handicap in spite of carrying away her bobstay. She won in 1881 and again in 1882 on a protest, having been fouled by *Bella Donna* on the Shoeburyness sands. This seems to have been the extent of her racing career, but it explains her reputation as a potentially fast yacht.

In the early part of 1883 there arrived in England a prominent Australian lawyer and politician, John Henry Want (1846–1905); he came from Sydney, his father Randolf John Want having emigrated in 1837 to establish a legal practice there. Randolf Want had been a successful lawyer and a founder member of the Royal Sydney Yacht Squadron, formed in 1862. His son's legal career had been even more successful and appropriately remunerative: he combined legal and political activities with various commercial ventures, some of a slightly suspicious character. Normally known as "Jack" or "Jimmy," John Want was a flamboyant and ostentatious sporting man, "over six foot in height, with a rugged jaw and flashing eyes." It was said that "to hear him bully a witness into prevarication, self contradiction and confusion, one would scarcely recognise the courteous, jovial fellow whose four in hand is always conspicuous at the race-course." He was a keen yachtsman, belonging both to the squadron and to the Royal Prince Albert Yacht Club, of which he was commodore from 1877 to 1881, and again in 1884. He owned a yacht called *Guinevere,* rated at 10 tons and built in Sydney in 1874; she was regarded as a somewhat spartan vessel, lacking pantry or toilet. According to his own account, Want came to England early in 1883 with a view to purchasing a fast 40-ton yacht to take back to Sydney with him but had difficulty in finding a suitable vessel for sale. Andrew Thompson, of the London Yacht Agency, suggested that he should hire a yacht in England and visit regattas around the coast in the hope of locating a yacht that would suit, and this was how he came to hire the 42-ton *Terpsichore,* which Thompson owned at the time. Want's story is not, however, convincing—he could indeed have purchased *Terpsichore,* which was a fast yacht and for sale, and at the time there were many suitable yachts for sale. The truth appears to have been that Want wished to locate a cheap yacht (he would have considerable expense in moving any vessel out to Sydney), and this was presumably what attracted him to the ageing *Mignonette,* which he saw and purchased at Cowes. The price for a yacht of her age would be around £300 to £400. The date of sale cannot be precisely established, since the transfer of ownership was not reported to the registrar general of shipping. I imagine this would have been done eventually, probably with a change in the port of registration to Sydney.

Jack Want's visit to England was not entirely a success. In *Terpsichore* he entered a number of races, gaining first prizes at Ostend and Ryde and a third at Southampton. At Torbay regatta on August 28 and 29 he beat *Beluga,* and the report in the *Field* raised the delicate question of the propriety of entering races in hired yachts, a practice at the time regarded as quite taboo. An acrimonious correspondence ensued, in which Jack Want legalistically relied on the "precedent" set by the entry of the well-known yacht *Norman* in regattas when on hire. *Norman*'s owner, N. N. Ewing, indignantly denied the truth of this, and in a letter in October from Bridles Manor more or less implied that Want had not just behaved in an ungentlemanly manner but was simply lying. The *Field* also adopted a hostile tone and even refused to publish one of his letters, which drew a subtle distinction between "let" and "lent" yachts; the correspondence then continued its unpleasant course in *Land and Water,* which, under the influence of Andrew Thompson, was more sympathetic. But the unfortunate Jack Want acquired little kudos from his yachting holiday in England.

He arranged for *Mignonette* to be sailed out in the spring of 1884: she was too large to ship as deck cargo. The delay meant that she spent another winter on a mud berth at Brightlingsea, steadily deteriorating. Want apparently planned to build a new yacht in Sydney—eventually the 43-ton *Miranda* was built in 1887. There may have been an element of prestige in acquiring an English yacht instead of a local product that induced Jack Want to sail out an elderly English vessel to the colony.

In November Tom Dudley heard of the sale of the *Mignonette,* probably through Andrew Thompson of the London Yacht Agency, who had arranged the sale; he successfully applied for the job of sailing her out.

Tom Riley Dudley, to give him his baptismal names (he sometimes signed as Thomas), was born on April 24, 1853, at Tollesbury, the son of George Dudley by his first wife Susannah (Carter). His second name was presumably taken from the Riley family, of whom the 1871 census records two households in Tollesbury: that of Daniel Riley, his wife, Charlotte, and their children; and that of John and Mary Riley. Daniel and Charlotte were probably Tom's aunt and uncle; both Rileys were mariners and oyster dredgers. George Dudley (b. 1822 or 1823) was employed in 1853 in the preventive service of the customs and excise, his job being thankless combating of smuggling, a popular pastime on the Essex coast. He came from Bradwell and had moved to Tollesbury between 1851 and 1853, there then being a coast guard station there. Tom had two elder brothers—William (b. ca. 1846) and George (b. ca. 1850)—and a sister Charlotte, who was two years younger than he was. She was presumably named after her aunt, Charlotte Riley. Tom's elder brothers were both mariners, and their father appears to have left the customs service soon after moving to Tollesbury; in the censuses of 1861, 1871, and 1881, he is described simply as a mariner, and he worked in the season as a yachtsman. Press reports in 1884 describe him as a yacht captain, who had commanded the yachts *Merle* and *Butterfly* (though there may be confusion here with his son); in 1884, at the age of 65, he was said still to be at work away from England on a year's cruise. The Dudley family lived in a house on Head Street, but the family had been disrupted by the death of Susannah Dudley, who died in 1859 when Tom was six. By 1871 his sister Charlotte was living with another aunt, Elizabeth Fisher; and George no longer kept up a home in the village. By this date his three sons would be wholly self-supporting.

Tollesbury in Tom Dudley's youth had a population of around 3,500, and the men were employed principally as agricultural laborers or as inshore seamen. The principal industry was the oyster fishery, the oysters being in fact farmed. When not directly managing the oysters, the dredgermen caught star fish (their principal predators) to be sold as manure and caught sprats or other fish. In 1876 some 70 smacks, employing 160 men, were operating from Tollesbury. Tollesbury's connection with yachting became important only in the late nineteenth and early twentieth centuries, and Tom Dudley was the first well-known yachtsman to come from the village. As his wife later wrote of him, "from his youth he has been hard-working and plodding, aiming to improve his position, but having received little or no education he tried in every way to supply this deficiency." In the neighboring village of Tolleshunt Major lived Thomas Dudley, a blacksmith married to a schoolteacher. He too was probably an uncle, and Tom may have been named after him. Thomas was literate and indeed acted as an enumerator in the census of 1871. Perhaps he and his wife helped Tom in his struggle for education, for he became able both to read and write fluently, if not very correctly: his spelling remained erratic.

Tom Dudley's career as a seaman began three years after his mother's death, in January 1863; he was a child of nine years and nine months when he signed on as a boy on the Dartmouth fishing smack *Royal Charter,* on which he worked for nearly six years on undocumented voyages, leaving in December 1868 when he was 15. He was not formally apprenticed. For much of the next year he did not go to sea, but on September 26, 1869, he joined the 60-ton schooner *Iris* of Goole (Captain E. Jackson), a London coaster, and worked on her first as an ordinary seaman and later as able seaman at £1.15s. a month until November 1870.

In the summer of 1870 he and his father worked on a "gentleman's yacht." Probably she was the yawl *Condor,* 92 feet overall and 155 tons. Owned by Sir Francis Gooch and commanded by Sailing Master Mackie, she operated mainly on the Clyde, and on her Tom Dudley, known as "Little Tom," established a reputation for courage he was to keep. A letter published in the *Daily Telegraph* on September 10, 1884, recounts how,

> Coming round to the Clyde the Condor was caught in a full gale of wind in St. Georges Channel and, with three reefs in the mainsail Captain Mackie . . . had to run before the wind. It was soon found desirable to pull down a fourth reef, but with the end of the enormous boom making a white furrow in the water not one of the crew would volunteer to go out and reeve the fourth reef earing. At last Dudley, though a comparatively fresh hand, went out and did this. . . .

This letter was written by one T. Dykes, a Scots sporting writer and yachtsman (he used the pseudonym "Rockwood"). He had sailed with Dudley and seems to have been a friend of the family; it may, however, refer to a later incident, for his period of service on the *Condor* is not satisfactorily documented.

Father and son left *Iris* in November 1870, and Tom, on his own now, joined the schooner *Lady Rodney* of Salcombe (Captain Thomas Cowling; 98 tons) as cook and steward. She was engaged on voyages to St. Michaels in the Azores, and a combination of evidence suggests that she was both undermanned and unhappy. On his second voyage Tom and another sailor, Frank Williams, deserted in St. Michaels on sailing day, March 24, and the police failed to apprehend them. Somehow Tom made his way back to Hull, probably on the *Annie*

Grant, and joined another schooner there, the *Mary Elizabeth* (Captain George Burns) on April 8. He left her too, probably deserting, at Antwerp on May 11, joining the *Jane Ann* of Sunderland (Captain Thomas Sinclair) next day and remaining with her on voyages to Seville and Cronstadt. His pay on the *Jane Ann* rose to £2 and then £2.5s. and to £2.10s. on his next schooner, the *Annie Grant* of Dartmouth (Captain Joseph Appledore; 148 tons), on which he remained until February 1873, making voyages to Newfoundland, Spain, Portugal, and Genoa. The yachting season of 1873 found him as able seaman on Prince Albert of Monaco's schooner yacht *Pleiad* of Torquay, and then it was back to a trading schooner, *Bohemian Girl* (Captain Nicholas Keen; 174 tons) at £4 a month on a voyage to Lisbon, employed as cook steward. Such employment would probably familarize him with butchery, for ships commonly carried live pigs or sheep on board.

In the 1874 season he rose in rank to boatswain on the 38-ton cutter yacht *Mosquito* of Greenock, owned by F. P. Dunne of Clonastic in Ireland, the period out of season between January 1874 and February 1875 being spent as able seaman on the schooner *London* (Captain James Ferguson). The 1875 season brought real success; Tom became mate of the leading racing cutter yacht *Fiona* (79 tons). She was owned by the enormously wealthy Edouard Boutcher, who belonged to some 13 yacht clubs. In 1880 he acquired a second *Fiona* (150 tons) for cruising; Fiona herself must have been his wife or mistress. The cutter *Fiona* was one of the most successful racing yachts of the 1870s, sailing under Captain John Heuston (or Houston) with a crew of eight. In 1875 she won £570 in prize money, the largest sum won that year. In some races a proportion of the prize went to the sailing master and, if a different person, the helmsman; a generous owner would in fact pass on all or some of the prize to the crew and might augment their earnings by celebratory gifts. Hence a berth on a leading yacht was highly coveted, and owners competed to secure the very best yachtsmen. As appears from the record of Dudley's service, yachting provided longer terms of employment than the commercial schooner trade. To be first mate on *Fiona* was a stepping stone to higher things. During the winter of 1875–76, he returned to commercial shipping as first mate of the schooner *Lizzie* of Teignmouth (Master J. Bedwell), leaving her on February 6, 1876.

From *Fiona* Dudley moved for the season of 1876 to his first command, *Camellia* of Greenock. He was probably the first Tollesbury man to become a sailing master, and it was said by Dykes that he secured the position through Captain Mackie's support. *Camellia* was a much smaller vessel, 28 feet overall and rated at 5 tons: she had been built in 1876 by Fife and Son of Fairlie for Mr. T. Lawson, who belonged to the Royal Rothsay Aquatic Club and Western Yacht Club on the Clyde. On her his reputation as "the little man who was built with the boat" continued to rise. One of the captains under whom he served (unhappily not identified) described him as "a sober, steady, respectable, God-fearing man; and a smarter or pluckier one never sailed a boat." His enthusiasm to reach a regatta in Dublin Bay in bad weather nearly brought disaster to *Camellia,* when the yacht was pooped, and "his boat was waist deep in water, and only careful steering, along with the use of 'the bucket' saved his life." Out of season, he served as mate on *Leader* of Plymouth (Captain R. E. Roberts; 212 tons). In 1877 he again was master of *Camellia* for a seven-month season and won 15 first prizes and 6 seconds, collecting £201 in prize money. On some occasions her helmsman was not Dudley but William Fife, Esq.—presumably a friend or relative of her owner—but no doubt Dudley instructed him. Her great rival was Mr. Baron Webb's *Freda,* with whom she sailed, and sadly lost, a private match at an impressive stake of £100. In the same year, between January and June, Tom continued to work as mate on the Plymouth schooner *Leader.* By the close of 1877, he had built up a record of some 14 years of service at sea, since he had joined *Royal Charter* back in 1863; presumably he also held shore jobs in the periods of unemployment as a mariner, perhaps as a cook.

It must have been in 1876 or 1877 that he met Phillipa Mary Julian, who was to become his wife. The Julians were a West Country family, and Phillipa, seven years Tom Dudley's senior, was the daughter of a Cornish miner, William Julian. She was born on April 12, 1846, at Trew near Breage in Cornwall, and had two sisters, Jenny and Lizzie. Perhaps her real father died early in her life, for she seems to have regarded Richard Julian (presumably an uncle) as her father and gave his name on her marriage certificate. He taught school in Plymouth, and so did Phillipa.

At Plymouth on December 27, 1877, in St. Saviour's Church, Dudley married Phillipa. His address on the marriage certificate is given as the village of Oreston, which is near Plymouth. Tom Dudley may have met her while working on the schooner *Leader.* The Dudleys' first home was the schoolhouse at Oreston, where Phillipa was schoolmistress. She presumably encouraged Tom to improve his career further, and early in 1878 he twice sat and failed the Board of

Trade examination for mates. But on March 7, 1878, at Plymouth, he finally passed the examinations and obtained his certificate, No. 04729, as "only mate," his competence being limited to fore-and-aft-rigged sailing vessels. In due course no doubt he would have proceeded to obtain a certificate as master mariner; in the event he never did.

From *Camellia* Dudley moved to command *Volga,* another Fife yacht built in 1878, 38 feet overall and rated at 10 tons, Thames measurement. She was owned by a Glasgow lawyer, Thomas Houston Kirk of 183 West George Street, and Dudley was her captain in 1878 and 1879. She was not raced very frequently but won seven firsts and six seconds in 1878 and one each in 1879. Tom's command of *Volga* was succeeded by a very much larger command in 1879 and 1880, that of the 84-foot schooner *Reindeer* (at one time called *Sea Mouse*). Built by Fife in 1870, she was rated at 106 tons and was owned by I. Macnab, a Glaswegian living in London; his yacht was based at Cowes and employed principally as a cruiser. Now that Dudley held a mate's ticket, such a vessel was within his competence. In 1879 he may also have commanded *Merle,* a 10-tonner owned by one Frank Harris of Halstead—perhaps for a single cruise; the reference may be to his father. He is also said to have commanded *Butterfly* about this time. During the years 1878, 1879, and 1880, Tom was also employed (presumably outside the yachting season) on the schooner *Sam Slick* of Plymouth, owned by William Hill of that city; under Captain Joseph Hill she traded between England and Spain.

In 1881 he became sailing master of *Nixie,* a 53-ton yacht with a crew of eight owned by another Glaswegian, Gavin Addie, but based at Southampton; this job came to an end with the owner's death in 1883. No doubt to recoup his loss, he offered in that year to sail Mr. J. Morrison's 20-ton cutter *Sayonara* to Montreal for £130; he may indeed have done so, but it is more probable that the voyage never took place. Then, in early 1884, he took command of the three-masted schooner-rigged auxiliary steam yacht *Myrtle.* Probably this was his first foreign yachting voyage, the last before the voyage of *Mignonette.*

Myrtle was a sizable vessel, advertised as 400 tons but in reality 209 net, and The Pleasure Yachting Company had chartered her for a Mediterranean cruise advertised on December 22 in *Land and Water.* The intention was to take on "a select party" of 30 paying passengers for a cruise which was to start from Southampton on January 7; great care was promised in the selection of those permitted to join. In the event Sir Charles Strickland appears to have booked all the accommodation for his own guests, and only 10 went. Their return was stormy, and *Myrtle* had to put into Corunna unexpectedly to take on coals. But she arrived safely at Dartmouth on April 23. Andrew Thompson acted as agent for this venture and appears to have been acquainted with Dudley on the Clyde; plainly he had a high opinion of Tom's abilities.

From his record it is easy to see how the *Daily Telegraph* could say of Tom Dudley that, "possessing the character of a bold and fearless man, he has been much sought after by owners of yachts." His career, however, shows a progressive move away from the prestigious world of racing to that of cruising. To secure captaincies of one of the very few of the leading racing yachts was a difficult task indeed; and in the 1870s and early 1880s, the golden age of the sport, five men dominated the scene: Henry Thompson (sailing *Vanguard, Cetonia,* and *Samoena*), George Cousins (*Florinda*), Charles Diaper (*Myosotis, Vol au Vent, Latona*), "Lemon" Cranfield (*Nova, Formosa, Miranda*), and William "Paddy" O'Neill (*Myosotis, Cuckoo, Annasona,* and *Samoena*). Cranfield, the most successful of all, collected no less than £8,123 in prize money between 1874 and 1883. It may not have been lack of ambition that held Tom Dudley back but marriage and resulting family obligations. The life of a leading yacht captain required absence from home from March to September or longer. The Dudleys did not stay in Oreston long; by 1880 they had established a home at 1 Myrtle Road, Sutton, in Surrey, where Phillipa had obtained the post of mistress of the Sutton (Newtown) Girls School. She preferred to work, though Dudley urged her not to do so. The Dudleys had three children—Phillipa Serpel (b. May 1880), Winifred Sara (September 1881) and Julian Tom (December 1882). To be near his family, Dudley needed a shore-based job for the winter, and he set up a greengrocer's business with a partner by the name of Smith. This venture proved disastrous, and Smith emigrated, presumably after a scandal. Long after transportation had ended, voluntary exile to the colonies was a means of escaping the past.

In about 1883 the Dudleys began to consider the same possibility. Probably on Phillipa's side of the family, they had relatives who had already emigrated to New South Wales, and these included an aunt, Mrs. R. W. Pettigrew, who lived or had premises at 38 York Street in Sydney. Mrs. Pettigrew was in business as a tent maker, and it was envisaged that Tom Dudley would move into the business, which could be combined with yacht fitting and sail making. He was therefore particularly attracted by the contract to take the *Mignonette* out, which offered a chance to see the possibilities at first hand. The terms offered were generous—£100 to take the contract on and a further £100 payable on delivery in Sydney. Out of this, Dudley had to pay his crew and provision the yacht but would still gain a substantial capital sum. A further arrangement was made for Dudley, if he did decide to stay in Sydney, to take on the captaincy of Jack Want's new yacht, to be constructed there. It was therefore as a potential emigrant that Dudley assumed the captaincy of the *Mignonette*.

He arrived at Southampton in command of *Myrtle* on April 27, and by April 28 he had finished his work with her. After returning home, he left Sutton again on Saturday, May 3, for his home village of Tollesbury. His father was away, but his stepmother would be there, and there were other relatives, including his aunt, Elizabeth Fisher, who had looked after his sister Charlotte as a child. With him he took his wife and his eldest daughter Phillipa, then aged four; his wife was to come with him on the initial stage of the voyage. It is just possible, though improbable, that his idea was to take the whole family out to Sydney on the yacht if he could convince his wife of the wisdom of this; there would indeed have been ample room for them, but little comfort. Alternatively, all that may have been involved was a short pleasure cruise, with no owner to get in the way.

Dudley initially intended to ship a crew of one able seaman and a boy; he was a man of economical bent, and the smaller the crew, the greater the profit. At Liverpool Street Station in London he met the two sailors he hoped to engage, who had just returned from Plymouth, and they took the train to Essex together. Meanwhile, the *Mignonette* had been fitted out at Brightlingsea by a friend, who sailed her the short distance to Tollesbury the previous evening. It was blowing a gale when the Dudleys arrived. The two sailors were themselves from Tollesbury; the boy was Jim Frost, and the able seaman his elder brother William. Jim was born on April 30, 1870, and was therefore just 14. The two brothers spent the night on board the yacht, while the Dudleys were more comfortably accommodated on shore. There they encountered some local feeling against the wisdom of the whole venture; in Tollesbury at least Dudley was thought to be acting in a foolhardy way, but he was not dissuaded. Precisely why there existed this feeling is not recorded.

Early on Monday May 5, the Dudleys set to sea for Southampton; the weather was warm and summery, but the sea was still very rough after the gale. During the course of the day, when running down Princes Channel in the Thames estuary some seven miles north of Margate, the yacht was struck by an extremely severe thunderstorm, which may well have alarmed Phillipa and her daughter. But the *Mignonette* pressed on around the North Foreland and passed through the Downs, between the Goodwin Sands and the south coast of Kent, where some 150 sailing vessels were sheltering after the storm. At 8:30 A.M. on Wednesday, the *Mignonette* reached Southampton and moored in the Itchen River at Northam, off Fay's Yard, then the leading yacht-building yard in the area. Here Phillipa and her daughter debarked from the yacht for home, leaving Tom to prepare the yacht for the long voyage ahead.

Perhaps it was intuited as a trip to remember, for the Frost brothers also declined to go any further. Varying stories have survived as to why this was so. One attributes the initiative to Jim, who decided against the wisdom of the venture. Another story attributes the decision to pressure from William's wife or to his illness; still another tradition, passed on to me by Joe Frost, one of Jim's sons, is that William and Jim walked to Brightlingsea to join the *Mignonette* but found she had sailed—this recollection could refer to the move of the yacht from Brightlingsea to Tollesbury but conflicts with the other evidence. Whatever the explanation, Jim Frost had every reason to congratulate himself, for he lived on for many years, becoming a well-known barge skipper, owner, and businessman. He died at the age of 92 in December 1962, the last man alive who is known to have sailed on the *Mignonette;* you can still see the faded sign over his business premises in the village of Tollesbury. Had he joined the crew for the voyage out, matters might have ended differently. His youngest son, Raymond (known as "Budge"), recalls him often speaking of the *Mignonette* as a good sea boat, and in the family Budge, when reproved, would tease his father with the remark, "Lucky you're here. I reckon you'd have tasted better."

At Southampton the *Mignonette* was now hauled out at Fay's Yard for repairs, though the obvious place to have had any necessary work done was in Brightlingsea, where she had lain all winter and where she had supposedly been fitted out already. Possibly the reason was that the voyage had revealed defects that needed attention. Her mizzenmast was removed, so leaving her cutter rigged, and the planking next to the keel (the garboard strakes) was replaced. She was also fully provisioned. All was completed by May 15, and the *Mignonette* lay to mooring off the village of Itchen Ferry. Though of course relaid since, this mooring still exists and is, I am told, currently used by Mr. Dan Candy, who owns the oldest surviving Itchen fishing smack. Near to the *Mignonette* lay *Wraith,* whose Captain, Harry Thompson, recalled many years later how he had teased his friend Tom Dudley over the dangers of the voyage on which he was embarking.

Meanwhile, Dudley had been trying to engage a crew. His original plan to ship a crew of two only had come under criticism, and he now decided to engage a mate in addition. On May 15 he went with three men he had selected to the customs house, where they formally signed the ship's articles before the shipping master, as legally required since 1844 by the merchant shipping acts. The *Mignonette*'s articles survive in the Public Record Office. They record the three crew members and some information about them. The mate was James R. Haynes, whose last ship had been the *Lord Eslington* of Newcastle. He was 29 and was to be paid £7 a month. Edmund Brooks, of Brightlingsea, was engaged as able seaman at £5.10s. per month; he gave his age as 39, and his last ship was *Athenia.* Richard Parker of Itchen Ferry was engaged as ordinary seaman at £1.15s. a month; he gave his age, incorrectly, as 18. He alone was quite illiterate and made his mark. These rates of pay were said at the time to be higher than normal—Brooks later said his pay was £1.10s. above the standard rates going at the time. The comparison he was making may have been with sailing vessels bound for Australia: figures for all ports for 1886, the nearest date for which such statistics exist, show that first mates were getting on average £7.6s.4d. a month, second mates £4.17s.6d., third mates £3.4s.8d., sailors £2.12s.9d., and boys anything between 5s. and £1.10s. In comparison with figures paid by yachtsmen, what was offered was not particularly favorable, though on the *Mignonette* food was provided. Dudley's estimate of the duration of the voyage meant that his complete pay bill was likely to come to a maximum of £57. The ship's articles specified the scale of rations: 6 pounds of beef, 2¾ pounds of pork, 1½ pounds of flour, and 1 pint of peas each week, plus 1 pound of bread on Sundays. Daily each man was to have 3 quarts of water, ⅛ ounce of tea, and 2 ounces of sugar. No alcohol was taken—Dudley was a teetotaler. The ship's articles also provided that Dudley undertook to find employment for his crew aboard a British vessel at ordinary wages for their return or pay their return passages, a standard arrangement.

James Robert Haynes, who came from Turnchapel in Devon, was a very experienced sailor, who had obtained his mate's certificate in Plymouth in May of 1875 and had qualified as a master mariner in Plymouth in February 1878. Turnchapel is next door to Oreston, where Dudley was living in 1877; I assume they knew each other. His experience was very varied—he had, for example, sailed on the schooner *Clara* of Bridgwater from 1880 to 1883, and then in that one year worked on the steamships *City of Hamburg* and *Lord Eslington* (Brooks's ship), the barque *Isipingo,* and the barquentine *Vidonia.* But his connection with *Mignonette* did not last long; the very next morning he changed his mind and deserted the ship; his reason is not recorded. For this, in theory, he could have been criminally punished, but Dudley simply recorded his desertion formally. The Board of Trade recorded him merely as "discharged"—perhaps it was felt he had a defense against any charge. He was now the third sailor to act on misgivings about the *Mignonette,* and though he was offered higher pay—£8 a month—he persisted in his decision, though it was not until the end of July that he found another ship, the barque *City of Aberdeen.* But on the same day, in Northam, Dudley found an equally well-qualified replacement, Edwin Stephens, who signed articles at £8 a month.

The new mate had been born on August 21, 1847, the only son of a seaman, Richard Stephens and his wife, Fanny (Penford), who then lived at 20 St. John Street, Southampton. Richard became a master mariner and worked for the Isle of Wight Royal Mail Steam Packet Company, popularly called the Red Funnel Line; this company is still in business. He captained *Ruby* and latterly *Queen;* so employed, he drowned in an accident at West Cowes on April 24, 1868. The family home was at 25 Bugle Street, where Edwin was brought up with his seven sisters, one, Penford Stephens, being older than himself. Edwin followed his father's footsteps, but as a deep sea sailor: in 1884 he romantically said of himself, "In fact all my life, till the last two or three years, I have been sailing to the southward." Reared in more affluent circumstances than Tom Dudley, he did not go to sea until he was 14, joining the prestigious Peninsular and Oriental Line on their steamship *Ellora* as a boy on February 1, 1862. This company, though registering its vessels in London, used Southampton as its base. His second ship, which we shall meet again in disagreeable circumstances, was another of their steamships, the *Euxine,* and he continued with the line as boy on the S.S. *Poonah* and S.S. *Pera,* becoming ordinary seaman in December 1863. He then left the line to work as able seaman on sailing vessels—*Rantipole* (1865–67) and then *Deerfoot* (1867), returning to the sailing barque *Indus* (1868–69) used as a collier by the line. On October 12, 1869, he was certificated as second mate and obtained a berth as such on the Union Line's *Anglian;* on December 15, 1870, he qualified as first mate. After two years as first mate on *Magnet* of Dublin, he returned to the line, joining the *Asiatic,* a new 2,066-ton vessel built for the mail run in 1873. He served on her for a number of voyages between 1873 and 1876, rising in rank from third to first mate, and for some of these the ship's articles survive in the Public Record Office. Thus in 1875 he completed the round trip to the Cape and Algoa Bay three times as second mate under Captain E. Manning; the voyage took about two months, and in the intervals he lived at his home at 4 Anglesea Terrace in Southampton. His pay was £7.10s. a month with allowances of £3.15s., and the job was prestigious and reliable. In 1876 he was moved to the *Danube,* again as second mate, and in the same year, in February he obtained his certificate as a master mariner. In 1877, his progress with the Union Line took another step forward, and he became first mate (or "first officer," as the grander lines were beginning to call the position) on the *European.* She was a 2,272-ton three-masted screw steamer, built in 1869 as the *Europe.* As first officer with a long and impeccable record, Stephens could look forward eventually to promotion to captain in one of the leading shipping lines of the period. But it was not to be, for in 1877 his career with the Union Line came to an abrupt and disastrous end.

On November 13, a bad day to choose, the *European,* under Captain R. W. Ker, had left Cape Town; Captain Ker, long the company's agent in South Africa, appears to have had little recent sea-going experience, and his appointment as master may have been to some degree honorific. In addition to the mails (which included some diamonds) the *European* carried 30 passengers and a crew of 76 hands. Having called at Madeira on December 1, on December 5 she was approaching the entrance to the channel. Her last landfall had been Cape Finisterre, where she had set a course of northeast by east, intending to pass 25 miles off Ushant. The last sun sight had been taken on December 3; since then visibility had been poor, and navigation was by dead reckoning only.

Since noon on December 4, Stephens had been in charge of the navigation. At 1:30 P.M. the ship was stopped for soundings, and no bottom was found in 100 fathoms: the charted position at the time, based on dead reckoning, indicated 73 fathoms as the depth that ought to have been found. Something was plainly amiss, but since she was outside the 100-fathom line, regarded as the indication of proximity to land, the *European* pressed on at 12 knots. Another attempt to find bottom failed at 4:30 P.M.; from this failure it logically followed that the ship's charted position by dead reckoning was now at least 47 miles away from its actual position. The actual position probably lay south-southwest of the charted position; the ship had been making less headway than Stephens realized because of the set of the current. But it never seems to have occurred to captain or first mate that the *European*'s position might be *astern* of where they thought it was, much less that it was also closer to land. A memorable conversation then took place. "We must," said Stephens, "be a long way from land." Captain Ker, a reticent man, replied "Yes." In fact at this moment the *European* was about 40 miless *short* of Ushant, just over three hours' sailing away, and, being set in by the current, was heading straight for the island, which was hidden by fog. Soundings were again taken at 7:45 P.M. and a bottom of shell and sand found at 40 fathoms. At this point, the captain and first officer conferred again and convinced themselves that they were now safely past Ushant. They located a convenient spot some ten miles north of Ushant on the chart with a depth of 50 fathoms (though with the wrong bottom), and there they placed the position of the *European*. Thus comforted, they pressed on again through the fog at 12 knots.

Stephens went off duty at the end of the second dog watch at 8:00 P.M. but remained on the bridge long enough to hear the call of the lookout, 10 minutes later, "Light on the port bow." The helm was put hard to starboard and the engines stopped; as the lookout cried out a second time, "Breakers ahead," Captain Ker rang for full ahead in a desperate attempt to clear the reef. The light had been the Ushant Light on *Pointe de Créach,* seen at a distance of 1½ miles. The *European* impaled herself on the Basse Meur rock and rapidly sank. She had hit the most westerly point of France; had she been just a little to the west, no accident would have occurred. Excellent discipline saved the mails and all on board, and in accordance with protocol, Captain Ker was the last to leave the doomed ship. No criticism could be made of officers or crew as to their conduct once the accident happened; it was indeed a model shipwreck. But the loss of a passenger vessel carrying the mails, even without loss of life, meant a formal inquiry.

The wreck enquiry sat in London on December 20 and 21, and the inevitable conclusion was reached that Captain Ker had been guilty of gross and culpable negligence. He lost his certificate for six months. As a junior officer acting always under his captain's authority, Stephens was not of course in any way censured; the decisions were taken by the captain. But command structures apart, Stephens was as guilty as his captain and conceded his errors at the hearing. The Union Line never employed him again; there was at the time a surplus of certificated ship's officers, and a leading shipping company could pick and choose. Later, his wife was to say that all their troubles seemed to begin with the loss of the *European*. The Christmas of 1877 cannot have been a very happy one for Edwin Stephens.

Nevertheless he obtained work of some kind, and although the Board of Trade records note no voyages at all between 1877 and 1881, he had in fact secured employment with G. T. Harper of Southampton, who traded in the Mediterranean and Black Sea, on the steamship *Ascupart* (and perhaps on other vessels), for which Stephens employed his master's ticket, which he had originally reported as lost with the *European*. It had apparently turned up, and he did not collect the replacement, authorized by the board on January 3, 1878, until September 21, 1881, as *Ascupart* was about to sail from Newport.

On November 2, 1871, in the Portland Baptist Chapel, Stephens married Ann Annan, daughter of a ship's chief engineer; she was almost the girl next door, for she was then living at 9 Bugle Street. By 1884, they had five children, of whom the youngest, Albert Richard, had been born on September 23 of the previous year. I have not certainly identified the other four, but they were probably Annie (1873), Elizabeth Jessie (1874), Florence Ethel (1876), and Charles George (1880); there may have been other children who did not survive.

Stephens was a respected local figure, active in the Young Men's Christian Association and a member of the Cape of Good Hope Masonic Lodge; he and his wife were a devoted couple. In 1881, he was at sea again as first mate on the *Ascupart*. The following year, he was first mate on another of Harper's vessels, the *Lady Josyan*, from which he was discharged in Malta. He then managed to obtain work in 1883 and early 1884 with the Red Funnel Line with which his father had served, working as mate on two of their steamers, the *Lord Elgin* and the *Carisbrooke*. The pay was considerably lower than that of a first mate on the Union Line; figures for 1889 show the Red Funnel Line paying their mates £1.10s. a week (ca. £6 a month), while an ocean-going passenger ship might pay a much higher monthly rate. By way of comparison, articles for the S.S. *Tartan* of Southampton in 1883 show the master receiving £15 a month; the first, second, and third mates £10, £8, and £6, respectively; and able seamen £3.10s.

It must by now have been clear to Stephens that although he could find work with difficulty, his career would never prosper if he remained in Southampton; so he decided to emigrate. Dudley tempted him further by offering him the captaincy of the *Mignonette* in Sydney—presumably he had a mandate from Jack Want—and agreed to pay him £8 a month if he shipped. Since he held a master's certificate and had considerable if unhappy experience as a navigator, Stephens was particularly valuable to Dudley, who may well have had anxieties over the complex task of establishing longitude at sea. So Dudley was anxious to recruit him. Stephens did not apparently reveal to his wife his plan to emigrate; he probably had difficulties enough in reconciling her to his going on the voyage. That would come later.

"Ned," "Neddy," or "Teddy" Brooks, christened Edmund James, was born at Brightlingsea on May 18, 1846, the son of James Brooks, a mariner, and Susanna (Small). He went to sea at an early age, apprenticed when he was 12 to a Captain Francis, master of the Brightlingsea oyster dredger *Greyhound*. Ironically, disaster overtook the *Greyhound* in 1884, the same year as the *Mignonette,* and shortly after Ned Brooks landed at Falmouth. *Greyhound* was run down by a steamer while carrying oyster brood from Brightlingsea to Whitstable, Captain Thomas Coppin, formerly captain of the *Mignonette,* being the first to sight the wreckage. Brooks's career is inherently difficult to trace, since he never became a certified officer, and his record as a naval reservist has been destroyed by the custodians of the public records in one of the tidying fits that have lost historians so much. He became a yacht hand and had been acquainted with Dudley since about 1872; he had known the *Mignonette* herself since she was built. In 1879, he had established himself in Southampton in lodgings with Sydney and Mary Egerton in Northam. According to rumors in Brightlingsea, he was married (though not to a local girl) and had deserted his wife; he claimed, however, to be a bachelor. In Southampton he worked on yachts in the summer and on Union Line steamers in the winter—in 1884 his last vessel had been the *Spartan*. As a yachtsman, he must have been very highly regarded, for he served four seasons (1879–83) under Captain W. O'Neill, who was one of the outstanding skippers of the time. His yachts were the famous *Myosotis, Annasona,* and *Samoena,* and he acted as second mate on *Annasona* in her most successful season. In 1883, his last year with O'Neill, *Samoena* was the most successful yacht, winning £1,325 in prize money. Brooks also worked as a rigger in Fay's Yard and was so employed when the *Mignonette* arrived from Tollesbury. This is how he came to hear of the job. At the time, the major source of interest in Fay's Yard was the construction of an extraordinary and extravagant yacht, designed by one Richardson of Liverpool, to replace Mr. J. Jameson's *Samoena* in the coming season. *Samoena* was a sizable enough vessel: a 90-ton cutter 81 feet in length. The new yacht, though rated smaller at 74 tons, was designed to carry even more canvas, and to make this possible she was fitted with a 72-ton solid lead ballast keel, at that time the largest external ballast keel ever built. Captain O'Neill was to command the new yacht, and Brooks could have had a berth as a member of the crew. She became *Irex,* and surviving crew lists of 1885 and 1887 show her under commission under Captain O'Neill with two mates (Ben Parker as second mate), nine or ten able seamen, a steward, and a cook. It is somewhat surprising that Brooks preferred to join Dudley on the *Mignonette,* even if the wages were higher, in preference to a comfortable and probably remunerative summer season on the *Irex*. But the explanation is that he too had been considering emigration, and Dudley offered him work on the *Mignonette* in Sydney if he wished to stay there. Perhaps his wife, if there was one, had got onto his trail.

The last member of the crew was the boy Richard Parker, then aged 17, who came from the village of Itchen Ferry in the Parish of St. Mary Extra on the eastern side of the river Itchen, just across the water from Fay's Yard at Northam. In the nineteenth century Itchen Ferry had a distinctive village character and was quite distinct from Pear Tree Green and Wolston. It was the home of a peculiarly close-knit community of seamen and their families. Many were fishermen or worked as watermen or ferrymen, while in the summer they became yachtsmen, providing many of the crews of the leading racing yachts of the nineteenth and early twentieth centuries. Three Parker brothers, for example, were members of the crew of the Kaiser's yacht *Meteor*—Bill Parker was captain, Ben Parker was first mate; and Dan Parker, known as "Bucky Eye" (for all the men of Itchen had nicknames) was second mate; they were cousins of Richard Parker.

So, like Tollesbury, Itchen Ferry was one of the few yachting villages that retained this traditional connection with the sport until quite modern times. Certain families in the village were particularly prominent, most notably the Diapers, the Jurds, the Parkers, and the Cozenses. In the 1871 census returns there are listed no fewer than 13 distinct households of Diapers, the most numerous clan, and eight of Jurds. The Parkers were represented by 11 households; tradition is that they fell into two sub-clans. Legend also has it that at some remote time Algerian pirates had raided the village and ravished the women, injecting swarthy characteristics into the local gene pool. The story is of course common in one form or other around the coasts. The Parkers, some of whom had (and still have) dark skins and blue eyes, were sometimes called in consequence by the odd name "Algerines" or "Algernines," a corruption of "Algerian." Indeed a 10-ton yacht named *Algerine,* captained by Charley Diaper, regularly raced in the Itchen regatta in the 1860s. The head of one of these Parker families was a gardener, and old Ann Parker, probably a widow, had been a laundress. The rest were families of fishermen, and at the age of around 12 the sons followed the family tradition and became fishermen too.

Richard Thomas Parker was born on March 31, 1867, the year *Mignonette* was built, into this rather special world, and was the son of Daniel Parker, always known as "Old Chick." Old Chick was a noted cricketer on Pear Tree Green at the top of the village, and he was also a yacht skipper, commanding the yawl *Medora,* owned by C. J. Phillips of Bugle Hall in Southampton. Richard's mother was Mary Parker, and she died in April 1874 at the age of 48, when Richard was only seven. Old Chick survived her, but he too died on May 14, 1881 at the age of 61, leaving Richard—known as "Little Dickey" (though he was taller than his captain, Tom Dudley)—an orphan. Richard had three brothers: they were Daniel, Stephen, and William ("Flop"). When their father died, Daniel was 22, Stephen 18, and Flop 16; besides having many relatives in the village, they could look after themselves and had been working for some years. Richard, at the age of 14, was young but working too. The elder brothers sometimes worked on yachts—in 1884 on the cutter *Ladye* and the schooner *Foam.* Richard was cared for by Captain and Mrs. Mathews, who lived in the village. Captain Jack Mathews too was a yacht skipper, commanding *Daphne,* on which Richard sailed in 1883. The Mathewses appear to have been related to the Parkers; an Emily Parker, daughter of Daniel Parker, senior, had married a Mathews. Richard also had a younger sister, whose name was Edith; she was two years younger than he was, and in 1881 still in school. In

1884 she was variously said to have been in London being educated in an orphanage, or to have been in London in service. Although there exists no direct evidence on the matter, she may well have been a domestic servant in the home of an engineer, John F. Haskins, but I have been unable to discover confirmation of this, and the Parker family today possess virtually no information about her.

The local church that served the community is situated on Pear Tree Green, named after a tree said to have been planted by Queen Elizabeth I. Known as Jesus Chapel, it had a school attached to it, where Mr. E. J. Petty made ineffective efforts to educate young Richard, who left school wholly illiterate; as we have seen, he could not even sign his name on the *Mignonette*'s articles. Richard appears to have run wild, as boys do, living rather rough, but he was well liked and seemed to have had no trouble in keeping himself. Physically he closely resembled his elder brother, Daniel, whose photograph survives, though only in old age. Richard joined the crew because he wanted to travel abroad; he had never sailed on a long ocean voyage, and he also thought he might emigrate. He also wanted, as he said, "to make a man of himself." This expression is also used by Dudley independently, and he must have talked him into the voyage as being in some sense a rite of passage, though it was to turn out a more definitive rite of passage than anticipated. Dudley said he would give Richard some schooling on the voyage and took books on board for this purpose.

For some days, while the subject was in the air, the Mathews tried to dissuade Richard from what they saw as a foolish venture. But on May 15, without telling them, he went to the customs house and signed on. He bragged to his friends that he would be paid £1 a week, but this was, as we know, not quite true. When he told his foster mother he had signed, she said, "Well, if you are determined to go, I hope everything will be all right and that, please God, you will come home again." By shipping on the *Mignonette,* Richard gave up a berth on the *Daphne,* which he could have had, for he was a favorite of the yacht's owner, a Mr. Hankinson. But Dudley promised him work on the *Mignonette* in Sydney if he wished to stay.

The crew was now made up, and the yacht thought to be ready for sea. But Dudley decided to postpone his departure until the Monday. He later said this was to enable him to spend the weekend at home with his family; this may have been a factor, but the real reason was more probably the well-established seaman's superstitious dread of starting a voyage on a Friday. So all four men spent the weekend at their homes—or, in the case of Ned Brooks, at his lodgings in Mrs. Egerton's County Tavern in Millbank Street. Edwin Stephens lived nearby in a small terraced house (which still exists) at 73 Northumberland Street, and Richard Parker across the water at Itchen Ferry. No doubt a watch was organized to care for the *Mignonette,* lying at her moorings in the Itchen River, with her frail dinghy drawn up on the shore.

Both in Tollesbury and Southampton there were those who thought the *Mignonette* quite unsuitable for the long voyage; three men had already left her, and as the time to depart drew near, no doubt there was much wagging of heads over the whole venture. When Dudley arrived back at 11:30 A.M. from his home, he learned that Ned Brooks had now backed out. He saw Brooks in Northam; what passed is not recorded, but Brooks said he would be ready by tide time that evening, which was about 5:00 P.M. Later, Brooks was to say, "I did not consider there was any risk in undertaking the voyage. Having always been brought up to the sea in small yachts and boats, I did not think there was any more danger in going to Sydney in the *Mignonette* than there would be in crossing the Channel. . . . My friends, however, or everyone who spoke to me on the subject, persuaded me not to go." This was defensive; what may have been his true feelings came out in a conversation many years later, as we shall see. Edwin Stephens also seems to have had problems in getting away from his nearby home. He had to be fetched twice but later said, "I never had the least anticipation that the *Mignonette* was not seaworthy. I made enquiries before I shipped—not being a yachtsman—whether it would be safe—and they all said yes, and that we should ride better than in a big vessel if she was properly handled." Perhaps it was difficult for him to part from his wife and young children. Richard Parker was the only real enthusiast. Excitement made him rise early and leave his home soon after 5:00 A.M. His kit was prepared by both Mrs. Mathews and one Mary Jane Diaper, in whose family the story of Richard's departure has been passed down to this day. If I have identified her correctly as the daughter of Charles and Ruth Diaper, she lived near the Mathewses and would have been 24 or thereabouts at the time; a possible explanation of her involvement is that she was at the time Richard's girl friend, an emotional connection that would explain her retelling of the story to her children later in life. More probably, she had merely a sisterly relationship with young orphaned Richard. As he left home and kissed his foster parents goodbye, some realization of what might be ahead seems at last to have overcome him. Mrs. Mathews recorded, "As he said Goodbye, he kissed us both, and hung upon our necks for several minutes, and, I shall never forget it; he seemed then sorry that he was going to leave us, and this was the first time he showed any regret for the resolve he had taken. That was the last I saw of him, for I did not see the *Mignonette* leave the river." History has not recorded his parting from Mary Jane Diaper, but I imagine she would have seen *Mignonette* towed down the Itchen river at about 5:15 P.M., on the turn of the tide, by the steam tug *Meryphic.* But, being raised in the customs of the sea, she would know that it brings ill fortune to stare after a departing vessel, and it may be that Mrs. Mathews, in emphasizing to the press that she did not even see the yacht leave the river, wanted to make it clear that she had not brought about the loss of the *Mignonette.* So Mary Jane Diaper also probably did not watch *Mignonette* put to sea, under all plain sail, or see her drop her tow near the moorings of the battleship H.M.S. *Hector.* There was a light southeast breeze blowing.

The voyage to which the *Mignonette* was now committed involved sailing somewhere between 14,000 and 16,000 miles, using the route around the Cape of Good Hope. There was no advantage in reducing the distance 1,000 miles or so by using the Suez Canal, for a sailing vessel requires reliable winds that the route through the Mediterranean did not provide. The canal at this period served only the luxury passenger trade to the Orient. Precisely how many miles the *Mignonette* would sail depended on the unpredictabilities of the weather and navigational errors. The normal pracice for the large sailing barques was to aim to pass close to St. Paul's Rocks in the western part of the South Atlantic, not very far from the coast of South America. They would then be in the southeast trade winds and would follow a curving track passing well south of the island of Tristan da Cunha, entering the "roaring forties"—the belt of strong westerly winds—in latitude 40 or more south. Once in the westerlies, the barques would pass well to the south of the Cape of Good Hope, at no point entering port or coming close to land, unless there was some emergency that made it desirable. Some captains would, however, aim to pass close to Tristan, instead of 500 miles or so to the south, to check the ship's chronometer against a landfall. In general, however, masters of large sailing vessels preferred to keep well away from anything solid. Those in pursuit of record passages would follow as closely as possible a great circle route, which took them as far south as ice conditions and personal courage permitted, for the precise great circle route from around St. Paul's Rocks to Sydney passes throught the Antarctic continent and cannot be followed exactly.

Dudley decided to adopt a quite different plan; he would sail first to Madeira and pass close to the Cape Verde Islands. After a short stop, he would sail on to Cape Town, whence he would set out on the last and most hazardous stage of his journey to Sydney. His route through the North Atlantic lay therefore considerably to the east of the orthodox one, and the discrepancy increased as he went further south, where it lay both east and north of the normal route. For this he was subsequently criticized. Thus "A Retired Merchant Captain" of Bayswater sounded off (as they still do) in the pages of the *Daily Telegraph:* "It seems to me incredible how any commander of a vessel who had had any experience in the Australian or East Indian Trade could possibly have got into such a position [as the one where the yacht foundered]." But Dudley was not a deep-water sailor commanding a large sailing barque; he was sailing a yacht and thought that he would be likely to meet less violent weather if he did as other yacht captains had done before him. His route was very similar to that followed by earlier captains of small vessels sailing to the Cape. The sailing barque's traditional practice took the ship into reliable winds, it was true, but also into the mountainous seas and continuous gales of the southern ocean; conditions were often appalling and not infrequently disastrous. Dudley's decision was understandable and quite irrelevant to the loss of the *Mignonette.* His route in the South Atlantic also lay well to the west of the steamers' route to the Cape, which, as it turned out, was to prove unfortunate; but sailing vessels were not navigated with a view to placing them in shipping lanes, where there was always a risk of being run down at night.

The *Mignonette* was by no means the first small yacht or sailing vessel to make the passage from England to the Antipodes. Some of these early small-boat voyages are little documented, such as that of the *Mystery,* a 17-ton lugger from Penzance that went to Australia in the 1840s, or the 25-ton *Why Not,* which, at some uncertain date, successfully reached New Zealand. About others more is known. The *Wanderer,* a 140-ton schooner, reached Australia to be wrecked on the coast in 1840, its owner, a Mr. Boyd, killed by the local aborigines. The 73-ton *Albatross* successfully sailed to Australia in 1840 and returned by Cape Horn in 1846. In about 1856 one Captain Stallard of Ryde took the 30-ton cutter *Gem* to Australia to sell—she was about the same size as the *Mignonette,* as was *Spray* (33 tons), which sailed from Cowes to Hobart under an eccentric skipper, Captain Wylie, in 1860. The voyage of the 72-ton schooner *Chance* in 1862 is better documented. She left Cowes on January 13 and arrived in Sydney on June 3, after spending three days at the Cape and 140 days at sea. *Vivid* in 1864–65 (25 tons' yacht measurement and around 16 tons' registered tonnage), a smaller yacht than *Mignonette,* was 130 days at sea, spending a fortnight at the Cape. *Alerte,* a 56-ton cutter owned by Mr. William Walker, left Falmouth on May 6, 1865, under Captain Alexander Campbell and a crew of six; crossed the line on May 31; and anchored in Table Bay on July 3, 58 days out. After spending 5 days there she put to sea again, reaching Sydney on August 23, having been 108 days at sea in all. This yacht is said to have logged, somewhat improbably, a run of 400 miles in two days, including a day's run of 240 miles, "the little clipper spanking along at a rattling pace." She returned to England safely under the command of her mate, Joseph Gentle of Gosport, after 115 days at sea. Her owner was commodore of the Royal Sydney Yacht Squadron. Dudley would no doubt have known of some of these voyages (which all, as far as it is recorded, involved a stop at Cape Town); he may even have known some of the sailors involved. The logs of several of these voyages had been fully published in *Hunt's Yachting Magazine.* Jack Want in Sydney would also know of some of them. By 1884 even the misanthropic sport of single-handed sailing was known. In 1877 Alfred Johnson sailed across the Atlantic alone in the 20-foot *Sentennial.* and, lest it should be thought that bizarre voyages are a strictly modern phenomenon, the Atlantic was crossed in 1866 by the weird sailing vessel *Red White and Blue* (under Captain Hudson, with Mr. F. E. Fitch and the dog Fanny as crew). This 27-foot iron vessel, which measured only three feet from deck to keel and had a beam of only six feet, was, incredibly, ship rigged and nevertheless survived to reach Margate on August 14, after having left New York improbably on July 12.

Small-yacht voyages across the oceans were not therefore all that uncommon; nor was *Mignonette* a particularly small yacht. She was, for example, only one foot shorter than Sir Francis Chichester's ketch *Gypsy Moth IV,* in which he circumnavigated the globe in 1966.

Dudley and his navigator, Stephens, hoped to reach Sydney in 110 days or 120 at the outside. This would have required an average daily run of around 127 (or 116) miles; for a yacht of *Mignonette*'s size, these figures were very optimistic, but not impossible. *Gypsy Moth* reached Sydney in 107 days in 1966; *Alerte,* a larger vessel, in 108 days in 1855. The record passage out (though to Melbourne) was much faster; the famous clipper *Thermopylae* took 60 days in 1869–70. But a displacement yacht's potential maximum speed (which is rarely reached, much less sustained) is primarily dictated by her length, and *Mignonette*'s was about 9½ knots. She could not possibly rival the runs of the clippers or larger sailing barques. Unhappily, her longest daily run is not recorded, but her progress out does indicate that she was a fast yacht, resolutely sailed.

Dudley must have kept a log, and from his recollection of this he could record the progress of the *Mignonette* fairly precisely. At midnight on May 19, she passed the Needles. At noon the next day she was off Portland Bill, and by midnight on May 20 she was abreast of Start Point. Next morning at 10:30, she met the schooner yacht *Lady Evelyn* and put letters on her for home. These were posted in Plymouth and later gave Phillipa Dudley the mistaken impression that Dudley had put in there. *Mignonette* was making good about four miles an hour, or 96 miles a day, and this in light winds. At noon on the same day she was near the Eddystone Light, her last contact with England and the point from which the ocean voyage began. Employing the traditional language of the sea, Dudley recorded this emotional moment: "At noon was off Edystone from whence we took our departure course set a berth off Ushant 22nd. 8 Am distance was run but owing to its being hazey did not see it." Perhaps this was a relief to Edwin Stephens. Dudley's account continues, "We had a fine passage to Madeira reaching the roads at Midnight on June 1st." *Mignonette*'s average daily run between Southampton and Funchal had been around 110 miles.

There, according to Dudley's own account, *Mignonette* remained a mere 12 hours, taking on water, fruit, and other provisions—probably meat, vegetables, and fish. The four men also sent messages home. Dudley cabled his wife, "All is well," and this cable reached Sutton on June 3. Stephens wrote to his wife, Ann, explaining the plan to emigrate and asking her if she would join him with their children. She replied to the Cape that she would, no doubt anticipating that the letter, by fast steamship, would reach there before the yacht arrived. It did, but Stephens never collected it. And Richard Parker wrote what was probably the first letter of his life to his foster parents. In his own hand, presumably copying from a draft by his captain, he told them that "he was happy and comfortable, that all on board were well, and that they had had a fine and pleasant voyage all the way." His tutelage had not been confined to learning his letters;

Dudley, a devout Anglican, took prayer books to sea, and each Sunday divine service was celebrated on board.

Dudley's is not the only account of the visit of the *Mignonette* to Funchal. Considerably more detail is supplied by Donald McCormick in his *Blood on the Sea*. In this book he claims that a curious and significant incident took place there. Dudley, it is said, rescued a 17-year-old girl from drowning. Her name was Otilia Ribeiro, an orphaned Portuguese flower seller. Later the same day, in the afternoon, the British consul visited the *Mignonette* to congratulate Dudley on his bravery. It was indeed an eventful day for Otilia; for earlier, Richard Parker had hit her on the head with a boat hook, not out of sheer *joie de vivre* but because she was trying to sneak onto the yacht. Otilia too had a wish to emigrate to Australia and hoped to secure a passage on the *Mignonette*. Dudley refused but gave her Jack Want's address in Sydney. We shall meet this lady again under the name of Ricardo Parker and follow her adventures as a spirited transvestite and transsexual. Much of her story is plainly either maritime myth or fiction, but the initial problem is to decide whether she ever existed at all. Matters are not improved by the fact that much of the detail of the incidents at Funchal, as recounted by Mr. McCormick, cannot be correct. For example, the consul—at this time one George Harvey Hayward—could not have visited the *Mignonette* in the afternoon, as McCormick claims, since by then the yacht had left. McCormick also gives an account of a picnic lunch that sounds more like a report from the Club Mediterranée than an account of the activities of a group of professional sailors of the nineteenth century; there is no possibility that this lunch ever took place.

McCormick cannot now locate the source for the story of Otilia; after nearly 20 years, this is not surprising and in no way shows that he did not have one, either in some contemporary document or in maritime folklore. It is clear too that he was in possession of a story about the rescue of a girl *before* he wrote the book, for in a letter to the press published on January 13, 1961, in which he solicited information for the book, he described Dudley as a man "who had risked his life to save a girl from drowning at Madeira during the yacht's voyage." I have a press clipping of this letter, given me by Captain C. C. H. Diaper of Itchen Fery. In *Blood on the Sea,* Otilia is referred to, though not by name, in two partially reproduced letters, to which Mr. McCormick had access, by Phillipa Dudley to a Mrs. Pettit in Sutton, one in 1886 and one in 1887–90. One letter also refers to two other supposed acts of bravery—one when Dudley is said to have saved a diver in Southampton Docks; the other, "when a small yacht he was in caught fire, and, though he ordered the crew to get away in the ship's boat, he stayed behind himself to fight the fire and salve the ship's stores." I have been unable to find any other evidence of these incidents, but this is not to say that they never happened, especially as I have not traced one pamphlet to which McCormick refers. It is rather surprising, however, that more was not made of them at the time, or of the story of Otilia. As far as I have been able to discover, none of the yachts commanded by Dudley was ever on fire, and the idea of "salving the stores" is bizarre. There does survive in the Home Office files a long letter from Phillipa Dudley extolling her husband's virtues, and one would expect to find in it mention of these three brave deeds. There is none. That there may have been some brief encounter at Funchal is not implausible, and brief encounters are the more enjoyable if they are romantic, too. With the assistance of the British Historical Society of Portugal, I have attempted to locate references to the affair in Funchal, and the story was carried there in 1884 on September 19 under the headline "Horrivel" ("Horrible") by a local newspaper, *Diario de Noticias*. The story was taken from the *Cape News* and noted the visit of *Mignonette* to Funchal on June 2. But of the rescue of Otilia there is no mention.

After leaving Madeira on Monday, June 2, the *Mignonette* continued to enjoy good sailing conditions and on June 8 sighted the island of San Antonio, the northernmost island of the Cape Verde group. The following day, she met an Italian sailing barque, 30 days out from Cardiff, and on Sunday, June 14, the *Bride of Lorne,* which had left Liverpool under Captain Frazer on May 5. They boarded her, and Captain Frazer took their letters and offered provisions, which they did not take, as they had no need for any. On Wednesday, June 17, the *Mignonette* crossed the line at a longitude of 26°40′ west. This they had reached on their twenty-ninth day out, with average daily runs of about 120 miles. For both captain and boy, this was the first crossing of the line; whether the boisterous and sometimes obscene rituals associated with this maritime event were celebrated is not recorded. Both Dudley and his second in command were devout men, and Dudley himself had a strong sense of decency. We can be quite sure that nothing indelicate or cruel would have been permitted.

The *Mignonette* was now moving into the South Atlantic, where it was winter, and in preparation for more arduous conditions Dudley decided to reduce the yacht's top hamper. So the topmast was brought down on deck, drastically reducing the height and weight of her rig. The *Mignonette* could now expect to be in the region of the strong and reliable southeast trade winds, which would carry her close hauled toward the Cape. For some days she did experience the conditions expected, though by June 21 the strength and direction of the wind combined with a heavy cross sea forced Dudley to run her a couple of points to the east in order to bring the seas more onto her quarter. On June 25 the wind became more variable, blowing at first from the northwest for four days and then suddenly changing to a very strong south-southeasterly gale. In these conditions, Dudley was forced to reduce canvas, first to a double-reefed mainsail and then to a storm trysail. Even this was at times too much, and the yacht, with all canvas off, lay a-hull. On July 3 the wind dropped away completely. The *Mignonette* lay in the eye of a severe storm; in the evening there was a light southwesterly breeze, which increased steadily until it was blowing strong. By Saturday, July 5, the *Mignonette* was laboring in heavy cross seas in a fresh south-southwesterly gale, and a little before 4:00 P.M. Dudley, in his own words, "made up my mind to heave to for the night and have a comfortable tea." And so, for this intensely British reason, work was set in hand to bring the yacht, then running before the gale, head to wind under minimal canvas. At the time she was carrying a reefed squaresail, a storm trysail, and a small number 3 jib. The squaresail had to be taken off, and the vessel left to ride under a backed jib and trysail. The crew had been organized into two watches—Dudley and Richard Parker had taken the afternoon watch from mid-day to 4:00 P.M., and Stephens and Brooks were below lying in their oilskins, attempting without success to sleep. At 4:00 Dudley called the watch and told Stephens to take the tiller lines and steer while sail was taken in and the maneuver completed. The other three men handed the squaresail and then busied themselves in making everything secure before Stephens brought the yacht head to wind, an operation that, in the conditions prevailing, would subject the yacht to violent stresses as she came broadside to the seas. Dudley had in his hand a small American axe (i.e., a hatchet and hammer combined), and he set about nailing canvas over the aft or "ladies" skylight (on yachts the aft cabin was traditionally the equivalent of the drawing room). By about 4:30 P.M. the work was finished. Richard Parker had gone below to "wet the tea," and Brooks had just returned on deck with lashings that he was going to use to reinforce those holding the dinghy. Dudley was about to give the order to luff up and bring the *Mignonette* around. He was just too late. In his own words.

> I heard the Mate who was at the tiller cry out look out I at once looked under the boom and saw a very high sea just about to brake over us I caught hold and had the weight of same on looking round me I saw all the lee bulwarks was washed away and heard the Mate cry out her side is knocked in the boat she is sinking not very plesent words at such a time I hastened to windward to my horror to prove his words only too true get the boat out was the thing in hand.

Stephens's account tallies with this; as the wave approached, he put the helm hard up in order to meet the wave square, but it broke right over the yacht. He recollected calling out, "My God! Her topsides are stove in; she is sinking," and he saw that the weather topsides and bulwarks abaft the beam had been shattered. He hung on by the tiller lines. Dudley and Parker were on the lee side of the boom, to which they clung, and it broke the force of the sea. Brooks saw the wave coming: "I saw a tremendous sea—reaching I should think, quite half way up to our masthead. . . ." He instantly took two turns of the lashing of the dinghy around each arm and thus survived as the wave swept the deck.

Dudley realized at once that the *Mignonette* was sinking and ordered the dinghy lowered. It was lashed upside down over the fore skylight; Dudley cut the aft lashings and handed his axe to Brooks, who cut those forward. The dinghy, which was of relatively fragile construction, with planking only a quarter of an inch thick, was got overboard, becoming holed on the port side in the process. It was not of course provisioned, and the first essential was water. So Dudley asked Parker to go below and pass up a breaker of water kept at the foot of the ladder that led down into the accommodation. Parker did this, and then threw the wooden cask into the sea. This was not—as some writers have supposed—an act of suicidal idiocy; any attempt to lower the water breaker into the dinghy from the deck of the yacht would have risked smashing a hole in her bottom. A wooden cask of water will of course float, and Parker thought it could be picked up later; the cask was in fact half full and would have floated quite high in the water. According to one of the press interviews he later gave of the incident, Dudley indeed *ordered* Parker to act as he did, and the fact that in his earlier statements he had not explicitly said this may indicate a retrospective awareness that an attempt to lower the breaker into the dinghy, though hazardous, might have been wiser. However, conditions at the time left little opportunity for such reflection.

Stephens, Brooks, and Parker then got into the dinghy, which was held on a line aft of the sinking yacht; and Captain Dudley, in accordance with the proprieties, was now the last man on board. He continued to act with his customary presence of mind and first wrenched the binnacle containing the compass off the deck and handed it into the dinghy; later he was to express astonishment at this feat of strength. He then went below into the cabin, which by now was breast high with water, and secured the sextant and chronometer, which were floating about in their cases. This was a particularly courageous act, since it involved descending a ladder below deck, with little hope of escape if the yacht rolled over. He also collected some six tins of provisions. Stephens, Brooks, and Parker, seeing that the yacht was about to go at any moment, called out several times to Dudley, "Come up, Captain!" Dudley, who had felt the *Mignonette,* as he put it, "sally-over," attempted to throw the tins into the dinghy—one only landed in it. He then got into the dinghy and backed her off with the oars. A minute later,, the *Mignonette* sank by the stern, about five minutes in all after the wave struck her; the dinghy was only a few boat lengths away on her port quarter when she sank.

The chronometer and sextant were picked up, and only one of the remaining five tins, which had floated. Also recovered was a piece of cotton waste (which was used by Brooks to plug the hole in the dinghy) and the wooden bed of the water breaker. The breaker itself they could not find, and it was never seen again; floating high in the water, it would have been carried off rapidly by the wind. Also recovered was the yacht's head sheets grating, which had floated clear. Immediate action was needed to hold the dinghy facing into the seas if she was not to be swamped, and Dudley went to work at once, probably assisted by Brooks, the most experienced sailor in the crew. Using wood from the binnacle together with the breaker stand and the head sheets' grating, he constructed a sea anchor that brought the dinghy's head to the sea and thus enabled them to survive the storm. A small dinghy cannot live in heavy seas in any other position. Dudley, in what seems to be the earliest of his accounts, describes the scene thus:

> to relise our position it was very bad sea like a mountain at times and water coming in faster than we could bail it out and night coming on

Important Message

FOR ______________________________

DATE ____________________ TIME ____________ A. M. / P. M.

WHILE YOU WERE AWAY

M ______________________________

OF ______________________________

PHONE NO. ______________________________

Area Code Number Extension

Telephoned		Please Call	
Called To See You		Will Call Again	
Wants To See You		Rush	
Returned Your Call			

MESSAGE ______________________________

____

____

____

Signed ______________________________

LITHO IN U. S. A.

WC-2424-P — Reorder From Ram Industries, Inc.

> it seemed our time was near but we must do the best we can and trust to God to take care of us and I feel sure he ruled the waves that night they would come within a foot of our little boat at times we had only one breake [i.e., bailer] on board but we managed to stop the whole up so we soon freed her again about 11 pm I should think by the moon a large shark came knocking his tail against our frail boat which made me think our time was near for him to be dining off our bodis, but I prayed that we might be speared to see all at home if possible live a better life in the future. . . .

Another account, again in Dudley's remarkable direct style, catches the man's character—a quick appraisal of the situation followed by decisive action: "About 11 pm as I should judge by the moon a great shark nearly as long as our boat came knocking his tail at our boats bottom the thought of a monster like him near us was not very agreeable I can assure you after a few hits on the head from our ore he left." Dudley was never given to indecision. The attendance of a shark was at this time universally regarded by sailors as an omen of impending death on board. And so the crew of the *Mignonette,* the minister of death repulsed, survived their first night, and the next day Dudley repaired the hole in the dinghy more effectively, cutting off the ends of his trousers to obtain material to do a good job. The position in which the yacht had sunk was, according to Stephens, the navigator, latitude 27°10′ south and longitude 9°50′ west. This was probably an approximation based on dead reckoning from her last established position. To the east lay Africa; they were about on the latitude of Luderitz Bay. Some 1,600 miles to the southeast was the Cape of Good Hope. Some 680 miles to the north on a bearing of 20° lay the island of St. Helena; about the same distance to the south, the islands of the Tristan de Cunha group. Though constituting the nearest land, St. Helena or Tristan de Cunha were equally unreachable in a shallow dinghy possessing no proper sails and incapable of making ground to windward under makeshift rig. They were in the belt between the equator and the southern ocean dominated by the southeast trades, which in July would blow at an average velocity of around 13 knots. Hence the nearest land, in any practical sense, was South America, more than 2,000 miles to the west. And although there was always the chance of meeting a sailing vessel, their course toward land would take them further and further from the normal steamship route to the Cape, which lay to the east. They were very much on their own. Parker, through ignorance, imagined that they would soon reach land or be rescued. Brooks, typical of professional sailors of the period, had no real idea where they were; navigational mysteries were left to the ship's officers, who normally did not inform their men of the ship's position from day to day. In all probability he thought of voyages in days, not locations or miles, but he did appreciate that they were a long way from land, and that the sea is an empty place. Dudley and Stephens of course fully appreciated their desperate position.

Why did the *Mignonette* founder? Dudley gave the formal reason on the Board of Trade form as "stress of weather," but this explains nothing. After the story broke in England, there was a certain amount of speculation on the matter, and various views were put forward. Edward Parnell, a master mariner of 16 Beaumont Place, Plymouth, wrote a letter to the Board of Trade suggesting that a formal inquiry be set up: "Now sir that the sea should knock a hole in the *Mignonette* or any other vessel when afloat and properly handled is a very improbable story." But though the view in the Board of Trade was that the *Mignonette* was not really fit for the voyage, on account merely of her size, she was not thought to have been technically unseaworthy and could not therefore have been prevented from leaving. Since the circumstances of her loss were in a sense well known and the loss of life, by the standards of the time, was trivial, no inquiry was ever held, and the cause was never officially analyzed, though an existing Marine Department minute concludes, "It seems doubtful whether the vessel was fit for such a voyage."

Since the weather conditions were in no way exceptional, an explanation must center on the yacht herself. Thomas Hall, her previous owner, attributed the disaster to her being a very stiff boat—that is, one that possessed a high initial resistance to heeling before the wind—having therefore little ability to "give": "She was strained, and as she had a quantity of lead (nearly two tons) on her keel, the strain literally pulled her in two, top from bottom." This explanation does not fit the accounts given of the disaster, and in any event a well-constructed yacht does not come apart in this way. Hall, unaware of the facts and supposing the *Mignonette* to have been carrying the huge spread of canvas employed for fair weather English yachting, also suggested that she was overcanvassed. But she was not; Dudley had seen to that. Another explanation, which appeared in the Australian press, suggested that she had been weakened when the elliptical counter stern had been built on to her original square transom stern. Dudley's drawings of the yacht, however, make it plain that the counter stern was well above the waterline, and a failure there would not have caused the yacht to founder.

The wave that swept the *Mignonette* cannot have been all that heavy, or the crew would have been carried overboard; furthermore, the relatively fragile dinghy remained undamaged on deck. The mere loss of the lee bulwarks would not in any way endanger the yacht, nor would damage to the weather topsides explain the rapidity with which the yacht was filled. Something disastrous must have happened on or below her waterline, and this suggests some structural weakness in the vessel. Since Aldhous yachts were noted for their strong construction, any weakness most probably arose from some deterioration occurring in the *Mignonette* in the 16 years since she had been built. Indeed it is certain that there had been some deterioration, since she was hauled out at Southampton for replacement of the planking next to the keel—the garboard strakes. Dudley may have discovered weakness here on the trip from Tollesbury to Southampton.

He himself gave a number of accounts of the reason why the vessel foundered, and the fullest of these indicates that he thought that the yacht's planking below the waterline had sprung loose from the frames:

> All I can account for the accident is this that "Migenette" was to aged for to have all lead ballast I myself felt when the sea ~~on the quarter just as if the afterend was being knocked away from the solled weight which would now allow the frames to spring~~ as if something bound her amidships and I ~~had~~ having extra stores etc. which all ment weight and had most all ~~in the~~ a Midships but I proved her to be a good sea boat as good as could be and think if she had been a new boat the accident would not have happened. . . .

Elsewhere he said that her butt ends lay open; that is to say, her planking had sprung away from her frames. Since she sank by the stern, we can be reasonably sure that what occurred was that her planking on or more probably below the waterline sprang open, parting either from the frames, the stern post, or the deadwood, rapidly allowing the yacht to fill. Dudley, as we have seen, attributed this failure to the strain put upon her by the internal lead ballast and stores carried. But properly secured planking does not of course spring loose, and it is logical to suspect that the fastenings failed because of weakness in them or in the vessel's timbers. Dudley may indeed have been somewhat on the defensive, since he was, as captain, responsible for the condition in which the yacht put to sea; he ought to have known of any weakness.

This explanation tallies with two curious pieces of oral evidence. In 1935 or 1936, a young apprentice shipwright, Mr. Vernon Cole, was planking a yacht in the company of an old man of around 73, one Dick Fox. Fox had been a foreman in Fay's Yard and had returned from retirement to work in Moodies Yard at Swanwick. Vernon Cole, then aged 18, had been told to keep an eye on the old man to ensure that he did not strain himself by moving large timbers. Cole countersank the planks—they were garboard strakes—with a view to screwing them (a somewhat unusual technique, I am told) securely to the yacht's stem, where they fitted into grooves, known as rabbets, cut into the timber. Fox told him instead to drill right through the stem and fix the planking by fitting copper rods from one side of the vessel to the other and clenching the ends. This, he explained, was a safer method and made it impossible for the ends of the planks (known as the hood ends) to fly off. He then explained that many years earlier he had used screws to fix the replaced garboard strakes of the *Mignonette* before she left for Sydney: her deadwood, he noticed, had been "a little sick." The *Mignonette,* he said, had foundered in 10 minutes when her hood ends had sprung, and ever since that he had always adopted this more reliable technique. Fox had indeed been ready to give evidence on the matter at the trial but had never been called. That he felt some anxiety over the repairs was reflected in the fact that he repeated on several occasions, "I'm sure in my own mind that I did everything right," and Vernon Cole tells me that the loss of the *Mignonette* preyed on his mind. The repairs would have been much discussed in Fay's Yard after the news reached Southampton, and Brooks's reluctance to sail may have been connected with doubts about the condition of the yacht. Fox's explanation tallies with an account given by Ned Brooks in 1906 to a member of the Parker family, when he too said that *Mignonette* was "unseaworthy." Brooks worked in Fay's Yard after his return and no doubt discussed the story with others who worked there: the public house where he lived was close to the yard. No doubt his view of the state of the yacht before he sailed and after he returned differed, but this is nothing surprising—no doubt Dudley also thought the yacht was safe, but the work showed that the "little sickness" in the timbers ought to have been taken more seriously than it had been.

Dudley himself may have felt some guilt in the matter too, for it is inconceivable that he would not have been told of any slight weakness in the *Mignonette* that came to light when she was out of the water at Fay's Yard. The relatively lengthy account that has been quoted he crossed out, and in the final draft which he sent to the Board of Trade he merely said that *"Migenette"* was rather aged. Age in a yacht is, by itself, nothing; the reality was that *"Migenette"* was unseaworthy and needed expensive repairs to her timbers. But Dick Fox recollected that he had been instructed to carry out repairs using her own timbers, and he therefore confined his work to some replanking; to replace the timbers would have been a very much more expensive job. Dudley, it is clear from other evidence, was an economical man and kept the repair work to a minimum. Had the yacht been brought head to wind a few minutes earlier, she would not have foundered on this occasion, but it is hardly conceivable that she would not at some later point have been struck fatally by as heavy a sea. The *Mignonette* was, for all practical purposes, doomed from the moment she put to sea.

It is ironic that Andrew Thompson, who, if anyone, was responsible for the voyage, had written on May 10 in *Land and Water,* "She is a fine, able little sea boat, but for all that the voyage is not likely to be altogether one of pleasure."

3
"The Horrid Deed"

Good skipper, use him truly,
For he is ill and sad
"Hush! hush!" he cried, then cruelly
He killed the little lad.

—"Ballad of the *Mignonette*"

Although they survived the first night, the position of the four sailors at dawn on Sunday morning was desperate indeed. They possessed no fresh water whatsoever, and their only supply of food consisted of two tins of turnips. Brooks, who had been acting as cook, knew what was in them, and his knowledge was hardly encouraging. But the fact that they had survived the night must have encouraged them to think that God was not wholly against them, and this is reflected in Dudley's account: "I feel sure he ruled the seas that night they would come within a foot of our little boat at times we had only on breake [i.e., a bailer] on board but we managed to stop the whole up so we soon freed her again." This passage also reflects Dudley's characteristic determination, which must have contributed greatly to their survival. The successful repulse of the shark was also, as we have seen, a good and significant omen. The sea anchor held the dinghy head to wind and was vital to their safety. Any attempt to run before the gale would have rapidly ended in disaster, and from July 5 until July 20 the dinghy was normally kept thus on the improvised sea anchor, one man continually steering with an oar in order to ensure that seas were met square on. At the time of the disaster, the wind had been blowing from the south-southwest, but on Monday, July 7, it veered to the southeast and continued to blow strongly from that direction, though moderating on July 13. Probably it was then that Dudley put the bottom boards up at the stern to catch the wind, ensuring that the dinghy faced up into it and made sternway down wind. The dinghy is shown being handled in this way in the drawings based on sketches by Stephens and published later by the *Illustrated London News* and the *Graphic*. The artist of the *Illustrated London News* ("I.R.W.") shows the bottom boards in use only when the dinghy was sailing forward during the last nine days: his drawing includes what is plainly a portrait of Stephens. J. Nash, the *Graphic*'s artist, shows them also in use when the dinghy was lying to this sea anchor.

Maritime tradition (though by 1884 not law) discharged castaways of any obligation to obey officers if their vessel foundered; authority thereafter rested on the personal qualities of the captain. But Dudley's authority over his crew was maintained, though weakened by their predicament. His men remained a disciplined body. They took turns steering, though Richard Parker was only relied on in this critical work when the weather moderated; one error could have been fatal to them all. A system of watches was established, and they seem to have adopted regular berths in the cramped conditions of the dinghy—Dudley and Brooks toward the stern, Parker and Stephens in the forward end; trim was a factor in survival. On the Sunday immediately after the disaster, Dudley's spirits must have been low, for he wrote a penciled letter to his wife on the back of the chronometer certificate, and its tone suggests that he did not expect them to last long. He hoped it would be found after their deaths: "July 6th 1884. To my dear wife—Dudley—Myrtle Road, Sutton in Surrey. Mignonette foundered yesterday. Weather knocked side in. We had five minutes to get in boat without food or water." Later he continued this letter, which, since they were rescued, never performed its function as a message from the dead. As reproduced later in the press, the spelling has been corrected, for Dudley as we know could not spell the yacht's name correctly. However, Dudley seems soon to have regained his composure, if indeed he ever publicly lost it. Phillipa Dudley was of course a biased witness, relying on her husband's account of the matter, but a letter she wrote later fits the independent evidence and in all probability gives a fair picture:

> His wonderful forethought bravery and unselfishness were very prominent. He it was who stayed in the yacht till almost too late, procuring

> provisions. He constructed the sea anchor with which to break the force of the huge waves and prevent them from engulfing them. He cut off the bottoms of his trousers to stop the hole in the boat; he urged the men to give up a garment apiece to be used for sails, and on their refusal, erected all the wood that could be spared from the bottom of the boat. After constant entreaties they gave up their shirts, which, with his own, he erected for a sail. The men, hopeless and tortured, were bent on committing suicide, but were buoyed up by him. . . .

The reference to suicide probably refers to their desire to drink seawater. It was only on July 19 or 20 that he succeeded in persuading the others to make a sail from their shirts; the dinghy then ran before the wind, making some four miles each hour. This increased the risk of a capsize, and the loss of clothing further reduced their comfort; Dudley's aim must have been to get westward as rapidly as possible in order to cross the regular track of the sailing barques.

Dudley insisted on rationing the food, and the first tin was kept until July 7, its five pieces of turnip being divided to last two days. Thereafter the precise dating of events becomes difficult, since there are discrepancies in the evidence. On about July 9, a Wednesday, Brooks spotted a turtle, which Stephens seized by the fins. It came aboard "as light as a fly." Of it, Brooks, no zoologist, said, "I can tell you we were pleased at the prospect of having something to eat, and you can have nothing better at sea in the shape of a fish than a turtle." Dudley killed it, and they attempted to catch its blood in the chronometer case. But waves were breaking into the dinghy, and seawater contaminated the major part, so the blood was not drunk. At the time it was universally believed by sailors that to drink any seawater at all was suicidal—seawater was a sort of poison. A nineteenth-century ballad, "The Raft" (also known as "The Wreck" or "A Sailors Life at Sea"), depicts the predicament of a castaway, left without food or water, who sees a ship passing him by.

> Oh, life is sweet when there is hope, heed not the words I raved,
> Speed on, before it be too late, speed on—I am saved!
> Help! help! good Heavens, they heed me not, their course is changed, and I
> Can hope no longer, O, this thirst, my throat is parched and dry,
> And yet there's water all around, 'tis easy to be had,
> No, no keep off, one draught of you, Oh God, would send me mad!
> Would send me mad, well what of that? 'twere better mad to be,
> Than live like this, a prey to hope, between the sky and sea.

> I'll drink ye, though the fiends of hell were lurking in each draught;
> We'll call it nectar, yes hurrah for a life upon the raft!

This embodied the conventional wisdom; it is now known that small quantities of seawater, particularly if combined with another fluid, can be drunk safely over quite long periods, as long as the practice is begun before the body has been allowed to become grossly dehydrated. This was dramatically demonstrated by Dr. Alain Bombard, who succeeded in crossing the Atlantic alone in an unprovisioned dinghy, living on seawater, fluid obtained from fish, and plankton. His account, *Naufrage volontaire,* was published in 1956, as the first assault on what he demonstrated to be a myth. The crew of the *Kon Tiki* also found it possible to use seawater. But in 1884 drinking any seawater was believed to be a sure recipe for madness and death, and to this day it is generally supposed to be extremely dangerous to consume any.

The flesh of the turtle was cut into strips and hung round the boat; as a sort of celebration, they also ate their second tin of turnips the same day. Though Stephens ate little of it, they lived on the turtle until between July 15 and 17, even eating the bones and chewing at its leathery skin. In the daytime it was hot, and the meat became putrid; some of the fat was so revolting that they threw it overboard. The total amount of meat from the turtle was not large, amounting only to about three pounds of meat each.

Chilled at night and burned by the sun in the daytime, the survivors' principal problem was not hunger but thirst, and by July 13, they had all begun to drink their own urine, a standard technique for prolonging life in such conditions. It did little to alleviate thirst—from a physiological point of view, the earlier this is done, the more useful it is in delaying dehydration; but understandably the men would only begin to overcome their revulsion when conditions had become very bad. Their lips and tongues became parched and blackened, their feet and legs swelled and their skins developed sores from constant exposure to sea and wind and from pressure in the crowded boat. Lack of vitamins and essential minerals must soon have reduced their bodies' ability to heal or to tolerate the grim conditions in which they just managed to exist. From time to time they caught some rain; but, as Stephens explained, "the rain accompanying the squalls seemed to pass on both sides of us. When a squall would approach us we would button our oilskin coats which we fortunately had on, the behind part before, and, spreading our arms out with the coat resting on them, we waited, with burning throats and stomachs, praying to the Almighty for water until the squall passed." Phillipa Dudley gave a similar, though second-hand account: "The very elements seemed to mock their sufferings—because as he [Dudley] often described it, they would eagerly watch the clouds gathering and seem ready to pour down rain in abundance and then while the poor sufferers in agony watched the clouds dispersed and left them in despair." Believing in the poisonous nature of seawater, they would not drink rain contaminated by it, and the quantities they caught were small—sometimes a wine glass full, sometimes as much as a pint. By about July 16, the turtle was finished, though some pieces of skin remained to be chewed; there was no food left and no stock of water.

In preparing for his examination for a master's ticket, Stephens had been given some instruction in techniques for survival. On his advice, he and Brooks soaked their clothes in seawater, but they found that this left them miserably cold at night. They and Parker also tried hanging naked overboard while a lookout was kept for sharks, and they found this gave some relief. They had no way of catching fish, and there is no contemporary evidence for Mr. McCormick's claim in *Blood on the Sea* that they ate plankton (a notion perhaps transferred from the *Bombard Story*). They caught some rain again, probably on July 18, but no more in the days that followed. Their condition thereafter worsened markedly; they began "to look very black at each other."

It was probably during the night of Sunday, July 20, that Richard Parker drank a considerable quantity of seawater and became violently ill. He suffered from diarrhea (which would dehydrate him still further) and lay groaning and gasping for breath, becoming delirious and then comatose. The sudden worsening of his condition prompted him to admit what he had done. Brooks told him he was a silly young fellow, but he replied, "I must drink something." Stephens, who suspected Richard might have started to take seawater earlier than this, later said, "I had been thinking of doing the same myself and I said to him on the quiet—I did not wish the others to know what I thought—'How does it taste Dick?' and he replied, 'Oh, not so bad.' I took a drop or so myself when nobody was looking, and found it burnt my throat like fire, and I made up my mind not to try again. If we had seen Parker drink it we would of course have stopped him. . . ." The three older men tried to comfort young Richard, who kept asking for a ship. Ned Brooks said, "Cheer up, Dickey, it will all come right." But, given the beliefs of the time as sailors, they must all have thought that Richard Parker was now doomed. Indeed, according to Brooks, Richard had been explicitly warned that drinking seawater would kill him. The same belief may, as I have suggested, lie behind the reference to suicide in Phillipa Dudley's account—suicide committed by drinking seawater. They were also struck by the fact that after drinking seawater Richard could not bring himself to drink urine again. Stephens too may have drunk rather more seawater than he admitted—he was the next weakest, suffering greatly from internal pains and swollen limbs. Brooks in fact thought that Stephens too was dying and held his hand for comfort as they prayed for help. So hope began to fade, and it was apparently on July 21 that Dudley completed his farewell letter:

> We have been here 17 [*sic*] days; have no food, we are all four living, hoping to get a passing ship. If not we must soon die. Mr. Thompson will put everything right if you go to him, and I am sorry, dear, I ever started on such a trip, but I was doing it for our best. You know, dear, I should so like to be spared. You would find I should live a Christian life for the rest of my days. If ever this note reaches your hands, you know the last of your Tom and loving husband. . . . Goodbye and God bless you all, and may life provide for you. Your loving husband. Tom Dudley

None of Dudley's written accounts of the story mentions any proposal being made to draw lots in order to select one to sacrifice to save the others. This is a most peculiar fact and not at all easy to explain, since it was in Dudley's favor to have recorded any attempts to have lots drawn. It raises the suspicion that the whole subject of lot drawing was for some reason something better not mentioned at all. Contemporary accounts of the landing at Falmouth also refer to a belief in the town that no such proposal had ever been made and, in consequence, to local animosity against the survivors. But the pilot, Gustavus Collins, said later in evidence that Dudley told him that he had wanted to cast lots, which the others refused, and all three survivors claimed thereafter that such a proposal had been made. Their individual accounts differ somewhat in detail; what follows is perhaps as near to the truth as one can get.

According to Brooks, it was some time before Richard drank seawater that they first broached the possibility of drawing lots as to who should be killed to save the lives of the others. In evidence before the magistrates at Falmouth given on Thursday, September 18, Brooks said that his captain mentioned this possibility several times. The first occasion, on about July 16 or 17, was just after the last of the turtle had been eaten. According to Brooks, Richard heard this conversation and did not then join in it; another version claims that Richard said that he would not participate in drawing lots. At this time Dudley's proposal was not that lots should be drawn there and then but eventually; the others thought it premature to discuss the idea. Someone said, "Do not let us talk about that yet. There is plenty of time." After Richard became ill, the matter was again raised by Dudley. His own account was that after drinking the seawater—probably, that is, on Monday, July 21—Richard said, "We shall die." His account continues, "I remarked, 'We shall have to draw lots boys.' This was ignored by all, and they said, 'We had better die together,' to which I replied, 'So let it be, but it hard for four to die, when perhaps one might save the rest.' " It was on this occasion that Brooks said (according to the account he gave in the Falmouth court), "Let us all die together." Later at the trial at Exeter, this was further elaborated: "Let us all die together. I should not like anyone to kill me, and I should not like to kill anyone else." Dudley's own account of the first discussion agrees with Brooks in placing it on about July 20, before Richard became ill: "About the 15th day when lots was spoke about we all was about the same in bodily health—Brooks must admit that I offered my life did the lot fall on me and I was quite prepared to die and have God for my witness but no-one else would hear of it but it was not to be done until the last possible moment." This suggests some sort of agreement to cast lots *eventually,* if it came to that. But Dudley's understanding of what had been agreed differs from Brooks's understanding, and Stephens's accounts do not carry the matter further. Indeed, another curiosity of the evidence is that, in his accounts of the story, Stephens never said anything at all about drawing lots: the evidence for the discussion of lot casting comes entirely from Dudley himself and from Brooks. Stephens later made a fairly full statement to the press but glossed over the fate of Richard Parker and the events which led up to it, as if he could not bring himself to say anything about it.

It appears, then, that Dudley initiated one or more discussions of the possibility that lots would have to be drawn and that Stephens and Brooks, and perhaps the boy Richard, argued that this was premature. But matters became worse, and Dudley raised this possibility again. This was on the day before Richard Parker was killed.

Dudley himself was uncertain as to whether Richard died on Friday, July 25 (this was the date assumed at the trial and is given on Richard's death certificate—which also gave his age wrong), or on Thursday, July 24. Stephens and Brooks settled for the Friday, too, but in my view the earlier date is more consistent with the evidence. Apart from the inevitable lapses of memory among dying men, the dating of incidents is made more difficult because the maritime day was conceived of by sailors as starting at 12:00 noon, not 12:00 midnight, and this causes further confusion.

Assuming July 24 to have been the date of death, it was on the previous day that Dudley raised yet again the question of lots. By then the condition of all the sailors was very bad, so that it was difficult for them to speak at all: "There was not much said that day." Dudley initiated discussion by saying there would have to be something done; his companions would know exactly what he meant. This was addressed generally, but Richard was by then lying in the bottom of the boat, groaning and probably comatose, so only Stephens and Brooks would hear. Dudley went on to argue that it was better to kill one than for all to die. Both Brooks and Stephens replied, "We shall see a ship tomorrow." Dudley persisted and said they would have to draw lots. Brooks's evidence at the trial was, "He said we should have to draw lots. I said I should not draw lots." So the matter was left for the time being. During the night Brooks, now the strongest of the survivors, was steering from about 1:00 A.M. until 6:00 A.M., and at about 3:00 A.M., while he was so occupied, Dudley held a conversation with Stephens that Brooks said he did not overhear. According to his own account, Dudley said, "What is to be done? I believe the boy is dying. You have a wife and five children, and I have a wife and three children. Human flesh has been eaten before." Stephens replied, "See what daylight brings forth." Brooks, it must be remembered, was thought, probably correctly, to be a bachelor.

Throughout the nineteenth century, the family destitution that was so often the result of shipwreck was a constant theme in popular literature. Thus the ballad of the *Betsey,* lost in 1821 off Fishguard, concludes, typically,

Now for to make a finish
Of these few lines I've penn'd
When a seaman he doth enter a storm
He meets with many a friend,

And if that he is lost at sea,
His friends will grieve for him full sore,
Perhaps they'd wives and families,
Their fate it is full sore.

The possession of dependents therefore constituted a highly rational ground for preference, and we shall meet it as a principle of selection again in an earlier case, discussed later in this book.

At about 6:00 A.M., Stephens relieved Brooks at steering, and he sat on the thwarts for a little time looking around for a ship. There was no sail in sight. Then, according to both Dudley and Stephens, an agreement was made by signs that the boy, who was lying at the bottom of the boat with his arm over his face, was to be killed. The three men's degree of participation in the decision to kill Richard Parker, and the precise sequence of events, is again not easy to establish; and it is possible that in spite of their apparent frankness, some details were in reality suppressed. They had a considerable amount of time later on the *Moctezuma* to settle what was to be said. Furthermore, their mental and physical condition at the time was very weak, and there may have been some confusion in recollecting matters that there was strong psychological pressure to forget. It is not surprising, therefore, that the stories they told differed slightly.

In the evidence he gave at Falmouth, Brooks did not deny that this silent exchange took place, nor that he understood that the boy was to be killed, though he said he did not know *when* this was to be done. His deposition taken at the magistrate's court reads, "I understood what was to be done by Stephens nodding to the boy. We did not talk about killing the boy at any time before that. I did not hear Dudley or Stephens discuss the question of killing the boy." Some considerable period later, in November, he gave evidence at the trial in Exeter, but there he was never really questioned about the silent agreement, except when prosecuting counsel asked, in relation to the time he was sitting on the thwarts after finishing his turn at the steering, "Did Stephens do anything?" He answered, "No. The Captain says to me. "You had better go forward and have a sleep." The question was obviously an attempt by counsel, working from the deposition, to elicit the information that Stephens had nodded at the boy. But Brooks failed to produce the expected reply. In addition to his evidence given on these two occasions, Brooks also made a long statement to the press published on Friday, September 12. He said he knew of the conversation in the night (perhaps he learned of this later, if he did not overhear it at the time) and added that, when he was lying in the bows of the boat, "Stephens made signs to me, which I understood to mean that the Captain intended to take the boy's life, as he was dying." The point of killing Richard before he died naturally, he explained, was to secure his blood to drink. But on this occasion he said that he did not believe Stephens agreed to the killing. Nothing Brooks ever said suggested that he dissented actively or protested at the killing in any way. What he said in his deposition before the shipping master is now undiscoverable, the document having disappeared. Years later, he was to tell a very different story.

Dudley's account of what preceded the death is different in emphasis. He clearly thought that both Brooks and Stephens had agreed to the killing but claimed that both had said that they could not themselves perform the act; their own accounts do not mention this. In his letter to the Board of Trade, he put the matter thus: "We arranged if nothing was in sight at sun rise and no rain came to put the poor lad Parker out of his mesury by killing him for such it was him having drank some salt water could not drink his owen about 8 a.m. nothing in sight and no rain. We Mate Brooks and I made signs between ouselves we had better do it but neither of them had the heart they said I will try and do it." His earliest account emphasizes the fact that he took the initiative: "For the last three days he lay gasping for breath and his frail frame was all but lifeless when I ensisted that we should put an end to his life and drink the drops of blood if any from his body. . . ." Stephens never denied that he agreed to the killing but also never claimed that Brooks did. Brooks's involvement was probably essentially passive—he neither agreed nor disagreed—whereas he had on two earlier occasions actively dissented from any proposal to draw lots, which would of course have endangered his life too. The discrepancy between his account and Dudley's may have simply turned on what counted as "agreement" in the conditions that prevailed.

Stephens's interpretation of what happened is again subtly different. He emphasized that it was difficult to recall precisely what did happen, but in a statement to the press, he hints that all three men were implicated, and he saw the stabbing of Richard more as an acceleration of death than as a direct killing. "The lad dying before our eyes, the longing for his blood came upon us, and on Friday morning, the twentieth day of our being cast away, the master hastened his death by bleeding him." In the deposition he signed in the customs house, Stephens said, "On the twentieth day deponent agreed with the Master that it was absolutely necessary that one should be sacrificed to save the rest, and the master selected Richard Parker boy as being the weakest Deponent agreed in this and the master accordingly killed the lad. . . ." Here it is clear that there were three stages: agreement that *someone* must be killed, selection of Richard by the master, ratification by Stephens. Stephens's description of the killing by bleeding may have as its context the widespread but inevitably ill-attested medical or nursing practice of "easing the passing," which in the nineteenth century relied on techniques different from those employed today. The law treated accelerating death as murder; popular culture did not necessarily accept this rigorous line.

So much for the evidence given in 1884. This is in one respect incomplete, since neither Dudley nor Stephens made any statement before the magistrates or gave evidence at the trial. Until the passing of the Criminal Evidence Act in 1898, it was the general rule that an accused person was not allowed to give sworn evidence at his own trial (though an unsworn statement could have been made by permission of the judge). Since all three men had ample opportunities before and after landing at Falmouth to discuss what they would say, it is possible, as I have suggested, that the full story of what went on before Richard Parker was killed was not told at the time. Certainly the more unpleasant details were suppressed.

There is some evidence—though it cannot be said to be compelling—that in fact lots *were* drawn. In a conversation that took place in 1906, some 22 years later, Brooks told a different tale. He said that Dudley and Stephens conversed and decided that lots would have to be drawn: "The boy was aware that something of this sort was being done. Four pieces of wood one shorter than the others were used. Brooks said that he knew it was rigged against the boy but could do nothing to alter it being too weak himself to care much. Dudley went forward and when the boy saw the knife he said 'What me Sir?' " For reasons that will appear later, this tale of a sham drawing of lots, bizarre though it may seem at first sight, is not wholly implausible; and it is just possible that Brooks hinted at the trial that something of the sort took place. In the course of examination in chief, the following series of questions and answers took place:

Q.	Was anything said about drawing lots?
A.	Yes, that day [the day before the killing].

Q.	What was it?
A.	He [Dudley] said we should have to draw lots.
Q.	You said something about a ship.
Baron Huddleston:	"We shall see a ship tomorrow," you said?
A.	Yes, and I believe Mr. Stephens did too. *Whether the Captain did or not I do not know* [italics added].

Anyone familiar with court procedures will know that witnesses, either because they are confused or because they feel they have been cut short, sometimes answer or elaborate an answer to an earlier question, and it is just possible that in the italicized passage above Brooks was trying to say that he did not know whether Dudley himself actually drew lots or not. In cross-examination Brooks did say explicitly that no lots were drawn, but this is not conclusive of the question. If some sort of charade took place at the time, then it is not difficult to see why, on reflection, this obviously disreputable part of the story was suppressed. Again, the fact that sham lots were drawn might well in retrospect have so embarrassed Dudley that he felt unable to mention the discussion of drawing lots at all in his numerous written accounts of what happened. The whole question of lots was, as it were, better passed over in silence; to this extent candor did not prevail. In the same way, Dudley's frankness understandably enough did not extend to a full account of the more revolting details of the dismemberment of Parker's body. Again, Stephens's curious statement that the Captain "selected" Parker may be a dark reference to the drawing of sham lots. I am inclined to suspect that Brooks's later account is true, particularly because he was at the time talking to a relative of Parker, when it was against his interest to mention sham lots at all. There is also some slight corroboration in the account given by Dudley of the killing itself, to which we must now turn. But before doing so, it is worth recording that a traditional version of the story that circulated in the 1930s in Southampton was that lots were drawn; they fell on the mate, Edwin Stephens; and he then killed Richard Parker, who had been drinking seawater. How the story came to be told in this form one can only speculate.

At about 8:00 A.M. Dudley pulled himself up by the dinghy's improvised shrouds and looked around yet again for a sail; nothing was to be seen. He told Stephens to be ready to hold Richard Parker's legs if he struggled and then killed him by thrusting his penknife into the boy's jugular vein, catching the blood in the chronometer case. Stephens described the process by saying, "the Master hastened his end by bleeding him."

Dudley wrote out eight distinct accounts of the voyage of the *Mignonette,* one of which, as we have seen, was sent to the Board of Trade. When describing the killing, these accounts vary considerably, the earliest being this: "I then offered a prayer for the poor boys soul if were to commit such a rash act asked forgiveness from our Maker I then said it must be done it may save three lives so we put an end to his sufferings which was not a moments work and all was over himself never moving from where he lay. . . ." His next account claimed the boy never spoke and died in five seconds; the next extended the period to 10 seconds, and the next to 30. The next two versions state that Parker "murmered what me?" By quoting this remark by the unfortunate boy, Dudley had brought himself to reveal that Parker was conscious and knew he was going to be killed. Brooks, as we have seen, later explained this remark by saying that Parker knew that lots were being drawn, and when he saw the knife was asking if he had been allocated the fatal lot. But Dudley's next statement is fuller and provides a different explanation, though a very bizarre one—he told Parker that he was going to kill him. This account reads,

> Brooks nor Mate could do the deed I said I would Brooks going in bows of boat and covering his face up and the Mate and I left to do the horrid deed I offered up a prayer for to ask forgiveness if any of us was tempted to committ any rash act and ask that all our souls may be forgiven I then said no Dick your time is come poor boy murmured out what me Sir and I said yes my boy but he did not move Mate was to hold his legs if he had but in less than 30 seconds I am sure he lay lifeless.

Another version, sent to the Board of Trade and possibly composed earlier, is similar but puts the duration of life at 15 seconds. The originals of all these accounts survive in the Public Record office.

Brooks heard Dudley's order to Stephens—"Hold his feet"—and then heard a noise on the inside of the boat that made him look up; what caused this noise remains unexplained. Dudley's prayer was presumably silent, or an afterthought, for Brooks never heard it. He saw that the boy had been stabbed, and he fainted. When he came to, he saw Dudley engaged in catching the blood and he and Stephens drinking it. Brooks at once asked for a share, saying, "Give me a drop," and noticed that the eyes of the boy were quite white. Brooks was given some blood; it was congealed, and there was little of it. He swallowed it as well he could. It might now be supposed that the three sailors, confronted with the corpse of their shipmate, would be in something of the same state of puzzlement as children confronted for the first time by artichokes—uncertain how to proceed next. But Dudley and Stephens seem to have had no such problem. They stripped the body, threw the clothes overboard, and at once cut out heart and liver, which they ate. Then Brooks took over the steering for the next two or three hours. It was presumably during this period that the body was dismembered, using the dinghy's brass oar locks, or crutches, as a block, in order to avoid damage to the thin planking. Providentially, the precise details have not been recorded. Brooks later described the scene as "a horrible sight and no mistake" but added, "But I did not think so much of it except just at the moment, though when I am by myself I think of it a good deal and my thoughts then of what I have seen and what we went through are very dreadful." In all probability much of the corpse was jettisoned quite soon, and it is recorded that what remained (perhaps strips of flesh) was washed and covered up to protect it from the sun. It must be remembered that all three men would have been involved in or at least had witnessed butchery; they were not of a twentieth-century delicacy, and Dudley had worked as a ship's cook. Later, when he was in prison, Dudley gave expression to his retrospective horror at the recollection of the scene: "I can assure you I shall never forget the sight of my two unfortunate companions over that gastly meal we all was like mad wolfs who should get the most and for men fathers of children to commit such a deed we could not have our right reason." The following day they caught a substantial amount of rain water, and thereafter, as Dudley put it with an unhappy choice of verb, "we feasted off the body and having no rain had to drink our owen water again." For the next four or five days they continued to live off the remains of Parker. Dudley and Brooks consumed most, Stephens very little. Brooks said, "I and the Captain fed on the body, and so did Mr. Stephens occasionally, but he had very little. We lived on it for four days, and we ate a good deal—I should think quite half—of the body before we were picked up, and I can say that we partook of it with quite as much relish as ordinary food." Inevitably, the remains began to decompose. Conditions in the small dinghy must have been extraordinarily repulsive.

Nevertheless, the three survivors seem to have been generally well satisfied with what had been done. Dudley was quite convinced that it had saved all their lives: "I feel quite sure had we not that awful food to exist upon not a soul would have lived untill we were rescued." And, according to Phillipa Dudley, who no doubt had further details from her husband, "after the deed was committed, both Brooks and Stephens grasped his hands many series of times in the day, saying he had saved their lives, and how they would show their gratitude in reaching home, if they ever did so." Brooks said as much both to the press and at the trial and added that, after drinking the blood, "I felt quite strong—in fact we all made use of the expression that we were quite different men." Dudley himself, recording how they had washed the decomposing pieces overboard and cut out the rotting bits, said it was better than nothing. "In fact we all said many times it and it alone kept life in our bodies." The grim thought must, however, have occurred to Stephens that he, as the weakest, was likely to be next on the menu.

But on the morning of the Tuesday, July 29, a sail was sighted. Dudley's account runs thus: "on 24th day as we was having our breakfast we will call it Brooks who was steering shouted a sail true a sail it was we then all prayed the stranger will be directed across our path." Brooks, who first saw the sail at about 6:30 in the morning, did not grasp its reality immediately; he was talking to himself and praying, but he then cried out, "Oh, my God, here's a ship coming straight towards us." Tom Dudley, practical and decisive as ever, did not confine himself to prayer. The vessel was some five miles away, coming up to windward of the dinghy. Dudley had the sail taken down in order not to increase the distance between them. They then set out to row to windward to get into her path, and Stephens waved a shirt. They did not succeed in getting directly ahead of her and endured the suspense of an hour and a half before she came up with them. In a peculiarly unhappy expression, Dudley said that during this period, "their hearts were in their mouths."

At last it became obvious that the ship had seen them, and shortly after being struck by a squall, it came up with them. Brooks then took the oars, while Dudley in the bows caught a rope, calling out, "Oh Captain, for God's sake help us. We have been twenty four days and have had nothing to eat or drink. Help us on board." The captain of the vessel replied in German and sent two of his crew down to assist them on board—Julius Erich Martin Wiese and Christopher Drewe. Brooks managed to scramble on board by the chainplates and was then carried by the carpenter; Dudley and Stephens were hauled up by ropes. They were given half a glass of water each and later more water, brandy, and food. The captain of the rescuing vessel and his wife, who was on board, took personal charge of the care of Dudley himself.

The rescuer was Captain P. H. Simonsen, and his vessel was the three-masted wooden sailing barque *Moctezuma,* 42.29 meters in length, 442 tons net; she had been built in 1864–65 in Apenrade by the master shipbuilder Skifter Andersen under the name *Fetisch,* originally for the Hamburg line of Peter Diederishsen; she was then the largest ship he had ever built. She had been sold on September 12, 1881, to the Oetling Brothers, who renamed her *Moctezuma;* in accounts of the case her name is usually misspelled as *Montezuma.* She was a much traveled ship, having in her time sailed to Pisagua, Hong Kong, Valparaiso, San Francisco, and Bangkok. Her present voyage had begun in Bordeaux, and she was returning to Hamburg from South America.

According to McCormick's *Blood on the Sea,* Captain Simonsen had earlier altered course to bring the ship near to the then uninhabited Île de Trinidade to settle a bet with the ship's doctor as to the existence there of mermaids. His story of the rescue is elaborated with much detail, some of it transparently inaccurate (the dinghy in his account was rowed to *windward* of the barque, whereas of course it was only rowed at all because it was to *leeward*). Again it would be quite extraordinary for a merchant vessel at this time to carry a doctor, and the talk of the alteration of course makes no sense if the distances involved and the ship's position are taken into account. All that is known is that the *Moctezuma* had started her return voyage from Punta Arenhas in Chile, a small seaport on the western shore of the Straits of Magellan and the most southerly port in all of South America. She was carrying a cargo of fustic and cedar to her home port. At the time of the rescue, her position was 24°28′ south and 27°22′ west—approximately 990 miles east of Rio de Janeiro, and it was her captain who first sighted the dinghy, supposing it at first to be a piece of wreckage. He was astonished to discover men alive in it. Since the loss of the *Mignonette,* they had drifted and sailed some 1,050 miles, covering about 43 miles a day; it would have taken as long again to reach land.

The dinghy still contained the pathetic mortal remains of Richard Parker, and Dudley later claimed that he had insisted on their preservation, in conformity with his general policy of concealing nothing.

Someone—most probably Brooks, the strongest of the survivors—must have doubted the wisdom of this and thrown most of the remains overboard, for all that was actually found in the dinghy was a rib and a few fragments of flesh. These Julius Wiese, on Captain Simonsen's orders, threw into the sea. Dudley entreated the captain to save the dinghy as a memento of this remarkable voyage—as we have seen Dudley was keen on mementos. And so it was that the dinghy was taken on board the *Moctezuma*.

Captain Simonsen, his wife, and the crew treated the three castaways with great kindness. They were all in very poor condition, with swollen feet, badly emaciated bodies, blackened mouths and lips, and skins suffering from continuous exposure to sun and salt water. Stephens was the weakest, Brooks the strongest; but for some days they could neither lie down nor stand without torment. For poor Tom Dudley, matters were made much worse by an accident the following day that gave him a serious wound, still under treatment two months later. In his own statement, Dudley was reticent about the nature of this accident, writing, "I myself happened with an accident which gave Captain Simonsen a great deal of trouble to him I owe a great deal in the kind way he treated me through the illness which was far from a pleasant task to perform and I cannot mention it here." More details of this embarrassing injury were passed down from William Danckwerts, a barrister engaged in the case, to his son, the late Lord Justice Danckwerts. The unfortunate Dudley had been sitting on a chamber pot that broke and lacerated his buttocks severely; more than two months later he had to stand throughout his trial at Exeter. At the time of the accident, he would be ill, and his body would possess little ability to heal; no doubt the wound became infected.

On board the *Moctezuma,* Dudley wrote out the eight accounts of the loss of the *Mignonette* to which reference has been made. These include one that he sent to the Board of Trade (it is now numbered "C" and stamped as received on September 8). Of the remaining seven, six are numbered, and one has the letter "D" and the roman numeral "I" on it. The numbering is not original and does not appear to correspond to the sequence in which the accounts were originally written. Dudley's purpose in writing these accounts seems to have been to prepare a letter to the yacht's owner, Jack Want, explaining the loss, as was normal; and the later drafts, numbered "2," "6," "C," and "D," end with either "I remain yours faithfully Thos. Dudley, Master late Migenette" or "Yours obediently Thos. Dudley,

Master." They are therefore draft letters of explanation, not confessions. Dudley also made two drawings of the yacht on a blank page, perhaps to be used to make a model of her; this was a standard shipboard hobby. Stephens also made some drawings, perhaps to show other sailors; the originals of these drawings have not survived. What else passed on the voyage home to England is not recorded, until the moment when the pilot boarded the *Moctezuma* to bring her in to Falmouth, where they were taken into custody by Sergeant Laverty on a charge of murder on the high seas. It was not to be a happy homecoming.

4
Before the Falmouth Magistrates

The Captain and Mate are now on their trial,
To killing the boy they give no denial,
'Tis a terrible story which they have to tell,
How they have suffered and how the boy fell.

—"Ballad of the *Mignonette*"

Once the harbor police had arrested the three men, it was their duty to bring the prisoners without delay before the borough magistrates, and arrangements were made for this to be done at 11:00 A.M. on Monday morning, September 8. It was then the duty of the magistrates to hold a judicial inquiry to decide whether the charges should be proceeded with or not and, if so, whether the men should be set free on bail or held in custody. This stage in the proceedings, the preliminary inquiry or the committal proceedings, originated at a time when the magistrates performed many of the functions of a police force, including that of actively investigating suspicions of crime, arranging for the arrest of suspects, and collecting evidence from prisoners and witnesses. The procedure was regulated by Jervis's Act of 1848. By 1884 the nature of such magistrates' hearings had changed to the more passive role of deciding whether the police (who now normally investigated crime) or the private prosecutor could make a sufficiently good case against the accused—a *prima facie* case—that it was reasonable to put them on trial before a judge and jury at the appropriate court of assize. The investigative function was no longer in their hands, though they did record the prosecution evidence in written depositions, which the witnesses signed. Although the magistrates no longer took the decision to prosecute, they did retain the option of simply dismissing the charges. Dudley appears to have been quite confident that, once the magistrates heard the evidence, they would do so. The point of a formal inquiry, as he saw it, was simply to set an official seal of approval on his conduct so that he could be set free, judicially exonerated from any blame in the matter.

While Dudley and his companions remained in a cell or cells in the borough police station, Sergeant Laverty continued to investigate and to assemble his evidence. He already had the knife, and the depositions signed in the customs house had been sent from there to the Board of Trade in London, together with Dudley's long and incriminating letter. These documents in their turn were sent on from the Board of Trade to the Home Office, as standard practice, for the Board of Trade was not responsible for prosecuting regular crimes alleged to have been committed on vessels at sea. There were, however, other properties still on the *Moctezuma;* and William Hodges, the waterman, was employed to row out to the barque early on Sunday morning to bring ashore the dinghy, its paddles, the pair of brass crutches or oarlocks, a chronometer, a sextant, and a bundle of clothing, all of which were handed over by Captain Simonsen, together with a list written in German. William Hodges also collected the two sailors Julius Wiese and Christopher Drewe; though neither spoke English, they were potential witnesses as to the contents and condition of the dinghy when it was found. Arrangements for holding them would have been settled with Mr. Robert Fox, the German vice-consul, of the leading local firm of shipping agents. All the property was handed over in the customs house, where Sergeant Laverty also seized a package of papers that fell out of the clothing: it comprised the seven additional draft statements by Dudley as well as his letter to the Board of Trade, all written in his own hand. All were incriminating and potentially exhibits in the case.

That evening Sergeant Laverty visited Dudley at the police station at 33 Market Street and, somewhat oddly, asked him what should be done with all his possessions. Dudley asked him to hand them all over to a Mr. John Burton. The sergeant insisted on retaining the papers and the knife but otherwise complied with Dudley's request. The dinghy itself was placed in the warehouse of a Mr. John Buckingham, a marine stores dealer, who had premises at Upton Slip. Presumably Sergeant Laverty, armed with numerous "confessions," did not think he would require the dinghy or the other items as possible exhibits. It is surprising that the dinghy itself was not detained by Mr. Cheesman in the Queen's warehouse, but the evidence is clear that this was not done.

John Burton, who now had custody of Dudley's property, was a celebrated local character. His shop, The Old Curiosity Shop, stood a short way from the police station at 27 Market Street. Here Burton stocked an extraordinary collection of curios. Over the door was painted "Wonders from Many Lands," and that was indeed the nature of the merchandise he sold. On an occasion in 1882 he even attempted to outbid the Plymouth Corporation and purchase John Smeaton's old Eddystone Lighthouse; in this venture he failed, and it now stands in consequence on Plymouth Hoe. The weird collection he held provoked one H. J. Daniels to publish bad verse in the *Western Daily Mercury,* of which this is an extract:

> There's a sword of Shere Ali, no more to be drawn
> And stirrups from Delhi, that city of blood,
> There are Japanese coins, not at all like our own
> And brutes from the forest and fish from the flood.

Later in the month of September 1884, he even had a sea serpent for sale, caught, he claimed, on the Manacles Reef. Much of his stock was acquired from sailors calling at Falmouth, and mementos of British cannibalism were just the sort of thing that Burton would covet; it was as an entrepreneur that he would have visited Dudley. But he was also a kindly and generous man and offered practical help. Burton probably put the men in touch with a solicitor, Harry Tilly, another prominent local citizen and a partner in the legal partnership of Fox and Tilly, whose office was also close at hand in Church Street. At first Dudley was so confident of his own rectitude that he saw no need for lawyers, but someone—perhaps John Burton—persuaded him otherwise. He was, as it turned out, going to need them badly.

The three men were also visited by Mayor Liddicoat, who seems to have been somewhat apologetic about their arrest; he continued to take a close personal interest in their comfort. On Monday morning they all appeared before him and seven of his magisterial colleagues on the bench, charged with murder on the high seas. The court sat in the Guildhall (now called the Old Town Hall). Sergeant Laverty described the conversation he had overheard and produced the penknife with which Richard Parker had been killed. He asked for a remand in custody and an adjournment until he had received instructions from the treasury solicitor representing the Home Office; a deputy, the Hon. H. J. A. Cuffe, actually handled the case. This request followed advice he had probably been given by the clerk to the magistrates, Mr. W. J. Genn, who had recently received instructions from the attorney general, Sir Henry James, to seek the advice of the Treasury lawyers in all murder cases. This new system had been announced in the House of Commons on March 17, 1884; it was intended to ensure that capital charges were competently handled by London lawyers, particularly when the sanity of the accused was in any doubt. This new system alone would have ensured that the case of the *Mignonette* would not be handled locally. However, the Board of Trade (and through it the Home Office) had already been informed, and the clerk told the magistrates that the treasury solicitor had been instructed already to deal with the prosecution and wanted an adjournment. He had no doubt been in touch with London by telegram.

For Harry Tilly the defense of the survivors of the *Mignonette* must have been a thrilling experience; he was now responsible for the defense of the three men in a case that was certain to be nationally or even internationally famous. He was clearly determined to defend them with vigor, and when his turn in the proceedings came, he boldly applied for them to be released on bail, though to do this in a murder case was at that time virtually unknown. He pointed out that all three men had been entirely cooperative and emphasized their weak health as an argument against their continued detention. They were, he said, "willing that all the facts should be brought before a proper tribunal." This application was carefully considered and must have secured some support behind the scenes, for the bench considered it "for some time." But it was eventually refused, and the men were remanded in custody for a further hearing to take place on Thursday, September 11. So they returned to the borough police station. There on Tuesday evening a macabre incident occurred. Daniel Parker, Richard's eldest brother, was on the racing yacht *Marguerite* at Torquay, where he somehow heard on Sunday evening of the death of his brother; fuller details were read out from the newspapers to the whole crew by its sailing master, Captain T. Diaper of Itchen Ferry, on Monday. Daniel traveled at once to Falmouth, arriving on Tuesday evening at the police station. There Dudley heard him talking to Superintendent Bourne and called out, "Why, that's little Dick's voice!" Daniel, who closely resembled his young brother in appearance as well as in voice, then met Dudley, Stephens, and Brooks and, astonishingly, shook hands formally with them all—Dudley first, then Brooks, then Stephens. What they talked about is not recorded. Daniel then remained in Falmouth for the hearing on Thursday.

Meanwhile in London the file concerning the case, marked "Pressing" in red to ensure attention, was circulating up the hierarchy of officials in the Home Office, and on Monday, Sir Adolphus Liddell, the permanent under-secretary of state, wrote on it, "Sir W. Harcourt to see." So it was that on Wednesday the home secretary himself, having discussed the case with the law officers of the crown, the attorney general, and the solicitor general, placed on the docket the decision to go ahead with the prosecution. "This is a very dreadful case. The law must decide what is the character of this terrible act. I presume these men will be committed [i.e., sent for trial by the magistrates]. In any case, I should wish the Public Prosecutor to take charge of the case so that it may be properly dealt with." From this it is apparent that Sir William assumed that an important point of principle was involved in the case—was this terrible act murder in the eyes of the law or not? There was a leading case to be made of the tragedy. Appropriate letters were then dispatched on September 13 to the director of public prosecutions and the Board of Trade by Sir Adolphus Liddell. The legal machinery had now been set irrevocably in motion, and the lawyers took over for the moment. Almost at once the Home Office was made aware of the apparent incongruity of accusing good Tom Dudley of murder, for on September 10 Mr. I. Macnab, whose schooner *Reindeer* Tom had commanded, wrote to the home secretary to express his astonishment at the affair:

> Thomas Dudley was at one time Captain of my yacht and while in my service I conceived the highest regard for him in every way . . . upright, truthful and honest as a man and kind to a degree to all under his command. He was generous too and gave freely from his small store to his less fortunate friends. . . . But it passes my understanding to conceive the horrors of the extremity that could induce so good and brave a man to do a wrong. I am sure of this that whatever view the law may take of the act Dudley could not have thought it unjustifiable. Neither selfishness nor cruelty had any part in his character.

The letter, prophetic of the problem that the case was later to present to the home secretary, was acknowledged and filed.

Back in Falmouth on Thursday, September 11, Dudley, Stephens, and Brooks again appeared in court. Superintendent Bourne's men held the public back until a little before 11:00 A.M., but then the crowd rushed the diminutive courthouse, which became "densely packed with an eager and expectant throng." Murder cases were a major source of interest and entertainment in Victorian England, and murder combined with cannibalism was about as entertaining as even Victorian criminals could offer. The drama was heightened by the presence in court of Daniel Parker dressed as a yachtsman, with his yacht's name, *Marguerite,* embroidered in red on his jersey; no doubt gossip told the crowd of his resemblance to Richard, and it is not often that a murder case occurs with the alter ego of the victim present in court. And, when the maritime background to the case is taken into account, it is hardly surprising that the population of Falmouth was particularly fascinated. The prosecution simply asked for a further remand until the following Thursday, September 18. Then it was Harry Tilly's turn. By now better prepared, and dealing for probably the first and only time in his life with a really interesting question of law, he made a spirited application for bail again. In part he relied on his clients' "wretched state of health" and the difficulties they had faced in unsuitable accommodation. But more significantly, he argued and indeed assured the lay magistrates that the charge of murder was a mere technicality. He asked them "to consider this principle—the great universal principle of self-preservation which prompts every man to save his own life preferably to that of another. At its worst the case was not one in which there was the slightest possibility that the charge alleged against them could hold." And since the charge was a technicality and they were not wealthy men, bail should not be set at a high figure. He supported his argument by reference to legal authorities—Sir Francis Bacon; the great Sir William Blackstone, author of the *Commentaries on the Laws of England;* and the contemporary guru of criminal law, Sir James Fitzjames Stephen, one of Her Majesty's judges and author of the monumental three-volume *History of the Criminal Law of England,* first published in the previous year. Harry Tilly was indeed something of a local intellectual. He was for many years, up to 1893, on the committee of the Falmouth and Penryn branch of the Royal Cornwall Polytechnic Society (which was dominated by the Quaker Fox family of Falmouth; the secretary in 1884 was his partner, Wilson L. Fox). His legal argument was a creditable performance.

What, if anything, the good grocer who presided (or his colleagues) made of all this learning we do not know; he was more familiar with such down-to-earth matters as the sale of wines and spirits—good port wine at 1s.4d. a bottle, "quality and strength guaranteed." But the clerk to the justices also had a contribution to make. He had been in touch with the Treasury solicitors and heard that they did not ask for a remand in custody: "They add that the question of bail is one which they desire to leave entirely in the hands of the Bench, and will raise no objection if they think fit to grant the application." This broad hint did the trick, making it unnecessary for the bench to delve into deep matters of criminal theory, and, after retiring for 10 minutes, they took the quite remarkable step of granting a release on bail to prisoners charged with a capital offense. Already the legal establishment's curious approach to the case of the *Mignonette* was beginning to emerge—a determination to secure a conviction for murder, combined with a humane and slightly inconsistent desire to see that Dudley and his companions did not suffer unduly in consequence.

The decision to release the men was received with loud applause. Dudley was to be required to offer bail of £200 himself, with a surety in the same amount. Stephens's and Brooks's bail was fixed at half the same sum. These monies did not have to be actually produced, merely formally promised by an archaic mechanism known as a recognisance—a contract to pay the Queen £200 (or £100) *unless* they appeared for trial when required. Failure to attend could lead to the forfeiture of the promised sums of money. John Burton stood surety for Dudley and, after some hesitation, for Stephens and Brooks as well; at first he offered to be surety for £50, if someone else would share the burden, but nobody in court came forward. A local paper, the *Falmouth News Slip,* commented approvingly, "What would we do without old Burton? He was the only man at the Court ready with £400 bail for the Mignonette's crew. He brought gladness and joy to the distressed crew." The men were now free to leave. Before they did so, Daniel Parker talked to Dudley about the wages due Richard, which had been left at the customs house. (Apparently Stephens's wages had been paid by Phillipa Dudley directly to his family.) Dudley's slightly parsimonious character comes out in the fact that he was reluctant to pay any wages for the period after the loss of the *Mignonette,* as appears from correspondence surviving in Falmouth; he was not in fact legally liable to do so. But no dispute arose over Richard's pay.

This matter settled, Daniel again shook hands ritually with the three men in open court; they had now been publicly exonerated by the head of Richard's family. They then left the court and walked without hindrance about the town. For the mayor, however, the day did not have a happy ending. By the late post he received a letter from Sheffield; it was anonymous. It contained "nothing but a series of disgusting oaths calling the Mayor by the most outrageous names for having issued the warrant . . . he had no right to take such a course, as the men had not committed murder. The writer concluded by saying that he intended to come to Falmouth next week to shoot the Mayor. . . ." It may be that the writer of this letter, who fortunately for the grocer failed to keep his promise, had had a similar experience as a castaway.

By now it was clear that in Falmouth public opinion was entirely on the side of Dudley and his men. At first this may not have been so. The *Western Mail* said, on September 8, "The question which was most extensively discussed by the public was 'Why did they not cast lots?' and in the mind of a very large section a feeling of strong antipathy to the survivors has been created on this point." Local opinion obviously thought this was the correct procedure. Once the full facts were known (including Dudley's attempt to cast lots), opinion changed; they all became heroes, and public sympathy took practical forms. The men were destitute and needed money for living and defense. The dinghy was put on show by John Buckingham to raise money, and the *Falmouth News Slip* exhorted its readers, "Go and see the Boat of the Yacht Mignonette at Buckingham's, and leave some coppers for the men." At the time a visiting showman, R. D. Patterson, had booked the Royal Polytechnic Hall for *Zealandia,* a "Grand Diorama of New Zealand," a "stupendous Work of Art" painted on 2,000 yards of canvas by a colonial artist, one J. S. Willis, depicting 50 scenes in the colony. The proceedings were also enlivened by the activities of such artists as Mr. Watson Thornton, "Humourist, Lecturer and Author," and Mr. Dan Everett, "Coloured Colonial Philosopher and Eccentric Comedian"; and by a performance of a farce, *The Ghost in the Pawn Shop.* Seats were 3s., 2s., and 1s.; and tickets were on sale at Messrs Uglow and Thuell's Music Store. On Wednesday, September 17, Patterson arranged a special benefit night for Brooks and Stephens; this was inspired by Dudley's reluctance to pay them any wages from the date of the loss of the *Mignonette,* which alone local feeling condemned. A photograph of the dinghy, exhibited there, was later sold as a postcard and still survives. According to one account, the dinghy bore bloodstains. The show produced a "handsome donation" and the exhibition of the dinghy £4.12s. Mr. W. Clark Russell, the celebrated marine novelist and journalist, sent a check for the three men and congratulated the people of Falmouth on their generosity, reminding them of their kindness on an earlier occasion in 1825 when they had cared for Colonel Fearon and the men of the 31st Regiment of Foot, shipwrecked when the *Kent* foundered on March 16 of that year.

Sympathetic feeling also found expression in a long editorial in *Lake's Falmouth Packet and Cornwall Advertiser* on Saturday, September 13. This supported the mayor over the arrest but argued, on lines different from Henry Tilly's, for the innocence of the prisoners. "It is utterly impossible that men can endure the tortures of nineteen days' starvation, the exquisite agony of a long continuing thirst, the anguish of mind and the prospect of excruciating death . . . without the mind becoming in a measure at least deranged; and without thus becoming to the fullest extent irresponsible for their actions." In any event, Darwin's "survival of the fittest" justified the killing. So the paper trusted that the men would be discharged by the magistrates once the business had been judicially investigated.

Dudley left for home late on Thursday afternoon, the last London train departing at 5:25 P.M. Mr. Cheesman, as ever nervous of his local reputation, turned up at the station to see him off. Dudley bore with him his sextant, his chronometer, and his letter to his wife. Phillipa and two friends met him at Paddington Station at 4:00 on Friday morning. The press was also there, and of course release on bail gave all three survivors a chance to publicize their version of the events, which they did. Dudley allowed his last letter to his wife to be published; it first appeared in the *Falmouth News Slip* on September 13. It was a touching document, and its publication can only have increased popular sympathy for him; it is something of a masterpiece in this genre, rivaled only by Scott's last message from the Antarctic. Passages have previously been quoted, but it is here reproduced in full from a newspaper version; the original has not survived.

> To my dear wife Dudley, Myrtle Road Sutton in Surrey. Mignonette foundered yesterday. Weather knocked side in. We had five minutes to get in boat, without food or water; 9th picked up turtle. July 21 . . . we have been here 17 days; have no food, we are all four living, hoping to get a passing ship. If not we must soon die. Mr. Thompson [of the London Yacht Agency] will put everything right if you go to

> him, and I am sorry, dear, I ever started on such a trip, but I was doing it for our best. You know, dear, I should so like to be spared. You would find I should live a Christian life for the rest of my days. If ever this note reaches your hands, you know the last of your Tom and loving husband. I am sorry things have gone against us thus far, but I hope to meet you and all the dear children in heaven. Dear, do love them for my sake. Dear, bless them and you all. I love you all dearly you know, but it God's will if I am to part from you; but I have hope of being saved. We were about 1300 miles from Cape Town when the affair happened. Goodbye and God bless you all, and may life provide for you. Your loving husband. Tom Dudley.

Messages from the dead of the sea actually did turn up in the nineteenth century from time to time—for example, the *Times* published one dated January 2, 1863, found in a soda water bottle: "Latitude 70 Longitude 25. Lord Help us All. The bark Ely of Card. Capt. P. Schrabt." None I have seen rivaled Dudley's. Phillipa Dudley had indeed already met the press on September 9; even then, letters of support and sympathy from friends and from Dudley's superiors and subordinates had begun to arrive in considerable numbers. Accompanied by journalists, the Dudleys took a cab to Victoria Station and caught the 6:10 A.M. train to Sutton. The captain was by now viewed with such awe that men took off their hats and stood bareheaded as he passed by in carpet slippers, for he was still unable to wear boots. When they arrived home, a doctor attended to his wounded buttocks, and all day a stream of sympathetic callers visited. In the evening, considerably distressed, Dudley told the press of his experiences.

Edwin Stephens and Ned Brooks too seem to have anticipated no hostility in Southampton, where they returned, near though it was to Richard's home just across the River Itchen. They went straight there, arriving on Friday at 12:30 P.M.; friends were shocked at their emaciated condition. Stephens was almost prostrate; he suffered from severe headaches and a general inability to concentrate on what he was doing. He walked on his mother's arm, accompanied by his brother-in-law, Mr. Fisher. Ned Brooks, in relatively good health, was met by friends, and a considerable crowd accompanied him back to his lodgings at 39 Millbank Street; there seems to have been a sort of heroes' homecoming. Stephens received the following letter (said to be typical of many) from a correspondent in Cowes: "The great privations you and your noble companions have undergone, and the great skill with which you handled your frail bark under such exceptional circumstances and under a tropical sun, will place you in the first rank of England's heroes." Both men also made full statements to the press, Stephens including little sordid detail but emphasizing that, in the event, he had not actually physically participated in the killing. Brooks was rather more explicit. The whole affair naturally filled the local press.

As the men dispersed, so did their rescuers. The barque *Moctezuma,* short-handed now, having left behind two of her crew, put out to sea again past St. Anthony's Head and turned east up channel for the voyage to Hamburg. She was pursued by the officials of the Board of Trade. Following a practice originating in the Foreign Office, they encouraged the rescue of castaways by a system that combined indemnities and rewards; it was not until 1911 that the master of a ship was put under a *legal* obligation to aid other vessels in distress by the Maritime Conventions Act, though a duty to stand by after collision had been imposed earlier in 1862. Captains of rescuing vessels were reimbursed for their costs and rewarded by the presentation of useful gifts. So, on September 8, it was noted in the file that a reward should be considered, and Mr. Cheesman was told to look into a possible claim for subsistence for the 38 days the men from the *Mignonette* had been on board the *Moctezuma.* Once the ship left, these inquiries were handled through the British consul in Hamburg. Whether Captain Simonsen ever did receive any money, I do not know; but he did in the end get a pair of binoculars. It should surely have been donated by the legal profession, to whom he had given the most remarkable leading case of all time.

By now, of course, the story of the *Mignonette,* or "The Terrible Tale of the Sea," was filling the world's press, and it is clear that in general public sympathy was strongly in favor of the three men. They had become widely considered as heroes. The murderer as folk hero need not particularly surprise us; in Victorian England, murder was a source of fascination with fewer rivals than today, and contemporaries were particularly titillated by the believed ubiquity of the phenomenon and the thrilling possibility that there was a good chance one's everyday acquaintances might include an undiscovered murderer or so. The barbarous rituals that still accompanied executions—including the solemn reading of the funeral services to the condemned man before he died—no doubt served to heighten the macabre fascination of the whole subject, and from time to time there were bungled executions to add to the horror. Dudley, Stephens, and Brooks were perhaps unusual in that they were respectable "murderers" with whom one could legitimately sympathize, and their release on bail made them available to public inspection and reverence in a manner denied in the case of such giants of the trade as Constance Kent, William Palmer, Franz Müller, Henry Wainwright, or the great Charles Peace himself. Had Dudley and Stephens been executed, their names would be better known today than they are; they were, however, mercifully to be denied that guarantee of immortality.

In assessing public opinion, we need to distinguish popular feeling, which was all one way, and the more variegated opinions of the intelligentsia. As far as the former is concerned, the most striking evidence is the feeling in Itchen Ferry itself, the home of the unfortunate Richard and his many relatives. There, if anywhere, one might expect to find evidence of violent hostility, particularly toward Captain Dudley himself; he had, after all, stabbed the boy to death. The *Southampton Times* recorded that initially feeling did indeed run high against Dudley and his crew but that, "while many of the briny fraternity complain that an equality of chance was not given to the four exhausted survivors by the casting of lots, others regard with more charity the unparalleled extremity to which they were driven, and contend that it would have been equally a crime to have sacrificed one of the other three, when it was evident that the boy . . . could not have survived many more hours." A week later, as the facts became more fully known, this hostility had gone, and in the village pity rather than a feeling of revenge was expressed. Even Richard's foster mother said, "I do not think that there is any really strong feeling at the Ferry against the poor unfortunate men, and all I have to say about it is that I really do not think they should have killed him. I can seem to see him looking up at Captain Dudley and saying 'What, me Sir?' " So spoke the broken-hearted Mrs. Mathews.

Popular feeling was also reflected in practical steps taken to provide for the men and finance their defense in court. The exhibition of relics in Falmouth had, as we have seen, raised "a handsome donation." In Southampton, one Charles Harrison compiled a ballad that sold in the streets and raised £4 for them. I have been unable to identify with any certainty the text of this ballad or the identity of its author, but out of the three street ballads I have located that arose out of the case, one was plainly published while the men were awaiting trial and may be by Harrison (though I think this unlikely). It is possible that he was connected in some way with the Amy Harrison who later owned relics of the affair. To the music of *Driven from Home* it ran,

Just for a few moments your attention I crave,
While I relate a sad death on the wave;
God help poor sailors—for we cannot see
What they go through when alone on the sea.
A terrible story, alas, has been told,
A worse one I'm sure we ne'er could unfold,
Of the sufferings of sailors on the ocean alone,
What they went thro' may never be known.

The waves rose like mountains round the poor shipwrecked crew,
Starving and thirsty, oh, what could they do,
They thought of their children, their homes and their wives,
They killed the poor boy to preserve their own lives.

It was but a vessel fragile and small
Not fit to sail the Atlantic at all,
The "Mignonette" yacht was a speck on the wave,
A coffin to carry poor men to their grave.
A storm she encountered she could not withstand
She sank on the ocean far, far from the land;
The captain and crew in an open boat lay
Exposed to the weather by night and by day.

For twenty-four days they were tossed on the sea,
Expecting each moment their last it would be,
Five days without water seven days without food,
By ravenous sharks the boat was pursued,
Mad with the thirst and the hunger as well,
What they did then is fearful to tell,
Between life and death on the desolate wave,
They killed the poor boy their own lives to save.

The captain went to him as he laid on his side,
"Dick your time's come" to him he cried,
I pray God forgive me for what I must do,
The story is terrible but alas it is true.
The poor lad was stabbed, they drank his life's blood,
He died as his manhood was yet in the bud,
Only nineteen he drew his last breath,
To give life to others he met with his death.

They lived on the body of the ill-fated boy,
To satisfy hunger his limbs did destroy,
It may seem strange to me and to you,
But we cannot tell what hunger will do,
What must it be when day after day,
Starvation slowly takes life away,

The burning sun on them, 'tis fearful to think
Tho' surrounded by water not any drop to drink.

The captain and mate are now on their trial
To killing the boy they give no denial,
'Tis a terrible story which they have to tell,
How they have suffered and how the boy fell.
They never forget those days on the sea,
As long as they live, wherever they be,
God bless poor sailors alone on the wave,
The ocean alas, is too often their grave.

Ballads were also compiled, and probably sold on their behalf, in Falmouth; this particular ballad could also be one of the Falmouth ballads. Appeals were also made in the papers. One appeared in the *Southampton Times,* particularly directed to helping Edwin Stephens and his five children, who also received help from the Cape of Good Hope Masonic Lodge, of which he was a member. The subscribers to these appeals included prominent local citizens—the Southampton list, for example, includes two local justices of the peace. An appeal was also organized by yachtsmen. The initiative seems to have been taken by the vice-commodore of the Corinthian Yacht Club at Erith, S. Harman Sturgis, and by Augustus G. Wildy, who was rear commodore of the Junior Thames; they wrote to the press, appealing for money for the defense of "men who in their time have been foremost in our great national sport of yacht racing for their pluck and zeal—men of good character or ability . . . now to be tried for their lives." The Thames Yacht Agency was also involved in the appeal. The fund was managed by Arthur H. Glennie in London and H. N. Custance in Falmouth. John Burton continued his efforts to help the men, telegraphing Brooks in Southampton, "Doing all I can to get a sum of money in hand to hand over to you all. Hope Southampton will do the same." The Peace and Harmony Lodge raised £5, and from Australia Jack Want did the decent thing by sending the £100 that was to have been paid to Dudley on delivery of the yacht in Sydney. Eventually, it appears that a surplus remained after all defense costs had been paid. Because of their involvement in the rich man's world of yachting, and also because Edwin Stephens was the son of a well-known sea captain in Southampton, the survivors of the *Mignonette,* though not themselves wealthy, received considerable help and direct support from the prosperous as they might not have if they had simply been common seamen. Association with the gentry served them well in this respect.

The views of the literate upper middle-class world were also reflected in press comment and in letters that found their way directly or indirectly into print. The *Royal Cornwall Gazette* noted that, in Cornwall, "the men of the ill-fated yacht have been real heroes." "Old Salt" wrote sympathetically to the *Morning Post* explaining that he had spent five years in the search for the Franklin expedition, lost in the Arctic since 1845; "Experience taught us that men would eat anything rather than die of hunger, for I have known things to be eaten—although we were not reduced to cannibalism—that would fairly sicken me now to think of." This view was opposed by a lady from Burton-on-Trent who wrote primly to the Falmouth magistrates to "suggest that at least some notice should be taken of this irregular proceeding." The irregularity, she thought, lay only in the failure to draw lots. In the *Daily Telegraph* of September 11, W. C. Russell, who wrote under the pseudonym "A Seafarer," published a florid defense of the survivors, arguing that it was "impossible to make a lawyer's question of this dreadful circumstance." His letter is full of passages like this: "Follow on till you come to the sunken eyes already repulsive with the fires of famine, to the gaunt and haggard faces, to the voices which can but whisper hoarsely as they seek to cast their accents the length of the boat. . . ." William Clark Russell (1844–1911), though now a somewhat forgotten figure, was then a very well known and extremely prolific novelist. Having been himself a sailor, he specialized in marine stories, such as *The Wreck of the Grosvenor* (1897) and *The Death Ship* (1888), which even has a heroine named Imogene Dudley, surely an echo of the affair. Since 1882 he had been on the staff of the *Daily Telegraph,* and his identity was well known. A lively correspondence developed, involving "A London Magistrate," "A Barrister," "Peluca," "Another Barrister," "An Old Salt," "An Old Seafaring Surgeon," and "A Law Student." Though reflecting a difference of opinion as to whether it was appropriate to bring the men to trial at all, and advancing most of the arguments that were to feature later in the trial, this correspondence reflects a general assumption that, whatever the law said, the men would suffer only a nominal punishment or no punishment at all. "Another Barrister," writing in the *Daily Telegraph* on September 12, argued powerfully that "our sympathy with these men ought surely not to make us desire to suspend or vary that regular course of procedure which, however superfluous it may appear in some cases, is in others the only protection against crime"; but he conceded that there was no danger whatever that the men would be made to suffer for their act—mercy had already pardoned them. Instead, his argument was that it was essential to bring them to trial and convict them, because a failure to do so would endorse "a new canon of legal irresponsibility" and "dangerously wide application": that one may take the life of another if his own life is in danger, if such an act is necessary to save himself.

A similar point was made by Lamed Nun Dhalet Yod, writing improbably from Bodmin to the *West Briton* on September 13; he would be happy if the men, if convicted, received "an hour's or other light imprisonment, *and thus assert the sacredness of human life.*" What he objected to was the acceptance of the idea that their act was justified, that the strong could kill the innocent weak. To avoid the canonization of this dangerous doctrine, a prosecution must be brought. Among the editorials, one in the *Standard* contains a passage that (noting in passing that "the Welsh, if we may believe the antique Chroniclers, were not free from this compromising trait") was mildly hostile in its argument: "It is impossible to justify such revolting acts: even wild beasts will often die rather than eat their own species. At the same time it is only the well fed moralist who will anathematise those who, in the fearful agony of famine, have proved faithless to their higher nature." Again, the assumption seems to have been that the men's act, though morally indefensible, did not merit any punishment. What was important was that the point of principle involved in the case should, for the first time, be authoritatively settled, and to this end the only possible procedure was to bring the case before the courts for trial and, in Russell's phrase, "make a lawyer's question" out of the tragedy of the *Mignonette*. That this intellectual view ran quite contrary to popular opinion is beyond question. It wholly baffled Tom Dudley, who regarded any legal proceedings as both unjust and pointless, the outcome being in any event quite certain. In one of his letters to his wife from Falmouth before bail was granted, he had written, "No harm can come to me, or any of us dear. They say it is my statement that has caused the enquiry. I have told the truth. If I had told a lie I should be sharing the comforts of home instead of being here." Dudley even took the desperate step, which must be unique in English legal history, of writing to the *Times* itself to express both his gratitude and his sense of outrage, and the letter was published on September 22: "May I through the medium of the Times express my thanks for numerous favours of sympathy to myself and companions for our past unparalleled sufferings and privations on the ocean, and our present torture under the ban of the law, being charged with an act which certainly was not accompanied by either premeditation or malice in the true sense of the word, as my conscience can affirm." He wrote a similar letter to the Plymouth papers suggesting that he was not of sound mind at the time. But the Home Office was quite unmoved and committed to legal proceedings that would ensure that the case of the *Mignonette* became a leading case.

Central to the approach of Sir William Harcourt, the home secretary, appears to have been revulsion against the popular idea that Dudley was a hero. It is of course not difficult to see why he could be so regarded—he had, as they say in the Westerns, done what a man must do. Confronted by the dictates of necessity, he had risen to the occasion and steeled himself to the terrible act of killing the boy when his companions shrank from the deed. He had fulfilled a captain's role. At a more intellectual level, and one that perhaps was not missed by the classically educated intelligentsia of the period, he had acted as Agamemnon did in sacrificing his own daughter, Iphigenia, to appease Zeus and ensure that the Achaean fleet reached Troy; the very horror of the sacrifice that had to be performed is integral to the heroic stature of the actor. But moral approval of Agamemnon's act in submitting to necessity belonged to a heathen culture from which, Victorians believed, Christianity had liberated them: hence only in a pagan culture should such an action be viewed as heroic. Contemporaries were not to know how the ultimate fate of Captain Dudley was to echo the Greek myth.

The prosecution was entrusted to junior Treasury counsel in the person of William Otto Adolph Julius Danckwerts, whom the Treasury solicitors briefed for the preliminary inquiry. A local agent, Mr. G. Appleby Jenkins, town clerk of Penryn, was employed to look after the interests of the Crown as local agent. Mr. Danckwerts was a barrister of the Inner Temple; he was 31 at the time and had been in practice for only some six years. He appears to have specialized in appearing in wreck inquiries and had close contacts with Walter Murton (solicitor to the Board of Trade), whose book on the subject he had worked on in 1883. Family tradition, recorded by Danckwert's son, who became a lord justice of appeal, preserved the fact that he was well aware of the strong local feeling in favor of the three men—so strong that it was said a conviction achieved could have put his life in danger in the West country.

It must have been apparent to Danckwerts at once, on studying his brief, that he was facing formidable odds. The Falmouth borough magistrates had to date behaved impeccably but, local feeling being what it was, could hardly be relied upon; and the evidence available to the prosecution was not such as to inspire great confidence. The two sailors available from the *Moctezuma* were likely to be reluctant witnesses with little to contribute, and that left only the eavesdropping Sergeant Laverty and the unsympathetic shipping master, Robert Gandy Cheesman, as prosecution witnesses. In effect, all the witnesses to the killing of Richard Parker were defendants. In the contemporary state of the law, it was quite out of the question for them to be required to give their account of what happened or give sworn evidence in court and thereby expose themselves to cross-examination to elicit the facts. Not until the Criminal Evidence Act of 1898 were prisoners on such a charge even allowed to give sworn evidence. As far as the preliminary inquiry was concerned, they were legally entitled to say nothing at all and would without doubt be advised to exercise this right. Danckwerts possessed, of course, the depositions made in the customs house to the shipping master, but these were open to challenge, since they had not been taken for criminal purposes, and consequently no caution had been administered. It was also arguable that they were not made voluntarily (there being a legal obligation to make them), and this also might exclude their use as evidence. The law also ruled that confessions were only admissible as evidence against the individual making the confession—not against others—and the account of the facts in the depositions was meager. Dudley's letter and his other draft accounts were perhaps the best evidence available. It was plain, too, that the defense of necessity would be raised; the legal status of this defense was problematical, and its application might well depend on the precise conditions in the *Mignonette*'s dinghy. Only a witness who had actually been there could speak convincingly about them.

Mr. Danckwerts therefore needed such a witness, and the only candidates were Dudley, Stephens, and Brooks. One of them must appear for the Crown, and the obvious choice was Brooks, who was of subordinate status and had taken no active part in the killing. Precisely what he had said in his deposition is now undiscoverable, since the document does not survive. It is just possible that it did implicate him and therefore had to be discreetly suppressed; in any event, it could not be tendered as prosecution evidence. More probably it ended up in the lost treasury solicitor's file. In opening his case before the magistrates at the renewed hearing on September 18, Danckwerts, without apparently elaborating the point, announced his intention of turning Brooks into a prosecution witness: "As to Brooks, having carefully considered his position, he had come to the conclusion that in point of law probably Brooks would have to be acquitted, and therefore he proposed to offer no evidence against him, and to ask the Bench to discharge him that he might be called to give evidence. It was fair to Brooks and to the other two prisoners, because they would then have the opportunity of eliciting the facts of the case." Another account of his speech puts Brooks in a more favorable light: "As to Brooks, I have carefully considered his position, and I am taking the responsibility on myself of saying I have come to the conclusion he was in no way an actor or participator in the crime of his two companions." Viewing the forthcoming trial as a dramatic exercise, Brooks was on his way to being cast as a rival hero of the story, and it would of course assist the prosecution of Dudley and Stephens if it could be shown that Brooks, starving like them, nobly held out against the temptation to which they succumbed.

The magistrates agreed to the discharge of Brooks, and their decision was met with hearty applause, which provoked Danckwerts to an appeal to the chairman, Mayor Liddicoat: "I beg, sir, you will ask the public to suppress these manifestations." The chairman obliged. "I must ask the public to suppress their feelings either way, or I must order the court to be cleared." Brooks appeared surprised by his discharge and made no protest at being recast as a prosecution witness. There is no evidence that any bargain had been struck with him, though it may have been.

Danckwerts then proceeded to put forward the prosecution case, assuring the magistrates that there was no question in law of there being any defense to a killing in the circumstances in which Richard Parker had died. He called his witnesses: Sergeant James Laverty, Mr. Robert Gandy Cheesman, Julius Erich Martin Wiese, and Edmund Brooks. Giving evidence through an interpreter, Robert Herschel, Julius Wiese proved unhelpful. He saw some flesh and a bone and threw it overboard but could give no evidence as to what it was; his companion was not called. Sailors were not sympathetic to criminal prosecution in cases of shipwreck. Under cross-examination, Mr. Cheesman strongly emphasized the fact that the men had not been cautioned before making their statements: "Witness begged to be allowed to state that when the statements were made to him he had no idea they would be used against the men on a criminal charge, or he should not have asked them the questions he did." The written accounts of the tragedy found among Dudley's clothing were handed in unread as exhibits. At the conclusion of the prosecution case, nothing of substance had emerged that was not already familiar through press accounts. But there had been a dramatic intervention by Dudley. When Robert Cheesman was giving an account of Dudley's reenactment of the killing he forgot which side of Richard's neck was stabbed. Dudley, as ever anxious that the whole and accurate truth be known, intervened from the dock, calling out "It was the left side."

In the event, Danckwerts does not seem to have had much difficulty in persuading the magistrates to send Dudley and Stephens for trial at the next assizes before a judge and jury. After referring to the sympathy all must feel for them, he went on, "The evidence could not leave the bench in doubt as to their course of sending the prisoners for trial. They had not met there to settle the case, but merely to decide whether there was sufficient evidence to send the men before a jury of their own countrymen." Though maintaining that in his opinion the killing was legally quite unjustified, he pointed out that this was a matter for a jury and a higher court to determine and not a suitable question for the Falmouth magistrates to resolve. His speech also contains a hint that the matter would be decided eventually not by a single judge but by "the judges of the land." One of the local papers, *Lake's Falmouth Packet and Cornwall Advertiser,* throws further light on Danckwerts's skilled handling of the matter: "Counsel displayed sincere sympathy with the accused: and intimated as plainly as he could, without saying it as much in so many words, that the clemency of the Crown would be extended to them in the event of a conviction . . . the learned gentleman took considerable pains to elicit every fact that could possibly tell in the prisoners' favour." Perhaps for this reason Harry Tilly's defense was not pressed, and after a short retirement the magistrates committed Dudley and Stephens for trial at the next winter assizes for Cornwall and Devon—the case to be heard at the sittings at Exeter. The mayor explained that the matter was too grave for the magistrates to decide. He was referring to the defense of necessity, which was clearly going to be treated as the crux of the case. Bail was again extended, and the two men were free to go. The hearing, which had lasted more than six hours, had been an ordeal for them both. Throughout the hearing, Stephens "exhibited a good deal of emotion" and frequently buried his head in his hands. Captain Dudley, who had to remain standing throughout because of his injured buttocks, maintained his composure until the end, when he burst into tears. The renewal of the two men's bail provoked further applause in the court.

Dudley and Brooks left Falmouth by the 7:08 A.M. London train next day; they were seen off by the shipping master, the calculating Cheesman, and Stephens, who was to leave later by boat, calling at Plymouth, where he could meet Mr. J. H. Cocksey, chairman of the Southampton magistrates, and Mr. T. Cleveland; both had been ready to offer bail if need be. Brooks traveled to Southampton, arriving at 5:00 in the evening, and again talked to the press of the kind treatment he had received. As he was now a Crown witness, his expenses were defrayed by the Treasury. He later traveled to Brightlingsea to visit his mother. Stephens arrived at Southampton on Saturday on the *Lady Wodehouse,* free passage having been arranged by Mr. J. E. Le Feuvre, another Southampton magistrate, a prominent Mason, and a shipping agent. Captain Dudley went to Colchester, presumably to visit relatives in Essex and his home village of Tollesbury, not yet linked to the railway. Expressions of sympathy continued to pour in, together with practical help. Stephens was still ill and destitute, but his Masonic friends came to his aid. Money was even pressed anonymously into his hands. An impromptu concert raised two sovereigns, and subscription funds were set up and advertised in the local press. The yachting community also assisted by establishing a defense fund. At first Dudley (who was not of course destitute) was ashamed to accept charity, but he gave way on condition that any balance remaining unspent should be put in trust for Edith Parker, Richard's younger sister.

On October 28, the *Times* announced that the trial at Exeter would open on Saturday, November 1, before Baron Huddleston; the date was subsequently altered to Monday, November 3. Mr. Arthur Charles, Q.C., was to lead for the Crown; Mr. Arthur John Hammond Collins, Q.C., assisted by Henry Clark, was briefed for the defense. Dudley and Stephens's leading counsel was, on the face of things, the best man that could be obtained. A bencher and former treasurer of Grays Inn (where he had been called to the bar in 1860), he was also a member of the Middle Temple and the leader of the Western Circuit at that time. In addition, he had been since 1879 the recorder of Exeter, where the trial was to take place. Nobody would be able to say that the two prisoners were not given the best legal talent to defend them. What sort of job Collins made of the defense we shall see; anyone with his familiarity with the English judiciary must have realized that as a matter of law he had little hope of success on the theoretical issue of legal guilt. Killing and eating cabin boys was not a practice likely to recommend itself to Her Majesty's judges.

5
The Custom of the Sea

Her body then they did dissect
Most dreadful for to view
And serv'd it out in pieces,
Amongst the whole ship's crew

—"Ballad of the Brig *George*"

The story of the *Mignonette* was essentially a tale of maritime disaster and of the ensuing fall from grace, through extreme temptation, of the victims. The nineteenth century was a great era for disasters. The Victorians, like ourselves, were always delighted to hear of the latest ones, and ample material lay at hand. Thus the index to the *Times* for 1884 lists, with a slight air of frivolity, the following remarkable examples of sudden death:

> Captain Berry, at Nyasa, from a huge Alligator seizing him in the Middle while Bathing.
>
> Thomas Farmer, at Chatham, from taking Liquid Ammonia instead of his usual Cough Mixture.
>
> Mr. A. W. Jesson, who Fell Down and Expired while Running at the Oxford Boat Race.
>
> Mary Jane Butterfield, by having her scalp torn away by a Lion during a panic in Wombwell's Menagerie at Bolton.
>
> Mr. Richards, Thrown into a Millpond as a Joke by Getting Entangled with the Weeds.

> The Revd. J. Selby-Watson, by Falling out of his Hammock in Parkhurst Prison.
>
> Josephy Jacklett, who Died from Holding some Dynamite over a Gas Flame, at Aldershot.
>
> Samuel Halliday Smith, Shot Dead by the Explosion of An Explosive Walking Stick.

These improbable events involved individual deaths only; major disasters killing large numbers of people at once usually involved mines, railways, and ships. Shipwrecks provided the most dramatic of all catastrophes, for like air crashes today, they killed large numbers of people at the same time. But aircraft are more efficient and leave less scope for the tales of heroism and precarious survival that grace the stories of the sea; storm and tempest also lent an air of grandeur that is lacking in most air accidents. There were indeed plenty of shipwrecks, and their monotonous frequency was reflected in the grim entry in the index to the *Times:* "Disasters at Sea, see each day's paper." In addition to the daily press, magazines such as the *Illustrated London News* and the journals of philanthropic societies gave extensive accounts of the horrors of sea travel, and there was an abundant literature of marine catastrophes, much influenced by the belief that literature must improve and instruct, not merely entertain. An example is the popular work *Notable Shipwrecks* by "Uncle Hardy" (a pseudonym for one William Senior), first published in 1873, *Being Tales of Disaster and Heroism at Sea.* This cataloged such notable wrecks as that of the *Royal George,* which capsized at Spithead on August 29, 1782, establishing a record, lasting nearly a century, of around 900 killed, and of the *Rothsay Castle,* which more or less fell to pieces on August 17, 1831, finally running aground and breaking up on Dutchman's Bank near Puffin Island in the Menai Straits. The tone was melodramatic and sentimental: "Fathers and children, husbands and wives, brothers and sisters, took loving farewell of each other; last embraces, heart-rending to give or witness, were exchanged; children were clasped to the arms of fond mothers . . . the air was rent with hysterical wails and piercing shrieks; people swooned, tore their hair, ran wildly to and fro, or prayed for pardon, for mercy, for aid." Also included was sharp censure and self-congratulatory moralizing: "The captain's conduct can only be accounted for on the supposition that his senses had deserted him. . . . What volumes it speaks for the innate love of order and discipline which the Englishman possesses, that they, in the face of this gross incompetence and obstinacy, kept up a show of respect for the captain's office!"

Many of these wrecks are now all but forgotten, but they were familiar enough in their day. There was the *Amphitrite,* which sank on August 31, 1833, off Boulogne, with 101 doomed women convicts aboard. The loss of a convict ship had of course the drama inherent in the death through "Act of God" of those who had escaped the gallows at home and thought they would live; there were quite a number of such sinkings—the *George III* and *Neva* in 1835 (killing 139 men and 145 women, respectively), and the *Waterloo* in 1842 (143 drowned). Ballads recounting the disasters to the first three survive and are published in Hugh Anderson's *Farewell Old England.* "The Melancholy Loss of the *Amphitrite*" concludes particularly grimly:

> This wreck will never be forgot,
> This dreadful tale of woe,
> We hope their souls in Heaven will rest,
> While their bodies rot below.

As for heroism, there was the sinking of the troop ship *Birkenhead* on February 26, 1852 (454 lives lost), where the men of the 74th Highland Regiment stood at attention on deck, the band playing, while the women and children were saved, and the captain very properly went down with his ship. Emigrant ships packed with human cargo produced some of the very worst catastrophes. The *Annie Jane* foundered in September 1854 (348 lost); the *Austria,* built on the Clyde in 1857 and "fitted with every appliance of modern science," caught fire on passage from Hamburg to New York in September 1858. The boatswain was fumigating the steerage with burning tar, and his misguided sanitary enthusiasm led to the disaster. "We are all lost!" cried the captain and fell overboard; he was nearly correct in his estimate, for of the 538 persons on board, only 67 were alive to be picked up five hours later by the French barque *Maurice.* The following year the *Pomona,* another emigrant ship, went ashore on the Wexford coast, killing 386 of those on board. The *Cospatrick* (1874) was destroyed by fire; only three out of a total complement of 479 ultimately survived. But they were more fortunate than any of the 569 or so persons on the *Great Queensland* (August 1875), emigrants who shared the ship with a cargo that included explosives. All that was ever found was some wreckage from the explosion.

Regular passenger vessels were in no way immune from disaster, either. On April 1, 1873, the *Atlantic,* through a wholly inexcusable navigational error appropriate to the date, hit Nova Scotia, killing 562 of the 933 persons aboard. This was the worst disaster to an Atlantic liner until the same shipping line's loss of the *Titanic* on April 14, 1912, when 1,490 died, surpassing all nineteenth-century records and never surpassed by a merchant vessel, though more passengers alone died on the *Empress of Ireland* in 1914.

The nineteenth-century British and European record was held by the affair of the *Princess Alice,* and memories of this disaster would be fresh in 1884. She was simply a pleasure vessel—a saloon steamer—and she left London Bridge for a cruise to Sheerness and back on September 3, 1878, carrying 600 or 700 pleasure-seeking passengers. She was returning up the Thames in the evening, and the band had just struck up the popular tune "Nancy Lee" when, at 8:20 P.M., she was cut in two by the steamship *Bywell Castle* just off Tripcock's Point in Galleons Reach, a mile or so below Woolwich Arsenal. It was never really established how many died, but by November 21, 632 bodies had been recovered, and the total deaths may have been as high as 700; no passenger lists existed. Even more—some 850 coolies—had died when the *Flora Temple* was lost in October 1859, but that was far away in the East.

Dramatic though these individual disasters were, they were insignificant when set against the background of continuingly regular, relentless loss of ships and life. Thus in 1884–85 561 British-registered vessels were totally lost; the tonnage came to 212,149. This total included no fewer than 398 sailing vessels, so the *Mignonette* was clearly not an isolated case. In particular years the numbers of ships lost could be much higher; in 1881–82 no fewer than 838 sailing vessels, with a combined tonnage of 204,236, were totally lost at sea. The statisticians were to note in 1889–90 that the total tonnage lost, 192,696, was the highest for 13 years. As steam replaced sail, the number of sailing vessels lost, which reached 443 in 1887–88, began to fall, but the losses continued high for many years after that. The sacrifice of life was appalling. In 1884–85, for example, deaths (from all causes) to crews of registered British vessels with United Kingdom ownership came to 2,769, and to passengers 1,490, making a total of 4,259. If one adds those who lost their lives on fishing boats, harbor boats, etc., but excludes yachts, the total figure rises from 4,259 to 4,632. Passenger ships in this period *never* carried sufficient life boats, and in merchant ship disasters it was very unusual indeed even for all the crew to escape a sinking ship. In general sailors adapted a fatalistic attitude to shipwreck, making little or no prior provision for such an eventuality. Furthermore, sailors usually could not swim and sensibly did not try to learn. It merely prolonged the agony.

Disasters at sea were therefore a normal and prominent feature of the Victorian world, and the press, popular and elite literature, the theater, and the arts generally ensured that the subject of shipwreck was continually brought to public attention. Thus the awful fate of the French frigate *Medusa,* lost in 1816, generated a classic account of shipwreck by A. Corréard and J. B. H. Savigny, published in a London edition in 1818, as well as a famous painting, *La Radeau de la "Méduse"* by Théodore Géricault. The celebrated story of Mrs. Fraser, survivor of the *Stirling Castle,* wrecked on the Australian coast ("The Fatal Shore") in 1836, led to that lady's exhibition in a peep show in London in 1837. Many a shipwreck gave rise to a popular penny ballad. For example, the *Royal Charter* was wrecked in Red Wharf Bay, Anglesey, on October 25, 1859, with a loss of 459 lives, en route from Melbourne to Liverpool, in a storm that claimed hundreds of vessels and was always known as "the Royal Charter Storm." An anonymous ballad writer publicized the event in a work of 27 stanzas. One noted the statistical positions:

> And such a melancholy wreck
> With loss of human life,
> Thank God, we do not often hear,
> Though wrecks are very rife.

Another noted the courage of the parson:

> And in the midst of that sad throng,
> Was heard the voice of prayer
> The Reverend Mr. Hodge did raise
> His supplications there.

Less admirable conduct was immortalized in an Irish ballad on the loss of the emigrant ship *Eliza:*

> When the Captain saw our danger it's from the ship he drew
> And launching out a small boat to save himself and crew,
> He left us to the ocean to perish one and all,
> But God he was our safeguard and prov'd his sad downfall.

When he saw our danger he never looked behind,
He thought to save his precious life in spite of sea and wind,
The Lord on high he heard our cry and prov'd his sad downfall,
The very night he lost his life in the Island of St. Pauls.

Some such ballads adopted an instructive stance, directed to bringing home to landsmen their good fortune in never having to face the horrors of the sea:

Our Captain from the long boats bow
To the helm he did run
Its now my lads, stick to your pumps,
Or else we are all undone,
Those words were scarcely uttered,
Than she struck on a rock,
The Lord have mercy on our souls,
The deep must be our lot.

Our gallant crew were twenty-five,
All on the deck did stand,
And out of all that number,
Only three did reach the land,
Our ship's name was the *Betsy,*
From New York we were bound,
So you see the dangers of the sea,
You landsmen all around.

Others reflected a fatalistic acceptance of the inescapable perils of the sea, as in this fragmentary ballad that has survived in the Devon Record Office:

A ship in dreadful stormy weather,
Is a most dreadful shocking sight
Just like an army of brave soldiers,
Going in a field to fight.
But soldiers when they are overpowered
Might fly from their most dreadful dooms
But sailors bold in stormy weather
Must all submit to watery tombs.

Resignation was not, however, the only possible reaction, and there were many remarkable accounts of sailors and passengers who survived shipwreck under almost incredible conditions. An example is the story of Amos Marcier, sole survivor of a crew of nine on the schooner *Leader,* whose story appeared in the *Times* on June 22, 1865. The *Leader* left Montreal for St. John's, Newfoundland, on November 22, 1864. By December 8 the vessel was in the open sea, hopelessly lost; it was snowing and blowing a hurricane. The *Leader* lay to under a reefed main staysail. A heavy sea carried away the deck house and all the crew except Marcier and three others, including the captain; only Marcier remained uninjured. There was no shelter whatsoever. On December 10 at 2:00 A.M. the schooner ran onto the shore at Well Cove, between Coal River and the Bay of Islands on the western shore of Newfoundland. The area was then uninhabited in winter, and of the four men who reached the shore through the December surf, one had no boots. Finding no help ashore, they returned to the wreck for shelter: unable to walk, the man without boots had to crawl. The sailors sheltered in the wreck with no fire and no covering. The captain soon died. Willett, another sailor, had a broken back and two broken thighs; he lasted in this condition for eight weeks, freezing to death on January 27. On the same day, the third sailor died, leaving Amos Marcier alone with the corpse beside him, where they remained until Marcier was eventually rescued on March 21 by a sealer. During this time he once took off his socks to examine his frost-bitten feet; four toes fell off in the process. Such an account, here much shortened, could easily be matched by others, equally horrific, reported in the press in the nineteenth century; the loss of the schooner *Leader* was in fact a relatively common affair. In Victorian England nobody could possibly have been unaware of the perils of the sea.

Before the nineteenth century, disaster and suffering at sea failed to generate public enthusiasm for attempts to increase safety and reduce the sufferings of passengers (apart from slaves) or sailors and their dependents, the last often reduced to destitution by the death or crippling of the family wage earner. In the nineteenth century this was to change, and the first expressions of the change included the formation of the British and Foreign Sailors Society in 1818 and the Royal National Institute for the Preservation of Life from Shipwreck in 1824, the latter through the initiative of Sir William Hillary. The London Sailors' Home (progenitor of the Sailors' Home in Falmouth, which cared for Dudley, Stephens and Brooks) was established in 1830 at Well Street next door to the Destitute Sailors' Asylum, which had opened in 1827. The latter was set up by three naval officers: Captain George C. Gambier, Robert J. Elliot, and Lieutenant Robert Justice. Voluntary organizations multiplied throughout the century:

the Shipwrecked Fishermen's and Mariners' Royal Benevolent Society in 1839, the Thames Church Mission in 1844, the Missions to Seamen in 1856. Public charitable appeals to care for those who survived shipwrecks, or their families, became a regular feature of life in Victorian England, and associations to organize charitable relief were established in all major seaports. Their work was assisted by ad hoc appeals, such as those organized to assist the survivors of the *Mignonette* and Edwin Stephens's destitute family. Provision by way of charity has survived even into the era of the welfare state, for the National Lifeboat Institution, the descendant of the organization set up in 1824, still declines to take state aid directly, though its work is now in fact assisted by the use of government service aircraft and helicopters.

The humanitarianism that produced voluntary assistance also led to an increasing degree of legislative and administrative regulation of the merchant marine. A series of passenger acts, starting in 1803, attempted to regulate living conditions on emigrant ships; and one of these acts, passed in 1835, was in part concerned with the seaworthiness of vessels engaged in this lucrative trade. But for the general prevention of shipwreck, the starting point was a report by a Select Committee of the House of Commons established in 1836, a year later than the first committee on mining accidents. This committee was set up to investigate the causes of shipwrecks, which had come to arouse considerable public concern, in part because of their increasing frequency. There was now more deep-sea shipping, and the emigrant trade had expanded; there were therefore more ships to sink and more passengers to drown. At this time the merchant marine was virtually unregulated by any legislation directed to improving safety and protecting passengers and seamen, though legislation did cover many other aspects of the maritime world and emigrant ships. In a lecture delivered in February 1887 to the Worshipful Company of Shipwrights, Thomas Gray (1832–90), who served as permanent assistant secretary to the Marine Department of the Board of Trade from 1867 to 1890, summarized the state of laissez-faire that then prevailed. The merchant marine depended largely on pauper apprentices for sailors, a system of directed labor little removed from slavery. There were no examinations or qualifications for masters, mates, or engineers. "Freight was the mother of wages," so sailors were not entitled to any remuneration if the ship failed to earn freight; hence the crew of a ship that was wrecked earned nothing at all for the voyage. Ships carried no lights. There was no international rule of the road of the sea. No statistics existed as to the number of ships lost, nor were any inquiries into shipwrecks held. A ship's master had no obligation to stand by after a collision, much less to give aid to a vessel in distress or to pick up castaways; and originally he had no encouragement to do so. No regulations laid down minimum scales for the supply of food, water, or accommodation to seamen; nor did any system exist to control tyrannical or brutal masters. Once they joined a ship, seamen could raise no questions as to the seaworthiness of the ship on which they were bound to sail and could be sent to prison if they went ashore to complain. In addition to the absence of special regulatory control, serious difficulties existed over the application of basic criminal law to activities on ships on the high seas. These difficulties were partly practical; partly they arose from the lack of adequate machinery to secure the arrest of criminals; and partly their source was the uncertain jurisdiction of English courts over crimes at sea. Of course at this period the development of regular policing on land had only just begun, with the foundation of the Metropolitan Police in 1829. It is hardly surprising that the high seas were largely beyond the reach of law of any kind.

The committee of 1836 revealed an extraordinary state of affairs. The incompetence of masters was remarkable; the committee heard how a 14-year-old lad called Storey had commanded a brigantine, the *Headleys* (or *Hedleys*) on a voyage from Belfast to Quebec. Lack of navigational skill was a common cause of disaster. In response to a question from the chairman, "Have you known instances of extremely erroneous reckoning, of ships finding themselves 300 or 400 miles from the place where they supposed themselves to be?" Mr. Coleman, an experienced witness, replied: "Yes, very many." The expense of navigational instruments (which ships' officers provided for themselves) meant they were often not carried, and ignorance of their use often precluded their purchase. Drunkenness was endemic; Captain Pelham, a naval officer, had firm views on the problem:

Q: You think the appetite for drink, on the part of seamen, is uncontrollable?
A: Insatiable.
Q: You think that nothing but the difficulty of getting it keeps them sober?
A: I am quite of that opinion.

He told how sailors would say, "The moment I get ashore I will go up to Wapping with my wages and lay my soul afloat." Ships frequently put to sea with everyone on board drunk (occasionally, of course, they still do). It must also be borne in mind that bulky sailing vessels, particularly if square rigged, were inherently dangerous and difficult to maneuver, and there was a tendency to blame sailors, not ships, for the disasters that occurred. In response to alarming evidence, the committee produced an elaborate analysis of the principal causes of maritime disasters under 11 heads, which included, for example, "Incompetency of masters and officers," "Drunkenness of officers and men," "Operation of Marine Insurance," "Imperfection of charts." Its members thereby recognized the absence of any single panacea, surely the beginning of wisdom in matters of safety. They recommended the establishment of a Mercantile Marine Board to tackle the problems in a variety of ways—for example, codifying maritime law, classifying ships, setting up nautical schools and examinations for competence, holding inquiries into shipwrecks and censuring or suspending ships' officers, and providing schemes to redress seamen's grievances. There were numerous later committees and commissions. A select committee of 1839 (under the chairmanship of Mr. G. Palmer) was especially concerned with the loss of timber ships from North America. No wonder, for statistics provided with the report showed that from January 1, 1835, to December 1837 no fewer than 164 such vessels had been wrecked in this dangerous trade; many were found only as unidentifiable floating derelicts. There were further investigations in 1843, 1845 (concerned with lighthouses), 1854 (the O'Connell Committee on Emigrant Ships), 1860 (to inquire into the working of the Merchant Shipping Act of 1854), 1873 (the Somerset Royal Commission on Unseaworthy Ships), and at the time of the loss of the *Mignonette,* yet another Royal Commission on Loss of Life at Sea (the Aberdeen Commission) was deliberating. An inquiry into the state of merchant shipping through letters to British consuls was also conducted by the Foreign Office in 1848 and repeated in 1869–70, and there were numerous other less central investigations, such as one into the practice of wrecking in the Hebrides in 1867. But the principal proposals all derive from the 1836 committee's acute analysis of the problems. For this remarkable report, much credit must go to its chairman, James Silk Buckingham (1786–1855), M.P. for Sheffield. Born in Flushing, near Falmouth, he had been to sea himself, beginning at the age of 10; he knew from direct experience about the perils involved.

Out of this continuous process of investigation emerged a mass of legislation, whose broad philosophy reflected the approach of the 1836 committee; a variety of remedies was applied and modified through experience. Although the Mercantile Marine Board was never set up under that name, the substance of the recommendation was eventually carried into effect by the Mercantile Marine Act of 1850, which made the Board of Trade responsible for the merchant marine. For the first time there was a department of state responsible for safety at sea and for the legal regulation of merchant shipping, and the Marine Department of the Board was established to carry out the board's new functions. Thomas H. Farrer, later Sir Thomas, joined the Marine Department in 1850 and, as secretary to the department until his retirement in 1886, was responsible for most of the later reforming legislation. Thomas Gray, who joined as a clerk in 1851 at 15s. a week, rose by 1867 to be its permanent assistant secretary; he not only formulated the rules for avoiding collision at sea but rendered them into verse so that sailors would remember them. An indefatigable administrator, he was a sailor in his spare time and wrote extensively both under his own name and the pseudonym A. de C. Elgate. A special legal department was first set up in 1875 under Walter Murton.

Implementing the recommendations of the various committees took many years. Wreck inquiries, for example, were first instituted by an act of 1846. Official examinations for masters and mates conducted by the Board of Trade replaced an earlier voluntary system run by Trinity House in 1850; their licenses could be canceled or suspended for incompetence, habitual drunkenness, or tyrannical habits. And though no complete code of maritime law was ever successfully passed through Parliament (though one reached a second reading in 1870), the Merchant Shipping Act of 1854 established a basic framework of regulatory law and was a partial code. Many of the details of maritime legislation are not of course directly relevant to the case of the *Mignonette,* but some do provide the essential context. But for the Mercantile Marine Act of 1850, there would have been no Board of Trade to concern itself with the loss of the *Mignonette,* which would have simply been a matter for its Australian owner to deal with. But for the system of wreck inquiries initiated in 1846 for steamships, later extended and amended by the Mercantile Marine Act of 1850 and the Merchant Shipping Act of 1854, there would have been no occasion for Captain Dudley and his companions to visit the customs house at Falmouth and make their depositions.

But for another provision of the latter act, Section 267, it is not entirely clear that an English court would have jurisdiction to try them in England at all.

More generally, the establishment of the Marine Department of the Board of Trade and the enactment of a mass of regulatory law reflected a long-drawn-out process that attempted to bring sea-going ships and what transpired on them within the effective control of the law. An eighteenth-century merchant vessel, though not wholly outside the law, was nevertheless not very obviously answerable to regulation of any kind as to its management. To a common sailor a ship was a sort of prison, and to its master something not far removed from an independent state. What went on in a well-regulated vessel was largely dictated by necessity, custom, and superstition. A curious example of their interaction is recorded in a legal work, James Ram's *Treatise on Facts as Subjects of Inquiry by a Jury:*

> A gentleman in New York desired to import some certain variety of the cat species . . . they were duly shipped, directed to him at New York. The vessel in which they were transported met with bad weather: the sailors insisted that it was occasioned by the presence of the cats, and it resulted in all the poor creatures being tossed overboard. We [i.e., the legal firm of the editor, John Townshend] were employed to enforce compensation for the loss of the cats: payment was for a time resisted on the ground that the destruction was *necessary* for the safety of the ship; eventually the parties compromised.

Sometimes what was jettisoned might be human beings. In an ill-run ship appalling conditions could arise from the effectiveness of the master and mates in enforcing their will, however evilly directed, and from their superior ability as navigators and ship handlers, which gave them the power of indispensability; legal penalties apart, mutiny was often impracticable.

The starvation of crews (not to mention emigrants) through the meanness of owner or captain constantly recurs in accounts of the horrors of the seamen's life. A ballad, "The New York Trader," in the Crampton Collection (now in the British Library), is specially devoted to the theme:

> Our cruel captain as we did find
> Left half our provisions behind
> Our cruel captain as we understand,
> Meant to starve us all before we made land.

The captain in this instance turned out to be a murderer, too, and was sensibly cast overboard when it was realized that his presence attracted bad weather. Nor was service on a sailing vessel necessarily voluntary. Thus Sir James Bisset's account of his early days at sea in the days of sail (*Sail Ho!*) records how he and the crew of the sailing barque *County of Pembroke* all but starved as late as 1903 through lack of provisions—whatever the Board of Trade then required—on a voyage from Callao to Falmouth, and how two additions to the crew were acquired from crimps and delivered on board for cash, totally unconscious. Virtual impressment of merchant sailors continued until quite recent times. More atavistic incidents are still recorded from time to time today. Well into this present century the conditions of life at sea, the vast distances involved, the absence of modern communications, and the essentially temporary and international character of seamen's work have combined to impede attempts to make landsmen's law rule on sailing ships.

The task of bringing ships under the rule of law has therefore been a long uphill task, never fully completed. It has also been one fraught with much controversy. The Board of Trade under Thomas Farrer and Thomas Gray was inclined to take a rather modest view: the value of legislation and legal interference was reduced if there was too much of it, if it changed too often, and if it encouraged those capable of looking after themselves to neglect their responsibilities. In particular, Gray put a related problem of legal technique thus: "Can loss of life at sea best be prevented by leaving everybody to his own devices in his calling, and if he does wrong by injuring, maiming or drowning his crew, punish him after he has done that wrong: or by previous interference with all ships?" In the period immediately before the case of the *Mignonette,* controversies over the protection of sailors and passengers had been inflamed by the activities of the radical Member of Parliament for Derby (1868–80), Samuel Plimsoll, "the sailors' friend," whose approach to the problem favored prior intervention. Relying to a considerable extent on the earlier work of James Hall, a Tynemouth ship-owner active in the late 1860s, he concentrated first simply on unseaworthy ships as a cause of mortality and started a campaign to amend the law with a resolution in the House of Commons in July 1870. His more effective appeal was to public opinion through the publication of *Our Seamen* in 1872, attacking the wicked ship-owners of the overinsured, overloaded "coffin ships," and this caught the public imagination. Plimsoll was no doubt careless with his facts, ill informed, and sometimes violent in his language; but perhaps successful campaigns require devils, conspiracies, and simple solutions. In reality ships were lost for a variety of reasons, and unseaworthiness was only one of them. The culmination of his efforts came in a dramatic scene in the House of Commons. Though he had helped to secure the appointment of the Somerset Commission, which was sitting at the time, Plimsoll was exasperated by its apparent lack of success. His attempts to bring about legislation to prevent unseaworthiness through overloading of ships had not succeeded, and on July 22 he lost or pretended to lose his temper. As Hansard records, he rose "with great excitement" to move the adjournment of the House. He spoke of the consignment of "some thousands of living human beings to undeserved and miserable death." He referred to ship-owners "of murderous tendencies outside the House, and who are immediately and amply represented inside the House, and who have frustrated and talked to death every effort to procure a remedy for this state of things." He said that at least one member was a "ship-knacker." Warming to his task, he listed ships by name: The *Tethys* and *Melbourne,* lost in 1874; the *Foundling;* and the *Sydney Dacres,* lost in 1875. He even named their owner, Edward Bates (1816–96), the millionaire founder of Edward Bates and Son, Liverpool, and Member of Parliament for Plymouth. He ended, "I am determined to unmask the villains who send to death and destruction . . . [loud cries of "Order" and much excitement]." Courteously challenged by the speaker, he refused to withdraw. After a disorderly altercation, Disraeli moved that he be reprimanded, and Plimsoll withdrew, calling out, "Do you know that thousands are dying for this?" while from the gallery leaflets were scattered into the chamber.

Scenes of this kind, described by a later speaker as "without precedent in the annals of this Assembly," blow over, as this one did. There are reasons to suppose that it was contrived, and it was certainly politically effective. There were indeed some wicked shipowners who sent overinsured, unseaworthy, ill-provisioned, and overloaded vessels to sea; and Plimsoll's load line, for which he remains famous, was one minor step toward increasing safety. From 1875 on a maximum load line had by law to be painted on most ships' sides, but it was not until 1890 that its actual position was dictated by law. Edward Bates, who had a very bad reputation as a starver of crews, defended himself in a speech in the Commons on July 30, 1875, conceding that he had indeed totally lost no fewer than five ships in 1874 and 1875 and had two others wrecked; one of those lost was the *Euxine*. Most were classed "A.1" at Lloyd's, and none was overinsured or unseaworthy. Plimsoll was forgiven, and the outcome was that some of his ideas not long afterward passed into law. But this legislation appears to have had no dramatic effect on the problem of maritime safety; indeed the statistics published in the First Report of the Royal Commission in 1885 would suggest, probably unfairly, that it had none at all. But Plimsoll's work formed part of a process, and as far as our story is concerned, his importance lies principally in the part he played in generating public sympathy for sailors, in much the same way as Florence Nightingale generated sympathy for soldiers.

Essentially there were two competing views about sailors and indeed even about their officers, not unlike those views that competed to explain the embarrassing phenomenon of the poor. According to one view, sailors were stupid, superstitious, barbarous, depraved, and degenerate. Thus an internal memorandum by Sir Denis le Marchant of the Board of Trade in 1849 reflected this attitude and used these harsh words to describe the quality of the ships' officers: "being in almost numberless instances deplorably deficient in scientific and general knowledge, careless of their cargoes, coarse in their habits, addicted to drink, prone to tyranny, and indifferent to the conditions of their crews." Many officers possessed no idea at all where they were, and near Istanbul there was even a shoal called the English Shoal, so called because English ships continually struck it. The sailors, le Marchant opined, were not much better: "Ignorance and habits of drunkenness and insubordination prevail among British merchant seamen to a greater extent than among Foreign seamen . . . they may fairly be charged with a reckless neglect both of their employers' interests and of their own." The immoral and licentious habits of seamen on return to port were of course well known; indeed sexual deprivation and lewd fantasy provide the principal themes of the sea chanty, which is hardly to be wondered at. But the very degeneracy of sailors, if that was how one looked at the matter, was a challenge, and even the hard realist le Marchant admitted some sympathy for them, reflecting the comforting view that they were more sinned against than sinning:

> The British seaman indeed labours under heavy disadvantage. He enters the service so young as to be necessarily almost illiterate . . . the articles under which he engaged himself are prepared by the licensed agent, who it is to be feared often contrives to appropriate his

> first month's wages under the pretext of cashing his tokens for clothes or goods, which are charged 50 per cent beyond their value . . . he signed the articles without attending to them. He considers himself imposed upon, and views the captain as his worst enemy. If the voyage is toward the tropics his sleeping accommodation is wretched. . . . Whatever money he saves from the lawyer is squandered in vice, and, however meritorious his services, if his life is spared beyond the period of his strength, he closes it in the Union.

Sympathy could indeed easily extend into actual admiration for the courage and hardihood of the valiant heroes of the sea, and a contrasting romantic vision of the seaman is encapsulated in the character of the honest tars in Gilbert and Sullivan's *HMS Pinafore,* though Gilbert slipped in for the gentlemen in the audience some coy references to their less honorable association with prostitution:

> Gaily tripping, lightly skipping,
> Flock the ladies to the shipping.

But if properly cared for and protected from vice, sailors could perhaps be redeemed. To this end immense missionary efforts were dedicated, and it may be, though the point is incapable of strict proof, that one of the consequences of the general if undramatic improvement in the lot of sailors was a feeling that their more barbarous behavior should be viewed somewhat less tolerantly in 1884 than in the past. And one form of barbarous behavior, which could be viewed tolerantly or intolerantly according to one's predispositions, was their settled practice of eating each other when they became hungry. It was a significant, if unusual, peril of the sea.

There is no doubt that the principal reason why the case of the *Mignonette* attracted such enormous attention at the time and continues to fascinate lawyers and others to this day is the fact that it involved this practice; cannibalism lifted it out of the category of a routine shipping disaster or a run-of-the-mill murder case. The popularity of the most recent major study of cannibalism illustrates the persistent interest in this macabre subject. It arose out of the crash of a Fairchild F-227 aircraft carrying a Uruguayan rugby football team in the Andes on October 13, 1972; the team was known as the Old Christians Club, consisting of alumni of Stella Maris College, a conservative Roman Catholic School run by Irish members of the Christian Brothers order, whose members regard the English amateur form of the game (Rugby Union) as morally uplifting. Some of those who survived kept alive by eating the bodies of those who had died, the initiative being taken by a medical student. The story filled the world's press, generated a number of books, and was made into a movie. The fullest account, *Alive* by Piers Paul Read, became a best-seller and was described by the *New York Times* as "thunderous entertainment" and by *Playboy* as "inspirational—spiritual if you will." As a theme in literature or pictorial art, cannibalism has a long and distinguished history, stretching back to the origins of European culture. Thus a form of it is involved in the tale of the Cyclops Polyphemus, who, Homer tells us, made a practice of consuming two of Odysseus' sailors each evening for his supper, *au naturel*. The Greek myths include, among other such stories, the tale of Chronos, who ate his own children; and Tantalus, who served his son at a banquet for the gods; the subject has constantly recurred in imaginative literature. A relatively modern comic example is the melodrama *Sweeney Todd, the Demon Barber.* This originated in its current form in 1847 as a play by George Dibdin, "A String of Pearls, or The Fiend of Fleet Street," but is based on a fifteenth-century story of a demon barber of Paris. A real case, in which cannibalism was combined with murder—if it really was murder—committed in the reign of Queen Victoria by a gentleman's gentleman and denizen of the Home Counties, not by some benighted savage who knew no better, was bound to be a winner. To the lawyers, the unique character of the case heightened the fascination; although the law books were ransacked to find similar cases, the operation met with little success. Here indeed was a *cause célèbre.*

Though to a mind focused solely on the law reports, the case was indeed more or less unprecedented, contemporary attitudes cannot be understood simply on that basis. For in addition to its prevalence as a theme in imaginative work, cannibalism as an actual phenomenon in two forms was very familiar to Victorians. The first form was socially accepted cannibalism, supposed to exist as a regular practice among "savages" or less "civilized" peoples. Travelers' tales and missionaries' accounts never tired of recounting the existence and character of the practice, and the engravers produced amazing pictures of the cannibals gnawing arms and legs or sitting down to human barbecue parties together with every sign of enjoyment. Thus Mrs. Fraser, a survivor of the *Stirling Castle,* had a particularly dramatic tale of life among cannibals to tell, one recounted in a contemporary broadsheet (quoted in full in Michael Alexander's *Mrs. Fraser on the Fatal Shore*). After the shipwreck, Mrs. Fraser having given birth "unto a lovely babe," the survivors reached

> . . . THE FATAL SHORE
> Its name is call'd Wide Bay,
> The Savages soon them espied
> Rush'd down and seiz'd their prey,
> And bore their victims in the boat,
> Into their savage den,
> To describe the feelings of those poor souls
> Is past the art of man.

Mrs. Fraser avoided being eaten, though there were hints of "facts . . . which, if we dared to publish them would excite an involuntary shudder of horror and disgust in every well regulated mind," though precisely what form of exciting ingestion was involved is left unclear. The assumption that "savages" were all cannibals is brought out in the celebrated explorer Burton's classification of the looks or stares he received as a white man in Africa—stare number 12 is "the stare cannibal, which apparently considered us as items of diet." As late as 1926, Northcote W. Thomas, government anthropologist in South Nigeria, writing the article on cannibalism in the thirteenth edition of the *Encyclopaedia Britannica,* assured his readers that "in our own days cannibalism prevails, or prevailed until recently, over a great part of West and Central Africa, New Guinea, Melanesia (especially Fiji) and Australia. New Zealand and the Polynesian Islands were great centres of the practice." It was principally around cannibalism among savages that there developed a vast literature, in which scholars or pseudo-scholars have produced elaborate and sometimes comical taxonomies of the practice. Wholly uncritical works of this kind have been published in very recent times. Thus M. Roland Villeneuve, in his *Histoire du cannibalisme* (1965), a work embellished with remarkable illustrations, though one that is difficult to take very seriously, divides cannibalism in pseudo-scholarly terms into *le cannibalisme alimentaire, le cannibalisme guerrier, le crime rituel,* and *le cannibalisme pathologique.* The last subdivides into two categories, *curatif* and *erotique.* The *curatif* category is an oblique reference to the practice, said to exist in smart circles in Paris, of drinking blood as a regenerative practice, though M. Villeneuve's illustrative material comes from foreign parts. Another system, at which W. Arens pokes fun in *The Man Eating Myth,* distinguishes gastronomic cannibalism from survival cannibalism and cross-classifies into endo-cannibalism (eating people in one's own group), exo-cannibalism (eating people in the other groups), and auto-cannibalism (eating oneself, mild practices like biting one's finger nails excluded). From this scheme arise such bizarre and comical concepts as "gastronomic endo-cannibalism." Hasting's *Encyclopaedia of Religion and Ethics,* published just outside the Victorian era, elaborates a complex scheme of motives for cannibalism, and these include "morbid affection, eating the dead out of sheer love," a practice said to have been recorded in Limerick in the early nineteenth century, and "cannibalism through sheer gluttony—the worst of all." This vice was attributed to the Fans in the Congo, and it remains a prevailing belief that once the taboo on consuming human flesh has been broken it is easy to become, as it were, addicted to it. Thus Northcote Thomas explained that exo-cannibalism and any great extension of endo-cannibalism must be connected to a desire for human flesh "grown into a passion." Presumably the psychoanalytic school would explain this myth as reflecting a widespread latent tendency toward cannibalism as a form of sado-masochistic behavior in all of us.

The orthodox theory of the nineteenth century seems to have been that cannibalism, once universal, had become restricted in range by the spread of civilization. Such a view was reinforced by alarming indications that it had once been practiced in Britain itself. There was, for example, the passage in Gibbon's *Decline and Fall* in which he noted the propensity of the Picts and Scots to attack the shepherd and not the sheep; and the celebrated tale of the Beans of Galloway (or possibly Ayrshire), Sawney Bean and his offspring constituting a whole family of professional cannibals, inhabiting a cave by the seaside littered with the remains of their victims. The story, which first appeared in a broadsheet in about 1700, is variously attributed to the reigns of James I of Scotland (1406–37) and James VI (1567–1625). If it has a basis in fact, it is presumably a story of famine. The same vice has been attributed to a remote period to the clan Kennedy around Girvan in Ayrshire, thought by some to have been the remote ancestors of the well-known American family. Even in Victorian England there were occasional atavistic outbreaks, as in the bizarre case of Thomas Dulton, reported in the *Times* on November 17, 1877, who in the White Lion in Warwick, for no apparent reason, attacked a Thomas Parker "and, getting his forefinger in his mouth, gnawed it like a dog for upwards of two minutes." He had previously bitten off a finger belonging to one Summers, and the *Times* thought his sentence of but one month's imprisonment (at hard labor) an encouragement to cannibalism.

But such incidents could, if anyone troubled about them at all, be categorized as pathological; and pathological cannibalism formed a special category of its own. Its most recent practitioner, a Japanese student named Issed Sagawa, who consumed his girl friend in 1981, has come to be called the Cannibal of the Bois de Boulogne. *Letters from Master Sagawa* by Juro Karawa, based on this incident, has recently won the leading Japanese literary award.

As far as maritime incidents are concerned, a number were recorded in the eighteenth century. The best documented involved the *Nottingham Galley* in 1710. Two versions exist, one published in 1711 and written by Jasper Dean, brother of John Dean (who was captain), and additionally vouched for by Miles Whitworth, who was on the vessel during her voyage: this also appeared in a printed edition in the same year and was republished on numerous occasions. Another version, also from 1711, was based on depositions by the mate, Christopher Langham; the boatswain, Nicholas Mellon; and a sailor, George White; when published, it was rather more expensive than Dean's account, costing 6d. versus Dean's 3d., and was a reply to it, as the title indicates: *A true Account of the Voyage of the Nottingham Galley of London John Dean Commander from the River Thames to New England, Near which Place she was cast away on Boon-Island, 11 December 1710 by the Captain's obstinacy, who endeavoured to betray her to the French, or run her ashore; with an Account of the Falsehoods in the Captain Narrative*. The two sources in general are not in conflict. The vessel left Gravesend on August 2, 1710, in convoy; off Whitby she sailed on alone to Ireland, leaving the convoy hove to in a gale, and took on a cargo of cheese and butter at Killybags. According to the Langham version, she sighted privateers en route, and it became clear that Captain Dean, his brother, and Whitworth, having fully or over-insured the ship and cargo, wanted to surrender the vessel to them. But Mate Langham resisted this plan successfully. She then crossed the Atlantic, leaving Killybags on September 25, and (according to Langham) sighted off Newfoundland what Captain Dean took to be a French ship. Again the captain prepared to surrender his ship, but the other turned out to be a London vessel, the *Pompey Galley*. No mention of all this sinister behavior occurs in the Dean version. The accounts vary as to when and where the *Nottingham Galley* made her landfall, but both agree that she ran ashore on Boon Island, east of the Piscalagua River, off the coast of Maine; it was little more than a rock about three miles from the mainland. The Dean account explains this as a simple navigational error. The Langham version, after recounting a violent quarrel between Captain Dean and the mate, in which the Captain knocked the mate unconscious with a periwig block, attributes it either to a deliberate intention to wreck the vessel (which is quite implausible) or to arrogant obstinacy in standing in too close to land in spite of the mate's protests. According to this version, Captain Dean said "that he wou'd not take his Advice though the Ship should go to the Bottom." He also "threatened to shoot the Mate with a Pistol, and told him, he would do what he pleas'd except they confined him to his Cabbin." The disaster occurred on December 11, between 8:00 and 9:00 P.M., and all managed to get ashore in safety, but the cook died the same night. Apart from a little cheese, they had virtually no food, and what they had soon ran out; in addition, they were unable to make a fire.

A boat was built from the wreckage and launched into the surf on December 21, with Captain Dean, his other brother Henry, Whitchurch, and George White aboard; the surf smashed the boat to pieces, "totally disappointing our Enterprise and destroying all our Hopes at once." In Captain Dean's account,

> We were now reduc'd to the most deplorable and mellancholy Circumstance imaginable, almost every Man but my self, weak to an Extremity, and near starved with Hunger and Cold; their hands and Feet frozen and mortified, with large and deep Ulcers in their legs (the very smell offensive to those of us, who could creep into the Air) and nothing to dress them with, but a piece of Linnen that was cast on Shoar. No Fire, and the weather extreme cold; our small stack of Cheese spent, and nothing to support our feeble Bodies but Rockweed and a few Muscles, scarce and difficult to get (at most, not above 2 or 3 for each Man a Day).

But in spite of all this a raft was made, and two men, one a Swede who had lost his feet from frostbite, left; both drowned though the raft was seen to reach the shore. Such vessels as passed did not see them. At the end of December the carpenter died, "a fat Man, and naturally of dull, heavy, Phlegmatic Constitution and Disposition, aged about 44." According to the captain's version, the men suggested eating him; the mate insisted it was the captain who initiated the idea, saying, "It was no Sin, since God was pleased to take him out of the World, and that we had not laid violent Hands upon him."

The captain himself skinned, dressed, and quartered the corpse. He added that he "first ordered his Skin, Head, Hands, Feet and Bowels to be buried in the Sea, and the Body to be quartered for Conveniency of drying and carriage." But he conceded that he did the job himself. The mate and his two fellow deponents at first refused to eat but soon joined in with, the captain claimed, "the utmost Greediness." He also said that cannibalism at once transformed the crew's character, which became "fierce and barbarous," adding that "nothing now being to be heard but brutish Quarrels, with horrid Oaths and Imprecations, instead of that quiet submissive Spirit of Prayer and Supplication we had before enjoyed." This reduction to animal behavior was denied in the Langham version, according to which they had never been a happy band of brothers under their tyrannical captain. The 10 survivors were rescued not long after, on September 4, by a shallop and recovered, though the captain's boy lost part of a foot. Langham, Mellon, and White gave depositions concerning their version of the affair before Samuel Penhallow, justice of the peace of Portsmouth, New Hampshire, on February 9 and further depositions in London on August 1, 1711. Their version was thus recorded just before Jasper Dean's account was published on August 2, 1711, and was denied by him in a postscript, where it was said that the vessel and cargo had not been overinsured; no doubt it was this controversy that helped to generate interest in the story. Captain Dean did not suffer from the attack upon him; he ended up as British consul at Ostend, dying there in 1761. The last edition of his own account appeared the following year, but the story is reported in numerous other collections of shipwrecks.

In the nineteenth century many more cases are recorded, the first I have noted being in 1807, when the *Nautilus* stuck on a shoal off Cerigotto (Antikythera) in the Aegean; initially there was some reason to expect rescue, "but neither the whale boat nor the promised vessel appeared to mitigate the sufferings of the famished men, who were now glaring with greedy eyes upon the lifeless bodies of their shipmates as the only way of relieving the cravings of inordinate hunger. As the day advanced, famine overcame their natural repugnance to this loathsome diet." The rapidity with which the sailors took to cannibalism in this instance was quite extraordinary. Nine years later, in 1816, there was a more celebrated incident still, the wreck of the *Medusa*. This is unusual in that it inspired Géricault's remarkable *Radeau de la "Méduse,"* originally exhibited as *Scène de naufrage* in Paris in August 1819 and now in the Louvre. The frigate

Méduse was wrecked on July 2, 1816, en route to Senegal, and a raft was constructed to carry from it those whom its boats could not accommodate. The boats, needless to say, were taken by the captain and more senior officers; and although the original plan was for the boats to tow the raft to safety, the lines were soon cut and the raft abandoned, with some 150 persons on board. Fifteen survived to be rescued on July 17, and by the third day many had started to engage in cannibalism; on the sixth a number of ill survivors, 13 in all, were thrown alive into the sea by common agreement among the remaining 15. An account of the disaster by Henri Savigny (a doctor who selected those to be jettisoned) appeared in the *Times* on September 13, 1816, and a fuller account by Savigny and Alexandre Corréard, *Naufrage de la frégate la Méduse faisant partie de l'expédition du Sénégal en 1816,* was published in translation in London in 1818. It has been reprinted in numerous editions. Cannibalism is not in fact depicted in Géricault's painting, though it appears in some of his preliminary studies.

In 1822 occurred "the lamentable shipwreck of the brig *George,*" a timber ship that left Quebec under Captain John M'Alpen on a voyage to Greenock, Scotland. It was beaten into a derelict hulk by a storm, and to this the survivors clung for many days; accounts vary from 38 to 59. The ballad telling the tale records events following the death of a woman named Joyce Rae:

> At length we drank the female's blood,
> To quench our raging thirst.
> Her wretched husband was compel'd
> Her precious blood to taste.
> And for the whole ship's company,
> The same did not long last.
> Her body then they did dissect,
> Most dreadful for to view,
> And serv'd it out in pieces
> Amongst the whole ship's crew.
> Eleven days more we did survive
> Upon this horrid food,
> With nothing to supply our wants
> Save human flesh and blood.

Five more sailors were consumed before Captain Hudson in the *Saltom* rescued them on November 14, only to be shipwrecked a second time on December 19 off Cumberland. The captain and one seaman survived, and another ballad gloomily ends,

> So now to conclude, as the danger is o'er
> Those poor men with the Saltom did get safe to shore.
> They have the sad case of the George to deplore,
> And we think they will go on the seas never more.

No doubt it was the eating of Mrs. Rae, and the double shipwreck, that made this story so popular. In 1835 the *Elizabeth Rashleigh*'s fate was reported in the Plymouth journal; she was another timber ship. After the vessel became waterlogged on a voyage from Quebec to Padstow, Master Rashleigh (the vessel was presumably called after his wife), two mates, and three seamen took to the longboat and were picked up after nine days on December 13 by the *Caroline,* after, "as the only means of saving their own lives, the survivors were obliged to the horrible experience of drinking the blood and eating the flesh of their deceased shipmates, even to the entrails!" The only alternative, potatoes, had unhappily run out, and there was nothing else to be had on board.

In 1835–36 the press reported that cannibalism had been resisted in the cases of the *Earl Kellie* and the *England.* In the former case the vessel, an old 550-ton East Indiaman, broached to on December 3 but eventually righted herself, waterlogged, after the loss of her anchor reduced her instability. Attempts were made to obtain provisions by diving into the hold—this, it must be noted, was in the North Atlantic in December. A vessel came up but gave no assistance; it had no boats. Merely to be spotted was at this period absolutely no guarantee of salvation; rescue might be too dangerous or even pointless if the other vessel had no provisions to spare. On Saturday, December 5, a contemporary account reads, "We were fortunate enough, to our great surprise, to catch three or four rats, which had saved themselves by some means; these proved very acceptable to us, especially their blood, to those who were fortunate enough to get it." When the mate died, completely insane, on Tuesday the eighth there was a proposal to eat him, but his body was in fact thrown overboard. On December 20 another vessel, the *Lord Melville,* declined to take the survivors off; it had no provisions left, so they might as well starve where they were. They were eventually rescued by the *Robert Isaac* or the *George Marsden* (accounts differ) the same day. In the case of the *England,* rescue occurred after 45 days in the boats in time to prevent cannibalism, which had been mooted but never practiced. Or so it was said.

In the same year it did, however, occur in the case of the *Home* (Captain Duncan), when five out of 17 survived the initial catastrophe; she was another timber ship from Quebec. The frequency of horror stories connected with this trade is explained by the fact that even gravely damaged timber ships would not sink, and consequently their crews were kept alive longer than they would have been on other vessels. It was also common for such vessels to carry deck cargo, which reduced their stability and increased the risk that the helmsman would lose control in a strong following sea and allow the vessel to broach to, whereupon the ship would almost inevitably become a waterlogged derelict. The published story of the wreck of the *Home* comes from a letter by John Gibbs to his wife, written from the Liverpool Infirmary: maimed and frostbitten, he recorded how, after 11 days in the mizzen top without food or shelter, "they were under the disagreeable necessity of opening two of their dead companions, and subsisting on their remains till they were taken from the wreck." The *Hannah,* yet another case, was an old leaky vessel of 260 tons; she had a crew of a captain, mate, eight seamen, and two boys ("boys" might be anywhere from about the age of eight upward). En route from Quebec to London she broached to on July 12, 1836, some 30 miles off Cape Breton, and lay on her beam ends. The captain cut away the hemp standing rigging to rid her of her masts, and, relieved of their weight, she righted herself in a waterlogged state with all water and provisions lost. It was 12 days before the survivors were rescued. They drank seawater, and on the fourth day John Roulards died "of fatigue" and was eaten. "A boy named Tarbuck soon after became delirious. He refused to partake of any part of the body of his shipmate, and was continually calling out for his father and mother. He exhibited the greatest dread at the prospect of his body being cut to pieces, and begged his companions to throw him over when he died. This last wish was complied with. He died on the 6th day." Another sailor became raving mad and died; the survivors were rescued on the twelfth day by the *Volunteer,* which landed them at Hull. On arrival, Timothy Madagan (the source of this account) and the other survivors received 5s. from Trinity House and 2s. from Charity Hall; they then went to London, where Madagan tried to take out a summons in the Thames Police Court against the owner of the *Hannah* for wages. In this he failed: at this time, as we have seen, the doctrine of maritime law that "freight is the mother of wages" prevailed. This meant that if his ship had foundered and thus earned no freight, no wages whatsoever were due, whether or not he or his fellow sailors had been responsible for the loss of the ship. This remained the basic legal principle until the law was changed by the Merchant Shipping Act of 1854; it probably originated at a time when mariners operated more as a partnership, sharing the risk of the adventure and its profit, but the doctrine survived with grotesque injustice into a world in which seamen had become simply employees. Timothy Madagan, confronted with this legal principle, said "that after he had risked his life for the profit of others in a bad ship, and been all but starved to death on the ocean, he could now obtain no help in his native city, where plenty abounded." But Messrs Ballantine and Brodrip at the Thames Police Court were unmoved; so, having made his protests, he left the office and disappeared from history.

Right through the nineteenth century the dismal story continued. Thus the *Times* for Thursday, April 24, 1856, printed a full statement made by Captain Edward Rudolf describing the loss of the barque *Blake* on a voyage from Ship Island Harbour, Mississippi, to Cork. After days of gales during which the sailors had been at work for three days with no sleep, and with over 13 feet of water in the hold, the *Blake* broached to at 6:00 P.M. on March 12 and in a hurricane the next day capsized completely, subsequently righting herself. The weather moderated, and on March 20 the captain recorded how, "this being the seventh day without anything to eat, I caught a half-drowned rat, which I immediately cut up and shared out to each one: it was a delicious morsel." Two vessels took no notice of them on March 22, and another vessel ignored them on March 25. On their thirteenth day since the disaster, they began to eat a sailor who had died—he was either José Ariva of Callao or Richard Foss of Bideford. The crew fed "very sparingly indeed, for the thought of it were almost as bad as death itself," and after 17 days the captain and seven out of a crew of 17 survived. They were rescued by the schooner *Pigeon,* which was saved by the *Mercury,* in its turn having run out of water. Other shipwrecks leading to cannibalism, not all of which I have tracked down, were mentioned in the Commons debate on the Unseaworthy Ships Bill in 1875 by Samuel Plimsoll, such as that of the *Anna Maria* where "part of the leg of a woman was found which evidently served the crew for food." Plimsoll mentioned two other cases, where the names of the ships were not revealed, in one of which "four bodies were found under the maintop, all dead, with part of one of their comrades hung up, as if in a butcher's shop." One involved a Whitby ship called the *Earl Moira* (Captain Terry) in which an attempt to rescue the survivors was made by the *Sarah* in November 1838. The captain of the *Sarah,* who sailed close by the waterlogged hulk, made prolonged attempts at rescue, and

> declares he never was so shocked in all his life, and hopes never to witness such a scene again, or spend such a day in the world . . . the remnants of the crew had taken refuge in the main top. . . . There were eight persons alive on the main top; but the most horrible sight was one swinging and hung by the neck, evidently as food for the rest. He had black whiskers, and his intestines had been taken out, and a piece of the shoulder cut off. To keep his body as fresh as possible, and place it out of the way, it was hung just under the trim of the foretop. . . .

Because of the weather conditions, the *Sarah* could not rescue any of the eight survivors; two of them, probably one being the captain, drowned trying to swim to her. Later the barque *Ranger* found the hulk on December 19; by then all were dead, and remains indicated that another sailor, a boy, had been cut up and eaten. The hulk eventually went ashore at Corunna in March 1839. Earlier, parliamentary select committee reports of 1836 and 1839 had specifically referred to these and other cases, such as those of the *Dalusia* (1833) and the *Lucy* (1834). In certain other cases—for example, the *Earl Kellie* in 1836 and the schooner *Leader* in 1865—contemporary accounts of their fate strongly suggest that cannibalism in fact took place but was concealed.

So normal was cannibalism that on some occasions survivors found it appropriate to take pains to *volunteer* denial that cannibalism had occurred; suspicion of this practice among starving castaways was a routine reaction. An example can be found in 1866. The *Jane Lowdon* was dismasted on December 21, 1865, on a voyage from Quebec to Falmouth; eventually she was found by the *Gresham* in a grotesque condition, with not a living soul aboard, on January 27. There were, however, five mutilated bodies on board. The derelict was reported when the *Gresham* reached Spithead on February 1. In fact eight sailors had escaped the initial disaster, but of these Captain Casey alone had survived, being earlier rescued from the hulk on January 18; he had been saved by a Dutch ship, the *Lola Elizabeth,* before the *Gresham* sighted the derelict, and landed in Holland at Nieuwe Diep. There he was visited in the hospital by the British consular chaplain from Batavia, the Rev. J. M. Arnold, who wrote to the *Times* of Captain Casey's miraculous survival. Eventually his wife and five children heard of this. Captain Casey was severely frostbitten and destitute, and an appeal was launched for him, with what success I do not know. Though he admitted the temptation, he denied engaging in cannibalism, in spite of hints that his tale of survival without food for 28 days was incredible; indeed he may well have eaten the ship's carpenter, James Beatt.

Cannibalism under survival conditions may simply take the form of eating the corpses of those who have died naturally. Though disagreeable and distressing, it is difficult to see any moral objection to this. As such, it has never been regarded as illegal, though it is said that in 1884, not long before the case of the *Mignonette,* when Mr. Justice Fitzjames Stephen ruled in *Regina v. Price* that privately conducted cremation was not by itself illegal, the home secretary, Sir William Harcourt, cynically remarked that the judges would soon approve of cannibalism as a means of disposing of the dead. But survival cannibalism may involve the actual killing of one or more of the survivors, with or without their consent, or the acceleration of imminent death by bleeding the dying person to secure blood to drink. In the nature of things, it can never have been easy to establish what precisely did occur in the grim conditions of shipwreck or famine at sea, particularly because the remains, such as they were, could usually be thrown overboard before rescuers had an opportunity to inspect them. However, there are a large number of cases in which it seems to be quite clear that deliberate killing took place, and some others that look fairly suspicious; obviously these recorded cases represent merely the tip of the iceberg. To these cases we now turn.

The earliest recorded, and one that was cited as a possible "authority" in the case of the *Mignonette,* comes from the early seventeenth century, and the only direct account is to be found in a medical work, Nicholaus Tulpius's *Observationem medicarum,* published in Amsterdam in 1641. Tulpius had the story from what he called "eye witnesses," and there is no reason whatever to doubt the truth of this, since a Dutch colony was involved. Seven Englishmen set out from the Caribbean island of St. Christopher (St. Kitts, earlier known as Merwars Hope) for a voyage expected to last one night only. But a storm drove them out to sea, and they were afloat for 17 days.

One of them suggested that lots should be cast as to who should die to satisfy the hunger of the others; the lots were cast, and the lot fell to the one who had proposed the scheme; lots were also cast to select an executioner. A victim was by his own consent killed, and his blood drunk and his body divided and eaten. It will be noted that the form of the story emphasizes the fairness of the proceedings and thus general acceptability. They were eventually cast up on the island of St. Martin; on landing, they were well treated by the Dutch on that island and sent home to St. Christopher. There they were accused of homicide by "the proctor"—presumably some sort of constable—and their judge (*ipsorum iudex*) pardoned them, their crime being "washed away" by "inevitable necessity." (*Sed dilvente crimen inevitabili necessitate, dedit ipsos brevi veniam ipsorum iudex.*) There would have been a local judge of the English community, appointed by Sir Thomas Warner, the governor, under a commission of 1627; the legal records of the Court of Admiralty that existed there survive in the Colonial Office Papers but start too late to include the story, in 1644. The incident probably occurred between 1629 and 1640.

A number of similar incidents were recorded in the eighteenth century. The *Gentleman's Magazine* for 1737 printed an account by Simon McCone, an Irishman from Drogheda, and Thomas Thompson, an American from Rhode Island, only survivors of the slaver *Mary,* which foundered near the Canaries after picking up a cargo of slaves at Cutchoe (Cochea) in West Africa. Together with four Englishmen and two Portuguese, they escaped in the ship's boat, abandoning the slaves and 15 crew members to their fate, and in due course they began to eat each other, starting with the Portuguese, the sixth man being killed in self-defense when he was himself attempting to kill Simon McCone. The two survivors reached Barbados on January 19, 1736, and appear to have made no secret of how they had survived. The same journal also carried the story of the *Dolphin* in 1759. This was a case not of shipwreck but of famine, which persisted until the survivors were rescued by another vessel, the *Andalusia*. The account in the *Gentleman's Magazine* for August reads as follows:

> Being reduced to the last extremity, they all agreed to cast lots for their lives, which accordingly they did; the shortest lot was to die; the next shortest was to be the executioner. The lot fell upon Anthony Galatea a Spanish gentleman, a passenger. They shot him through the head, which they cut off and cast overboard; they then took out the

> bowels and ate them, and afterwards, ate all the remaining parts of the body, which lasted but a very little while. The Captain [Captain Barron] saw they were casting lots a second time, but it happend very luckily that he bethought himself a pair of breeches that were lined with leather. . . .

So they ate the leather instead. One cannot but be suspicious about the selection of a passenger—in some other cases, as we shall see, this sort of suspicion recurs; the lot mysteriously falls on the obvious victim. This again was a case in which the executioner as well as the victim was selected by lot—the shortest lot for the victim, the next for the executioner. Six years later, in the case of the *Peggy,* the crew had the solace of alcohol but, after the pigeon, the cat, the tobacco, the candles, and what leather they could find had been eaten, no access to other food. Led by the mate, the crew burst in on the captain, and, with "countenances of the most frightful ghastliness" announced that they would have to draw lots. Captain Harrison attempted to buy time, but the crew left him and then returned, saying they had already cast lots and that "the lot had fallen on the negro who was part of the cargo." The unfortunate slave attempted to escape but was dragged on deck and shot by a sailor by the name of Doud. It strains credulity to suppose that lots were fairly cast. After another sailor, James Campbell, ate the liver raw, elaborate culinary activities commenced, including an attempt to pickle the body. Three days later Campbell went mad and died; fearing to contract madness from his body, the others threw it overboard. "Used with the utmost economy," the slave's body lasted from January 17 to January 26, and then lots were cast again. The captain, who had so far resisted any involvement, now gave way to prudence, and on this occasion "considered that if the lots were not drawn in his presence he might not himself be fairly treated." Presumably he too had been suspicious about the first occasion. The lot fell on Richard (or David) Flat, a "seaman much beloved on board." Flat accepted with resignation and asked Doud to shoot him. But Doud could not bring himself to do so, and after a short prayer some attempted to catch fish—if they were successful, Flat's death could be postponed. But the strain on the unhappy Flat was too much. By midnight he was deaf, and in two or three hours raving mad. His death was postponed, and they were rescued by the *Susanna* just in time to save him. When crew members rushed in to tell the captain of the sail in sight, he misinterpreted their behavior and nearly shot them, fearing it was now his turn. On the *Susanna,* which brought them home to London under Captain Thomas Evers, Doud himself died. But Richard Flat survived, together with Captain Harrison and two other sailors, Ashley and Wentworth. The story of the *Peggy,* which was very well known, may have been used by Byron as a source for the scene of shipwreck in *Don Juan.*

The *Tiger* was shipwrecked in 1766, and in Peter Viaud's story of it, once matters became critical, "it came into Viaud's recollection that mariners had cast lots who should die to keep their comrades from famine. His eyes lighted on the negro youth. . . ." His companion, Mme la Couture, had the same idea about the same time, and the formality of casting lots was dispensed with, though some time was directed to "bitterly bewailing his fate." The unfortunate man, who appears to have been a slave, was killed and indeed smoked.

The story of the survivors of the Nantucket whaler *Essex,* sunk by a sperm whale on November 20, 1820, has been immortalized indirectly as a scene used by Herman Melville in *Moby Dick.* The crew escaped in three whaleboats, one of which disappeared. In the one that contained the captain, George Pollard, bodies were eaten; and eventually, on February 1, lots were drawn among three survivors. Owen Coffin was shot by Charles Ramsdell and eaten by him and the others, who survived. Cannibalism also took place on another boat from the *Essex* that bore one Owen Chase, the first mate, whose account of the affair was published as *Narratives of the Wreck of the Whale Ship Essex.* Another account, by Thomas Nickerson, who was in the same boat as Chase and was at the age of 17 helmsman when the disaster occurred, has recently been discovered and donated to the Nantucket Historical Association by Ann Finch; this was written up many years after the event, in 1880. The story of the *Essex* was widely known and gave rise to popular ballads, which gave it international currency and thus emphasized the legitimacy of lot drawing. One printed in Truro, Cornwall, has the story in this form:

> We ranged through, no food could we get,
> Confined there a long time, nothing for to eat,
> Till we all cast lots to see who should die,
> Which made our ship's crew for sorrow to cry.
>
> The lots were drawn one man was to die,
> For his wife and poor children most bitterly did cry,
> To kill him says the captain or take away his breath,

> But to starve with hunger is a deplorable death.
>
> Then his messmates they killed him and cut off his head,
> And all the ship's crew from the body did feed,
> And at eight different times lots amongst them were drawn,
> For to keep them from starving that's the way they went on.

In this popular form the story was widely disseminated among the seamen of the world. In the accounts by Owen Chase and Thomas Nickerson—both based on what Captain Pollard told them—lots were drawn by general consent to select both the victim (who was Captain Pollard's nephew) and the executioner, and Owen Coffin accepted his fate. The Nickerson account reads,

> The Captain with his three surviving companions after a due Consultation agreed to Cast Lots—the awful lot fell upon a young man named Owen Coffin who was a nephew of Captain Pollard, who with great fortitude smiled at his fate at this awful moment the Captain wished to exchange lots with him but to this Coffin would not listen for one moment. He placed himself in a firm position to receive his death and was immediately shot by Charles Ramsdell who became his executioner by fair lot.

Since only Captain Pollard and Charles Ramsdell survived, the knowledge of what happened depends solely on these two accounts, both second-hand.

In 1826 occurred "a most horrible shipwreck of the ship *Francis Mary,*" accounts of which appeared in the *Globe* and *British Traveller* and were republished in broadsheet form in Penryn and Bristol. A timber ship, she left St. John's, Newfoundland, on January 18 and was disabled on February 5. Two vessels spoke with the derelict but offered no assistance, and beginning on February 21, the crew began to die. John Wilson died on February 22 and was quartered and hung up for food; the next day, I. Moore died, and his liver and heart were eaten. Matters went from bad to worse, and when the cook, James Friar, died, Ann Saunders, his betrothed and a passenger, cut his throat and claimed prior property rights in his blood. She seems to have been a particularly tough character; it was said that she had "more strength in her calamity than most of the men. She performed the duty of cutting up and cleaning the dead bodies keeping the knives in her monkey jacket, and when the breath was announced to have flown, she would sharpen the knives, bleed the deceased in the neck, drink his blood and cut him up as usual." Another version of the story records how, when Ann, "heard of Frier's [*sic*] death, [she] shrieked a loud yell, then snatched a cup from Clarke (mate), cut her late intended husband's throat, and drank his blood, insisting that she had the greatest right to it." The survivors were rescued by the 42-gun frigate H.M.S. *Blonde,* under her captain Lord Byron; Lieutenant Gambier, who picked them up in the ship's cutter, remarked, "You have yet, I perceive, fresh meat." To this the reply was "No sir, it is part of a man, one of our unfortunate crew. It was our intention to put ourselves on an allowance even of this food, had you not come to our relief." Ann Saunders was not the only woman to survive; the captain's wife, Mrs. Patterson, did too, and, having eaten the brains of an unfortunate apprentice who had survived no fewer than three previous shipwrecks, opined "it was the [most] delicious thing she had ever tasted." Only six survived, and of the others it was said, "From want of water, those who perished drank their own urine and salt water: they became foolish, crawling on their hands round the deck (when they could) and died generally raving mad." One suspects some were killed. They disappeared from history: their rescuing ship lived on to achieve notoriety in the first Opium War.

Recourse to murder and cannibalism did not necessarily bring about survival, though when it did not, usually nothing was ever discovered of the fate of the crew. Occasionally evidence did survive. A peculiarly grim case, involving in all probability both mass murder and cannibalism, occurred in 1828–29, on the island of Anticosta in the gulf of St. Lawrence. Four men landed on the island and visited a hut at Godin's Post. Inside they found "the carcases of four human beings with their heads, legs and arms cut off, and the bowels extracted, hanging by their thighs in the room, and the others cut up in the same manner." There was also a store in a trunk, and a pot with flesh in it. This larder had not, however, saved the last survivor, who lay dead in a hammock. The *Times,* at the instigation of the Lloyd's agent at Pictou, published an account of items found at the site, where numerous other human relics were strewn about; this account derived from an affidavit sworn before a local justice of the peace. It transpired that the remains came from the *Granicus,* which had been wrecked on the island, then largely if not wholly uninhabited in winter, about November 20, 1828. Between 17 and 20 persons had been on board, and the last survivor was a sailor whose name was Harrington, the son of Mary Harrington of Barrack Street, Looe.

Bloodstains on the roof and other evidence suggested that a number of his companions had died after a violent struggle; he presumably simply froze to death.

There were at about this time numerous cases of simple cannibalism, not involving murder; 11 years later, however, in 1836, there occurred the case of the *Brig Caledonia,* recorded in the proceedings of the Select Committee on Timber Ships of 1839. It was a typical story of a waterlogged timber ship, where the men near to death had their throats cut for blood. They were self-selected; when it was the turn of the ship's boy, James Rimer, he was saved in the nick of time by the arrival of the Russian *Dygden,* which rescued the survivors. A broadsheet, "The Horrible Shipwreck of the Caledonia," was printed in Bristol by John Bonner on November 20, 1837, the day after the six survivors landed at that port, where they were lodged, crippled with frostbite, in St. Peter's Hospital. It records only one actual killing but confirms the story that on the thirteenth day they were about to kill the ship's boy. It does not appear to have occurred to anyone to bring any legal proceedings against the master, Captain David Cock, and what was left of his crew of 12. Typically, the officers survived—captain, first mate, and second mate; and the Bristol *Mercury,* which also printed the story (reporting two killings), helped to organize a subscription for the sailors and a purse for Captain Thornberg of the *Dygden* in appreciation of the courageous rescue carried out in heavy seas by the *Dygden*'s first mate, Otto Reinz Spoof. Rescuing men from a derelict in the days of sail was a complex and hazardous operation, particularly in merchant vessels that rarely carried spare men. Sails had to be taken in by clewing them up to the yards and the vessel hove to by bracing around some of the yards; then a boat had to be put overboard, manned, and maneuvered to leeward of the hulk, an operation in which the boat could easily be damaged or destroyed, while the rescuing vessel, now undermanned, was unable to help. Understandably, many captains would not take such a risk unless conditions were favorable.

The previous year saw the wreck of the sailing barque *Francis Spaight,* the strangest and best documented of all the stories of cannibalism after deliberate killing and preceded, in accordance with the traditions of the sea, by the ritualized drawing of lots.

Francis Spaight (1790–1861) was a merchant of Limerick who owned the estate of Derry Castle and became involved as a shipowner in the timber trade from North America. He is principally remembered today because he is featured in books dealing with Irish emigration and the Great Hunger, for he gave enthusiastic and frequently quoted evidence to the Select Committee on Colonization from Ireland in 1847. In that year ships carried some 2,000 Irish peasants out of Limerick; as Spaight explained, they represented clear profit, since the ships would otherwise have had to sail westward in ballast.

At one time or another he or his firm owned various ships—the *Bryan Abbs,* the *Governor,* the *Jessy,* the *Jane Black*—and the *Francis Spaight* and *Derry Castle* were specially named to reflect their ownership, a common enough practice; Edward Bates, a Liverpool shipowner whom we have met, even had a ship called *The Bates Family,* with the ultimate vulgarity of an appropriate group figurehead depicting nine members of his family. Whether the *Francis Spaight*'s figurehead, recorded as "A Man's Bust," was a portrait I do not know; it probably was. She was a wooden three-masted, square-sterned vessel, 108 feet 9 inches overall, of 345 tons burden; she was ship rigged. She had been built at Monkwearmouth (now part of Sunderland) in County Durham in 1835, and in light of her subsequent history, it comes as no surprise that her builder's certificate on completion was signed on April 13 of that year. She was registered at Limerick on May 4, with Francis Spaight owning 44 of the 64 shares in her and Alexander Denny of Glasgow the balance of 20—ships were divided traditionally into 64 shares. She was classified A.1 by Lloyd's. Spaight's ships normally worked the passage to Quebec; and although it was later said that she had been originally intended for the West Indian trade, it was to this port that she made her maiden voyage under the command of Timothy Gorman of Limerick, who, with Daniel Gorman (surely his brother) worked for Francis Spaight. Both came from Kilrush, on the Shannon, Daniel having been born there in 1795 and Timothy on September 23, 1799. From records in Limerick, in the Public Record Office, and the National Maritime Museum, it is possible to reconstruct Timothy Gorman's career in some detail. It began in June 1813 when, at the age of 13, he was apprenticed for three years on the *Waterhouse,* a North Shields ship. Then, between 1817 and 1820, he was in turn mate on the *Dandy* of the same port and the *Waterloo* and *Eliza* of Limerick. In August 1820, at the age of 20, he had become a ship's master, commanding the *Diana* (1820–21), *Mary Ann* (1822–23), the *Dublin Packet* (1824), the *Janet* (1825–26), the *Agnes* (1826–33), and then the *Breeze* (or, as he spelled her name, *Breige,* 1832–35). The *Agnes* was the first of these vessels in which Francis Spaight appears to have had an interest, and she was used on the North Atlantic run to Quebec. The size of Gorman's commands increased progressively from *Diana,* at a mere 94 tons, to *Agnes* at 203, *Breeze* at 321, and his next command, the *Francis Spaight* at 457.

On his first voyage in his fine new ship, Gorman reached Quebec in early July, and the starving condition of his passengers attracted the special attention of the emigration agent; he complained to the customs officer at Limerick, who ought to have remonstrated with him for putting to sea inadequately provisioned. On her second voyage that year, the *Francis Spaight* carried some 216 emigrants to Quebec; many came from the estate of Derry Castle, which Spaight purchased in 1844 and systematically cleared of peasants. She must have sailed from Quebec very much later in the season than was customary, for it was November 24 when she left St. John's, Newfoundland, with her cargo of timber for the return journey; she carried a large deck cargo. She had a crew of 18, of whom four were boy apprentices; at the time, merchant vessels were required by law to carry a proportion of apprentices. They included Patrick (or Pat) O'Brien, aged 14, who had been bound apprentice to Francis Spaight for four years on September 7, 1835, presumably about the date the vessel sailed from Limerick. No doubt he came from the Limerick workhouse.

At 3:00 A.M. on December 3, when running before strong winds under mizzen topsail, the ship broached to, partially capsized, and lay on her beam ends. She was then swept by seas coming aboard, and William Griffiths, the mate, and two seamen, Pat Cusack and Pat Behane, were drowned. She lay thus for an hour, the survivors clinging to the side of the vessel and the rigging. Captain Gorman had difficulty in persuading his men to take the only action that would save the ship, which was to cut away her masts and, by reducing the weight of her top hamper, enable her to right herself. In such a crisis the captain of a sailing ship, who would normally never work with his hands, had to lead his men by example, and in the event he and one seaman, Daniel Mulvihill, succeeded in cutting the lanyards by which the shrouds supporting the mizzen topmast were secured to the mizzen top and futtock shrouds; this improved her stability, and she righted, but by now she was full of water with only the poop and bulwarks showing above water. Neither food nor water was saved, and the 15 survivors, standing in water, clung to whatever they could, as seas swept over her. Next morning a sail was seen, but it was too far away to sight the derelict. Some rain

1. A drawing by Tom Dudley of the yacht *Mignonette,* which shows her with topmast housed as rigged just before and at the time of the disaster. The heavy line at the stern may represent the bulwarks that were carried away, or some form of canvas dodger. Public Record Office, London (KB6/6/006543).

2.
The devious Baron Huddleston, engraved by Horace Petherick in 1884. National Portrait Gallery, London.

3.
Sir William Harcourt, Home Secretary in 1884. Drawing by S. P. Hall. National Portrait Gallery, London.

4.
Alferd G. Packer in prison garb, photographed in Canon City Penitentiary in about 1886. By permission of the Denver Public Library.

5.
Sir John Duke Coleridge, Lord Chief Justice of England in 1884, who sentenced Tom Dudley and Edwin Stephens to death. National Portrait Gallery, London.

6. The sailing barque *Alliance,* which, under her earlier name *Moctezuma,* rescued the three castaways. By the ship portrait artist, Reuben Chappell. By courtesy of Mr. T. Larsson-Fedde.

7. The *Mignonette* dinghy, exhibited in September 1884 in the hall of the Royal Cornwall Polytechnic Society in Falmouth.

8. The sailing barque *Drot,* formerly the *Almira Robinson,* the last of the nineteenth-century cannibal ships, by Halvor Mikkelsen. Built in Bath, Maine, she sank in a hurricane in the Florida Straits in August 1899. Reproduced by courtesy of the Norsk Sjøfartsmuseum, Oslo.

9. The paddle steamship *Euxine,* photographed possibly in Marseilles, before 1868. Subsequently refitted as a sailing barque, she burnt out and sank in the South Atlantic in 1874. Reproduced by courtesy of the Peninsular and Oriental Shipping Company's Information Services.

10.
E. Boutcher's seventy-eight-ton cutter yacht *Fiona,* engraved in 1868 by Josiah Taylor and showing the yacht in the Royal Thames Yacht Club match on June 17. Tom Dudley became mate of this celebrated racing yacht. The National Maritime Museum, London.

11.
The yacht *Mignonette* sinking by the stern. Based on drawings by Edwin Stephens. Originally published in the *Illustrated London News*.

12.
The *Mignonette*'s dinghy at sea. Based on drawings by Edwin Stephens, who is portrayed twice (full face) by the *Illustrated London News* artist. The lower picture clearly shows the sea anchor constructed from the triangular headsheets grating and the water breaker base.

13. The trial of Tom Dudley and Edwin Stephens in the castle at Exeter. The lady behind Baron Huddleston is presumably Lady Huddleston. Dudley and Stephens appear with the moustached Julius Wiese; the bearded Ned Brooks is shown in the witness box. Arthur Collins is separately depicted.

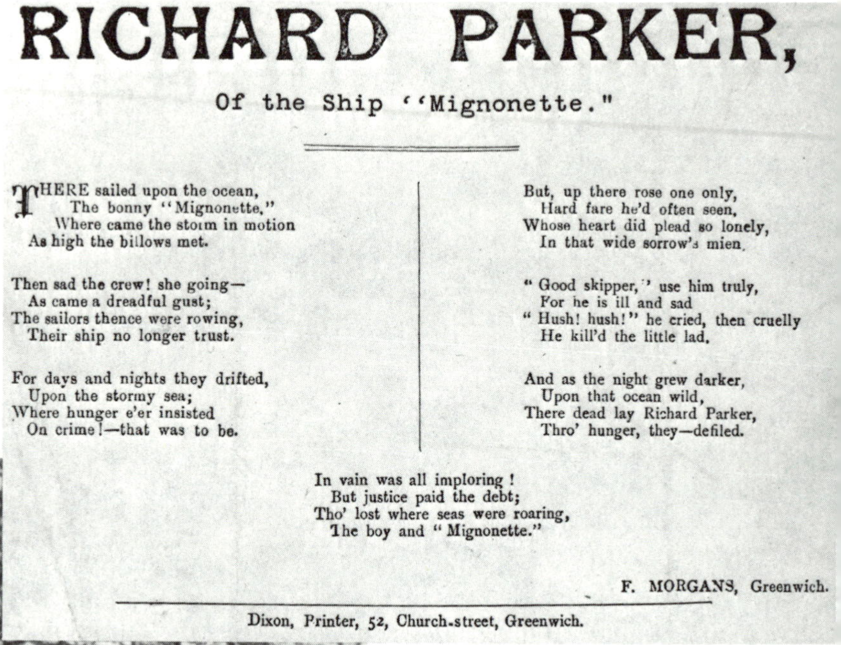

RICHARD PARKER,

Of the Ship "Mignonette."

THERE sailed upon the ocean,
The bonny "Mignonette,"
Where came the storm in motion
As high the billows met.

Then sad the crew! she going—
As came a dreadful gust;
The sailors thence were rowing,
Their ship no longer trust.

For days and nights they drifted,
Upon the stormy sea;
Where hunger e'er insisted
On crime!—that was to be.

But, up there rose one only,
Hard fare he'd often seen,
Whose heart did plead so lonely,
In that wide sorrow's mien.

"Good skipper," use him truly,
For he is ill and sad
"Hush! hush!" he cried, then cruelly
He kill'd the little lad.

And as the night grew darker,
Upon that ocean wild,
There dead lay Richard Parker,
Thro' hunger, they—defiled.

In vain was all imploring!
But justice paid the debt;
Tho' lost where seas were roaring,
The boy and "Mignonette."

F. MORGANS, Greenwich.

Dixon, Printer, 52, Church-street, Greenwich.

SACRED
TO THE MEMORY OF
RICHARD PARKER
AGED 17.
WHO DIED AT SEA
JULY 25TH 1884. AFTER
NINETEEN DAYS DREADFUL
SUFFERING IN AN OPEN
BOAT IN THE TROPICS
HAVING BEEN WRECKED IN
THE YACHT MIGNONETTE
"Though He slay me yet will
I trust in Him."
JOB XIII 15.
"Lord lay not this sin to
their charge."
ACTS VII 60.

14.
This ballad was probably intended to be sung, but no particular tune is suggested. Reproduced by permission of the British Library (from *A Collection of Topical Songs,* shelfmark 1874 e 4).

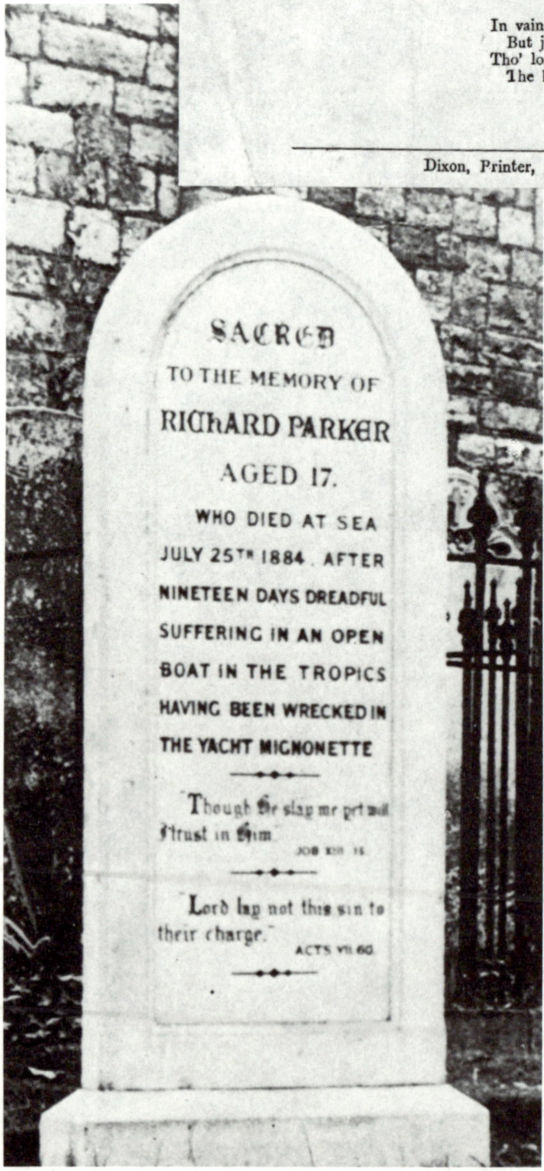

15.
The memorial stone for Richard Parker set up over the unmarked grave of his mother in the churchyard on Pear Tree Green, Southampton. Photographed before the stone was damaged by a falling tree, and showing the remarkably clean condition.

was caught in a tureen cover, and on the seventh day another vessel passed four miles away but took no notice of them. The behavior of the survivors deteriorated as conditions grew worse, with vindictive attitudes directed toward Patrick O'Brien. According to one account, it was on December 19, the sixteenth day since the accident, that the Captain said,

> They were now such a length of time without sustenance that it was beyond human nature to endure it any longer—that they were already on the verge of the grave, and that the only question for them to consider was whether one or all should die? . . . His opinion was that one should suffer for the rest, and that lots should be drawn between the four boys, as they had no families, and could not be considered so great a loss to their friends, as those who had wives and children depending upon them.

The report continues,

> It is clear that although O'Brien agreed with the casting of lots, he did not agree that this be limited to the boys, but protested against it, and only acquiesced when it appeared that if he did not the men would proceed in a more summary way.

Other contemporary versions place the first drawing of lots on December 18 or 22, and the vagueness as to dates is hardly to be wondered at. Lots were cast, apparently only among the four boy apprentices: George Burns, Johnny Sheehan, Patrick O'Brien, and one other; and the lot fell to O'Brien. In one account, the ritualized procedure for drawing the lots is minutely described. O'Brien was blindfolded and on his knees, and a sailor drew out sticks. As each one was drawn, O'Brien was required to call out the name of one of the four boys and the name that coincided with the shortest lot was to die. The first lot was drawn and he called for "little Johnny Sheehan"; it was laid aside without announcing whether it was the shortest or not. When the next lot was drawn, in response to the question, "On whom is this lot to fall?" he called out, "On myself." The sailor announced that this was the death lot. There is some suggestion that the procedure was contrived to select O'Brien. The captain then ordered the cook to bleed O'Brien to death: the cook, one John Gorman, refused. The captain told him it was his duty, presumably because it was the function of the ship's cook to prepare meals for the crew, and the other sailors said that if he failed to do so they would kill him. He reluctantly gave way. O'Brien appears to have acquiesced in all this, and he took off his jacket and bared his arm. The cook made an unsuccessful attempt, at which point O'Brien said to the cook that "he could not be looking at him without putting him to pain," took the knife himself, and, at the captain's suggestion, made an attempt on his left arm. This again proved futile. He suggested that, if he rested a little time, he might bleed, saying how a doctor in Limerick had once bled him successfully after initial failure, after he had rested. The captain then suggested that they had better cut O'Brien's throat, the job to be done by the unhappy John Gorman. At this point, Patrick O'Brien became terrified and began to resist. "The first man," he said, "who laid hands on him would be the worse for him: that he'd appear to him at another time; that he'd haunt him after death." But he was seized, and John Gorman, still protesting, was forced under threats of death to kill him. Blood was caught in the top of the tureen, and the majority fed on the corpse, though a sailor by the name of John Mahony refused. Matters grew worse, and the crew began to drink seawater; John Gorman began to rave, and two or so days later, as his death was approaching, his throat was cut and his blood drunk. The same day—this would be perhaps on December 21—one Michael Behane went mad and on the next day, another of the boys, George Burns. He too was bled to death, and Michael Behane had only avoided the same fate by dying unexpectedly. It was also said in one account that lots were drawn again after this among all survivors, and that the death lot fell on one of the mates. But a sail was seen by James Hourigan and John Mahony, and rescue came in time to save the mate. A Limerick paper, the *Limerick Times and Daily Herald,* later claimed that at the time of the rescue the captain was "in the act of eating the liver and brains of his apprentice." The rescuing vessel was an American brig, the *Agenora.* A peculiarly macabre feature of the story is that the men were so terrified of this ship passing by that they used the hands and feet of O'Brien to wave to the American vessel, which presumably sailed close by the derelict before heaving to and lowering a boat for the actual rescue. They had lasted 20 days, and of the original crew of 18, 11 survived. They were by then "in a state of abject wretchedness, and some so mutilated by the frost, and otherwise rendered helpless, as to be unable not only at present to obtain present bread, but to labour for it during the rest of their lives." The *Agenora,* under Captain John Jellard, brought the 11 men to Falmouth, as Dudley, Stephens, and Brooks were to be brought 58 years later; there they landed on Wednesday, January 6. There was no Sailors' Home then, so they were lodged in the workhouse, and Captain Gorman collected money for them. There they remained for some time, and the story was reported in some of the West Country papers—the *Cornubian* and the *West Britain and Cornwall Advertiser*—but not in all. No attempt whatsoever was made to conceal what had occurred, and the captain wrote from Falmouth a letter to Francis Spaight explaining the loss of the ship and the expedients by which some had survived, just as Tom Dudley proposed to do in 1884. This letter was published in the Limerick press, with the excision of the details of the killings—"Here we withhold, at the desire of Mr. Spaight, and out of respect for the feelings of the public, some shocking facts in connection with this frightful occurrency," said the *Limerick Times* on January 11. The *Times* exhibited no such delicacy of feeling, and the story was soon widely known.

The *Agenora* put to sea again on Tuesday, January 12. As for the men, no attempt was made to detain them in Falmouth. They eventually came home to Limerick late in January. There, too, although Francis Spaight was himself a justice of the peace, no legal proceedings against captain or crew were apparently even contemplated. Press reports emphasized the sufferings of the survivors; "The appearance of some of these unfortunate mariners, men and boys, is ghastly and spectre like with a singular woe-be-gone expression of countenance" and sang the praises of the captain ("Captain Gorman, who is happily saved, has always been an especial favourite with the citizens.") and his ship ("the finest belonging to our city"). Francis Spaight published an appeal for the survivors and families. On January 15 "Humanitas" also penned an appeal to the *Limerick Times;* he recounted how "none but an eyewitness could form an adequate idea of the piteous wailing of the friends and relatives of the ill-fated men, on the arrival of the disastrous and appalling intelligence." "Humanitas" also revealed that some of the crew who came from Kilrush at the mouth of the Shannon were known in yachting circles—like Dudley, Brooks, and Parker, they had worked as yachtsmen. He was probably Crofton M. Vandeleur of the Royal Western Yacht Club. Seventy pounds was raised—he contributed £20 to Francis Spaight's rather mean £10. Particularly distressed by the whole affair was Patrick O'Brien's mother, a widow from Thomondgate named Catherine (or Margaret). She went to Francis Spaight's country house, "where her hysterical cries were truly heart-rendering."

Similar scenes took place in Kilrush, Tarbert, and other villages on the Shannon.

The story of the *Francis Spaight* featured in parliamentary select committee reports in 1836 and 1839. On the latter occasion some further details were revealed by Thomas Edward, secretary of the Royal Society for the Preservation of Life from Shipwreck, based on an account of the rescue by John Cousins and G. Warren, passengers on the *Agenora*. The rescue had been extremely hazardous, Captain Jellard himself setting out in tremendous seas in a ship's boat with three volunteers—William Hill, the mate; John Towell, a seaman; and Samuel Hicks, a passenger. This was all investigated at Teignmouth by four Devon magistrates and a minister of religion, the Rev. E. D. Rhodes, and the society had voted the captain a gold medal and his helpers silver medals. But at no point was there any suggestion that criminal prosecution of the survivors was appropriate.

The *Francis Spaight* herself survived the tragedy; though waterlogged, there was no reason why she should sink, and at some date between 1836 and 1838 she was recovered, pumped out, and repaired. On January 7, 1838, as a result of an order of December 28, 1837, by the commissioners of customs, she was reregistered at London, her new owner and master being Joseph Shepherd of Colet Place, off the Commercial Road. He may well have salvaged her himself, and it is understandable that Francis Spaight may not have been eager to retain any connection with so ill omened a vessel. On August 8 she was remeasured and registered yet again, and she became the property of a consortium. She continued in service under Captains Shepherd, Neville Reid Sayers (June 1839), Thomas Winn (from 20 July 1840), and finally Henry Patterson (from 31 October 1844), sailing once to New Zealand and several times to Bombay; crew lists for some of these voyages survive. But few sailing barques of this period seem to have died in their home ports, and the *Francis Spaight* was no exception. Early in January 1846 she arrived at the Cape of Good Hope on a voyage from Manila and anchored in Table Bay to take on provisions. The wind got up to a heavy onshore gale, and at about 8:30 A.M. on Wednesday, January 7, she parted from her anchors and was driven onshore. A whaler reached her and took off all her crew of 15 except for the carpenter, James Robertson, who refused to leave the wreck: the whaler capsized in the surf, and Captain Patterson and all but one of his crew, one John M'Leod, drowned, in company with the six-man crew of the whaler. James

Robertson was the only other survivor. Among the four apprentices who lost their lives in the wreck of this sinister vessel was another Richard Parker.

As for Captain Timothy Gorman, he too was a surviving type, like his ship, and soon recovered from his grim experience; and his long, precarious career is usefully illustrative of the conditions of life at sea at this period. Francis Spaight entrusted him with the *Borneo,* another vessel employed in the emigrant and timber trade to Quebec. On March 29 he signed a crew of 21 and put to sea again. His crew included three new apprentices—Edmund McNevin, William Vickers, and John Edward—who, if they had any choice, do not seem to have been discouraged by the fact that their captain had eaten two of their immediate predecessors. A new cook was engaged, 50-year-old Angus Ferguson of Greenock, though history does not record whether his captain's view of a cook duties was made clear to him. On his return to Limerick on about July 28, Captain Gorman was reminded of the earlier voyage by Catherine O'Brien, and on July 30 he took proceedings against her in the Limerick magistrates court. According to the only extended account, "Captain Gorman said he had had no peace for the last week on account of the defendant, who threatened to take away his life and his children as well." She denied this, saying "that all that she did was to fall on her knees, to beg he would tell her about her son that was killed, and instead of doing so, he abused her." She was duly bound over to keep the Queen's peace in the only legal proceedings to arise out of the death of her son. At the same sessions the captain also took proceedings against his first mate, Thomas Greggs, for alleged insubordination, for which he too was found guilty, fined £3, and sentenced to imprisonment.

Timothy Gorman continued as master of the *Borneo* from 1836 to 1841, making two voyages a year to Quebec with remarkable regularity; by 1844, if not earlier, he was a part owner in her, to the extent of eight shares. He would leave Limerick in late March or early April and return in mid-July, leave again a few days later, and be back home in November. In 1842, Francis Spaight purchased a new 579-ton ship, the *Jane Black,* from John Martin & Co. of Belfast and Thomas Conrad Lee of Quebec, built and first registered at Quebec in 1841; her registration was transferred to Limerick in April 1842, and Timothy Gorman became her master. His old ship, the *Borneo,* continued in the North Atlantic trade for some years but was lost in the end in the Straits of Belle Isle in July 1846. With his new command Timothy Gorman was not so fortunate, for on her first voyage of 1842 she went aground at Pointe des Montes on the Ile aux Coudres some 50 miles short of Quebec early in March and was reported a total loss, though crew and passengers were saved.

However, she must have been salvaged but was apparently wrecked yet again on her second voyage, which began on September 12; a note on the crew list in Gorman's hand, dated November 12, records that "the articles of the crew from Limerick to Quebec with all other papers belonging to the ship were destroyed when the Ship became a wreck." But the *Jane Black* again survived and from 1843 to 1858 sailed regularly on the emigrant route, normally to Quebec, but once in 1844 to New York; on one voyage she carried Gorman's son William, a minister, who "took the voyage for the benefit of his health" and had to keep the log after his irascible father had sacked the mate, Daniel Martin. Emigration from Limerick reached its peak in 1847, the worst of the famine years, when 11,728 individuals took ship from the port. Thereafter the numbers declined, and by 1858 a mere 104 left; and the trade, once highly profitable, all but disappeared.

Usually Timothy and Daniel Gorman would manage two voyages a year, and on some occasions Daniel would be in the customs house to witness the signing on of the crew of the *Jane Black* before he took his ship *Jessy* down the Shannon and out to sea again. In 1845 the *Jane Black* again ran into trouble, catching fire in Quebec; the fire, which devastated the city, destroyed the ship's certificate of registration, and she was reregistered on March 22, 1846. As reregistered, she was some four feet shorter at 120 feet, and her original scroll head had been replaced by a woman's figure—presumably Jane Black, whoever she was. The alterations may have been the result of the fire in 1845 or the earlier accident. From crew lists some picture of the problems Timothy Gorman encountered can be reconstructed. Thus on her first voyage in 1845 Gorman signed on a crew of 24 between March 29 and April 3, and with James Lloyd as first mate sailed on April 4 with 400 emigrants crammed into the ship in some haste, Gorman apologizing to the shipping master for failing to complete the crew list properly. Typically, six seamen deserted in Quebec (it was a cheap way to emigrate), and one was left behind; substitutes had to be obtained from crimps at the exorbitant rate of £7 per month (seamen normally got £2 to £3, and the first mate only £5). In the same year, Daniel Gorman took the *Brig Governor* across on the same run; and in 1847 another Gorman, Thomas, sailed as second mate on the *Jane Black*. Francis Spaight continued as the sole owner for some time, but in February of 1849 Timothy Gorman bought 12 shares from him, and four years later Daniel acquired four shares. In 1850 compulsory certification of ships' officers came into force, and on February 19 Timothy Gorman was officially approved as a master mariner, the Board of Trade not holding his earlier aberrant activities in any way against him. For some years all seems to have gone well, except in 1851, when Gorman was fined £16 under the Passenger Acts for exceeding the permitted complement of emigrants by eight.

But in 1858 his ship was overwhelmed in the North Atlantic while returning from Quebec carrying, presumably, a cargo of timber. Precisely what happened is not recorded, but on November 10 the *Edisto* of Cronstadt, at 45° north, 41° west, passed the recently abandoned hulk of the *Jane Black*. Her topmasts were gone, her bulwarks carried away, her hatches were off, her decks were swept by the sea, and she was full of water; both her anchors were also missing. Presumably she had suffered much the same fate as the *Francis Spaight,* and her topmasts may well have been cut away and her anchors jettisoned in an attempt to right her. But the indestructible Timothy Gorman and his entire crew of 15 survived the disaster, which had occurred on October 22, leaving the crew on the deck of the waterlogged hulk of their ship with two gallons of fresh water and a small quantity of biscuit, saturated with seawater, to sustain life in the grim conditions of the storm-swept North Atlantic. They survived for nine days, and there was ample time for all, particularly the apprentices, to reflect upon their captain's earlier experience in similar circumstances on the *Francis Spaight*. But if the possibility of drawing lots was raised, the fact is not recorded, and on October 31 the American ship *Flora McDonald,* bound from Liverpool to Baltimore, took them off; it was driven by storms to seek refuge in St. Thomas in the West Indies, from whence their arrival on December 17 was reported to Lloyd's and published on January 3. From there they came back to Southampton on January 1, 1859. They reached Limerick to be signed off at the customs house on January 7. There Captain Gorman was described by the Limerick *Chronicle* as "still in a nervous state," as well he might be, having nearly returned a second time as a cannibal; and the quivering hand with which he signed the papers before Shipping Master J. W. Walshe confirms the newspaper's account. As for the *Jane Black* herself, she seems to have been as indestructible as her captain and to have decided to return home, with or without crew, and lay herself to rest in Ireland. The *Nicaragua* sighted her on November 17, with fore and main topmasts gone and decks swept. The *Maritona* passed her "in a sinking state and derelict, with only her lower masts standing" on November 23. Early in December the *R. A. Hiern* sighted her again, and on January 19, 1859, the *China* met with her again. Eventually, on January 27, she ran aground in a cove on Clare Island off County Mayo, no doubt to the delight of the local peasantry, and there she broke up. What little is left of her presumably lies there still.

His experience on *Jane Black* kept Timothy Gorman at home for two years only, and he returned in 1861 to the Quebec run in *Challenger.* In 1862, for example, he set sail in company with Daniel Gorman, in command of the *Jessy,* on April 7, arriving on May 21. *Challenger* was an ageing vessel, built in 1848, and rather larger than the *Jane Black,* at 721.29 tons: originally registered at Cork, she had been acquired by Francis, William, and James Spaight in 1860; and they sold Timothy Gorman eight shares. On her second voyage she was lost on the return trip early in September near Renews Head north of Cape Race, and her crew must have been taken off or escaped in boats, for they were discharged at St. John's on September 6. Presumably she too became waterlogged. This ended Gorman's connection with the Spaight family—on February 16, 1861, Francis Spaight had died. Gorman's next ship, *Creole* (428 tons), was not registered at Limerick or owned by the family: she belonged to Londonderry. In 1863 and 1864 he took her to Miramichi in New Brunswick and Quebec, discharging his last crew at Warrenpoint, where the mountains of Mourne do come down to the sea, on January 22, 1865. And there the long career of this remarkable and much shipwrecked old cannibal ended, sadly far away from his home in Limerick. One log of a voyage of his survives intact, and with it one can still set sail in the *Jane Black* on her journey in 1857 down the Shannon, out across the Atlantic and up the St. Lawrence to Quebec; return with him through the violent gales he so long survived; and read how on March 19 in "light winds and pleasant weather" Thomas Miskell (aged 22) fell at 3:00 P.M. from the main yard and was killed, to be buried at 4:00 A.M. next morning as the watch changed, or how at 2:00 A.M. on Wednesday, June 25, Wilson Hallard (aged 24), "not capable of his body turned away from the wheel could not steer the ship." Was it perhaps some similar incident that led to the catastrophe to the *Francis Spaight?* And in Limerick itself the eighteenth-century customs house where he so regularly signed on his crews is still there, and so is Spaight Quay; indeed the firm of Francis Spaight and Sons is still in business in the City, dealing appropriately in timber and hardware, though it is no longer in family hands. And further inland above Killaloe on the eastern side of Loch Derg you can see Derry Castle and the lands from which Francis Spaight exported crime and distress at £3.10s. a head just before the terrible time of the Great Hunger, from which they were providently thus saved.

The tale of the *Francis Spaight* is perhaps the most striking of all the nineteenth-century cases, and it belongs to a period in which such incidents appear to have been particularly common in the North Atlantic timber trade. It was, however, by no means the last such case. In addition to the case of the *Mignonette* in 1884, there was the *Euxine* (1874), where lots were drawn and a boy eaten, and, in the same year, the suspicious case of the *Cospatrick,* where cannibalism certainly occurred and possibly death was hastened by bleeding. In 1878 the American press reported the grim case of the schooner *Sallie M. Steelman* (or *Stedman*), which suffered severe damage on January 20 in a gale off Cape Hatteras on a voyage from Charleston, South Carolina, to Baltimore, and became a drifting derelict on which Captain S. G. Higby and his crew of six began to starve to death, their only provisions being coffee. On January 30, when they had been out 43 days, a black sailor, George Seaman, lost his reason and threatened to shoot the captain. On deck he called out to another black sailor, Walter Sampson, to come on deck: Sampson did so and, fearing Seaman was going to shoot him, pulled a pistol borrowed from the steward, Sylvester R. Herbert, and shot Seaman dead. After the body had lain on deck four hours, Sampson cut off the head, which Herbert and another sailor, David Barrett, wrapped in canvas and threw overboard. Barrett then butchered the corpse and salted some flesh; this was boiled and fried, Barrett claiming it tasted "as good as any beefsteak he ever ate." They were rescued on January 31 by the schooner *Speedwell,* on passage from Cadiz, and eventually reached New York. Press reports suggested that the men might be brought to trial, and when interviewed, "the seamen, while they answered inquiries put to them, seemed to do so unwillingly, and continually enquired if any punishment was likely to be inflicted on them for the act of cannibalism." But no proceedings were ever apparently brought, presumably because Sampson's story was accepted. The internationalism of the seafaring community is brought out by the fact that this American tragedy generated a Danish street ballad, set to the music of the song "Amanda Was Sitting with a Garland of Roses," which added a sad but romantic detail—George

Seaman was to have married Susan Illit on the ship's return; she stood waiting for him on the shore, not knowing of his death.

In the nature of things, some of these stories of the sea may be inaccurate in detail; no doubt in the aftermath of shipwrecks there was a fair amount of lying and romantic embroidery, designed to place the informant in a better light or to emphasize the horrors from which he had escaped. We shall never know for certain whether the lots on the *Francis Spaight* were really fairly drawn or whether the elaborate ritual actually took place. But our concern is that of establishing the historical context for the case of the *Mignonette,* and for that purpose what really happened hardly matters; what was really important was belief and myth, not reality. Viewed in this way, it is quite clear that the situation confronting the survivors of the yacht *Mignonette* was one for which they were well prepared and that in a general sense Dudley and his companions knew the proper thing to do; someone must be killed that the others might live. They also knew that to obtain blood to drink, a living victim was preferable; to wait until death occurred was unwise. They knew too the appropriate preliminary course of action, which was to draw lots, a practice viewed as legitimating killing and cannibalism, particularly if agreed upon by a council of sailors. Nor was the tradition of the sea as it applied to such critical situations confined to seamen, as a sort of professional secret (no doubt mariners would know of other more private stories, which circulated orally on shipboard or in seaports). The incidents I have described were all public knowledge. There was nothing whatever secret about the matter. What sailors did when they ran out of food was to draw lots and eat someone.

In addition to these arguably true tales of suffering and horror at sea, murder and cannibalism had featured in both popular and more sophisticated fictional literature. At a popular level, the traditional English ballad dealing with the subject is known as "The Ship in Distress" or "You Seamen Bold" and tells of the sufferings of the crew of a merchant ship under Captain Divers that eventually reaches Lisbon. It includes this stanza:

> Their cats and dogs, O, they did eat them,
> Their hunger for to ease, we hear,
> And in the midst of all their sorrow,
> Captain and men had equal share;
> But now a scant has come upon us,
> A dismal tale, most certainly,

Poor fellows they stood in torture
Casting lots to see who should die.

The individual selected in this ballad had a large family and was saved in the nick of time, while saying his prayers, when a sail was spied to windward. The version quoted was published in 1891, in John Ashton's *Collection of Real Sailors' Songs,* from an early nineteenth-century broadsheet; and other variant texts have been published, some with music, as by Roy Palmer in his collection *The Valiant Sailor.* One version, given me by Dr. Van der Merwe of the National Maritime Museum, identifies the intended victim as Robert Jackson; he is saved, and the ship comes into St. Vincent, Cape Verde. "The Ship in Distress" is indeed the English form of a ballad that exists in a variety of forms throughout Europe and Scandinavia. In Portugal, it is the "Ship Catherine," being connected with a royal vessel that existed in the early 1500s; in Catalonia, it is "The Cabin Boy"; in France, "The Short Straw," "The Little Ship," or the "Little Corvette"; in Denmark, "The Seafarers"; in Sweden, "Sir Peter's Voyage"; in Iceland, "The Merchant's Tale." In most of these versions, the intended victim escapes at the last minute, or his escape is assumed, but the details differ. In some the lot falls on the captain; the cabin boy offers himself as a substitute, climbs the mast for a last look around, sees the Towers of Babylon and the captain's daughter, and marries her. In others, the boy is offered the daughter and money as reward for acting as a substitute but asks for the ship instead. In the Catalonian version, the captain is saved by the devil, who takes his soul. A Scandinavian version has the king of Babylon in command; lots are drawn, and the unfortunate seaman who draws the fatal lot cannot decently be eaten, since he is closely related to the other sailors; one who is not related offers to die in his place and is sacrificed. (This problem of gastronomic incest arose in reality in the case of the whaler *Essex.*) These old traditional ballads, which survived into this century as a living form of folk art, instructed sailors as to what ought to be done, and their message was reinforced by other ballads dealing with specific cases—such as the ballads of the *Essex* and the *George.* The instruction provided by ballads could be very specific indeed. A ballad of the *Essex* contains this stanza:

Then his messmates they killed him and cut off his head,
And all the ship's crew from his body did feed,

And the eight different times lots amongst them were drawn,
For to keep them from starving was the way they went on.

And sailors indeed did just that—they cut off the head as a preliminary to eating the corpse. Or that at least is what they said they did, for one can never be quite sure where truth was sacrificed in an attempt to appear to live up to the custom of the sea.

Many folk ballads dealing with marine disasters must have been lost, but I have been able to locate two that recount the story of the *Francis Spaight*. "The Sorrowful Fate of O'Brien" was published in a collection edited by James N. Healy (*Irish Ballads and Songs of the Sea*), though without identifying the shipwreck that generated it. The ballad generally gives an extraordinarily accurate account of the disaster:

You landsmen all on you I call and gallant sea-men too
Till I relate the hardship's great that lately we went through:
From Limerick in the breeze to St. John's we set sail,
On the twenty-seventh of November in a sweet and pleasant gale.

It happened many miles from land, on her beam end she lay,
Our fore and main mast instantly we had to cut away;
When her masts went overboard, to rights she came again,
Three foot of water in her hold till daylight did remain.

Early the next morning we viewed our awful state:
Ben Cusack he was drowned and Griffin, our first mate.
Down below we could not go where our fresh water lay,
And as for meat we'd none to eat, for all was washed away.

All we got safe from out the wreck was three bottles of Port Wine
And every time that we got weak, we took a drop each time.
We had not water for to drink but what fell from the sky,
And no dry spot then could be got to either sit or lie.

On the third day of December, it being on the ninth day,
Without tasting any kind of food; the hunger upon us did prey
Our captain cried: "Cheer up my boys; let those four boys cast lots
They have no wives: to save our lives one of these four must die."

While lots they were preparing, these poor unfortunate boys
Stood gazing at each other with salt tears in their eyes
A bandage o'er O'Brien's eyes they quickly then did tie
For the second lot that was pulled up said O'Brien was to die.

He said unto his comrade boys: "Now let my mother know

> The cruel death I did sustain, when you to Limerick go."
> Then John O'Gorman he was called to bleed him in the vein
> Twice he tried to take his blood, but it was all in vain.
>
> Our captain cries: "Cheer up, my boys, this work will never do;
> O'Gorman you must cut his throat, or else you will die too."
> The trembling cook, he took the knife, which sore did him confound,
> He cut his throat and drank his blood as it flowed from the wound.
>
> Early the next morning the weather it got clear,
> And the American Aginora, in sight she did appear
> Providence sent her that way for to protect our lives
> We're safe once more on Limerick's shore with our children and our
> wives.

The other is less accurate and is reproduced in the appendix; a copy survives in the National Library of Ireland. Later we shall see that the case of the *Mignonette* too generated ballads, and some of these have been traced.

The boundary between folk art and high culture was blurred in 1845, when W. M. Thackeray composed a version of "La Courte Paille," which became well known under the title of "Little Billie" or "The Three Sailors of Bristol City." "Little Billie" was first published in 1849 by Samuel Bevan in *Sand and Canvas: A Narrative of Adventure in Egypt with a Sojourn amongst the Artists in Rome;* and it is said to have been composed in Rome, to be sung to the traditional tune of "Le Petit Navire" (or "La Courte Paille"): numerous variant versions passed into currency, one of which is published by Stan Hugill, the last of the chantymen, in his *Shanties from the Seven Seas.* Another version, containing the lines "I see the Towers of Babylon / And the coast of Barbary," was apparently adapted in 1884 to the story of the *Mignonette,* but my attempts to locate a text have so far failed.

Perhaps even better known is "The Yarn of the Nancy Bell" by W. S. Gilbert, the best known of the Bab Ballads. This was first offered to *Punch,* whose editor turned it down as being "too cannibalistic for his readers' tastes." In fact *Punch,* on March 11, 1865, had published a poem, "The King of the Lumbagees," that contained the couplet "We were talking of eating the skipper / With winegar, mustard and pipper." Be that as it may, "The Yarn of the Nancy Bell" appeared in March 1866 in *Fun.* It includes these lines:

For a month we'd neither wittles nor drink,
Till a-hungry we did feel,
So we drawed a lot, and according shot,
The Captain for our meal.

The ballad ends with an ingenious argument as to who should be the final victim, in the middle of which the cook, who is winning the argument, is popped into the pot. I have not been able to find an obvious contemporaneous model for Gilbert's ballad, though I have been told that the *Nancy Bell* was a real ship that sank in the Indian Ocean. Gilbert was not unfamiliar with the sea, owning the schooner yacht *Pleione*. *Fun* also published "The Cook's voyage" on December 5, 1868, a similar piece with recipe.

In more modern times the theme has been taken up by Stephen Leacock in *Soaked in Seaweed: An Upset in the Ocean* (*An Old-fashioned Sea Story*); and there is a reference to the custom, as one would expect, in Conrad's *Lord Jim* and his short story *Falk*. But far and away the most extraordinary fictional tale on this theme is Edgar Allen Poe's "Narrative of Arthur Gordon Pym," first published in magazine form in 1837. It has been said that this story owes something to Poe's acquaintanceship with Jeremiah N. Reynolds, a man prominent in the world of Antarctic exploration. He raised support for and went on the James Eights and Palmer-Pendleton Expedition of 1829–31. It was a rigorous experience, and it may be that he told Poe tales of the behavior of men in extreme privation. Poe's tale includes a remarkable description of the plight of starving castaways: they even catch a turtle (Poe calls it a tortoise), as did Dudley and Stephens. Eventually one of the three survivors says that he "has now held out as long as human nature could be sustained, that it was unnecessary for us all to perish, when, by the death of one, it was possible, and even probable, that the rest might be finally preserved." Splinters of wood are used for the lots. The man who proposed the scheme draws the fatal lot. He is killed and eaten. His name, incredibly, is Richard Parker. This bizarre coincidence did not escape contemporaries in 1884; "A Reader" drew attention to it in the *Times* of December 9, 1884. More recently, a distant relative of Richard Parker won a *Sunday Times* competition dealing with coincidences by recounting this story.

It is clear then that, in the Victorian imagination, cannibals abounded and that, as far as sailors were concerned, the matter went well beyond the imaginary. If properly conducted, cannibalism was legitimated by a custom of the sea; and the popular literature, augmented by the unrecorded tales seamen told each other, ensured that there was general understanding of what had to be done on these occasions and that survivors who had followed the custom could have a certain professional pride in a job well done; there was nothing to hide. In a recent book entitled *The Man Eating Myth,* W. Arens has argued that cannibalism, as a socially accepted practice, is a myth; he excludes from this thesis "survival" cannibalism. I should myself argue that maritime survival cannibalism, preceded by the drawing of lots and killing, was a socially accepted practice among seamen until the end of the days of sail; it is therefore not an exception but a counter-example. Outside the maritime world, the position is confused by the existence of such eccentric cannibals as Liver Eating Johnson or Dapick Absarcka, the Crow Killer (John Johnston, ca. 1820–1900). This mountain man consumed the livers of Crow Indians whom he had killed, not through hunger, much less gluttony, but as a matter of principle, for it was Crows who in May of 1847 had murdered and scalped his wife ("Crow, or this child never ate beaver tail" he is said to have observed at the time).

6
Man-Eaters of the Frontier

Six miners went into the mountains
To hunt for precious gold;
It was the middle of winter,
The weather was dreadful cold,
Six miners went into the mountains,
They had nor food nor shack—
Six miners went into the mountains,
But only one came back.

—Traditional Ballad Collected by Olive Woolley Burt in 1952 and Thought to Refer to the Story of Alferd Packer

The circumstances in which cases of survival cannibalism occurred are not peculiar to the sailor's world; they arose whenever men were to be found in frontier conditions. The sea was one continuous frontier, always dangerous, hostile, and lonely; but similarly inhospitable conditions could arise on land, as in war—for example, in the 1812 retreat from Moscow, as described in the *Memoirs of Serjeant Bourgogne, 1812–1813,* or in times of famine. In less populous parts of the world, such as the American West, conditions not infrequently become precarious, so that men faced imminent starvation. There and in the Polar region in the nineteenth century there were many more Europeans working in wilderness conditions and depending on their own resources than is the case today. A remarkable instance of cannibalistic recidivism in frontier conditions was the case of Alexander Pearce, an Irish felon transported for seven years to Van Diemens Land in 1820 after being convicted in 1819 for stealing six pairs of shoes, and subsequently sentenced to serve the remainder of his sentence in the penal settlement at Macquarie Harbour on the west coast of Tasmania. Conditions there were brutal, and shortly after his arrival, Pearce and seven companions absconded and took to the bush. According to a confession by Pearce, ultimately the sole survivor, published in the second Report of the Select Committee on Transportation in 1838, it was a convict by the name of Robert Greenhill who first proposed cannibalism "and said that he had seen the like done before, and that it tasted very like Pork. . . ." Little is known about Greenhill except that he was sentenced at the Middlesex Assizes in October 1820 to 14 years' transportation and appears to have been a sailor, a fact that would explain his apparent familiarity with cannibalism. Greenhill soon after killed one Alexander Dalton (who had flogged other prisoners and was hated for this reason), and he was bled, dismembered, and eaten: "Mather, Travers and Greenhill put his Heart and Liver on the Fire to Broil, but took them off and cut them before they were right Hot." One Kennely and a convict named William Brown then left the party, and some days later Greenhill, assisted by Mathew Travers, killed Thomas Bodenham. John Mather now became edgy; one of the recurrent features of such stories is the realization, once the first victim has been killed, that another member of the party will die next. He suggested to Pearce that they should separate, saying, "You see what kind of a Cove Greenhill is, he would kill his Father before he would fast one day." This plan was not followed, and soon after Mather was killed by Greenhill and Travers, after having been given the customary opportunity to say his prayers. Greenhill not long afterward killed Travers and continued the journey with Pearce, carrying as much of the corpse as they could. Relations between Greenhill and Pearce now, understandably, became somewhat strained. As Pearce put it, "I watched Greenhill for two nights as I thought he eyed me more than usual, he always kept an Axe under his head when he lay down. . . ." And so Pearce prudently engaged in a preemptive strike and killed and ate Greenhill. Other accounts differ. One claimed that the first killing was of Thomas Bodenham, after lots had been drawn: "This unfortunate Man did not appear in the least affected, he used no kind of Language by way of Soliciting their Compassion as many would think he would. . . ." He merely asked for time to say his prayers, and the experienced Greenhill acted as executioner because "he had been placed by Fortune in a Similar Situation before. . . ." If this is true, it must refer to Greenhill's maritime career. The other killings took place without lot drawing, more or less in the same way. Two other confessions, dating from 1824, provide shorter accounts. In one, lots were drawn by agreement on two occasions, those preceding the killing of Bodenham and Mather. In the other, Greenhill proposed that lots be drawn, but it is left unclear whether this suggestion was followed or not. The whole story in its various versions has many points of contact with nautical accounts of such incidents, even down to details such as the eating first of the heart and liver; it is by no means impossible that Robert Greenhill had indeed been involved in an incident of a similar character at sea.

Pearce was not brought to trial on this occasion; and Dan Sprod, in his scholarly study of the story, suggests that the explanation was the inadequacy of the evidence. He was sent back to Macquarie Harbour, from whence he again escaped in the company of one Thomas Cox, on November 16, 1823. Shortly after, he gave himself up, on November 21. He had quarreled with Cox and killed him, and when apprehended he had a piece of Cox's body in his pocket. He led his captors to Cox's mangled remains, "which the inhuman wretch declared was the most delicious food." Pearce had not eaten his companion out of necessity but from preference; the story conforms to the belief that cannibalism, once practiced, easily becomes a habit. Pearce was tried for murder before the supreme court of Van Diemens Land on June 20, 1824, Chief Justice Pedder presiding. He pleaded not guilty, and his defense appears to have been that he killed Cox in self-defense (a complete exoneration) or in a sudden quarrel, which would then have meant a conviction for manslaughter under the legal doctrine of only "chance medley." Chief Justice Pedder apparently directed the jury that the choice lay between murder and manslaughter. But the jury of seven commissioned officers found Pearce guilty of murder, and he was sentenced to be hanged and his body anatomized. During the latter process in the colonial hospital, his skull, missing some teeth, found its way into the collection of Dr. Samuel George Morton, an American phrenologist. Morton's catalog recorded the information, derived from one Henry Crockett—a surgeon who attended Pearce—that Pearce too had been a seaman. If true, it would explain further the similarity between the accounts of the first escape and nautical tales—it must be borne in mind that all the versions of the story derive from Pearce himself. His skull still exists in the Museum of the University of Pennsylvania. Pearce inevitably became something of a folk hero, and his immortality was assured when his exploits were worked into Marcus Clarke's novel *For the Term of His Natural Life,* where he appears as Mat Gabbett, with "his slavering mouth, his slowly grinding jaws, his restless fingers and his bloodshot, wandering eyes. . . ." This novel of life in a penal colony was first published in book form in Melbourne in 1847 and in London in 1875. Numerous other fanciful stories have evolved around the tale of the Man-Eater of Macquarie Harbour, the only clear instance (with Robert Greenhill) of a recidivist cannibal I have managed to locate.

The American frontier also produced numerous cases of cannibalism, two of which have become particularly well known. The earliest was the classic story of the Donner party, cut off and starving in the High Sierras during the winter of 1846–47. Stories of the misfortunes that occurred circulated widely at the time, but knowledge of the case was heightened by the 1879 publication of a very successful essay in investigative journalism, Charles Fayette McGlashan's *History of the Donner Party: A Tragedy of the Sierras,* which originally appeared in serial form in the *Truckee Republican* between January and June 1879. In book form in that year, it sold out in two weeks; there was a second edition in 1880 and a third in 1881. How well known the Donner story was in England in 1884 is uncertain. Since those days, McGlashan's book has appeared in nine further editions; and again in 1940 and in 1947, reprints were published, with introductions and bibliography. In 1911, interest was also revived by a remarkable book by Eliza P. Houghton (née Donner), who as a child survived the disaster. Of the Donner party 36 died in the mountains, and in all probability cannibalism and perhaps murder took place. An unfortunate individual named Lewis Keseburg became the scapegoat, largely as a consequence of lies told by an enormous, unsavory mountain man, Thomas O'Fallon, who later visited the scene in search of loot. But no legal proceedings were ever taken against Keseburg or the other survivors. Keseburg was eventually vindicated after his death, and although the story of the Donner party has given rise to an extensive literature as a classic of the old West, his name has largely sunk into obscurity.

This has not been the fate of Alferd G. Packer, the Colorado man-eater. His was the second notable tale of cannibalism in the West, and he has become the most celebrated of all the nineteenth-century American cannibals.

Not long before the story of the Donner party (which had never wholly died) had been given a new lease on life by McGlashan's book, there arrived in Colorado at the encampment of Chief Ouray of the Utes on the Uncompahgre River (near the site of the modern town of Montrose) a party of 21 prospectors from Salt Lake City. They were very hungry, having been living off horse feed and badger soup, which even old timers on the frontier did not regard as a treat. They had been surrounded earlier by a group of Ute braves, "a-yellin' and a-whoopin'," as Packer put it, and escorted to Ouray's camp, the Utes being suspicious that they might be settlers; relations with the Utes were at the time precarious. The prospectors were traveling with several wagons, and they intended to set out for Breckenridge in the San Juan mountains of southwestern Colorado to prospect for silver and gold; once this was known, the Indians became friendly. It was mid-December 1873, and Chief Ouray, together with his second wife, Chipeta ("White Singing Bird"), was well known as a conscientious if perhaps misled peace maker and a particularly agreeable man. He advised against starting to cross the mountains so late in the season. Some took his advice. Others were reluctant to do so; and one party, led by one Loutsenhizer, eventually set out for the Los Pinos Indian Agency post, some 75 miles away, which was reached eventually after a near disaster en route when the party was all but overwhelmed by a blizzard. They survived only through persuading a wolf to drop a leg of lamb it was carrying, and through killing a cow with their bare hands.

A second party left Chief Ouray's camp a few days later on February 9, 1874. This party consisted of Frank Miller (also known as "The Butcher," "Butcher Frank," or "Reddy"), Shannon Wilson Bell, James Humphreys, Israel Swan ("Old Man Swan"), George Noon (known also as "California"), and A. G. Packer, variously called "Al," "Alfred," and "Alferd"; he himself actually did spell his name "Alferd." They would be by any standards a rough lot. Packer is said to have been born on November 21, 1842, in Allegheny County, Pennsylvania, and to have been originally a shoemaker. Some obscurity hangs over his family background, but, according to his own account, recorded in 1893, he was born in Harrisburg to a rich and influential Pennsylvania Dutch family, his uncle, William Fisher Packer (1807–70), being the son of James Packer, governor of Pennsylvania during 1858–61. The family was in fact not Dutch but English in origin, being Quaker. Alferd may possibly have been related distantly to the millionaire Asa Packer, founder of Lehigh University. There were many Packers in the state; in the seventeenth century there had been Packers at Groton; and the state boasts Packersville, Packers Ferry, and Packerton. Alferd's father was probably either John Packer, a merchant of Elemington, Clinton County, or Judge Hezekiah B. Packer, of Williamsport. At the age of 12, Alferd ran away from home, his unhappiness being in all probability connected with the fact that he suffered severely from epilepsy. He drifted to Chicago, and when the Civil War came, he joined the Union

Army at Winona, Minnesota; his unit was the 16th G.S. Infantry. The same year, 1862, he was discharged as "incapable of performing the duties of a soldier because of Epilepsy." Packer always lied about his epilepsy and claimed that the reason for his discharge was typhoid. A second attempt to join the army in 1863 also led to discharge in the following year as a severe epileptic. He drifted around taking various work, as a coach guard, for example, and as a guard for the teams of Fred Creighton, engaged in setting up telegraph poles across the plains. He ended up as a prospector in Colorado. In the winter, he hunted or trapped, acting at one time as hunter for Carmichael, the Union Pacific contractor. In 1873, he had been working in Utah on the lead smelters and claimed to have suffered acute lead poisoning, a story perhaps true but more probably invented to explain his frequent and severe fits. From there he joined the party heading for the San Juan mountains; Packer's function was to act as a guide. It was not a job at which he excelled. By his own account he had earlier in 1864 set out during the gold rush called the "White Pine Excitement" to reach the diggings under the misapprehension that they were located in Idaho; they were in fact in Eureka, Nevada. Guiding was never his strong point; given the chance, Alferd got lost.

Chief Ouray advised the six men against setting out at all, but as they insisted, he gave them advice as to their route, drawing a map on the ground with his finger. There were two trails through the mountains, and of these the party decided to follow the shorter and more hazardous upper track to the Los Pinos Indian Agency. The other route was 25 miles or so longer, though Packer appears to have thought that the difference was much greater—40 miles—and that the short route was only 40 miles long. The party set out hopelessly ill equipped, without even snow shoes; the country at the time was wholly uninhabited. On April 16, 1874, Packer arrived alone; it was early in the morning, and he had taken some 55 days or more on a journey expected to last about a week. He was carrying fire in a coffee pot. Something had gone seriously wrong en route, for Packer had lost his employers. Some explanation was called for. According to later accounts, Packer looked suspiciously well fed and fit after his ordeal; indeed, instead of asking for food, his first request was for whisky. He said that after his party had lost the route, he himself had become lame; his companions had left him to seek food and had never returned. So he had set off on his own, surviving the appalling winter conditions by living off roots and berries and the occasional rabbit or squirrel. He thought his companions had headed south and would eventually turn up at Silverton in the Animas Valley.

On the same day, another prospector, one Preston Nutter, arrived from Chief Ouray's camp—he had taken only two weeks on the journey. Preston Nutter and Packer soon set off for Saquache, their next destination. But suspicions became aroused for various reasons. Nutter noticed that Packer had Butcher Frank's knife, which Packer implausibly explained by saying that Frank had left it stuck in a tree. Along the old Indian trail over Los Pinos Pass Utes picked up pieces of dried human flesh. On the frontier, suspicions of cannibalism would not be in any way abnormal; stories of cannibalism would be well known; and several such cases are documented. On arrival at Saquache, Packer lodged at James Dolan's saloon, where he whiled away the time drinking, carousing, and playing a form of poker called "freeze-out." He appeared to have too much money on him. Other members of the original party arrived, and they all began to doubt his story. One peculiarly suspicious circumstance to those not familiar with Packer's navigational skill was the fact that he had become lost at all, for two other parties had made the journey without losing their way. Packer also excited the suspicions of Otto Mears, who ran the store of Mears and Gotthelf in Saquache, since Packer was, according to Mears, in possession of two pocketbooks containing bills and drafts that he ought not to have had. Threats of lynching were in the air when no news arrived of his companions having reached safety; the belief grew that he had killed his companions and stolen their money. Suspicion was increased by his lack of popularity with the other members of the original party who had now reached Saquache. Consequently Packer was questioned by "General" Charles Adams, the resident Indian agent. Adams persuaded Packer to return to Los Pinos, where he was questioned. Eventually, he made a sworn written statement, signed before Judge James P. Downer on May 4, 1874. Various inconsistent accounts of what this "confession" amounted to have been published. In fact a written text, possibly a copy of the original, does still exist and is printed in full in Judge E. F. Kushner's study of the case, *Alferd G. Packer: Cannibal! Victim?*

> Old man Swan died first and was eaten by the other five persons about ten days out of camp. Four or five days afterwards Humphreys died and was also eaten; he had about one hundred and thirty-three dollars ($133). I found the pocketbook and took the money. Some time

> afterwards, while I was carrying wood, the butcher was killed—as the others told me, accidentally—and he was also eaten. Bill shot "California" with Swan's gun and I killed Bill. Shot him. I covered up the remains and took a large piece along. Then I travelled fourteen days into the Agency. Bell wanted to kill me with his rifle—struck a tree and broke his gun.

This was apparently a short written summary of the oral "confession," drawn up by Adams; and various accounts of what Packer actually said to Adams also exist.

According to one (told by Frank Hall), Alferd claimed that old Israel Swan died of starvation and was then eaten. Then Humphreys died and suffered the same fate. Then, when Packer was away collecting firewood, "Butcher" Miller was killed by Noon and Bell, and he too was eaten. Then Bell shot Noon. This left Bell and Packer, and with a touching faith in the sanctity of contract, they made a pact not to kill each other. But near Lake San Cristobal Bell attacked Packer, who killed him in self-defense; a rifle was broken in the struggle. Packer then set off, carrying as much of Bell as he could, and eventually reached Los Pinos. Another version (recorded by E. V. Dunklee) has it that Alferd claimed Swan was killed by a skull fracture while he was out collecting wood. Two days later the other three men decided to kill Miller, who was selected on gastronomic grounds as being best to eat—he was killed with a hatchet. The story continues as in the first version, with the addition that Packer said that "he had grown quite fond of human flesh, and . . . that he found the breasts of the men the sweetest meat he had ever tasted." Yet another version (recounted by Red Fenwick) has it that Alferd claimed that old Israel Swan died naturally, as in the first version; so too did Humphreys. Miller was then killed, selected because he had rheumatism and was holding up the party. The story then continues as in the other accounts. Another version (told in the *Graphic*) has it that Humphreys was killed accidentally. It is also said that Packer made various other statements, in one of which he said that lots were cast to select who was to die; certainly, many years later, he claimed that a proposal to draw lots was made. Probably the explanation for all this inconsistency is that Packer, not a man with a strict regard for truth, told various versions of the same basic tale to Adams during his interrogation, and afterward to those who were present at the Los Pinos agency at the time, such as Otto Mears and Preston Nutter. Consequently various versions passed into circulation.

"General" Adams believed that cannibalism had occurred, "as Mr. Packer looked quite fat when he arrived here and since shown traces of mental aberration, which is said to be the consequence of eating human flesh." Others doubted it completely, viewing Packer simply as an acquisitive killer who had lived off the country. One Nathaniel Hunter, who sat opposite him at supper the night after his arrival at Los Pinos later stated, "I was satisfied his tale was fishy. I did not believe that a man could have as good an appetite as he had after gorging himself with human flesh, nor be as good natured after undergoing as great hardship as he said he had experienced."

Alferd was made to lead a search party for the bodies and, it was hoped, the broken rifle that would confirm his claim of self-defense. But this expedition was a failure, some thinking that Packer deliberately led it astray. So he was arrested, probably illegally, and placed in the custody of the sheriff of Saquache, though the evidence against him was weak. But in late August of 1874 the remains of Packer's companions were discovered near Lake San Cristobal (now sometimes known also as Hungry Packer Lake) three miles south of present-day Lake City. One version is that three prospectors were camping there, Nicholas, Bell, and Graham, and their dog found the bodies; another account attributes the discovery to John A. Randolph, an artist on a sketching holiday in the Uncompahgre Mountains. He certainly sketched the corpses, and his macabre drawing, together with views of the scene, was published in *Harper's Weekly* on October 17, 1874. Yet another source attributes the finding to George Mitchel, F. P. Wells, and Captain C. H. Graham. It may be that some time passed before anybody troubled to take action about the remains, so various individuals thought they were first on the scene. Randolph's picture bunches the corpses together—they were in fact more scattered, though essentially in one location, wholly falsifying Packer's story that the deaths took place at intervals on the trail. Preston Nutter, who was there, later said that their heads had been cut open "as with a hatchet" and that fragments of blanket had been driven into the cleft in Israel Swan's skull; in Randolph's picture, however, Swan's skull is missing. Bell had been shot in the back and lay some distance away; Miller's skull was missing (it was eventually found, bearing axe cuts, by one Depping). By August, the remains would of course have been interfered with by animals, but when the inquest was held, the jury came to the conclusion that the men had been murdered by Alferd Packer, the assumption being that they had, with the exception of Bell and perhaps Miller, been murdered in their sleep. So a new warrant was now issued for the arrest of Packer for the murder of the five men; he was in fact already in custody. But before it could be served Packer escaped, almost certainly with the connivance of Sheriff Wall of Saquache, who, according to Packer's account in 1893 "advised him to leave." Food and of course whisky, regarded as essential in the old West, were provided, and Packer disappeared.

He was eventually located in 1883 at Fort Fetterman, in the Wyoming Territory. He was using the name of John Schwartze, and he was identified by Jean ("Frenchy") Cabazon, whom he had met as a member of the original party from Utah and again at Los Pinos, and with whom he had quarreled nine years earlier. Cabazon remembered his high-pitched, whining voice, and in due course Packer was arrested at Waggonhound, 30 miles from Fort Fetterman, and brought back manacled, to face trial. He was interrogated again and made a further statement, and in this he claimed that on the day in question he had been out of camp all day. When he returned, Bell, who had been acting oddly when Packer left, was sitting by the fire roasting part of Frank Miller's leg. Miller's body and those of the others lay about with extensive hatchet wounds. Bell attacked Packer, and the latter shot Bell in self-defense. Subsequently he lived off the bodies of the dead, and he admitted taking some $70 from them.

Packer's arrest caused a sensation, and he was at once portrayed in the press as a monster, contemporary headlines including such matter as "The Fiend Who Became Very Corpulent upon a Diet of Human Steaks," "A Cannibal Who Gnaws on the Choice Cuts of His Fellow-Man," and "The San Juan Ghoul." Thus the legend of the Colorado Man-Eater, Cannibal Alferd G. Packer, was founded. He was tried in due course for the murder of Israel Swan. The trial took place at Lake City, a town that had sprung up since 1874 only three miles from Dead Man's Gulch, where the murders were supposed to have taken place. Packer was represented by local attorneys, Aaron Heims and A. J. Miller. The grand jury had in fact approved five separate indictments for murder, but proceedings were limited to one only. The trial, of which a complete transcript survives, opened in the courtroom of Hinsdale County on April 9, 1883, before Judge Melville B. Gerry, and feeling against Packer ran high. His case was that he did not kill Israel Swan and that he had killed only Bell in self-defense. He gave evidence for some six hours, and it must have made something of an impression, for the jury, which retired at 7:00 P.M. on Thursday, April 12, took some considerable time to convict him, giving their decision with nice timing at 9:00 A.M. on Friday April 13. No doubt apart from sheer prejudice, the inconsistency in his statements and prosecution evidence that Bell had been shot in the back told against him—though he was not tried for killing Bell. He was convicted of premeditated murder, and this finding, based apparently on the assumption that the killings were planned in advance, as Judge Gerry believed, had the consequence of making the conviction capital. Perhaps this was the issue that most concerned the jury. But the evidence, as the judge said, was all very indirect: "Whether your murderous hand was guided by the misty light of the moon, or the flickering blaze of the camp-fire, you only can tell. No eye saw the bloody deed performed; no ear save your own caught the groans of your dying victims." The assumption on which he was convicted was that the victims had been asleep and the motive theft.

Packer was sentenced to death by Judge Gerry shortly after 4:00 P.M. on Friday, and the judge delivered a remarkable homily:

> God is not mocked, for whatsoever a man soweth, that shall he also reap. You Alfred Packer, sowed the wind; you must now reap the whirlwind. . . . Close your ears to the blandishments of hope, listen not to the flattering promises of life, but prepare for the dread certainty of death . . . prepare to meet the aged father and mother, of whom you have spoken and who still love you as their dear boy. For nine long years you have been a wanderer upon the face of the earth, bowed and broken in spirit: no home, no loves, no ties to bind you to the earth. . . . "

And so it went on, concluding, in the traditional manner, with the sentence that he be "hung by the neck until you are dead, dead, dead, and may God have mercy upon your soul." Contemporary folklore had it that the threefold repetition justified three attempts to hang a man if the first failed. This all took a lot out of Judge Gerry, having more effect upon him than upon the unfortunate Packer, though Alferd did weep at the remarks about his parents (apparently wholly unfounded, since his parents had disowned him).

At this point Larry Dolan, Saquache barkeeper and old drinking companion of Packer, ran out of the court, crying out, "They're gonna hang Packer!" He was somewhat intoxicated at the time. Possessing as he did a greater grasp of style than Judge Gerry (a prominent Democrat), he gave to the local drinking men in his saloon in Lake City an immortal rendering of the sentence:

> The judge, he says, "Stand up, y' voracious man-eating son of a bitch. Stand up." Then, pointing his finger at him, so raging mad he was, he says, "There was seven democrats in Hinsdale County, and you've ate five of them, God damn you. I sentence you to be hanged by the neck until you is dead, dead, dead, as a warning against reducing the democrat population of the state. Packer, you Republican cannibal, I would sentence you to hell but the Statutes forbid it.

So it was that Packer was moved off to the Lake City jail, there to await death. It is recorded that he secured peace and quiet in his cage by threatening to eat an imprisoned drunk whose behavior was noisy.

But, as it happened, Packer escaped execution on the local gallows on May 19, though the customary formal invitations to attend were printed and issued and a suitable rope purchased and exhibited. His lawyers, who seem at this stage to have done an excellent job, found a flaw in the proceedings—indeed, it was perfectly obvious from the start, as they had told Judge Gerry. Although the point was not formally decided by the Colorado supreme court until October 1884 (in the case of Al Garvey, who had been convicted of murder in legally similar conditions), their contention that the trial was invalid was set out long before this. It was that Packer had been charged with murder under a provision in the laws of the Territory of Colorado, which had been repealed in 1881 as a consequence of new legal arrangements made when Colorado became a state in August 1876. The legislation of 1881 failed to permit trial for murder after that date of a person accused of the crime committed *before* 1881 (in Packer's case, 1874). So Packer's trial had been a complete nullity. Although execution was stayed, the supreme court took its time in dealing with Packer's appeal; and at the time of the case of the *Mignonette,* Alfred Packer was languishing in a cage in a new, more secure jail in Gunnison City, waiting the outcome of these proceedings, which would decide if his lawyers were right. He was in the capable hands of Sheriff Doc Shores, a noted old-time law man, whose principal task appears to have been to protect the unfortunate Packer from the lynch mob outside. The legal technicality that had saved Garvey and was to save Packer was viewed with irreverent merriment by the local population, the Garvey case being reported in the Gunnison *Daily Review Press* under the headline "The Murderer's Mirth—The Supreme Court says Murder is not a Crime if Committed before the 28th Day of May 1881." Packer had many visitors in his cage, becoming something of a tourist attraction. The

Denver *Republican* recorded in July 1886 how "thousands of tourists who have visited this city in the meantime have called to see this criminal, more than whom there is probably none more noted in the jails of America." Ludicrous accounts of his appearance circulated: "He walks like one sneaking away or creeping upon a victim. Anyone possessing even a moderate knowledge of human nature would say he belonged naturally to the criminal class."

To what extent knowledge of the Donner tragedy and the case of Alferd G. Packer existed in England in 1884 it is not easy to say. Lord Chief Justice Coleridge, who was to preside over the final disposition of the case of the *Mignonette,* had spent the period from July 8 to October 28, 1883, in the United States on a grand tour—perhaps the first such by an English chief justice. He was received with great hospitality by universities and bar associations, and those who have suffered such functions know the tendency of lawyers at convivial gatherings to avoid matters of high intellectual importance and devote the evening to squalid anecdotes. I should be very surprised if he escaped being told the story of the sentencing of the Colorado Man-eater. But this it is impossible to prove. But any idea that cannibalism was a peculiarly English problem was certainly dissipated by the major scandal involving the American Greely expedition to the Arctic, if not by the Packer case. News of this broke in the English press in 1884, as Dudley and Stephens were approaching Falmouth, and the story dominated the American press during August and appeared all over the world. Press coverage even included the publication of pictures of some of those members of the expedition who had been consumed.

Lieutenant Adolphus Washington Greely, an army officer, had been appointed in 1881 to command an Arctic expedition. It was formally called the "Lady Franklin Bay Expedition" but was normally called after its commander. At this period, Arctic expeditions were a major source of interest and controversy, and the Greely expedition was the U.S. army's riposte to a naval expedition, there being, as ever, strong interservice rivalry. The navy venture was the Jeanette Expedition, partly financed by Gordon Bennett, owner of the *New York Herald,* and it was commanded by Lieutenant George Washington deLong. It had set out through the Bering Straits in 1879 and was last seen on August 17 of that year; nothing had been heard since. A tendency to vanish was typical of such Polar expeditions, and some of those left at home felt guilty if no rescue was attempted. Others thought that these ice follies were a scandalous waste of money and life and that "rescues" only encouraged further folly. Eventually, in June of 1884, seven survivors out of the original party of 25 were rescued at Cape Sabine by the navy (one died shortly after rescue). Of the remainder one had drowned, one been deliberately shot for stealing, one had died of exposure, and the others of starvation. Greely himself survived, and he and his men returned to a heroes' welcome; some of the bodies were brought home for burial. But rumors of cannibalism began to circulate, and on August 12, the story broke on the front page of the *New York Times* under the heading "Horrors of Cape Sabine." Not only had there been cannibalism, but there had been deliberate concealment of the fact by the authorities. Grisly autopsies of what was found in the coffins of some of the returned dead fueled the story, and the scandal became worse when it was hinted, quite against evidence, that the individual who had been shot had been killed for food. Precisely what did happen has never been satisfactorily established, but the evidence is available in the papers of Congress and is discussed in A. L. Todd's excellent book *Abandoned* (1961). It is at least clear that Greely himself was innocent, and his request for a court martial was refused—American law was thought not to run to Cape Sabine. In mid-August 1884 the story filled the world's press. On August 29, just as the excitement of the Greely case was beginning to die down, the London *Times,* lest the subject should grow cold, informed its readers, "Whatever may be the truth of the story as to the Greely expedition, a well authenticated case of cannibalism is reprinted by the *Courier des États Unis* from the Rocky Mountains. A short time back a man half dead from inanition and apparently insane was found wandering upon the banks of the Kicking Horse River. When brought to himself, the unfortunate man stated that he was a Californian miner named William Owens." He had eaten his companion, Joseph Williams, who, after six days without food, "threw himself on the ground and died of exhaustion within a few minutes." As this appeared in the English press, the *Moctezuma,* carrying Dudley, Stephens, and Brooks, was approaching the English Channel.

7
The *William Brown* and the *Euxine*

Le sort tomba sur le plus jeune;
En sauce blanche il fut mangé

—"Le Petit Navire"

In spite of the frequent occurrence of survival cannibalism, often preceded by deliberate killing, and the abundant evidence of a nautical custom legitimating the practice of killing under necessity, the survivors of the *Mignonette* have always been regarded as the first and indeed only individuals who have ever faced trial for murder for a killing committed in such circumstances. The fame of the case of *Regina v. Dudley and Stephens* largely turns on its uniqueness, its only rival being the American case of *U.S. v. Holmes* in 1842, which, though it did not involve cannibalism, did raise for lawyers the same theoretical question: Was necessity a possible defense against a charge of homicide? As we have seen, there had been other cases in which cannibal murderers have been brought to trial—Alexander Pearce and Alferd Packer are examples—but their trials did not raise this question; instead, the issue was whether they acted in self-defense or lacked deliberate intent to kill. Cases of psychopathological cannibal murderers have been not infrequent—a modern English example is that of Patrick Byrne in 1960, but his trial, though it gave rise to a leading case of mental abnormality and responsibility for murder, had nothing to do with the defense of necessity. Cases of survival cannibalism that have given rise to any form of legal proceedings are surprisingly very rare, notwithstanding the notoriety of many incidents of the practice, such as that involving the *Francis Spaight*. No general explanation for their rarity is possible. But the conditions under which such killings occurred, the absence of effective systems of public prosecution, and possibly greater tolerance combined against the initiation of prosecutions. The nineteenth century was to see changes that eventually brought the custom of the sea before the judges; for example, it was the Merchant Shipping Act of 1854 that first imposed an obligation on a shipping master to take some action if it appeared that death had occurred through violence. Previously it had been nobody's business.

The first prosecution to raise the putative defense of necessity directly (though not involving cannibalism), was that of Alexander William Holmes in 1842. Alexander Williams, alias Alexander William Holmes, was a Finn, born in Gothenburg and in 1842 aged 26. He had shipped as an able seaman on an American sailing ship, the *William Brown* of Philadelphia, in which city lived her captain, George L. Harris, aged 44. Built in New York in about 1826, the *William Brown*'s tonnage was just under 560. Her owner, Stephen Baldwin, sold her to Joseph P. Vogels on December 30, 1840. Having loaded a full general cargo, she left Liverpool for Philadelphia at 10:00 A.M. on March 13, 1841, an imprudent breach of maritime tradition, bound for her home port. Her first mate, Francis Rhodes, was aged 32 and an American from Kennebunk, Maine; her second mate was an Englishman, Walter Parker. The crew, including the officers, consisted of 17 men; typically, they were a mixed band: Charley Smith, aged 20, came from Sheerness, England; William Miller, aged 16, from Aalberg, Denmark; Isaac Freeman, aged 28, from Stockholm, Sweden; James Norton, aged 22, from Tipperary, Ireland. The crew also included two black Americans: Joseph Marshall, aged 37, the cook, from Beaufort, South Carolina; and Henry Murray, the steward, aged 22, from Georgetown, Maryland.

In addition to cargo, the *William Brown* carried 65 passengers. Most were Irish emigrants, but there were some Scots too, including the Edgar family from Lochmaben, comprising Mrs. Margaret Edgar; her three daughters; and a niece, Jean or Jane Johnstone Edgar, who was also a servant; all going to join Mr. Edgar and his brother, established as farmers in Germanstown, Pennsylvania. Among the Irish, there were unaccompanied men, such as John Welsh, all married, who were emigrating and leaving their wives behind, no doubt in the hope of bringing them over later; others were traveling to join families already in America. Bridget McGee, aged 19, from Drogheda, was to join her father, a livery stable keeper in Philadelphia; Biddy Nugent, aged 17, was traveling with her uncle, John Nugent, to join her mother, who ran a lodging house in the same city. Included were complete families: for example, the Leyden family of 16 people, driven by unknown necessity or inhumanity to leave Colonel Stewart's property in County Tyrone; and the Carrs (or Corrs), 11 in all: mother, father, five children, two nieces, and two nephews, all refugees from another landed estate in Tyrone. The Conlins, another family, numbered 15. Some passengers may have been reasonably affluent, like Mrs. Anderson and her five children on their way to join Mr. Anderson, a medical man in practice in Cincinnati. Most, however, would be poor or very poor victims of the grim conditions that existed in Ireland even before the years of the Great Hunger, though not so poor as those who emigrated by the cheaper route to Canada.

Initially the *William Brown* had a very rough passage, and conditions for the passengers were bad; one child died. But nothing exceptional occurred until Monday, April 19. That evening the ship was running before a south-southwesterly gale at between eight and 10 knots; John Stetson was at the wheel. The night was dark and foggy, and it was the second mate's watch, though Captain Harris himself was on deck. At about 9:45 P.M. she ran into a patch of ice and, in spite of Stetson's efforts, twice struck ice floes; her position at the time was at 43°30′ north and 49°39′ west, about 300 miles southeast of Cape Race, Newfoundland. The first impact was very violent; it flung Mary Carr, who was hanging a lamp at the time, over the provisions box in the steerage and even knocked Walter Parker, an experienced sailor, off his feet. The first mate and a sailor immediately inspected the damage, as did the captain, as the sails were clewed up and secured by gaskets. It was found that the bows had been stove in and water was pouring in. Sailing ships at this date did not possess collision bulkheads; and although the crew, aided by some of the passengers (like Ellen Black) exhausted themselves at the pumps, it was all to no avail. The ship was sinking. Julia McCadden spoke to the captain. She "asked him what he was going to do for them, who replied that he could do nothing, and that they must do the best they could for themselves." In panic passengers rushed on deck, leaving behind Isabella Edgar, too ill to climb the ladder out of the steerage. Most had gone to bed, and were barely clothed. They saw the sailors clearing away the boats, which were got overboard and brought alongside. This task took from 9:45 P.M. to about 10:20 P.M. There were two boats, a jolly boat rigged as a sailing cutter, and a shallower longboat propelled by oars. The jolly boat was between 19 and 20 feet long, the longboat 22½ and some six feet in beam.

Launching the boats was a complicated operation, involving cutting away part of the ship's rail; the jolly boat was lowered with four crew members in it and one of the emigrants, Eliza Lafferty. It must soon have become obvious that the two boats could not possibly hold all 83 persons on board. This was normal; the received wisdom was that it was wholly impracticable to carry an adequate complement of boats. With the fatalistic attitude adopted to shipwreck by sailors, nobody even tried; in consequence, when a passenger ship sank at sea, it was inevitable that some must be selected, either by circumstances or deliberate action, to die. Human nature being what it is, the crew usually took priority in survival; women and children (and for that matter, male passengers) normally came last. Nor was this necessarily unreasonable, for the management of small ships required experience, and their navigation required officers possessing instruments and the ability to use them. Classic tales of survival, the most remarkable perhaps being Captain Bligh's 3,600-mile open-boat voyage after the mutiny on the *Bounty* in 1789, dramatically illustrate this point.

The jolly boat obviously offered the best hope, and at first all the officers and the majority of the crew got into it, together with the enterprising Eliza Lafferty. But then a rearrangement took place. The captain, the second mate Walter Parker, six sailors, and the favored Eliza stayed in the jolly boat; and John Smith, the ship's boy, was moved into it. Though potentially this action was of sinister implications, it must be said in fairness that the boat was otherwise provisioned. Mrs. Matilda Patrick, Eliza's sister, asked that she and her husband might join Eliza, but the captain refused. The first mate, Francis Rhodes, together with eight sailors and 33 passengers, moved to the longboat, presumably so that Rhodes could navigate and command it. He was given a chart, a compass, a quadrant and a watch, told by the captain that he was 200 miles from land, and given a course. This all indicated that Captain Harris did not propose to keep him company. The longboat, though little bigger than the jolly boat, was quite disproportionately crowded, having 41 or 42 on board.

The two boats were veered off on lines, leaving on board the *William Brown* some 30 or 31 passengers. The decision as to who should be left does not seem to have been taken in any systematic way. Bridget McGee, who had got into the longboat, was ordered out and back on the sinking ship by Holmes, but she refused; so, too, did Biddy Nugent. Julia McCadden was also ordered out of the longboat by one of the sailors, but she remained. Holmes in particular behaved kindly and very courageously, going back on board the sinking ship to rescue the sick Isabella Edgar, who called out, "I am coming, Mother, I am coming." Mrs. Edgar, together with her other two daughters, Susannah and Margaret, and her niece and servant girl Jane (or Jean) had managed to get into the longboat: the sick Isabella had not. Holmes brought her off the ship on his back, sliding down the falls of the ropes by which the longboat was lowered. One of her sisters in the longboat was crying out for her. He gave his coat to a passenger and was the last man to leave the sinking ship. Mrs. Anderson, left on board, offered Holmes as much as he could earn in a year to take her off, but he replied that money was no object; it was lives he wished to save. She and her children were left on board. After this, the boats were pushed off and held on long lines, and at some point Francis Rhodes called out, referring to those left on board, "Poor souls, you're only going down just before us." The abandoned shrieked in vain for rescue, and at about 11:20 P.M., the *William Brown* stood on her bows and sank; they were all drowned. There was a curious and eery silence just before she went. The line securing the longboat was cut only just in time to prevent its being sucked down in the vortex created by the sinking vessel.

In the process of embarkation, families had been split up. Thus, though Charles Conlin had got into the longboat, his 14 relatives all went down with the *William Brown;* Ann Bradley, who was saved, had a sister on board; and Owen Carr, aged 11 or 13, was separated from his parents and his five brothers and sisters. Later he deposed pathetically that "all his friends were lost in the ship."

The two boats remained moored together during the night. There is a conflict of description as to the state of the weather, but there was a squally north wind, and a heavy sea was running. It may also have been raining and hailing. The longboat leaked and had to be bailed continuously, the passengers taking their turns. They were quite inadequately clad, some half naked. The mate gave a coat to Mrs. Edgar (he had two), and other sailors gave spare clothing away. Jack Stetson gave young Owen Carr a pair of stockings; a sailor gave Jane Edgar a coat. Holmes cut up his oilcloth pants to cover Julia McCadden (also called Judy McAdden—there was considerable confusion over the correct form of names). At dawn, around 5:00 A.M., a conversation took place between Captain Harris and the first mate, Francis Rhodes. Rhodes took a gloomy view of the chances of survival of the longboat; it was, he said, "impossible for the boat to live." In his view, the longboat was grossly overcrowded; it had lost its rudder and was unmanageable. The gunwales were within five inches of the water. Later on the passengers, at least some of them, put forward a less pessimistic view, but the mate's opinion is to be preferred. The captain proposed to set out for Newfoundland: he is reported to have said, "His boat was light, and he will go." The mate replied, "I think you might keep company with us today." But the captain was unwilling to do this and knew that the mate and longboat could not follow him. The mate also told the captain that unless he took some of the passengers into the jolly boat, it would be necessary to cast lots and throw some overboard. The captain replied, "I know what you mean" or, according to another witness, "I know what you will have to do. Don't speak of that now. Let it be the last resort." Yet another version has it that Rhodes said, "Captain Harris, we will have to draw lots." He replied, "I know what you mean. I don't want to hear any more about it." The gist of the various accounts is the same—Captain Harris did not explicitly take any responsibility for what might have to be done. According to Julia McCadden, Rhodes had raised the question of drawing lots the evening before as well, with much the same result.

A list was made by the captain of those in the longboat—he missed one name—and then he sailed off; within 10 minutes he was out of sight in the mist. Later he admitted that he thought the longboat had no chance at all of reaching land, and the chance of being picked up he put at 1%. He knew that the longboat, in its overloaded condition, would not ride head to wind, the only safe attitude if the wind rose. After four hours' futile attempt to head for Newfoundland, the sailors consulted and then set off south; at Holmes's suggestion, the captain's idea of heading for land was not followed. The crew rowed in turns; their course would take them further and further away from land but into warmer water and across the shipping routes. The evidence suggests that in fact Rhodes was not a competent navigator, and he later admitted as much.

An attempt was made to rig a makeshift sail, but it was taken down because of the risk of a capsize. Under oars, and with the wind behind them, they appear to have made a good almost three miles an hour. It rained heavily all day, and that afternoon the wind rose again; at night they met ice. Persistent trouble appears to have been caused by a drainage plug in the bottom of the boat. During the first night it had come out and been lost; the leak was temporarily blocked with caps, and Holmes made a new plug with an axe. The boat continued to leak, and another larger hole, about eight by four inches, was discovered at some point in the day; there is considerable conflict of evidence as to how serious the leakage was, though one would expect a hole of this size to be very serious indeed if below or near the waterline. According to the mate's later account, "finding that the boat was literally surrounded by small and large masses of ice, and that the water was gaining upon her, I thought it improbable that she could hold out, unless relieved of some of her weight. I then consulted the sailors, and we were all of the opinion that it was necessary to throw overboard those who were nearly dead, until we had room enough to work the boat and take to our oars." And so, starting at about 10:00 on Thursday evening, when it was fairly dark, the sailors began to throw the passengers overboard. Fairly precise details of how this was done have survived, though there are inevitably discrepancies in detail.

After the discussion between the mate and the sailors, an interval occurred. Then the mate, who had been bailing, suddenly said, "This work [i.e., the bailing] won't do. Help me God. Men, go to work." This initially produced no reaction. The mate repeated the instruction: "Now you must go to work." He later denied that what he did was to issue an *order,* claiming that he merely pointed out the position they were all in: "If they did not lighten her, they would all be lost, remarking at the same time that it was better that a few should be saved, than that all should perish, telling them also that they had as much to say in the business as he had . . . that he did not order the men to throw any overboard, but stated, that from the position in which they were, whatever was necessary to be done must be done immediately or that the boat would swamp. . . ." According to a story that appeared later both in the American press and in the London *Times* on July 24, 1884, one of the sailors, John Messer, held out against killing without drawing lots, but the mate threatened to kill him for his intransigence. But this story was almost certainly fabricated.

It was later claimed that the choice of those to be thrown overboard was dictated simply by practicalities, those nearest to the sailors being selected, by chance predominantly men. But it seems fairly clear that the sailors deliberately decided to jettison the men, rather than the women, though the mate may not have been involved in this decision. Whether he gave what counted as an order or not, his remark could easily be interpreted as one, for he was in command, and the sailors had undertaken the captain's directive to obey him. Isaac Freeman, for example, thought an order was given. There were 16 adult men, and from what occurred it looks as if it was agreed that all were to go. Having initiated the proceedings, the mate himself took no further active part in the operation; the passengers were neither informed nor consulted. The sailors directly involved were Charley Smith, Alexander Williams (Alexander William Holmes), Joseph Stetson, and Henry Murray, the cook. Isaac Freeman also later admitted assisting. According to Stetson, the first attempt was abandoned because of resistance. The sailors then tried again, and the first man to go was Owen Riley, a married man whose wife lived in Philadelphia. He was told to stand up and must have known what was about to happen, as he asked Mr. Edgar to beg the sailors to preserve his life; he also called to Isabella Edgar and to Julia McCadden. She also realized what was happening, for she called out, "Good God, are they going to drown the man?" He was thrust overboard, soon followed by a Scotsman, James Todd. James MacAvoy was probably the next. He begged five minutes' grace to say his prayers and button his coat and, at the instance of Henry Murray, he was given it. He said "Lord, be merciful to me, a sinner" and may have thrown himself over. Soon after, Frank Askins was seized by Holmes. He appears to have been the only passenger to put up serious resistance; Holmes called for help. Askins said, "I'll not go out, you know I wrought well all the time. I'll work like a man till morning, and do what I can to keep the boat clear of water; I have five sovereigns, and I'll give it for my life till morning, and when morning comes if God does not help us we will cast lots, and I'll go out like a man if it is my turn." Holmes replied to the effect that it was lives he was interested in, not money. Frank's two sisters, Ellen and Mary, then attempted to intercede; Mary, the younger, said that if her brother was to go she should go too; she was willing to die instead of him. Holmes and his assistants, having thrown Frank over, said that the sisters might as well go too. Mary may have gone voluntarily, unwilling to live now her brother was dead. Ellen, before she went, begged pathetically not to be thrown over, as she was practically naked. A cloak was thrown to her, though it was not her own. James Black was then seized: his wife Ellen offered to die with him. His own account reads, "He heard a mournful noise and found himself seized by one of the crew, who told him he must go overboard as it was necessary to lighten the boat . . . he asked him to let his wife go with him, when Mr. Rhodes called out, don't separate man and wife, they can't live long." He was spared, as was James Patrick for the same reason. During the night, another eight men were killed in the same way—George Duffy (who pleaded for his life as he had three children on shore, and because his niece, Bridget McGee, for whom he was responsible, was in the boat), Martin MacAvoy, Robert Hunter, Archibold Carr, John Wilson, John Welsh, and then James Smith. One called out "blood-an-ouns, let go of me and I'll go myself." The operation was still in progress as dawn broke the next day. Then it was the turn of Charles Conlin. He said, "Holmes, dear, you won't put me over." Holmes replied, "Charles, you must go." Mary Carr seized Holmes and pleaded for him, saying he was the last of a family of 15, but Holmes did not relent, and Charles Conlin was thrown into the icy waters of the North Atlantic.

Later, when it became fully light, two more men were found, apparently either hiding or hidden; they may have been in a dying condition, and Holmes later claimed one was actually dead. But according to Sarah Carr, the sailors "told the women not to hide them, as they would not leave a d...d soul of them in the boat." Holmes did not join in the last stages of what seems to have degenerated into a man-hunt. Hugh Keegan was thrown out by Joseph Stetson and John Nugent by Charley Smith. Nugent's niece, 17-year-old Biddy Nugent, heard him plead for his life and for him to be left to care for her orphaned self. As Nugent was thrown into the sea, the mate said, "Lord, cruel, cruel." One account suggests that one boy was thrown over but managed to cling under the bow and survive. This is improbable, but, if so, the boy could only have been Owen Carr, unless the reference is to one of those who died. Later a story circulated that those flung over clung to the sides of the longboat and their hands were cut off, but this story was denied and seems to have no foundation. In the conditions prevailing, they would in any event have rapidly lost consciousness.

The story told by the sailors was that all those jettisoned were nearly dead; although some of the passengers agreed with this, the probability is that this was not the case. The passengers were divided in their attitude as to what had been done—some at least said on Wednesday that the crew should be made to die the death they had given to the others. In particular, Bridget McGee repeatedly said that

Holmes should be punished; her uncle had been killed before her eyes. Accounts of the whole incident give the impression that, although Francis Rhodes was nominally in charge and initiated the killings, Holmes was in reality the effective leader until after the three Askins had been killed; he then appears to have tried to stop the killings, but Stetson and Murray carried on. Charley Smith later claimed that the passengers, after praying, all accepted their fate voluntarily, but this is quite unconvincing.

It was now possible to deal properly with the persistant leakage of water into the boat, which became manageable; the sailors could row southward. But at about 6:00 in the morning, very shortly indeed after the last two passengers had been jettisoned, the longboat was sighted by Captain George T. Ball from an American ship, the *Crescent;* he was aloft, conning his ship through the ice. At some considerable risk, he picked them up at about 7:00 A.M.—an hour or so later rescue would not have been possible. Immediately afterward, the longboat itself was crushed by the ice. Thus, in the event, the sacrifice of the passengers had probably made no difference to the survival of the others. When the *Crescent* was sighted, Holmes, the grim realist, prevented the survivors from standing up, calling out: "Lie down, every soul of you, and lie still. If they make out so many of us on board, they will steer off another way, and pretend they have not seen us." He even pushed Mary Carr down when she tried to stand. Numerous contemporary tales confirm the potential realization of his fears. But Captain Ball lavished every kindness on the survivors, even burning his own longboat for fuel to warm them. Their condition by this time was very bad. Owen Carr had no recollection of the rescue at all; the others could not walk. The *Crescent* was herself trapped for some time in the ice after the rescue. Captain Ball took them to Le Havre; en route, on May 2, he met another American vessel, the *Ville de Lyons* (commanded by a Captain Stoddard), to which he transferred some of the survivors. He secured a statement from Francis Rhodes as to what had happened, and Rhodes and eight sailors signed it; this was probably entered in the ship's log. Two passengers, James Patrick and James Black, also signed. They had reason to be grateful—their wives and James Patrick's child had been saved; and apart from the boy Owen Carr, they were the only males spared. The other 15 did not sign; the women were either unwilling or were ignored.

The *Ville de Lyons* reached Le Havre on May 10 and the *Crescent* on May 12. Captain Stoddard at once informed the American consul,

Ruben G. Beasley, of the story, and in consequence Francis Rhodes and his eight sailors were arrested and imprisoned. Rumors and news spread rapidly as to the nature of the "horrible catastrophe." In England, the *Morning Post* expressed concern: "Truly the circumstances must be made out in the clearest way to palliate such an act. We have emigrant ships sailing every week, and if it is held as law that 'might is right' it had better be declared so, and that the crew are justified in extremities in throwing overboard and as many, as they think right, without casting lots, or making any choice than their will." Back in Le Havre, the two consuls concerned, Beasley and his British counterpart Gilbert Gordon, interrogated the seven sailors from the *Ville de Lyons* individually at the American consulate, and on the arrival of the *Crescent* the mate, Joseph Stetson, and several passengers. Their evidence was recorded in signed depositions. Of the passengers, only Nancy Bradley and the infant child of the Patricks did not sign depositions. With the exception of Nancy Bradley and Biddy Nugent, all the passengers included explicit statements exonerating the sailors of all blame. There is a suspicious formalism about these statements, particularly in the case of Sarah (or Sally) Carr, who is recorded as having said "that she does not attribute any blame to anyone for what occurred as she believes that throwing some of the passengers overboard was a necessary act to preserve the rest and that if it had not been done, that all would have perished." These are not the words of an Irish peasant girl.

Be that as it may, the consuls were apparently satisfied by the depositions and by a report from the three ships' masters on the state of the crushed longboat (which had been recovered by the *Crescent*). On May 16 they issued a joint statement setting out what had happened, concluding, "throughout the affair we have not discovered any fact capable of drawing down blame upon any one whatever." The press commented, "The frightful necessity of sacrificing part of the passengers for the safety of the rest is fully proved." That appeared to be the end of the matter, except that "Homo" on May 18 wrote a pompous letter of protest to the London *Times* about the action of the consuls. "Homo" was not persuaded that "any circumstances whatever can possibly justify so gross an outrage." He congratulated his countrymen that no such thing "has ever been heard of, and I trust never will, on board an English ship." He was particularly shocked by the uncivilized nature of the act: it was what might have been expected "among the savage and heathen inhabitants of the South Seas," the earliest example of the use of this comparison that

I have noted. He went on to argue that one group of castaways ought not to be allowed to decide who was to die, particularly when it was the duty of officers and sailors to look after the passengers. And, if sacrifices had to be made, at least lots should be cast. Needless to say, "Homo" did not explain how, in the conditions obtaining in the longboat, this was to be done. His chauvinism was hardly justified, since it was from a British ship, the slaver *Zong* of Liverpool, that Captain Luke Collingwood had 132 African slaves thrown alive into the sea in 1781, allegedly out of necessity; this action later gave rise to a King's Bench suit, *Gregson v. Gilbert,* on the policy of insurance on the cargo (the slaves being insured for £30 each). In spite of the efforts of Granville Sharp, no prosecution for murder was ever brought.

Back in London, the press reports brought the matter to the attention of Lord Palmerston, then foreign secretary. He was outraged, and on May 18 a sharp letter was sent to Consul Gordon asking for confirmation that he had indeed signed the joint statement, continuing, "I am directed by Lord Palmerston . . . to state to you if you did sign it, you appear to his Lordship to have gone out of your way to put your name to an attempt to justify a transaction which was revolting in its character and of which the perpetrators cannot be absolved from great apparent guilt except by the result of a judicial investigation. I am to add that Lord Palmerston very much disapproves of your having signed that letter." A further letter of May 25 took an even stronger line. In a dispatch on the matter, Consul Gordon had entirely failed to give any account "of the steps you took in this business to investigate a transaction in which so many British Subjects were violently put to death by Foreigners." It was Consul Gordon's duty to bring the matter to a "strict investigation before a judicial Tribunal," and he was to take steps to have this done at once. Lord Palmerston, whose maiden speech in the Commons back in 1808 had defended the Copenhagen affair as being "in Conformity with the law of nature, which dictates and commands self-preservation," conceded that "it may possibly have been necessary for the American Crew to sacrifice a certain number of passengers . . . had however horrible such an expedient may have been yet if the necessity were fully established a veil might be drawn over the transaction." But he insisted on the need to investigate the matter judicially before this was done; the men should not be exonerated by purely administrative or executive decision. His wrath came too late; the men had left. All that happened was that the consul was authorized to remunerate Captain Ball for the cost of his longboat (about £19.16s.) and the cost of subsistence (£25.9s.) for the survivors; the depositions ended up in the Foreign Office archives. Consul Gordon apologized and explained that he had relied on the experience of Consul Beasley, a gentleman of the highest honor and character, with 30 years in his job. So Palmerston wrote on the docket, "This was a calamitous event, and nothing more needs be said about it." That appeared to be the end of the matter.

But as it turned out, the matter was by no means closed. In Le Havre, a subscription had been raised, and the emigrants set out again for Philadelphia, where they arrived in July—Bridget McGee on July 13, the others perhaps on the same date. Francis Rhodes, Charley Smith, and William Miller also traveled to Philadelphia; what became of the other sailors, particularly Joseph Stetson and James Murray, does not appear. Fate had been kinder to them or most of them, than to those in the captain's jolly boat. Those who had sailed off with Captain Harris had been rescued after six days by a French fishing lugger, *La Mère de famille,* and landed at S. Pierre in Breton Island, but they were badly frostbitten and one subsequently died in the hospital. Captain Harris, Walter Parker, and Eliza Lafferty also eventually reached Philadelphia on the *Childe Harold.* There must have existed in the Irish community in Philadelphia bitter resentment against the sailors for what could be viewed as an outrage, in which a captain had deserted his passengers, and his crew then killed them. There were also hints of racial favoritism—survival of the Scots preferred over that of the Irish; traditional religious hostilities lie behind this suspicion. Of the survivors Bridget McGee, Julia McCadden, and Nancy Bradley all resented what had been done, though Julia, no doubt to get away from Le Havre, had exonerated the sailors in her statement there. How precisely it came about is obscure, but it must surely have been pressure from kinsfolk that led to the involvement of the district attorney, William M. Meredith, in the matter. In the end Holmes alone was arrested and eventually, on October 18, 1841, indicted before a grand jury on a number of charges of murder and one charge of larceny of a quilt owned by James Patrick. Perhaps it was larceny that put him in the hands of the authorities. Francis Rhodes, Joseph Stetson, and James Murray seem simply to have disappeared, as sailors did; they were never brought to trial. The captain had committed no offense known to the law.

The grand jury found two true bills for manslaughter only and threw out the others. On December 9, depositions were taken from Captain Harris and Walter Parker; eventually, after long delay, Holmes stood trial on one indictment only for the manslaughter of Francis Askins. The trial opened on Wednesday, April 13, 1842, before Chief Justice Baldwin and Justice Randall of the U.S. Circuit Court for the Eastern District of Pennsylvania, and it lasted until April 23. For the prosecution, evidence from the survivors was given by Bridget McGee, Mary Carr, Owen Carr, Ann Bradley, Julia McCadden, Sarah Carr, and Biddy Nugent—those to be expected to support the prosecution. The defense relied on depositions from Captain Harris and Walter Parker (by then at sea), the Edgar family, and Eliza Lafferty. Again the defense team selected itself.

Holmes was ably and indeed flamboyantly defended by David Paul Brown, assisted by Messrs Hazehurst and Armstrong; in court, reporting the proceedings, was the famous American law reporter, J. W. Wallace. The proceedings were enlivened by "the unusual but agreeable appearance of a large number of ladies." Holmes, of whom it was said "his frame and countenance would have made an artist's model for decision and strength," admirably suited the need for a half-heroic figure; witnesses sang his praises. The defending counsel positively wallowed in the drama of the occasion; their speeches including such passages of oratory as this:

> Translate yourself, if you can, by the power of imagination, to those scenes, those awful scenes to which this proceeding refers. Fancy yourselves in a frail barque, surrounded by towers of ice Olympus high, and still magnified by the fear natural to man—exposed to the bleak and pitiless winds, surrounded by forty wretches as miserable as yourself—deepening your own afflictions by the contagion of grief. . . .

Mr. Meredith concluded his reply with similarly strong stuff:

> Was the sister of Askins insensible when she asked for a garment to cover her almost naked limbs, as they were about to plunge her into the deep? No! . . . They were sacrificed in the full possession of their faculties; sent into the presence of the Omnipotent, unanointed, unprepared; and there has gone up from the depths of the great ocean into which they were cast, a cry for justice, which this jury cannot—will not, disregard!

Florid oratory was the tradition of the period. Essentially the defense was that the killings had been justified by necessity and that the law recognized such a justification, even, so the defending counsel argued, if the alternative to killing was *not* inevitable death. Matters had to be judged on the well-founded apprehension of death, which the prisoner Holmes reasonably anticipated at the time.

Judge Baldwin, in a complex charge to the jury, accepted the view that necessity *might* operate as a complete defense, "But before the protection of the law of necessity can be invoked, a case of necessity must exist, the slayer must be faultless, he must owe no duty to the victim, be under no obligation of law to make his own safety a secondary object, and if in any of these particulars his case is defective, he is answerable by the law of the land." They had to consider whether in the circumstances it was the duty of the sailors to prefer the passengers or whether, in order to work the boat, it was imperative to keep the sailors alive in preference to the passengers. Among those who were in an equal position, among whom there existed no rational method of selection, the best mode was to draw lots, as long as circumstances made this possible. This, the judge thought, was generally accepted. But if the sailors are essential to the working of the ship or boat, they are not required to join in the drawing of lots—they must then be preserved as the instrument for preserving others. It was for the jury to decide how these general principles applied to the case and whether there really had been a necessity to kill anyone at all. The mate's order, if such it was, would be lawful or unlawful under the same principles: if unlawful, it did not exonerate Holmes. The jury convicted Holmes; why, it is of course not possible to tell. Nor, to be fair to Judge Baldwin, did he give any hint as to how the case should be decided by them; he trusted the jury to apply the principles he had set out and come up with the right answer. The jury took a long time to reach a decision, some 16 hours, and recommended mercy for Holmes. He was sentenced to six months' imprisonment at hard labor and, somewhat oddly, fined $20. He had already been in custody some six months, and although President Tyler refused him a free pardon, the fine was apparently remitted. Attempts to procure a retrial failed. The point taken in legal argument was that Judge Baldwin should not have introduced the idea that sailors and passengers might be in a different position in law. It was argued that necessity, if it existed at all, reduced everyone to a state of natural equality. But the court of review approved Judge Baldwin's approach and seems to have thought that the conviction was just because, as the facts stood, the sailors wrongly preferred their own lives to those of the passengers. Whether this is how the jury looked at the matter we shall of course never know, for juries give no reasons.

U.S. v. Holmes is in its own right a leading case, and in some respects the elaborate charge to the jury expressed a more sophisticated appreciation of the problems confronting survivors of maritime disasters than did the later English decision. The case is notable too as the only one in Anglo-American law that explicitly accepts the existence of a defense of necessity of homicide and as the only case that explicitly accepts the propriety, in appropriate circumstances, of selecting victims by lot. But the desultory judicial opinion affirming the charge, together with the inconclusive presentation of the problem as essentially a matter of jury decision rather than legal determination, deprived *U.S. v. Holmes* of the chance to become the central case.

It was some 30 years later that a chance arose for an English court of law to grapple with the problem; as it happened, the chance was lost. Quite unknown today is the story of James Archer and August Muller, who were fortunate enough to escape the fame of Tom Riley Dudley and Edwin Stephens. For the leading case in which they were cast to appear never happened: *Regina v. Archer and Muller,* or *The Case of the "Euxine,"* as it would have been called, is not to be found in the law reports, and memories of it have entirely passed away. The story is a curious one. It concerned the loss of a collier, which belonged at the time to Edward Bates, M.P. for Plymouth, who was, as we have seen, a prominent Liverpool ship-owner and Samuel Plimsoll's *bête noir.* Long after the Suez Canal opened in 1869, the steamships that used it to bear passengers to the East were unable to carry enough coal for the complete journey; they refilled their bunkers at Aden. The coal that they used was brought there, rather surprisingly, by sailing vessels using the long route round the Cape of Good Hope. It seems a strange arrangement but nevertheless made economic sense, since the steamships existed to provide a fast luxury service, and similar systems have operated in modern times. The *Euxine* was a ship-rigged sailing vessel, engaged in this disagreeable trade of carrying coal to Aden for the Peninsular and Oriental Line. She was elderly, originally built in 1847 at Greenock as a paddle steamer for the same line that had used her on the Istanbul run and later on the first leg of the overland route to India: she also carried military stores in the Crimean War and troops during the Indian

Mutiny. Sold in 1868 for £4,275, her engines had been removed, and Bates rebuilt her. Though elderly, the *Euxine* was in perfectly seaworthy condition, though she no longer held Lloyd's A.1 classification. Her long career had been uneventful except for an incident in 1854, when she left Southampton grossly overloaded with military stores for the Crimean War ("more like a log on the water than a ship") and was in grave trouble in the Bay of Biscay, so grave that the passengers protested in a letter to the *Times,* published on January 31. On the voyage that was to be her last, she left South Shields on June 11 or 12, 1874, under the command of Captain Peter Murdoch.

The next news of the *Euxine* came in September of that year, when the Board of Trade received a letter from the shipping master of St. Helena, Robert Noble. He reported the arrival there on August 18 of two boats containing the master and 22 members of the crew of the *Euxine,* which had been abandoned on fire, some 850 miles away at latitude 31°20′ south, longitude 7°40′ west. He reported that "the men appear to have suffered much from being so long in open boats—some of them being hardly able to walk." It was absolutely necessary to provide them each with a change of clothing, which he had done. The men, he said, had been saved by the master's "coolness, self-possession and decision"; when they were discharged on arrival, the distressing scenes that sometimes happened on such occasions, when the seamen, free at last from disciplinary restraints, let the captain know exactly what they thought of him, did not take place. They had good reason to be grateful, for Captain Murdoch had succeeded in locating the island, no mean feat of navigation; the chance of survival of castaways was enormously increased if they had a competent officer to lead them.

The loss of the *Euxine* had come about in a typical way. On August 1, when she was running in heavy seas under fore and main lower topsails, her cargo shifted, and the next three days were spent in the dreadful work of leveling off the cargo in the holds while the ship lay to in heavy seas. On August 5, smoke was seen coming from the cargo, which had ignited spontaneously. This was then a common source of disaster; between July 1, 1873, and June 30, 1874, seven colliers on foreign voyages were known to have burned, 32 were missing, and 330 lives lost. Course was altered for St. Helena, but all attempts to control the fire failed, and on August 8 the crew of 30 abandoned ship. But they kept close to the *Euxine* in the hope that the fire would die away, her hatches having been battened down close. On August 9, the ship was boarded and inspected, and the captain then abandoned all hope of saving her; by then she was in flames. Captain and crew set out in a convoy of three boats for St. Helena. The third boat was under the command of the second mate, James Archer, and it contained seven other members of the crew. Contact with it was lost the same night. It was not seen again, and Captain Murdoch supplied the shipping master with a list of the men who had disappeared with it.

Apart from making arrangements for the captain's deposition to be taken on his arrival home in Liverpool, as was required under the Merchant Shipping Act of 1854, the officials at the Board of Trade in London were not particularly excited by this run-of-the-mill maritime disaster, except that Robert Noble in correspondence had raised a tricky point of principle. In nineteenth-century ships the captain normally carried his own stores and provisions, and sometimes his own cargo. Peter Murdoch had provisioned the three boats from his own personal stores at a cost, he said, of £45. He asked to be compensated for this loss by the Board of Trade. This naturally alarmed the officials, as risking the administrator's ultimate nightmare: "The Creation of a Dangerous Precedent." They firmly maintained that he must take the matter up with the owners. Whether Edward Bates paid up, we do not know; I somehow doubt it, for among sailors Bates was principally known for his meanness and tendency to starve his crews.

Nothing further was heard of the fate of James Archer and his seven companions until November 3, when the Dutch barque *Java Packet,* under Captain Carel August Trappen, arrived at Batavia Roads in the Dutch East Indies on a voyage from Texel. She had on board James Archer, the 24-year-old second mate, and four other survivors from his crew. They were August Muller, aged 22, of Cuxhaven; Alexander L. Vermoulin, also aged 22, of Ostend; Manus (or Manshus or Mangshus) Schutt, aged 30, of Rostock; and Victor Sangström (or Sandström), aged 27, of Russian Finland. In a world where illiteracy was common, there is confusion in the spelling of the sailors' names. They had been rescued by the *Java Packet* on August 31 and, like Dudley and Stephens 10 years later, had no reticence about telling the appropriate official, in their case the acting British consul in Batavia, William J. Fraser, precisely what had happened in the period of 22 days that had elapsed between their parting from the other boats and their rescue. It was an ugly story.

The boat in which they were cast adrift was 30 feet long, with raised canvas bulwarks; she possessed two masts and a foreboom, carrying mainsail, staysail, and jib. James Archer possessed navigational instruments and a chart, and the boat was well provisioned with a ham, a cheese, two cases of biscuits, a number of tins of meat (variously stated as 12 or 20) and more than four pounds of plug tobacco. There were also tools and a can of oil, no doubt shipped for use in smoothing the waves by being leaked from a canvas oil bag. The water supply consisted of two small casks and was therefore minimal. After losing contact with the other two boats, Archer shaped a course northeast by north for St. Helena, strictly rationing his men to conserve food and more particularly water—each man had three-quarters of a pint a day only. After 12 days' uneventful sailing, he thought that they were on the latitude of the island and by dead reckoning placed the boat 30 miles to the east. But they could not find land, and the navigational skills of the second mate were obviously incapable of establishing longitude—a complex operation sometimes beyond mates, although included in the requirements of a mate's certificate. So, after two days spent searching fruitlessly for St. Helena, the decision was taken to sail northwest by north and head for Brazil before the trade winds. This entailed a further voyage of more than 2,000 miles, but there was at least no risk of missing South America. Rations were reduced to half a biscuit and one glass of water each day, and at first all went well, though conditions now must have seemed very unpromising. Soon the weather worsened; on August 27, at 11:00 P.M., the boat capsized. The boatswain, Peter Jackson (or de Jago) had been steering at the time, and he was drowned; there are hints of suicide. The others righted the boat, but shortly afterward the boat capsized again and was again righted. It capsized yet again. In this series of disasters, George Reynolds, a boy shipped as able seaman, also drowned, and Alexander Vermoulin was saved only by the efforts of Manus Schutt, who was a particularly strong swimmer. The five survivors clung to the upturned boat all night and righted her in the morning, but they were now in a desperate position, having lost compass, sextant, masts, food, and water. Unless rescued in the next day or so, they had little hope of survival.

The following day, Sunday, August 30, a small sail was set, and the five survivors continued their voyage, now become all but hopeless. The men included a small, dark-skinned Italian boy of about 20, who spoke very little English. The captain's list gives his name as Francis Gioffous, but in the papers concerning the case this is usually rendered as "Shufus." Both versions are corruptions of an Italian name, which could have been Zuffo or Ciuffu. On the ship's articles, which survive, what could be a signature gives his name as Franco Gioffey. He was not a popular member of the crew.

By the next day, August 31, Muller had become delirious and had drunk considerable quantities of seawater. According to James Archer, he then "offered his body to serve as food for the others and entreated the others to kill and devour him." This offer was refused, but soon after it was suggested that lots be drawn. Archer, Muller, and Vermoulin said that Manus Schutt first proposed this; Schutt claimed implausibly that the idea originated with Francis Shufus. All agreed, or so the ultimate survivors claimed. Archer's account then goes on,

> Having no other means to make a lottery of we hit upon using small sticks of different sizes, deciding that the one who drew the smallest should be the victim. After having made the sticks ready I held them in my hand while the others drew—on comparing them together found that the Italian Francis Shufus held the shortest stick. Having also agreed that the lottery should be thrice repeated and that when it should then prove that either three or two of us had drawn the shortest sticks these should cast lots amongst themselves, so that the victim should be singled out, we found that the same man had for a second time picked out the same object. Francis Shufus, when his turn came for the third drawing, hesitated to join and would not draw, upon which the man Sandström proposed he would do it for him. This he did and the shortest stick was found in Sandström's hand. . . .

Apart from the detail that, according to Schutt, it was Vermoulin who drew for the boy, all the others told the same story. Archer claimed that Francis Shufus "bore it all with great calmness and showed the utmost resignation." Vermoulin's account was that "the Italian, from the few words he said, and gestures he made, said he would undergo his fate." Sangström said, "The Italian appeared to be a little agitated." There was then a pause, variously estimated as two hours (Archer), 10 minutes (Vermoulin), and one hour (Schutt), and during this time the horizon was searched for a sail, Francis Shufus being left to pray. Archer later described the scene: "We stood upon the thwarts, Shufus prepared himself to meet his fate by praying and speaking in Italian. He gave us no parting message to be sent to his friends, most probably as he hardly knew more English than to say 'Yes' and 'No.' His bearing was of a man whose mind was made up." Shufus was then tied up, and Muller killed him: "I held the knife and gave him a cut across the nape of the neck, but as the knife was not very sharp I had to put it round his throat—Sandström caught the blood in a pannikin." In oral evidence, Schutt put it more simply: Muller killed him by cutting off his head. Archer adds the detail that, before killing Shufus, Muller offered to die in his place: "This Shufus refused and laying himself down in the bottom of the boat gave himself up to be tied. . . . He did not struggle or scream." Estimates as to the time of the killing vary; it was in the morning, perhaps about 10:00 A.M. All drank the blood; Muller cut out the heart and liver, and these were eaten. The head and feet were cut off and thrown overboard, the trunk and limbs put into the lockers of the boat. A few hours later (Vermoulin's estimate was five), they were rescued by the *Java Packet*. It must have been obvious enough that there had been cannibalism; the survivors clearly made no attempt to deny the killing, though Sangström claimed that an attempt had been made to persuade Francis Shufus to kill himself.

The story told by the survivors plainly consists, at least in part, of an account of what ought to have preceded the killing of Francis Shufus rather than what actually did; at the same time, it is strikingly candid in identifying the killer and admitting that the boy did not die naturally. What precisely did happen—a sham lottery or none at all—can never be known; but a letter in the Singapore press from Captain G. H. Harrington, which may derive from conversation with the men, may tell the real story: "They cast lots the second time and still the lot fell on him. He then jumped overboard and attempted to drown himself but was seized by his shipmates, and dragged into the boat, his throat mercilessly cut. . . . This story is told from their own lips, and horrifying to relate, they seem to consider that they were justified in committing the atrocious murder for the sake of appeasing their own wants."

It is perhaps surprising that Archer, the man in charge, who apparently neither suggested the killing nor took any very active part in it, should have joined in telling a story that is obviously in part untrue; presumably he felt that as the man in charge he was inevitably implicated and needed to tell what appeared, at least in the maritime world, to be an appropriate story.

On November 7, the men were put on the *Namoa* for Singapore, where they arrived on November 10. Accompanying them was a letter from the acting consul, William Fraser, together with the depositions taken before him. The matter now passed into the hands of Henry Ellis, who held the office of master attendant or shipping master at Singapore. He was a retired naval officer and a master mariner of long experience; he appears in Conrad's *Shadow Line*

(1916). Confronted with this startling case, he consulted with the attorney general of Singapore, Thomas Braddell. The conclusion reached is set out in the covering letter he wrote on November 14, when he posted the depositions to the Board of Trade in London. The attorney general concluded "that there was no necessity for any Judicial Enquiry and that the men who committed the deed are free to engage themselves on any vessel requiring their services." So the men remained in Singapore in the sailors' home, recovering from their ordeal and seeking a ship that would offer them employment. The depositions and Captain Ellis's covering letter did not reach the Board of Trade until early in January 1875.

The Board of Trade was not the first government department in England to receive official news of the additional survivors of the *Euxine*. The governor, Colonel Sir Andrew Clarke, sent a full account of the matter, together with copies of the Singapore *Daily Times* of November 16, to the Colonial Office in Despatch 334 of 1874, dated December 12. Accounts also appeared in the London *Times* on December 22 and 29, presumably reaching London by cable. The matter had in fact been brought to the governor's personal attention only on November 20, after the attorney general had decided that no legal proceedings were needed, and he had been uneasy about the release of the men. The following day, the governor ordered the men to be placed under police surveillance and cabled the Colonial Office that he had done so. The governor may also have seen and been influenced by Captain Harrington's letter in the Singapore *Daily Times* on November 13, which had contained a clarion call for action:

> I trust that, for humanities sake, and for the credit of my brother seamen, of whatever nationality they may belong, that steps be taken to bring these maneaters [*sic*] to justice, and that from Singapore may go forth the decision that under any circumstances, however great the sufferings may be, seamen are not allowed to sacrifice one of their number that one may live.
>
> I am fully aware, after having had some forty years' experience of a sailor's life, that during the dull night watches they are in the habit of relating such horrible stories of suffering which may have come to their ears, and by others recounting them they imperceptibly come to the conclusion that they are justified under certain emergencies in sacrificing one of their number . . . the sooner they are disabused of the idea the better.

He recommended prayer, not cannibalism, in such emergencies. There was also a leader published on November 17, calling for a judicial inquiry: sailors, it argued, should know whether such sacrifices were lawful or not. They needed legal guidance on the matter. The governor agreed in principle, especially as he suspected "that the unfortunate lad had—even were the course taken under any conditions justifiable—not met with fair play in this instance." But he was opposed to holding a trial "in a remote dependency." A trial before a British Court was essential, particularly because the second mate, James Archer, was the only British seaman in the boat (and ought to have prevented the killing). Furthermore, he argued, there were no precedents to guide a local court, which might not know what to say.

The Colonial Office reacted to this by cypher telegrams of December 17 and 25, conveying instructions to the governor to hold a judicial inquiry on the spot, and the papers were sent from the Colonial Office to the Board of Trade. The official concerned, the Honourable Robert H. Meade, assistant under secretary, noted on the file "To B. of Trade. But this sounds like the old *Satsuma* case over again. The men could not be sent to England to be tried as there are regular courts in the Colony." The reference is to a mutiny which took place on the sailing vessel *Satsuma* at 5:00 A.M. on January 29, 1874. Another collier, on the run to the coaling station at the Cape, she had left Sunderland late in 1873. When Captain William Leslie had announced his intention of logging a sailor, James Willey, for misconduct, the crew mutinied and tried unsuccessfully to kill him with a hatchet. The mutineers subsequently became dispersed throughout the world, two turning up in Hong Kong; and it was obviously in some ways desirable, if expensive, to ship them all back to England to stand trial together. But the legality of doing so was open to question, and the colonial secretary, the earl of Caernavon, took the formal opinion of the law officers of the Crown, Richard Baggally and John Holker. Their opinion was that where there were local regular colonial courts, those men charged with crimes on the high seas must be tried where apprehended. One sailor, John Johnstone (alias Anderson) was indeed eventually tried and convicted under this ruling in London on November 26, 1874. This opinion plainly covered the case of the *Euxine*. So, for the time being, the case was regarded as no longer the concern of the Colonial Office; it concerned only the authorities in Singapore.

Back in Singapore proceedings were therefore put in hand to bring the men to trial. The decision to do so was announced in the local press on January 8, and the case was scheduled for hearing before the court of the police magistrate, Captain Douglas, on January 15. His function corresponded to what was to be exercised 10 years later by the magistrates of the borough of Falmouth—he had to record the evidence of the prosecution witnesses and, if he thought it appropriate, commit the men for trial before a judge and jury. But although the colonial government had received firm instructions from London, the attorney general and his colleague, Mr. Gottlieb, began to encounter what seemed to them to be insuperable difficulties in proceeding to a trial by jury in Singapore. There, as we have seen, the original view had been hostile to taking proceedings at all; the attorney general, without seeing the papers, had relied on the experience of the master attendant: "The best thing to do was to say nothing about the matter." On December 20 the attorney general, after reflecting further and receiving orders from London, penned a minute, saying that the case was one "which, dreadful as it is, might be palliated with the plea of necessity." He had been originally inclined to feel that there was no need to "vindicate the law," but on reflection he now agreed with London and thought it better to put the case before a court that could take a final decision, rather than simply forget it. It was better "to put in evidence the exact facts of the case, especially as to the fairness of the drawing of lots and the conduct of the 2nd mate and Muller. . . ." Two of the sailors should be selected as "approvers" (i.e., as prosecution witnesses) and the others charged with murder; and even if a jury refused to convict, it could at least be said that the facts had been properly looked into. The governor agreed but still thought it better if they were tried in England, whatever the Colonial Office thought about the matter.

The attorney general thought that if the governor's solution was to be adopted, the consul in Batavia would have to commit the sailors for trial in England under Section 268 of the Merchant Shipping Act of 1854 and suggested he be asked to do this. Again, in another minute, he expressed doubts about the outcome of a local prosecution, pointing out that he had no adequate evidence unless some of the men turned Queen's evidence. But on December 26, the governor instructed that proceedings be taken locally, in accordance with his instructions from the Colonial Office, notwithstanding the fact that Mr. G. Phillips, who appears to have assisted the attorney general as well as acting as a puisne judge, expressed himself unable to see how a charge could be brought. The depositions taken in Batavia were by themselves of no use without evidence from the acting consul in Batavia or his staff as to how these were obtained. James Archer had made a statement in Singapore to the master attendant, but its usefulness was limited by the rule that a confession was admissible evidence only against the individual concerned. He needed better and more evidence and suggested (as had the attorney general) that the best course was for the police magistrate to select whoever seemed the least guilty to turn Queen's evidence. Those selected could be told that if they gave evidence for the prosecution "in an unexceptionable manner," they would be recommended for a pardon. This rather dubious scheme was reflected in the public proceedings. After various adjournments, these began on January 30. The case for the Crown was handled by Mr. Gottlieb, who was Crown solicitor or solicitor general. He explained that the prosecution was brought "to show that in no case was human life to be taken without the act undergoing the most searching judicial enquiry into the causes and motives which led to its being committed." He then called his only witness, Captain Ellis, the master attendant, and it became immediately obvious that the prosecution case was in very poor shape indeed.

Captain Ellis had copies of the depositions made in Batavia by the accused men, but the originals had been sent to London, as we have seen; these copies were ruled inadmissible as evidence. All that Captain Ellis himself could say was that James Archer had voluntarily told him that Muller had killed Shufus; this was not a confession by Archer nor admissible as evidence of a confession by Muller. What was available hardly amounted to a *prima facie* case, and the hearing was adjourned to enable the prosecution to collect some more convincing evidence from Batavia and to try to get one or more of the prisoners (though not Archer, the officer in charge; nor Muller, the killer) to turn Queen's evidence in return for a pardon. During these proceedings, the men were defended by a Mr. Donaldson, who brought out some interesting information in his cross-examination of Captain Ellis. It transpired that Ellis himself had once been a castaway; and when asked if the men were responsible for their acts, he was able from his own experience to say, "Certainly not. I feel sure they were not in a position to know right from wrong." He was also asked, "Do you know as a matter of naval history whether instances of shipwrecked men drawing lots as to who should die for the rest?" He replied, "Yes. About twenty or twenty-five years ago these cases were most common. I have never heard of men being punished for so doing." Mr. Donaldson then asked him, "Have you actually met such seamen?" He replied, "I believe I have seen a European seaman who helped to eat another man."

The local press a few days later carried the story of the emigrant ship *Cospatrick.* A sailing barque of 1,199 tons, she had left Gravesend, England, on September 11 for New Zealand under charter to the Colonial Government to carry emigrants. She had a crew of 44, and at the time of the disaster she had 435 passengers on board. These included many children. She also carried a highly inflammable cargo, which included 1,732 gallons of linseed oil and 5,732 gallons of rum and spirits. Some of the emigrants plundered the spirits, and the ship caught fire on November 18, some 2,000 miles south of St. Helena. Only two boats got away; neither was provisioned or carried any water, though one carried the carcass of a sheep, which had to be jettisoned to make room for passengers. On November 27, only five survivors out of a total complement of 479 were rescued by the *British Sceptre,* and of these five two died after they were landed at St. Helena on December 6. The survivors had practiced cannibalism, and this was widely reported. Although it was not suggested at the time in the press or elsewhere that there had been killing as well, the only deposition by a survivor to refer to cannibalism indicates that there probably was. Edward Cotter stated, "The biggest, fattest and healthiest looking went off first. It was not from them that the blood was obtained, but from the other men. I only ate twice. I drank whenever a vein was opened." This case was known and no doubt discussed in Singapore, as it was in England, where in February a formal public wreck inquiry was held. In terms of loss of life, it was indeed one of the worst disasters to a passenger ship that had yet occurred.

The police court resumed its hearing of the case of the *Euxine* on February 11. This time Schutt had been persuaded to turn Queen's evidence (Vermoulin and Sangström presumably refused), and this was just sufficient for Captain Douglas to reconcile his conscience to committing the other four men for trial on a charge of murder at the next criminal sessions, due to open on April 12. But behind the scenes the prosecution case was still in a state of considerable disarray, and there was little chance of a conviction unless the Crown could acquire some more convincing evidence. One possible source was the acting consul in Batavia.

He proved, however, less than amenable. The governor communicated with him on February 17, asking him to furnish all possible evidence as to how the depositions were obtained. He was also to telegraph whether he himself would come to Singapore for the trial. He failed to do so and wrote a wholly uncooperative letter on February 27:

> In reply I beg to inform you that the statements of the men as forwarded to the Marine Magistrate in November were voluntarily made by them in this office under oath, that they conducted themselves quietly when here and that as neither myself nor any member of my establishment can give any further material evidence connected with the matter, I did not deem it necessary to telegraph you as requested.

The *Java Packet* was about to sail, and it was impossible to obtain witnesses from her. The consul's only offer was to obtain an unhelpful affidavit from Captain Trappen, which he did. This reduced the attorney general to a state of desperation, and on March 3 he minuted, "I do not know under the circumstances what is to be done." The depositions by the men in themselves were, in his view, mere waste paper, and all he had was Schutt's evidence (merely as an accomplice) together with evidence from Captain Ellis, a reluctant witness. He tried the acting consul again by cable on March 4, who replied, characteristically, by letter on March 13. The *Java Packet* was still there, but none of the sailors would leave it voluntarily to act as witnesses. The acting consul added that it was impossible for him to come, and his clerks were needed in his office. "Anyway," he added cunningly, "it would be useless for him to come unless some of the sailors would come, too." This intransigent attitude did not in any way harm Acting Consul Fraser's career; shortly afterward he succeeded to the office of consul in Batavia, a position he held for many years. A certain degree of resistance against being controlled at long range by cable was essential in an imperial administrator, who not unnaturally often thought that the man on the spot knew best. Within limits, local initiative was tolerated.

In London there had also been developments; the package containing the original depositions of the five men had eventually arrived at the Board of Trade via Singapore, and the papers were commented upon by W. C. Monkhouse, who noted,

> I suppose that we should send this to the Home Office, but no steps will be taken by that Dept.
>
> There is a horrible sanity about all these proceedings but the men were not, I believe, responsible for their actions. No social advantage

> can be derived from prosecution or punishment. To live must be sufficient punishment.

Thomas Gray, the assistant secretary in charge of the Marine Department of the board, took a slightly different and more alarming line: "It is not likely that any jury would convict, and if a Court of Law were to stamp this custom with clear authority it might be made a pretext for getting rid of troublesome people. I should be inclined to leave it alone. The details are too disgusting to take to court." The permanent under-secretary, Sir Thomas H. Farrer, agreed with the conclusion. Prosecution in "one of the very saddest and most disgusting incidents that I have known" would only harrow the feelings of the public. "The act was done under the direct pressures of necessity and it is too abhorrent to all the feelings of human nature to be repeated except under similar circumstances—punishment, if practicable—or exposure—are not needed and would have no effect in future cases." The president, Sir Charles Adderley, agreed. Thus there emerged a departmental official view hostile to prosecuting in such cases, one which reflected the recognition that this particular maritime custom was best not turned into a lawyer's case. The papers were sent on to the Home Office as a formality, since that was the department concerned with crime and criminal law. At this time, the Board of Trade did not know that proceedings were in fact to be taken in Singapore. A clerk at the board noted on the ship's articles after the name of the boy, "killed by the crew for food."

Early in January, papers again circulated in the board, which had by then been informed that the governor had been instructed by the colonial secretary to take criminal proceedings. Thomas Gray's attitude had now hardened. "My view is that no crime was committed in killing and eating a fellow seafarer under these circumstances." The president noted that "this fortunately settles the question raised in former papers so far as we are concerned." It does not seem to have occurred to anyone to arrange for the return of the original depositions to Singapore, where they were desperately needed for the trial; the originals were admissible as evidence. Presumably, they were safely back with the Board of Trade after perusal by the Home Office. And so it came about that the supposed criminals were in Singapore and the evidence for their crime in Batavia and London. Such were the problems of a far-flung empire.

The authorities in Singapore were consequently forced into abandoning a local prosecution, and the final decision to drop the proceedings was taken by the Executive Council in March and announced in the *Straits Observer* on April 22; the proceedings were stopped by entering a *nolle prosequi*. This decision was communicated to the Colonial Office by dispatch on May 1, which reached the Colonial Office on June 7. There exists a long minute setting out in detail the arguments for dropping the local prosecution and holding a trial in England instead. It contains several compelling arguments. The inadequate evidence was confined to the testimony of Schutt, an accomplice (whose evidence would in law require corroboration) and the "confession" of James Archer to Captain Ellis (which in law was not admissible as evidence against Muller). Second, under local law the crime involved was probably not murder anyway, quite apart from any possible defense of necessity. The Penal Code (Section 300) defined it as culpable homicide, not murder, "where the person whose death is caused being over the age of eighteen years suffers death or takes the risk of death with his own consent." Hence the jury would probably either convict the defendants of this offense only or, more probably, acquit them entirely—especially as Captain Ellis's evidence would be sympathetic. It would be most undesirable if, as a result of an acquittal, the idea got around the seafaring community that it was legally permissible to kill and eat fellow sailors. This was particularly urgent as Singapore was a major seaport, from where the news would spread rapidly around the world, quickly reducing the life expectation of ships' boys.

The attorney general was also concerned about the status of any local legal decision to the effect that it was unlawful and criminal to act in this way. He put his point thus:

> The law as laid down in an English Court would have more weight in all parts of the world and would probably be considered binding in all parts of the British Dominions, whereas the law as laid down by the Court here would not be binding even upon the Court itself, and this being the first case of the kind which has ever been proposed to be tried, it is important that the principle to govern cases of this sort in future should be authoritatively upheld.

So he wanted the men sent to England by the naval vessel *H.M.S. Adventure*, which was then in the East. If, as he suspected, the detention of the men on the *Adventure* proved to be illegal, it was highly unlikely that they would sue; and even if they did, an English jury was unlikely to award them damages.

In fact the men were not put on *Adventure* but on a merchant steamship, the *Nestor.* The *Nestor* left Singapore on May 22; news that the men were consigned to England reached the Colonial Office only on June 7. The Colonial Office was quite clear that sending them to England was illegal, and after a lapse of a week, a cable was sent to Singapore telling the authorities there not to send the men home: a draft letter was prepared for the Board of Trade, suggesting the men simply be left in Singapore. By cable on June 16, Singapore revealed that the men had left almost a month earlier. The Colonial Office now set about the task of passing this embarrassing and illegal situation to the Board of Trade, which had in fact known rather earlier of the departure of the men from Singapore and on June 14 had written to the Colonial Office on the subject—the letter apparently no longer exists. The Colonial Office had in fact suggested to the Board of Trade in May that any attempt to send the men home ought, if possible, to be stopped. So it was well placed to pass any blame, and this was done in a letter to Thomas Gray of the Marine Department on June 19. After pointing out unctuously that the Colonial Office had done its best to prevent the illegal action of the Singapore authorities, the letter continues to hint at slackness by the Marine Department: "It does not appear from your letter whether the Board of Trade took any action in consequence of the telegram which Sir Andrew Clarke states in his despatch of 1st of May that he sent to advise the Board of Trade but Lord Caernavon presumes the Board of Trade will now communicate with the Home Office and determine what steps are to be taken in the matter." The Colonial Office was in fact also aware that the Home Office would be displeased if the home government had to bear the cost of a trial that should have taken place in the colonies at colonial expense. The Board of Trade did not itself conduct criminal prosecutions in England for such crimes as murder or manslaughter, and so in the end the case of the *Euxine* became the concern of the Home Office. The Board of Trade arranged that the registrar general of shipping should report the arrival of *Nestor* in London, and on June 29 the papers were passed to the Home Office. The *Nestor* arrived on July 9 and was reported by the shipping master. On July 10, at 12:50 P.M., the registrar general telegraphed the following to the Board of Trade: "Mr. Paule, New Inn, Solicitor to the German Government, called to ascertain whether Board of Trade had possession of papers relating to commitment of the remainder of the crew of the *Euxine.* Men arrived yesterday in the *Nestor.*" J. C. Pawle of Pawle and Fearon was presumably under instructions from the embassy to look after the interests of August Muller. By 3:23 P.M. the registrar, having received no reply, became restive; he therefore sent a second telegram. "Is there any reply to telegram about case of Euxine. The five men charged with murder are now here. Please say what we are to do with them." At the Board of Trade one of the clerks, Mr. Ashley Maude, was told to deal with the matter. Having no doubt made inquiries, he replied, somewhat unhelpfully, "Case in abeyance at H.O. Cannot say how men are to be disposed of." In the Home Office, the papers had no doubt been circulating, but since a file or docket on the matter no longer exists, if it ever did, it is not possible to reconstruct the stages in its circulation or tell who was consulted. For the time being, the five sailors were probably kept effectively, if not officially, under arrest. On July 13, however, a decision was reached by the home secretary himself, R. A. Cross. It was communicated to Thomas Gray by Sir Henry Selwyn Ibbetson, Bart., M.P., who was parliamentary under-secretary of state (the permanent under-secretary was Sir Adolphus Liddell—who was still in office in 1884). With meticulous accuracy, Sir Henry wrote as follows:

> I am directed by the Secretary of State to thank you for your letter of the 29th ultimo, forwarding correspondence in original, now returned, respecting an Italian seaman who was killed and partially eaten on board a boat containing some of the survivors of the wrecked vessel Euxine. In reply, I am to acquaint you with reference to your further letters of the 10th inst. regarding the arrival of the survivors in London per the steamship Nestor that after careful consideration of all the circumstances the Secretary of State does not consider that this is a case in which it would be advisable to institute proceedings against these men.

That was that. The men were, one assumes, simply released, apparently on July 22, and fingers crossed lest they sue for false imprisonment. Apparently they never did, and the press failed to pick up the story. But before they disappeared, three of the foreign sailors were persuaded to sign an official form discharging Edward Bates and the ship's officers of any further legal liability. Their transport to England had cost £30 each, and perhaps the four foreign seamen were discreetly assisted in finding berths to work on other ships or returning home. If so, the records I have traced do not record this.

Why was the prosecution thought not to be "advisable"? The difficulties over evidence that impeded a prosecution in Singapore had no doubt become even more acute by July 1875. Vice-Consul Fraser and his clerks were in Batavia, Captain Ellis in Singapore, and Captain Trappen and the crew of the *Java Packet* heaven knows where. The evidence had been dispersed; all that existed in London were the men and their depositions; to cap it all, their detention in the *Nestor* had been wholly illegal. A prosecution would have been a fiasco, causing embarrassment all around. Conceivably, too, more sinister political delicacies were involved, and this may explain the transmission of the decision through the *parliamentary* under-secretary of state. The *Euxine* was owned by the Conservative member of parliament for Plymouth, Edward Bates, a major Liverpool owner of sailing vessels; Bates was indeed to become a baronet in 1880, no doubt for the usual reasons, shortly before losing his seat on an election petition. Now in 1875 the campaign against wicked ship-owners by Samuel Plimsoll, "the sailors' friend," was in full swing; and Edward Bates was Plimsoll's archetypal villainous, indeed murderous, ship-owner. 1874 had been a bad year for Plimsoll's campaign—the shipping survey bill had been lost in June by three votes; on July 1 the Royal Commission Report had gone against him. Disraeli's government had promised a new merchant shipping bill, but no progress had been made with this, and by July of 1875 Plimsoll was exasperated by the dilatoriness of the government and the influence, as he saw it, of the ship-owning lobby. His great parliamentary explosion, which included an attack on Edward Bates, was to take place on July 22, when Disraeli announced the intention to drop the merchant shipping bill for that session, a decision presumably reached some days earlier; this led to both Plimsoll's suspension and an outburst of popular support for his war against the ship-owners. Had the case against the survivors of the *Euxine* been proceeded with, it would have been as notorious a case as that of the *Mignonette,* which in 1884 was to be internationally reported. The case of the *Euxine* would have been even more of a *cause célèbre.* The crew of a ship owned by a prominent Conservative ship-owner, himself notorious among seamen for starving his crews, had actually been reduced to eating each other. This would hardly have been welcomed politically, whatever the outcome of the case might be or whatever real blame attached to Edward Bates himself. In fairness to him, the loss of several of his ships seems to have been the result of spontaneous combustion of coal, a danger then not fully understood. It was all better forgotten. Curiously enough, Samuel Plimsoll either did not know of the story of the *Euxine* or, if he did, kept quiet about it in public. She was not one of the five lost Bates ships Plimsoll specifically named on July 22 in the Commons when he attacked Bates, yet it is almost incredible that he should not have picked up the story. Edward Bates himself, when defending his honor in the Commons on July 30, did mention the loss of the vessel, but not its disagreeable aftermath. He had indeed on the previous day moved that a select committee be set up to look into Plimsoll's charges against him, and, had the House acceded, the full story would of course have come out. By then, with popular feeling strong against the government, public knowledge of the dropping of the case would have been as embarrassing and open to sinister interpretation as proceeding with the charges. One can well understand Disraeli's enthusiasm for heading off the motion for a select committee; he succeeded in resisting the idea, and Edward Bates's request for a select committee may of course have been contrived. Disraeli also gave in on the merchant shipping bill, and by July 30, Plimsoll was triumphant. We can only wonder whether the terrible story of the Italian boy Shufus played some part behind the scenes in Disraeli's desire to appease Plimsoll. But of this there is no direct evidence. Since then, the story has been forgotten, though in 1884 it would have been familiar to Sir Adolphus Liddell, permanent under-secretary in the Home Office, who may have had secrets to tell about the whole untidy story of the attempt to bring the survivors of the *Euxine* to justice and a determination not to preside over any kind of fiasco involving the latest cannibals to land in England, Captain Tom Riley Dudley, Mate Edwin Stephens, and Able Seaman Edmund James Brooks, one of whom had indeed served on the ill-fated *Euxine*.

James Archer's subsequent career (the only one I have been able to trace) does not appear to have suffered from his deviant gastronomic activities. Like Timothy Gorman, he had never been convicted as a cannibal murderer, though his history must have been perfectly well known in maritime circles. His second mate's certificate, lost when the *Euxine* was abandoned, was renewed, and he obtained his first mate's certificate in Dundee on September 14, 1876, followed by his master's certificate on November 28, 1878. He served as an officer on numerous ships, his first command being *Lotus* (1879–80). In 1882 he was back in Singapore as mate of the *Lanarkshire,* and in 1884 he was there again as first mate on the *Kremlin,* a 1,188-ton vessel owned by William Raeburn of Glasgow. Thereafter, until the end of his sea-going career, he was an officer and eventually captain of a number of steamships owned by Scots owners such as James Mudie of Dundee—the *Gary,* the *Thane,* the *Vesper,* and the *Aurora.* His last ship was *Matin,* which he commanded from 1894 to 1911, when at the age of 60 he retired at last from the sea. His views on the trial of Dudley and Stephens, which took place when he was out in the East on a voyage to Saigon and back, are not recorded, but he may have been relieved not to have been the central figure in a lawyer's case; it was the sort of fame one could do without. It is inconceivable that the papers concerning the *Euxine* were not consulted in the Home Office in 1884, but no reference to the story is recorded in that year in any contemporary source I have located except the Plymouth *Weekly Mercury,* which records that an old retired Singapore magistrate, presumably Captain Douglas, who had once handled a similar case, visited Tom Dudley in prison. I suspect that the Home Office file, if there ever was one, passed into the hands of the treasury solicitor's department, there to be lost. It had all been a rather embarrassing business, but the production of leading cases requires careful management and an element of good fortune.

8
The Devious Baron Huddleston

Then the Judge, like any Jackdaw,
Oh, he lays down, what is law,
In a rotten stick your trust is,
And though you don't get Justice,
You're sure to get plenty of Law.

—from J. Ashton, *Modern Street Ballads,* 1898

Frustrated 10 years earlier in their attempt to bring the custom of the sea before a court of law for condemnation, the officials of the Home Office and that of the treasury solicitor may have taken particular pains over the prosecution of the latest cannibals to land in England, but most of the preparatory work is undocumented. On October 28 the *Times* announced that the trial of Dudley and Stephens would begin on the following Saturday, November 1, at Exeter assizes before Baron Huddleston; that Arthur Charles, Q.C., would appear for the Crown with Charles Mathews; and that the two prisoners would be represented by A. J. H. Collins, Q.C., and Henry Clark. Their fees were no doubt defrayed by the defense fund, though an offer had been made by a barrister from the Middle Temple to defend them without fee; he had himself been shipwrecked in the steamship *Sirius,* the first such vessel to cross the Atlantic. That had been in 1838; on January 16, 1847, the *Sirius* ran aground on the Irish coast at Ballycotton Island, and the wreck was at once plundered. I have been unable to identify the barrister in question. The counsel involved in the case were all of high reputation. In Arthur John Hammond Collins the defense had acquired the services of the leader of the Western Circuit; Collins also was the recorder of Exeter at the time and a well-known figure in the West Country. Plainly nobody would be able to say that Dudley and Stephens lacked adequate legal representation, an important fact, since the ultimate authority of the decision would be enhanced if everything possible had been urged on the men's behalf. Arthur Collins was in fact to be knighted the following year when he gave up his practice at the bar to become chief justice of Madras in British India, a post he held until 1899. It was not a moment of his life when he would have been at all eager to make a mistake.

The judge selected to conduct the trial, Baron Huddleston, was a somewhat colorful if unattractive individual, and although there is no direct evidence of this, it is highly probable that some careful thought was given by the lord chief justice as to his selection. F. W. Ashley, Horace Avory's clerk, records of him that he was in the habit of wearing gloves in court, suiting their color to the case: "There were black gloves for murder, lavender for breach of promise, and white for the more conventional cases." Which color he chose for this occasion is not recorded. He was what was known as a "strong judge"—that is to say, an opinionated, domineering man who was able to persuade juries to reach the decision that he thought correct. In so doing he was merely carrying onto the bench the qualities that had earned him success at the bar, where he had built up a large criminal practice. In its course he had returned numerous burglars to their friends and their relations, his forensic triumphs including the remarkable acquittal in 1859 (on her third trial) of Mercy Catherine Newton, indicted for matricide. More recently, in 1871, he had secured the acquittal of Edward Pook of murder in a *cause célèbre*. He had also appeared in the famous poisoning case involving William Palmer in 1856. His criminal practice had begun with dock briefs secured through a commission arrangement with a friendly entrepreneur, the turnkey at the Old Bailey. Indeed, John Walter Huddleston had come a long way from relatively humble beginnings. After matriculating in 1835 at the age of 18 at Trinity College, Dublin, he came to England without taking a degree. He entered Grays Inn in 1836 and was called to the bar in 1839, working as an usher in a school. By 1857, he had taken silk and become a bencher of his Inn. Though best known as a criminal practitioner—where purely legal ability is hardly required—he also appeared in civil cases of significance, notably the great case of *Indermaur v. Dames* (1866), where a public-spirited journeyman gas fitter fell down a shaft in a sugar refinery and thereby enabled Sir James Shaw Willes to rationalize the law relating to the liability of occupiers of property for injuries to their visitors. Huddleston entered politics in 1865 as a member for Canterbury, after fighting numerous hopeless seats; he lost Canterbury in 1868 and later, in 1874–75, sat as a member for Norwich. His parliamentary career was negligible, a mere incident on the route to the top, where he arrived twice. The first occasion was in 1872, when, at the age of 57, he married 31-year-old Lady Diana De Vere Beauclerk, daughter of the ninth duke of St. Albans. Whether her father would have agreed to this match is uncertain, but he had fallen off his horse hunting in 1849, succumbing to an epileptic fit in consequence, and was therefore not available for consultation. But socially unusual marriages ran in the family; the duke himself had married an actress, Miss Mellon, who was, providentially, enormously wealthy. The duke had been 26 at the time and Miss Mellon 50. Huddleston and Lady Diana were married by a notable snob, Bishop Wilberforce or "Soapy Sam," as he was then called, who in recording the event in his journal did not even trouble to record the name of the insignificant bridegroom. Huddleston, it is said, was never reticent in calling attention to his alliance with the duke, and Lady Diana not infrequently sat on the bench with him; a lady portrayed in the only contemporary drawing of the trial may indeed be Lady Diana. Huddleston's second triumph came in 1875, when he became a judge of the Court of Common Pleas and was consequently knighted. The same year he was transferred to the Court of the Exchequer and acquired the title of baron; this was the name then applied to judges of this court. Huddleston acquired this title just in time, since it was abolished the following year as a consequence of the reorganization of the judicial system brought about by the Judicature Acts (1873–76).

His connection with the seafaring world was limited but may have been significant. He was the son of a merchant captain, Thomas Huddleston. The elder Huddleston had also served in the navy, but probably not as an officer, though he is described as *Navalis praefectus* in the records of Trinity College, Dublin, in 1835. The baron himself had also been connected with the navy from 1865 to 1875 as judge advocate of the fleet, where, in the words of his *Times* obituary, "although he knew less of the lines of a ship than of the parts of a horse, he managed to hold his own. . . ." Men who have risen socially in life, as Huddleston had done, sometimes fall into a tendency to reject the world out of which they have risen, and Huddleston was a snob. It is not perhaps too fanciful to suppose that when Huddleston was confronted, at the Exeter assizes in 1884, with the ugly reality of the sailor's world which he had learned many years earlier from his father, his reaction was less than sympathetic. And presumably the only judge who had been directly involved with naval discipline was the obvious man to be sent there to do what had to be done, particularly as he had a reputation for getting his own way with juries and was well known in the West Country. He had sat as assize judge for the Western Circuit on a number of occasions and may have had relatives there, as his mother came from St. Ives. Sir William Grove had originally been selected to take the Western Circuit, and the change in plan may have been contrived.

The proceedings at Exeter, where Dudley and Stephens surrendered to their bail, fell into two stages. The first involved the consideration of the prosecution case, on its own, by the grand jury of the county, whose job it was to decide whether they should be put on trial at all (in which case, the jury found "a true bill" of indictment); if the jury rejected the case ("ignored" the bill), the charge was dropped. Since the question of whether the men should be tried at all had already been considered by the Falmouth magistrates at the preliminary inquiry there, the activities of the grand jury simply duplicated the functions of the magistrates, a ludicrous state of affairs that is explicable only historically. Grand juries originally had the function of formal accusation of crime, by 1884 a function long taken over by other institutions—here the police and the Home Office. The legal system has always been slow to adapt to changes, and grand juries were not finally abolished in England until 1948, long after their function had passed to others, though virtual abolition had come somewhat earlier, in 1933. The grand jury normally did simply what it was told by the assize judge and went through the calendar of cases with the jury and delivered a speech or lecture to the jurymen, known as "the charge." This was public, but the deliberations of the jury took place in private, and by 1884, the meetings of the grand jury had become largely a social event; prominent members of county society met with the Queen's representative, the assize judge, and participated only ritually in the administration of justice. There were luncheons and balls to add to the convivial nature of an event, incidentally enlivened by the trial of local members of the criminal and other dangerous classes. The grand jury was not a proletarian institution; in Blackstone's words, it consisted of "gentlemen of the best figure in the county." Thus on this occasion the 23 jurymen included the Honourable L. A. Addington; Sir Henry

B. T. Wrey; Sir Massey Lopes, Bart., M.P.; Sir John Duckworth; Sir George Stucley Stucley; Sir John Budd Phear; Lieut. Col. Charles A. W. Troyte; and Mr. Henry Samuelson, M.P. All would be county magistrates.

But grand jurymen could in principle exercise independent judgment, and Baron Huddleston was no doubt anxious lest the jury (which could operate by majority) might throw out the indictment for murder completely or accept only a charge of manslaughter. If this happened, the chance to turn the killing of Richard Parker into a leading case would be lost forever; careful management was going to be needed.

On the assumption that the case were to survive the deliberations of the grand jury, the indictment against Dudley and Stephens would then proceed to the second stage—the actual trial of the men, taking place before the petty or trial jury. This comprised 12 jurors, as is the rule today, but there have been significant changes in the system. In 1884, the jurymen were all male, qualified through a property qualification. Their decision also had to be unanimous; any dissent meant a retrial. Though again not a proletarian body, the petty jury, socially much less elevated than the grand jury, could be troublesome and was by no means as malleable as a grand jury. Given the strong local sympathy for the accused, which had already influenced the conduct of the case in Falmouth, Baron Huddleston must have been aware of the serious risk that the jury might disagree and convict the accused of manslaughter only or even, worst of all, decide to acquit the men entirely, thereby legitimating the custom of the sea. This risk was aggravated by the fact that sympathy was not confined to the lower orders of society—indeed, it is recorded that every captain under whom Dudley had ever served was present in Exeter to give evidence on his behalf. Discussion of the case in the press too had made it obvious that support was broadly based. From the point of view of authority, the Exeter jury was a positive menace to the rule of law. And although there is no direct evidence on the point, Baron Huddleston very probably also knew of the fiasco of the *Euxine,* only 10 years earlier.

The social arrangements attending the assizes ensured that there were opportunities to talk about the case informally and judge local feelings, or even guide it in the bar mess, at private dinner at the judge's lodgings, at the luncheon for the grand jury. Baron Huddleston cannot have wanted to preside over a fiasco and thereby allow a potential leading case to escape yet again. He had a further problem.

The policy of using the disaster of the *Mignonette* as an opportunity to secure an authoritative statement as to the law made it essential that the case should somehow come before a higher court, where not one but a bench of judges could declare the legal position with something approaching finality. The opinion of a single judge, delivered on assize, was not regarded as binding on other courts or judges and would only leave the law in an uncertain state; the problem was similar to what would have arisen if the *Euxine* case had been settled in Singapore. So Baron Huddleston had first to prevent the case from simply collapsing and then contrive to ensure that it did not end before him alone at Exeter. It does not appear whether the strategy he adopted was based purely on his own individual ingenuity or on prior conversations with the lord chief justice or Home Office officials.

The first hurdle, then, was the grand jury, which convened on Monday, November 3. Baron Huddleston remarked that "both in regard to the number and magnitude of the offences the calendar was a very serious one" but added that few of the cases would present any difficulty. He advised them to throw out an indictment against one Thomas Badcock for raping Ann Dunn, a case "of so extraordinary a character that during a professional and judicial career of nearly half a century he never recollected having seen its parallel." They did. As for the indictment of Edward B. and Clare Edwards for murdering their children, he indicated that it might be best to find a true bill against both, though Clare might have a defense: the jury failed to take the hint and threw out the indictment against Clare. He suggested that they might look closely at the indictment against Walter James Mathew for manslaughter: the bill was thrown out. He then turned to "another case of paramount importance, in which Thomas Dudley and William [*sic*] Stephens are charged with murdering a boy at sea." He described Dudley as "a man of exemplary character, great experience and courage" and described the sequence of events from the time when Dudley became master of the yacht to the landing at Falmouth. He claimed that "Brooks clearly took no part in the death of the boy," adding in reference to the killing, "indeed Brooks seems to have sternly dissented from it." Good stories need a hero, and Ned Brooks was by now well on his way to playing that role. The baron then gave a formal ruling on what he considered to be the law applicable to the case: "It is a matter that has undergone considerable discussion, and it has been said that it comes within a class of cases whereby the killing of another is excusable on the grounds of necessity. I can find no authority for that proposition in the recognised treatises on the criminal law, and I know no such law." He went on to consider the legal authorities that might be relevant to the existence of the supposed defense of necessity. He began with the case of the seven Englishmen of St. Christopher, mentioned by Baron Pufendorf in his *Law of Nature and Nations,* the account deriving ultimately from a seventeenth-century medical writer, as we have seen. This he rejected as no reliable report existed: "Although he says the men were English sailors, he does not say where the case was tried, nor of what nation were the judges." Next, he considered the American case of *U.S. v. Holmes* (1842), arising out of the loss of the *William Brown.* He misunderstood this case so badly that one suspects he never personally read the report. "That American case, however, was a charge not of murder but of manslaughter, on the ground of the failure, on the part of the prisoners, to discharge the statutory duty of preserving the life of a passenger." In fact, as we have seen, this was rubbish. In the context of this case he also took the opportunity of ridiculing the idea that killing might be justified if the selection was made by lot: "The learned American Judge in giving his reasons, said, 'It would be an appeal to Providence to choose the victims.' Such a reason would seem almost to verge on the blasphemous. I cannot but consider that the taking of human life by appealing to chance would really seem to increase the deliberation with which the act was done." Then he considered the discussions of the concept of necessity in the Report of the Criminal Law Commissioners (1878–79), which suggested that it was "better to leave such questions to be dealt with when, if ever, they arise in practice by applying the principles of law to the circumstances of the particular case" and a similarly unhelpful discussion by Huddleston's fellow judge, Sir James Fitzjames Stephen, in his *History of the Criminal Law,* published the previous year. Huddleston then went on to argue that it was only in cases of self-defense that homicide would be justifiable. He concluded,

> It is impossible to say that the act of Dudley and Stephens was an act of self-defense. Parker, at the bottom of the boat, was not endangering their lives by any act of his: the boat would hold them all, and the motive for killing him was not for the purpose of lightening the boat, but for the purpose of eating him, which they could do when dead, but not while living. What really imperilled their lives was not the presence of Parker, but the absence of food or drink.

It will be noted that this passage extends the concept of self-defense beyond cases where an attack is involved; a threat by mere existence would suffice. Huddleston justified his statement of the law by references to Blackstone's *Commentaries on the Laws of England* and the American *Commentaries on Criminal Law* by Joel Prentiss Bishop ("a high American authority") and explained away a somewhat incoherent analysis by Sir Francis Bacon, set out in his *Elements of the Common Laws of England* (1630). There was also reference to the stock example of the sailor who pushes another sailor off a plank after a shipwreck, the plank being inadequate to support both; this comes from Cicero's *De officiis*. Baron Huddleston's opinion would have gone as far as to justify excusing the pushing sailor in such a case, since his victims' very existence could be said to endanger life.

This charge to the grand jury is the first full English judicial discussion of the defense of necessity. To have given a formal and public legal ruling on the facts of a case that had not yet been put in evidence seems highly exceptional and indeed irregular; and althought it is possible that there were precedents, I know of none. Huddleston's behavior is explicable only on the assumption that it was already settled that the facts of the case were established and the outcome obvious. His opinion was used, somewhat modified, as a basis for the better-known opinion of Sir Chief Justice Coleridge, delivered later in the course of the case. Baron Huddleston must have been working on it before he traveled to Exeter, where copies of Baron Pufendorf's works and American legal treatises would not have been at hand. It may well have originated as an opinion by counsel before the prosecution was undertaken, prepared either for this case or earlier for the *Euxine* case. There had also been a considerable body of discussion of the principles involved in the press. For example, "Peluca" had written to the *Daily Telegraph* on September 10, drawing attention to the reference of the American case of *U.S. v. Holmes;* and that paper had carried a series of letters from "A London Magistrate," "A Barrister," "Another Barrister," and "A Law Student," discussing the legal position in a reasonably intelligent and well-informed way. It was Sir George Sherston Baker, Bart., a barrister, who in a letter to the *Times* on September 9 had located the original source of the story of the sailors of St. Christopher in the writings of Nicolaus Tulpius. The letter of "Another Barrister" on September 12 had argued powerfully against recognizing the defense of necessity on the facts of the *Mignonette* case as a justification or excuse. While conceding that shipwrecked sailors in conditions of famine would not be directly influenced by a legal decision, he argued that to admit the defense would be to introduce a new and wholly immoral "canon of legal irresponsibility," one giving men a right to do wrong, and capable of dangerous extension. Press comment had also made plain the frequency of cannibalistic killing in survival conditions—a *Standard* leader of September 9 had, for example, referred to such incidents as that of the *Medusa* raft, the Donner case ("a terrible carnival of cannibalism"), and the recent Greely case. One way and another, any assize judge would have had ample material to reflect upon before coming to an opinion. Nor could anyone who kept up with the press have been unaware of the widespread acceptance of the custom of the sea. A letter by E. C. R. published in the *Spectator* on September 27 had defended it, arguing bizarrely that the sea air caused particular problems by whetting the appetite, so that the suffering was "aggravated by the fresh air and free surroundings." A leader in that periodical on September 13 had attacked the apologists for cannibalism, saying,

> But so complete is the belief of sailors in the right to kill and eat comrades, that "Captain" Dudley, believed to be a most respectable man, who spoke most kindly to his victim, and asked God's pardon before he took his life, without any compulsion, voluntarily, related the whole story. . . . We have little patience, we confess, with the modern tolerance of cannibalism which came out in the discussion of the recent case in the Arctic regions.

Baron Huddleston's charge was delivered not only in advance of any establishment of the facts of the case but also without any opportunity for counsel on either side to argue the disputed point of law—defending counsel in particular had no chance to put forward any contrary argument. The theory of the common law is that judges know the law, and counsel merely refresh their memories; so this was in no way improper, though it can hardly be regarded as very fair. Presumably Huddleston gave an exhaustive ruling on the law at this early stage in order to persuade the grand jury to let the case go forward, but an incidental result was that there was little point in Arthur Collins attempting at the trial to argue that the law was otherwise. The judge had by then committed himself, and Collins's only hope was to raise the matter at some later stage in the proceedings before a higher court. This, of course, was exactly the end that Baron Huddleston was pursuing.

The grand jury, after deliberating in private and hearing prosecution evidence, obligingly found a true bill; Baron Huddleston was over the first hurdle, and his charge to the jury was published in the local and national press, thereby making it officially clear that Dudley and Stephens, not yet tried, had committed murder. The grand jury's compliance was also secured by indications, given no doubt by Baron Huddleston, that no harm would come to the men themselves. Some months later Tom Dudley, on January 24, 1885, petitioned the home secretary from his cell in Holloway Prison thus:

> On November 4th at Exeter Mr. Collins J.P. [Charles Robert Collins, the 23rd member of the Grand Jury] came and saw me after the True Bill had been found and he explained to me how necessary for them to do so but said Dudley you have our sympathy but prepare for the awful sentence which must be passed to uphold the laws of England. And rest assured as soon as things can go through their form you will be granted a free pardon we are all sure.

The vindicatory function of the proceedings is made clear in this statement. The indications that a pardon would be forthcoming, given at Exeter, are not of course recorded directly but fall in line with the policy pursued ever since the case taken over by Treasury counsel at Falmouth—officialdom wanted a legal decision, not the punishment of the two unfortunate men involved.

The trial itself was to take place in the courtroom in Exeter Castle and was arranged to open on the following Thursday. Exeter was no doubt buzzing with excitement, and many people concerned in the trial (as well as others) would have traveled there specially. Thus Robert Cheesman and his chief clerk, Samuel Tresidder (having of course obtained formal leave of absence) had set out from Falmouth on the 5:15 P.M. train on Saturday; also in Exeter were all the captains under whom Dudley had ever served. It is difficult today to re-create for those who have never witnessed such a scene the dramatic quality of a trial at the assizes before a red judge in the days when the old barbaric rituals were still kept up and the death sentence was still the supreme expression of the awful power of the law. I personally will never forget my experience as a schoolboy seeing the late Mr. Justice Croom-Johnson in action at an assize court; it was quite terrifying. To be in the presence of a judge was to be in the presence of a man who could order you to be killed (and some few would do so with pleasure); and lest there should have been local misunderstanding, on Wednesday Baron Huddleston, attended by his chaplain with the black cap, had sentenced to death the wretched Edward Bath Edwards, aged 34, for cutting the throats of his two children, Albert and Sydney. He was eventually to be reprieved and his sentence commuted to penal servitude for life, but that was still in the future; the conditional pardon only arrived in Exeter on December 9. His was the only case tried in the castle that day, capital cases always being full-dress affairs, long drawn out in comparison with less serious matters.

The trial of Dudley and Stephens, set for the following day, was of course the principal attraction, and a considerable crowd gathered outside the court. Admission to the show was in the main by ticket only, but a few seats were kept for the general public, and these were overfilled. The *Times* reported that "the Court was densely crowded, even ladies being present throughout." Many had been turned away. The proceedings began at 10:30 A.M., and the *Exeter and Plymouth Gazette* noted that "the accused are superior looking men, with fine intelligent faces"—Dudley looked the older of the two, though he was not; he had to stand throughout the whole case because of his injury. Both listened to the case with interest and anxiety but exhibited little emotion. A drawing of the scene survives, unhappily of poor quality. After the formal charges of murdering Richard Parker on the high seas on July 25 had been put and they had pleaded not guilty, the jury was sworn. The first man into the box was Samuel Widgery, who was almost certainly the foreman—he had been sworn first on Tuesday and again on Wednesday. Indeed the composition of the assize jury did not change much from case to case; precisely the same jury sat for all the six county cases heard on Tuesday and again for the murder trial on Wednesday. Then, for some reason, George Lock was replaced by Edmund White for the trial of Dudley and Stephens on Thursday; the other 11 jurymen were unchanged and had therefore heard the death sentence pronounced on Edwards the previous day. They could have been under no illusion as to the gravity of the charge. The continuity in composition and chairmanship of the jury would no doubt have assisted the development of a satisfactory working relationship between judge and jury that was of considerable significance in the case; judge and jury had by now grown used to each other. A similar practice has been shown to have existed in the eighteenth century by J. H. Langbein, but I was surprised to find it still in operation at this period.

Arthur Charles, Q.C., opened the case for the Crown, and in doing so he stated firmly that in his submission the two men were plainly guilty of murder. In putting forward this opinion, he reviewed such legal authorities as he had been able to locate, in much the same manner as Baron Huddleston had done at the grand jury hearing, concluding that no defense of necessity was available. He also raised and dismissed another possible defense—that the men had been temporarily insane at the time—a possibility not considered by the judge on Monday. Here the legal position was governed by what are known as the "McNaghten Rules," laid down by the judges in answer to questions put to them by the House of Lords in 1843 in connection with the trial of one Daniel McNaghten. Essentially the defense of insanity, under these rules, applied only if it could be said either that Dudley and Stephens had not known what they were doing at all or had not known that what they did was "wrong." Dudley's statement and Stephens's deposition before the receiver of wrecks ruled out the former claim, and the fact that Dudley had admitted to saying a prayer for forgiveness was relied on to show that he knew what he did was "wrong." "That it was done by persons of sound mind there is no doubt," contended Mr. Charles. However, he softened his speech by yet another hint of ultimate clemency: "Considerations of sympathy and compassion for the shocking and terrible sufferings which these prisoners have, undoubtedly, undergone, may well be urged as a most powerful plea for the remission in this case of the extreme penalty of the law . . . ," and he made no attempt to minimize their sufferings. At the end of his speech, Baron Huddleston turned to Arthur Collins, and a brief discussion took place on the law.

Baron Huddleston:	Mr. Collins, I presume you traverse the law [i.e., disagree with the prosecution's view]?
Mr. Collins:	Yes . . . I rely on these cases, and I say that if necessity compelled these men in taking the life they were justified in so doing.

By "these cases" Collins was referring to the seventeenth-century case of the seven men of St. Christopher, passages in *Blackstone's Commentaries,* and the Report of the Criminal Law Commissioners in 1878–79.

Baron Huddleston:	I mean that is the doctrine you set up.
Mr. Collins:	That is the doctrine I set up.

But Baron Huddleston had already formally stated that Arthur Collins's view of the law was wrong, and he now made it quite clear that Collins was to be given no opportunity to argue in its favor. Come what may, Huddleston was going to tell the jury that no such defense existed in English law. He could not however entirely muzzle the unfortunate defending counsel, and this bizarre exchange took place:

Mr. Collins:	. . . Your Lordship will take a certain course—whether the prisoners were justified or not under the necessity of the case—
Baron Huddleston:	Certainly not. I shall lay down as a matter of law there was no justification. I shall lay that down distinctly and absolutely.
Mr. Collins:	I must address the Jury on that point.
Baron Huddleston:	Yes. I shall rule it distinctly. I am firm on that point. That is my own opinion of the law, and I must rule firmly on that point.
Mr. Collins:	Yes. I will address the Jury upon my view of the case. Your Lordship will, of course, adopt what course your Lordship pleases after that.

So Collins would tell the jury that there was a defense of necessity and invite them to acquit, and then the judge would instruct the jury that Mr. Collins had been talking nonsense and that, since it was agreed all around that the facts of the case were not in any real dispute, it was their duty to convict.

Arthur Collins never suggested that the circumstances under which the killing took place might in law operate not as a complete excuse or justification of the killing but as a ground merely for reducing the crime to manslaughter. This was a conceivable argument and would have involved drawing an analogy between starvation and provocation; the latter in law did have this reducing or mitigating function. But if Collins expected a free pardon anyway, there was little point in running such an argument, and this may be the reason why he did not do so. Nor did he try to raise the defense of insanity, although in fact Dudley's prayer was offered only conditionally—he had never conceded at any time that what he had done was morally wrong or illegal. But again, Collins may not have thought it in his client's interests to raise this defense, which would have led to indefinite detention in a criminal lunatic asylum. Better to try for an acquittal and fail safe with a pardon than that.

In the course of the exchange with counsel for the defense, the judge produced an ingenious procedural suggestion that, if accepted, would in his surely hypocritical view spare the jury the pain of having to convict Dudley and Stephens and "hear again the awful sentence of death pronounced against them" i.e., as the jury had the day before. It would also enable a higher court to decide whether Baron Huddleston or Mr. Collins was right on the law. The jury cannot but have been struck by the apparent unfairness in not allowing Collins an opportunity to argue in favor of his view of the law and try to persuade Baron Huddleston he was right. To appreciate the nature of the Huddleston plan, it must be known that in 1884 the obvious system for reviewing a trial judge's ruling on the law—an appeal to a court of criminal appeal staffed by a number of senior judges—did not exist. Though many attempts had been made to establish a court of criminal appeal, the judges had always succeeded in blocking these attempts, which did not succeed until 1907, when the climate of opinion had been changed, partly through the scandal involved in the false conviction of Adolf Beck. Some of the functions of an appeal court were, however, performed by other agencies—for example, to give but one instance, by the home secretary, who could recommend a pardon if a sentence was plainly illegal. In particular, there was an institution known as the Court of Crown Cases Reserved, which could give authoritative rulings on the law in cases where it was thought to be uncertain. A trial judge could (and the decision rested with him) "reserve" a point of law for this court to consider; it was then argued before the lord chief justice and four other judges, normally the senior judges of the Queen's Bench who were available. If the five judges disagreed, the matter might be settled after reargument before 15 judges. This court had originated without a statutory basis as an informal gathering of judges to whom a colleague referred a difficult point. In 1848 the informal practice was regulated by a statute that made imperative a prior conviction by the jury, if a decision was to be reviewed. This then became subject to whatever the senior judges might say as to its propriety. An acquittal could not be reviewed, and presumably it was fear that the jury might balk at convicting Dudley and Stephens, even as a formality, that led Huddleston to make an alternative suggestion. This was designed to satisfy the jury that the defense arguments would be properly considered and to avoid embarrassing the jurymen by requiring them to reach a hostile verdict. At the same time, it was designed to bring the case of the *Mignonette* before a really authoritative tribunal, which could once and for all settle the legality of the custom of the sea.

The alternative that Baron Huddleston suggested was for the jury to find a special verdict, which could then be considered before a bench of senior judges in London. Normally, a jury simply found a general verdict, simply "guilty" or "not guilty." However, a procedure had formerly existed whereby a jury found the facts—that is to say, stated what in their view had happened—and left it to the judge or judges to say what legal conclusion as to guilt or innocence should be drawn from those facts. Such a finding of facts was called a special verdict, and the procedure had never been abolished, though it had long been obsolete. Indeed the last instance of its use had been nearly a century earlier, in *Hazel's Case* (1785). Lord Abinger in 1837 in *Regina v. Allday* had suggested to a jury that a special verdict be found, but the jury on that occasion declined the invitation, and he had accepted this: "I cannot direct them to find special facts in a case of felony [i.e., a capital case]." A celebrated eighteenth-century constitutional struggle, which culminated in Fox's Libel Act of 1792, had in a rather different context established the right of a jury to return a general verdict. Huddleston therefore had to persuade the jury to accept his idea, for in theory he could not force them, and Arthur Collins made it further clear that he had no right in a criminal trial to make any concessions to the prosecution. "I am powerless to consent," he said, and Baron Huddleston accepted this: "I do not ask you to. I shall take it on myself to do it." Huddleston then explained to the jury that he meant he would take it on himself to give the accused men the best opportunity to have their counsel's view of the law considered, by following the procedure he had indicated. Neither the judge nor Arthur Collins took any trouble to spell out to the jury their undoubted right to reject the Huddleston plan. The unhappy Collins was of course caught in a cleft stick. Given the intransigent attitude of Huddleston, his only hope of a chance to argue the point of law lay in going along with the Huddleston plan. The baron was completely within his rights in refusing to reserve the point for the Court of Crown Cases Reserved; and if he did so, the case would end in Exeter. Collins could of course fight vigorously to persuade the jury to acquit completely, but this was risky, given a judge as domineering as Huddleston. Looking at the matter realistically, he may have felt that his clients were one way or another bound to be convicted of murder and that their interests would best be served by adopting a cooperative attitude and relying on a free pardon at the end of the day. It is of course possible that a bargain had been struck between prosecution, judge, and defense.

It now being clear what procedure would be followed, the prosecution evidence was then called, much as it had been in the preliminary hearing at Falmouth. Counsel entered both the documents that showed the *Mignonette* to be a British-registered vessel and the articles signed by the crew. The jury also had the depositions of Dudley and Brooks before the shipping master and Dudley's letter to the Board of Trade; the judge ruled it unnecessary to read out Dudley's other statements that had been found with his clothing and were exhibited in the case. Evidence was given by Julius Wiese, Gustavus Collins, Robert Gandy Cheesman, Richard Hodge, and Sergeant Laverty. But the star testimony came, of course, from Ned Brooks. He did all that was expected of him, and in particular when asked, "When this talk took place about casting lots, what did you say?" he replied, by now word perfect, "I said, 'Let us all die together. I should not like anyone to kill me, and I should not like to kill anyone else.' " He was now the supreme hero of the terrible tale of the sea, if not quite in Grace Darling's class, near it. In cross-examination, Collins did not attempt the hopeless task of challenging the substance of Brooks's evidence. His questions were devoted to bringing out the appalling nature of the conditions in the dinghy and the fact that Richard Parker was dying. When it came to the eating of the boy, the exchanges went thus:

Mr. Collins: But you were all very bad I suppose?
Brooks: Yes, we were all very bad.
Collins: You could not resist the sight of the blood? I believe you asked for some, you were in such a state.
Brooks: I could not. I was obliged to ask for some.
Collins: Horrible as it was, you were obliged to have some?
Brooks: Yes.

Further questions elicited Brooks's view that, but for cannibalism, none would have survived:

Collins: And for those four days was life kept in you by this unfortunate boy's body?
Brooks: Yes, no doubt, it was Sir, I believe so.

On the question of lots, Brooks at one point denied that any had been drawn, and, as to the boy's consent, he was curiously evasive in reply to questions by the judge.

Baron Huddleston:	Did the boy consent to it or was he asked?
Brooks:	I am sure I could not say now.
Baron Huddleston:	But there were no lots drawn?
Brooks:	No.

As to whether the boy would have died first, he replied, "He seemed weakest. I could not say."

Given the lack of any real challenge to the prosecution's account of what had happened, and knowing that the judge would not allow him to argue the legal issue of necessity that was central to the case, Arthur Collins was placed in the unhappy position of being bereft of anything to do on behalf of his two clients. He could not call Dudley or Stephens to give sworn evidence on their own behalf, though a practice existed whereby they could perhaps have given unsworn evidence. There was no point in calling medical evidence as to the effects of starvation (though it was apparently available), since no defence of insanity was to be raised. So he was reduced to raising merely subsidiary legal issues. One of these somewhat disconcerted the judge.

This was the question of jurisdiction—had the court power to try the men at all? Collins conceded that the court had a power to try a case of murder arising on the high seas on a British ship and, further, that the *Mignonette* herself was a British ship. But, he contended, the dinghy was not itself a British ship, particularly in view of the fact that the Merchant Shipping Act of 1854 defined a ship as including "every vessel used for the purpose of navigation not propelled by oars." Nor was the dinghy to be regarded as part of a British ship. This threw Huddleston and prosecuting counsel into total confusion, and it took some time for Huddleston even to grasp the point. Behind this confusion, albeit in a convoluted way, lay a general awareness that the assize court in Exeter would have jurisdiction over the case only if it fell within the jurisdiction of the old Court of Admiralty (nobody present knowing precisely what that was) or if some modern act of parliament gave the court jurisdiction. After an adjournment, counsel for the prosecution weakly claimed that the court's jurisdiction was based on an act of parliament of Henry VIII's reign (28 Hen. VIII c.15); in fact, the position was not settled by this act at all. Baffled by the whole business, Baron Huddleston agreed to arrange for the special verdict to be so drafted as to enable the matter to be considered by the higher court too, since he did not really know the answer.

Arthur Collins's other subsidiary point dealt with the correct order of speeches to the jury, a matter upon which great energy was expended. He wished to have the last say immediately before the judge's summing up and direction—no doubt he hoped to persuade the jury simply to acquit and decline the invitation to find a special verdict. His claim was based on the fact that he had called no witnesses—this normally gave the right to the penultimate speech. Mr. Charles, however, relied on the theory that in any prosecution where the counsel was briefed by the Treasury and acted on the authority of the law officers of the Crown, the prosecuting counsel was specially privileged and had a final right of reply immediately before the judge summed up. Prolonged wrangling on this issue, at the time a very contentious one, led to Baron Huddleston's ruling in favor of the prosecution. Having lost the point, Arthur Collins then addressed the jury, inviting them to find the accused men not guilty, the killing having been committed under necessity: "Although they all knew that unfortunate men had in many instances been driven by stress of hunger and thirst to feed upon their fellow creatures, no government of any civilized country had in any case prosecuted the unhappy survivors on a charge of murder." He contended that, "according to the evidence laid before them, there was an inevitable necessity that one life should be sacrificed in order that the other three might be saved, and that they were justified in so doing in selecting the weakest. . . . It is evident that these men, on their return to this country, did not dream that they had committed any criminal offence. . . ." Baron Huddleston appears to have been somewhat irritated by this appeal over his head to the jury and told them that they "were not at liberty to disregard his ruling, though encouraged to do so by learned counsel for the defence." And so the attempt was foiled, and the jury was presented by Huddleston with a clear direction that they must either convict of murder or accede to his suggestion and find a special verdict:

> If I was to direct you to give your verdict, I should have to tell you, and you would be bound to obey me, that you must return a verdict of guilty of wilful murder. Now I hope I may deserve from you some consideration for putting you in the position of merely finding the facts, and not finding the verdict of guilty of wilful murder, and if

> you will be kind enough now to follow me in the facts that I have prepared and give your consent to each paragraph as I read these to you, then when the whole of these paragraphs or facts are found by you, the matter will be referred to the Court for the purpose of the Court saying what is the law upon the subject and that must be some satisfaction I hope to you.

Baron Huddleston, then, without pausing to ask the jury whether it was agreeable to this procedure or not, produced (like a conjurer with a rabbit) a draft special verdict that he happened to have with him. This draft, which still exists, had been prepared by him the night before and dictated to his clerk, who had written it out in a paper book. Baron Huddleston proceeded to work through it, paragraph by paragraph, inviting counsel on both sides to make any suggestions they liked for its improvement. The transcript records no protest from counsel or jurymen, and the judge had therefore succeeded in the task of creating, out of the material and procedures available to him, the "facts" of the leading case of *Regina v. Dudley and Stephens*. Whatever happened at a higher level in the system, this much at least was now achieved: the matter had been effectively taken out of the hands of the jury. All that they could now do was to express views as to the formulation of the precise text of the special verdict and, somewhat oddly, since neither Dudley nor Stephens had yet been convicted of any crime and were therefore in legal theory innocent men, recommend them to mercy. Baron Huddleston delicately avoided putting their recommendation in such a way as to bring out the absurdity of asking for mercy for the innocent.

Baron Huddleston:	I see that you are going to suggest to me—that you wish to accompany your finding with some expression.
A Juror:	That is just my idea.
Another Juror:	And mine.
Baron Huddleston:	And I take it you are very desirous that I should convey to the proper quarters your strong feeling of compassion for the position these men are placed in.
The Jury:	Yes.

And so they were recommended to a mercy which, at that time, they did not yet need.

The special verdict, as approved by the jury, was intended to become the conclusive or definitive account of the facts of the case of the *Mignonette,* on which the guilt or innocence of Dudley and Stephens would in due course come to be determined as a matter of law. The full text, as recorded at the time, is given in an appendix to this study, and in the main its precise terms were not a subject of any dispute. Counsel made no suggestions for its improvement, and the jury agreed to it, paragraph by paragraph, apparently mostly by nods, for the shorthand transcript records little actually said. At one point the foreman did say that all the jurors thought Richard Parker was likely to die first, and this was incorporated. The foreman also said that, in the jury's view, "they would have died if they had not had this body to feed on." Baron Huddleston mendaciously steamrollered in reply, "That is as I put it." It was not; he read out the text, which was as follows: "That if the men had not fed upon the body of the boy they would, *probably* [my italics] not have survived. . . ." The jury weakly gave up the point, and that was their only positive contribution. The original draft, considerably amended, indicates how carefully Huddleston had prepared the text. Thus, for example, the original draft was amended to include the words "Captain Dudley asked forgiveness for us all if either of us was compelled to commit a rash act and that our souls might be saved." This was a cunning amendment, since it was designed to rule out the defense of insanity under the McNaghten rules. The jury would not know this, though counsel would.

To judge from the extent of amendment and redrafting, most care was devoted by Huddleston to working out precisely what the jury should be made to say about the necessity of killing Richard Parker. This was the most delicate question, and if the full text of the special verdict is studied in its context, it is characterized by an extraordinary omission. The whole case turned on the question: Was it necessary, in the circumstances, to kill Richard Parker? This central question could of course be analyzed into two questions. First, was it necessary to kill anyone? Second, if yes, should Richard Parker have been selected? Whether viewed as one question or two, one would expect the jurymen to have been given an opportunity to state their view as to the correct answer or answers. But the special verdict contains no finding one way or the other as to whether it was necessary to kill Richard Parker or anyone. This extraordinary omission was not accidental. It is clear from the draft that originally Baron Huddleston had in mind presenting the jury with a question to answer: "Was there any absolute necessity for killing Parker rather than any one of the other three men?'' Presumably suspecting that this was dangerous, since the jury might answer yes, he changed his mind and instead drafted a statement, giving the right answer: "It was no more absolutely essential to kill Parker than any one of the other three men.'' This might, he no doubt hoped, cut out any possible finding that it *had* been necessary to kill anyone. Further reflection by the baron led him to conclude that even this approach was dangerous; the jury might not agree and might say it had been essential. It was safer to give the jurymen no chance whatever to say whether killing anyone was necessary or not. And so a further amendment produced this draft: "Assuming any necessity to kill anybody there was no greater necessity for killing the boy than any of the other three men.'' Baron Huddleston set about selling this text to the jury, which he succeeded in doing by a disreputable trick:

> Now comes another question which I shall ask you to tell me. According to the view some people take and in that very case I have referred to where a man was in this strait, they ought not to allow the stronger to have power over the weaker, but they ought all morally speaking to have the same chance and that there was no more necessity that they should kill the boy than that they should kill one of themselves. All they required was something to eat: but the necessity of something to eat does not create the necessity of taking and excuse the taking of the boy. That is the question—was there any necessity of taking that boy rather than drawing lots. I should think you would consider no. Therefore, I propose to add this.

He then read out his final draft. So the jurymen assented, presumably thinking that they were agreeing to uphold the custom of the sea, which required lots to be drawn.

By this ingenious tactic Baron Huddleston had headed off any risk that the jury might find it had been essential to kill someone, even Richard Parker, and also any explicit suggestion that lot drawing was appropriate. Now in the theory of the law, questions of law are for the judges to decide, and questions of fact are for the jury. The distinction between what is viewed as one or the other is fraught with difficulty; but in the case of the *Mignonette,* a straightforward view would be that it was a matter of law whether there existed a defense of necessity (distinct from self-defense) that entitled one to kill to save life and a question of fact whether, in these particular circumstances, it had actually been necessary to kill either anyone at all or specifically Richard Parker. But if the jury had found as a fact that it had been necessary to kill someone or, worse still, necessary to kill Richard Parker, it would have looked extremely peculiar for the judges to announce subsequently that, in spite of such a finding, the law forbade what was necessary or essential. Law that said what was necessary should not be done would seem an ass. Indeed, Baron Huddleston may have been dimly aware that such a decision would rather look as if the judges were convicting someone whom the jury had, in a sense, already acquitted. Given the obscurity over the boundary between law and fact and the respective roles of judge and jury, it was safer to allow the jury no chance of expressing an opinion on the matter.

The final words of the special verdict indeed left the whole matter open: "But whether, upon the whole matter, the prisoners were and are guilty of murder the jury are ignorant, and refer to the Court." This did not even hypothetically convict the accused if the law was that there was no defense of necessity or acquit if there was. Had the court eventually decided that there was in law a defense of necessity that entitled the prisoners to kill one of their number, the verdict would have led to an absurdity, there being no finding of fact as to whether it had been necessary to kill anyone at all. But Huddleston knew perfectly well that the outcome of the case was already determined and that this problem would never arise.

And so the proceedings ended with the renewal of bail for Dudley and Stephens—this time the surety was Thomas Houston Kirk, a partner in the legal firm of Simpson, Kirk, and Donaldson of 183 West George Street, Glasgow, whose yacht Dudley had captained. The two men were free to leave the court, and Baron Huddleston, having scored something of a triumph, went off to try a City case in the Guildhall. Next day the *Times* congratulated Huddleston on his firm stand on the law: "The English law as laid down by Baron Huddleston is averse from entertaining the notion that peril from starvation is an excuse for homicide. It would be dangerous to affirm the contrary, and tell seafaring men that they may freely eat others in extreme circumstances, and that the cabin boy may be consumed if provisions run out."

During the trial Baron Huddleston, in the course of seeing the idea of a special verdict to the jury, did not make it at all clear which superior court would in due course finally determine the guilt or innocence of Dudley and Stephens. Since the use of special verdicts had been so long obsolete, he may not have been himself entirely clear on the matter, or clear as to the proper procedure to be followed to bring the case before whichever superior court was to hear it. At the close of the trial, Dudley and Stephens were bailed to reappear at the next Cornwall assizes at Bodmin, to be held "after the Judges of Her Majesty's High Court of Justice shall have given a decision upon the question of a special verdict which has been found against them [*sic*]." It seems to have been envisaged that the judges in London (in whatever court they sat) would give a decision, and if it went against Dudley and Stephens (as it was obviously going to), they would have to travel back down to Bodmin or another assize town and be sentenced there for their crime, unless of course they received a free pardon first. Possibly Baron Huddleston thought so bizarre an arrangement tolerable, since Dudley and Stephens would be receiving a free pardon anyway, and one more train journey would not hurt them; more probably, he expected the immediate granting of a free pardon. Although he never explicitly said so, it is reasonably clear that he was persuaded that the power to try cases conferred by the commission of assize—the formal document authorizing judges to go on circuit and determine criminal cases—conferred only a power to try them locally, on the circuit, and that the essential parts of the trial, including the sentence, must take place on the circuit. To satisfy this requirement, the case of *Regina v. Dudley and Stephens* would have to conclude, as it had begun, in the West Country.

But in order to keep his procedural options open, once the last case had been heard at Exeter, Huddleston adjourned the assizes from his lodgings in Exeter to his room at the Royal Courts of Justice in the Strand in London, fixing November 25 as the date at which the matter could be taken up again. Theoretically this provided for a continuation of the Cornwall assizes in London, and this Gilbertian make-believe would seem to have been at odds with Baron Huddleston's idea that assizes must be taken locally. But he does not appear to have been troubled about discussing the point of law in London, as long as the essential steps in the trial took place locally. Adjournment to London also served to hedge bets—the technicalities were easier sorted out in London than in the wilds of the West Country, where law books and legal advice were not so easily come by.

Meanwhile steps must have been taken, in anticipation of the London hearing, to have the special verdict written out on parchment in preparation for whatever solemn argument that was to take place in London. Elegantly engrossed, the special verdict was then stabbed mercilessly through the middle to produce, using the mediaeval system of data storage, a complete file of all the indictments presented at Exeter; the massive and now filthy bundle, in which has been put the paper book used to draft the special verdict, is in the Public Record Office. Such a file was procedurally in order if the special verdict was to be brought before the judges by the process known as *certiorari,* employed back in the eighteenth century, when special verdicts had last been used, and indicates that somebody imagined that this old procedure would be followed. This certainly was the expectation of James Read, the deputy clerk of assize at Exeter.

At some point after the conclusion of the trial, but before the special verdict itself was engrossed, Baron Huddleston realized that he had made a serious and possibly disastrous blunder. In the original draft of the special verdict, the *Mignonette* had been described as an "English Merchant vessel." For some reason or other, Baron Huddleston had second thoughts and deleted this, substituting the description "yacht." The version read out and assented to by the jury read, "an English yacht" and went on to say that the sailors "were compelled to put into an open boat." It did not say that the *Mignonette* was a registered English yacht, and it did not say that the boat was the *Mignonette*'s boat. Both points might prove to be quite critically important in relation to the question of jurisdiction—if the *Mignonette* might be, for all the superior court officially knew, any old English yacht (perhaps registered as a French vessel) or if the dinghy was any old dinghy, the English courts might have no power to try the men at all. Thus Baron Huddleston quietly altered the text so that the special verdict now said that the *Mignonette* was "a registered English vessel" and that the dinghy was one "belonging to the said yacht." Both the original paper book and the minute book of the deputy clerk of assize clearly show the amendments. Baron Huddleston was not, however, eager to draw attention to this possibly critical cosmetic work, and it was too late to ask the jury whether it agreed or not.

On November 25, the Cornwall assizes opened again in number 2 court in the Royal Courts of Justice in the Strand before Baron Huddleston. The attorney general appeared for the Crown and admitted that there was a problem: "My lord, there is some difficulty in determining positively what is the right course of procedure. . . ." The difficulty arose because the structure of the courts had been radically altered by three recent acts of parliament, the Judicature Acts of 1873, 1875 and 1881; that is, since the old procedure by special verdict had last been used. In consequence, the mechanism that had been used in the eighteenth century to move a case from assizes to a bench of judges in London, sitting as the Court of Queen's or King's Bench, no longer seemed appropriate.

This requires some explanation. In the days before the judicature acts, an assize court was an entirely distinct institution from the Court of King's (or Queen's) Bench, sitting in London and, when operating as a multi-judge court (known as sitting *in banc*—as a bench), comprising the chief justice and the other judges. The basis for the jurisdiction of the two courts was quite distinct, and the Court of King's (or Queen's) Bench was the senior court, possessing a general supervisory function over lower courts, including an assize court. By a procedure initiated by a writ of *certiorari,* the Court of Queen's Bench had a power to move the formal record of an assize court before it, and on this it could adjudicate. So when a special verdict was recorded in the old days, this record could be moved from the lower court of assize to the distinct and senior Court of Queen's Bench, and the matter would be there determined.

All this had now changed. By Section 3 of the act of 1873, which came into force in 1876, the Court of Queen's Bench, as a distinct institution, had been abolished. It and all assize courts had been fused into a single institution, known as the High Court of Justice. This single court operated both in London and out on the circuits in what were still loosely called "assize courts"; but whether the judges went on circuit or sat in London, they were simply the visible manifestations of a single unified High Court of Justice. So it no longer made any sense to move the case of *Regina v. Dudley and Stephens* by writ of *certiorari;* there was in legal theory nowhere to move it from or to. Move about physically as it might, the case was in the same court all the time. The Queen's Bench only survived not as a court but as an administrative internal division within a court—the single High Court of Justice. These divisions, of which there were a number, had a variety of functions; judges belonged to one division or another, but they did not constitute distinct courts.

Normally the High Court of Justice visibly manifested itself or operated through single judges sitting alone. But there was embodied in the Judicature Act of 1873 (by Section 40) an arrangement by which the high court could function as a bench of five judges to deal with difficult points of criminal law and give a solemn decision regarded as binding on all criminal courts. However this procedure applied only when the court was exercising the powers of the Court of Crown Cases Reserved, which, as we have seen, had been established by an Act of 1848—indeed, this five-judge tribunal continued to be called the Court of Crown Cases Reserved (and sometimes the Court of Criminal Appeal) until it was abolished in 1907. But for a case to be brought before it, there must have been a *conviction,* and Dudley and Stephens had not been convicted. So it was not available.

No doubt somewhat baffled by the problem posed by Baron Huddleston's ill thought-out ingenuity, the attorney general suggested that matters might be handled satisfactorily by adopting a strange, hitherto unknown form of procedure. Assize judges were given their authority to try cases as judges of the High Court of Justice by being listed on the commissions of assize issued on behalf of Her Majesty—for crime, these were known as the commissions of *oyer* and *terminer* (authority to hear and determine) and gaol delivery (empty the gaols). In 1884, it was the practice to put all the judges of the Queen's Bench Division on the commissions; hence, if Baron Huddleston had succumbed to gout or another disability, any other available judge could have caught a train down to Exeter and conducted the assizes there validly as the local visible embodiment of the ghostly unified High Court of Justice. The attorney general suggested that the case could be conducted in London as a continuation of the Cornwall assizes but that Baron Huddleston should call in a few other high court judges to rally round, as it were, and help run the proceedings, thus providing an authoritative multijudge court: "I presume your lordship would seek the assistance of other judges sitting with yourself to determine the case and if they sat as Commissioners under the Commission, and if, too, the Assize being adjourned, they would have jurisdiction both as to time and place to continue the sitting as if they were sitting as Commissioners of Oyer and Terminer and Gaol Delivery." He argued further that, once the jury had given its special verdict, Huddleston could have simply ruled on the law himself and sentenced the men to death at Exeter; he and any other judges he cared to call in could do the same in London. This idea would have kept the case in a court of the same level, but a larger, more populous one. The attorney general no doubt hoped that such a larger court's decision would carry more weight as a precedent, for a decision on assize by a single judge was not binding on other judges at all.

Baron Huddleston was understandaby somewhat puzzled. He had imagined the case coming before a higher court, not simply the same assize court, expanded to become more populous. Neither he nor anyone else had ever heard of a criminal court picking up additional judges as it went along. He was also worried about the location of the proceedings—what he called "venue." Surely the Cornwall assizes should take place in Cornwall, not London. But he agreed to adjourn the "Cornwall" assizes once again to London on December 4. This obviously made matters neither better nor worse. It did not involve any decision as to the right procedure.

In the course of these inconclusive proceedings, it became clear that Arthur Collins had suspicions about the surreptitious amendment of the special verdict. He asked for a copy of the shorthand note of the hearing, and the following comical exchange took place:

Baron Huddleston:	Shorthand notes of what?
Mr. Collins:	Of the trial.
Baron Huddleston:	What do you want the shorthand notes of the trial for?
Mr. Collins:	I wish to read it, my lord.

On this note of menace, which cannot have been lost on Baron Huddleston, the proceedings ended. *Regina v. Dudley and Stephens* was now, procedurally, a complete mess.

The case was now set down for solemn argument on December 4, and Dudley and Stephens, who had been bailed to reappear at Bodmin, were told to come to London instead (no legal basis for this order ever appeared). The lord chief justice, Lord Coleridge, made arrangements to sit himself as presiding judge, assisted by Baron Huddleston (whose views had now been formally stated twice) and three other judges: Grove, Denman, and Pollock. These were selected by their seniority. What court the lord chief justice thought he was convening is unclear, but he presumably imagined that he was to preside over the Cornwall assizes, conducted in London before five judges, only one of whom had attended the first part of the trial at Exeter. Behind the scenes, nervousness still prevailed over the validity of all this, and it may have been the lord chief justice himself who became uneasy, though there is no direct evidence of this. Be that as it may, it was in the lord chief justice's court that the matter was next raised.

On December 2, having arranged for a shorthand writer to be present, the attorney general explained that he now thought "there would be some peril" in following his own earlier suggestion. What the peril was he never explained; but a note in the *Times Law Reports* by W. F. Finlason probably gives the correct explanation. It had been discovered that the commission of assize for Cornwall listed not only all the judges of the Queen's Bench Division but judges from other divisions, too—for example, the Chancery Division. Thus, if anyone Baron Huddleston cared to call from those listed could hear the case in London, in theory it could have been determined by judges who did not belong to the Queen's Bench division at all. But perusal of the statute book had revealed that the Judicature Act of 1873 transferred the old power of the Court of Queen's Bench, which used to rule on special verdicts in the eighteenth century (sitting *in banc*), to the new High Court of Justice operating through a divisional court of the Queen's Bench Division. Hence *Regina v. Dudley and Stephens* should be determined by judges of that division only. Alternatively, he may have been worried about the unprecedented nature of the swelling, moving, Cornwall assize court.

The attorney general must have informed Arthur Collins of his application, but there is no evidence that Collins attended, much less contested the matter, and the only possible explanation is that a deal had been made between them—of precisely what form is obscure. The attorney general presented his new idea by asking the lord chief justice "to allow the case to be taken by that Court which represents the old Court of the Queen's Bench." He wanted it clear when the five judges sat that they were to be called not an assize court but something else. How this labeling was to be done he did not quite know: "I do not know what outward sign is made in constituting a Court." But he suggested specifically that all should be judges assigned to the Queen's Bench division and that "the Court, certainly so far as it can be constituted, should sit not as the Court of Queen's Bench, but as the Queen's Bench Division." What court he had in mind was not very clear, and Lord Coleridge pointed out that "the Court of Queen's Bench no longer exists." The attorney general replied that "there was a transfer from the Old Court of Queen's Bench to the Queen's Bench as a division, and it is to this court as a division now taking on itself the duties of the Court of Queen's Bench that I shall have to bring this Record of the Trial at the Assizes." So the lord chief justice agreed to announce that the court on December 4 would be sitting as the Queen's Bench Division, the inheritors, as it were, of the old Court of Queen's Bench. In the course of the discussion Lord Coleridge indicated that he agreed with the attorney general's uneasiness about the original scheme. The proceedings must take place in the Queen's Bench division. The fact that most of the trial had already taken place on circuit was not mentioned as a difficulty.

Even after the case had been finally determined, some uncertainty seems to have prevailed as to what court did sit on December 4, and in 1885 a special note was published in the law reports, explaining that, "though the assizes had been adjourned until 4 December, the day on which the case was argued, the argument was heard by the judges not as commissioners of assize, but as judges of the Queen's Bench Division of the High Court of Justice." But what was the ghostly relic of the old Court of Queen's Bench? In fact the Judicature Act of 1873, which governed the matter, had made special provision for what were called "divisional courts" to handle matters that had been handled in the past by judges of the Queen's Bench sitting *in banc*—it described these matters as "such causes and matters as are not proper to be heard by a single judge." But the act quite specifically provided that these divisional courts should consist at most of two or three judges. Even if the case of *Regina v. Dudley and Stephens* had been transferred lawfully from judge and jury in Exeter to a bench of judges in London, the court that heard it was wrongly constituted. This may have been a simple mistake, but more probably it was done deliberately to confer on the decision an authority as a precedent equivalent to that of the Court of Crown Cases Reserved, for this quest for authority was the whole point of the operation. Arthur Collins either willingly went along with this or was simply incompetent. His general failure to raise the fundamental procedural difficulties is more easily compatible with the first suggestion; it is a point to which we must return. Since the validity of the procedure was never really challenged, one cannot say whether Collins would have succeeded if he had objected. It is a curious fact that, when the court system was reviewed again in the Judicature Act of 1925, it was specifically provided that an excessive number of judges did not invalidate a decision of a divisional court. I suspect that memories of 1884 may explain this.

9
A Lawyer's Question

Tried by a jury and five judges as well
What they have suffered it is hard to tell,
They have been condemned and sent back to gaol,
And quickly respited they need not bewail,
The Queen in her mercy can soon set them free
And so end this terrible tale of the sea.

—"The Terrible Tale of the Sea"

For the argument before the five judges on December 4, the Crown was represented by no fewer than four counsel, led by the attorney general himself, Sir Henry James. With him appeared Mr. Arthur Charles, Q.C.; Charles Mathews; and William Danckwerts, who had handled the case originally in Falmouth. This unusual array of legal talent reflected the official view of the importance of the case. Arthur Collins, Q.C., again led for the defense, assisted by two junior counsel, Henry Clark (recorder of Tiverton) and Lionel Edward Pyke. The choice was not accidental. Henry Clark (1829–1900) came from Efford Manor, Plymouth, and was a yachtsman of the Royal Western Yacht Club. Lionel Pyke (1854–99) practiced at the admiralty bar and specialized in wreck inquiries. He too was a yachtsman, associated with the Royal Thames, owning the 36-ton *Albicore*. When the proceedings opened, there was some uncertainty as to whether protocol required the prisoners to be present; Dudley and Stephens were outside the court on the advice of their counsel. Collins pointed out that they had been bailed to appear in Cornwall, not in London, but did not press the point that it was somewhat mysterious how the duty to turn up in Exeter had become a duty (or perhaps a right) to turn up at the Royal Courts of Justice in the

Strand. So the two prisoners, who must have been somewhat puzzled by all this, came into the court and sat down near their counsel. The hearing then began with the production of the elaborate record of the proceedings at Exeter, prepared by James Read, deputy clerk of assize. Tucked into the file, where it still remains, was the original rough draft of the special verdict. The clerk of assize of the Western circuit, William Channell Bovill, formally produced the record and passed it to J. R. Mellor, master of the Crown office, who proceeded to read it. This ritual must have taken some considerable time, as the document rehearsed the full commission of assize authorizing the assizes to be held, naming the assize judges, whose authority it was, and went on through the finding of the grand jury until it eventually reached the trial itself and the special verdict. The named commissioners of assize included not only the Queen's Bench judges but also the master of the rolls and lords justices of appeal and even Arthur Collins himself; and they were authorized inquiry into a remarkable catalog of mischiefs, including "Clippings, Washings and False Coinings" as well as engaging malefactions like "Riots, Routs, Retentions, Escapes, Contempts, Falsities, Negligences, Concealments, Maintenances, Oppressions, Champarties," etc. The text of the special verdict itself had been written up in two hands on different sheets, crudely joined, the second obviously representing second thoughts.

Why this business had been engaged in soon became clear. Once the special verdict had been read out, Arthur Collins, having confirmed that it had indeed been tampered with, objected to the inclusion of the words "a registered British vessel" and "a boat belonging to the vessel," and Sir Henry James at once conceded the point. "He believed they were not in the verdict as given by the jury, and they had been added from the judge's notes, but he did not think they were material, and was willing they should be omitted." Baron Huddleston made a half-hearted attempt to justify the amendments, relying on an old precedent for amending such verdicts from the judge's notes (*Hazel's Case,* 1785, the last case in which a special verdict had come before a King's Bench). But he agreed that the words had better be removed, and they were. This excised the first illicit amendments. To be fair to Baron Huddleston, *Archbold's Criminal Pleading and Evidence,* the standard treatise on criminal law, did suggest that a certain measure of tampering was in order if based on the judge's notes.

Arthur Collins now raised a more radical textual difficulty, which turned upon the relative function of judge and jury in a criminal trial. The special verdict, as recorded in Exeter by James Read, concluded with the words "But whether upon the whole matter the prisoners were or are guilty of murder the Jury are ignorant and refer to the Court." This formal conclusion had indeed been read out verbatim at the trial, and as far as the transcript indicates, the jury had accepted it—no doubt the jurymen had no particular views on the text but understood that the judges (the court) would determine the guilt or innocence of the two men. Baron Huddleston had probably used this formal conclusion because it was that employed in two cases in Leach's law reports that he had consulted, *Rex v. Pedley* in 1782 and *Rex v. Hazel* in 1785, the most recent precedents to be found. But at some point before the hearing in London it had occurred to somebody that such a "verdict" appeared to hand over the determination of guilt or innocence entirely to the judges. Surely the jury should decide on guilt or innocence—to give *verdicts*—not judges. Further research into the precedents revealed that in *Rex v. Mackalley* (1612) and *Rex v. Oneby* (1727) this point had been taken care of by concluding the text with a *conditional* finding or verdict. In *Rex v. Oneby,* the text concluded, "Whether this is murder or manslaughter the jury pray the advice of the court, *and find accordingly*" (italics supplied). By including a conditional finding, the roles of the judge and the jurymen were kept conceptually distinct: the judges said what the law was, the jury gave the verdict of guilt or innocence, and the judges gave the judgment of ensuing action. Behind the scenes, the record of the special verdict prepared for the London hearing had been discretely altered to include such a conditional finding, saying, in effect, that if the judges ruled that in law the men were guilty of murder, manslaughter, or nothing, the jury found an appropriate and conforming verdict. This must have represented a change late in the day, after Crown counsel had studied the text as it emerged from Exeter, and thus explains the curious physical condition of the record. The original conclusion was presumably destroyed. Arthur Collins was able to show from the verbatim transcript that no such conditional verdict had ever been put to the jury at Exeter or agreed to by the jurymen. His point is confirmed by James Read's own minute book, which contains the text as read out in Exeter.

Since, Collins argued, the jury had never been asked what verdict they would give if the judges ruled one way or the other, it was impossible to tell and wrong to behave as if they had reached such a conclusion. Indeed, in the absence of a conditional finding of guilt or innocence, there had been no verdict of the jury at all, and the proceedings at Exeter were a mere nullity. This argument, at first sight an oversubtle essay in legal metaphysics, in reality raised a serious question: a jury in an ordinary murder case could always acquit entirely or find the accused guilty of manslaughter only, whatever the court said was the appropriate law or whatever verdict the judge indicated should be reached. Whether a jury had the mere power or the *right* to ignore the judge's indication (the orthodox American theory in the nineteenth century) was not wholly clear. But they could certainly do it. The form of the special verdict, in failing to give the jury its final say, transferred this final say to the judges, and that was in principle objectionable. As Collins put it, "unless there was a finding [i.e., a conditional "finding" or "verdict"] the judges would give the verdict." No doubt tact restrained him from using strong terms to describe the deliberate falsification of the record.

This point worried the judges, particularly Mr. Justice Grove, though all appeared to regard it merely as a point of form, not one of substance. After some argument, Mr. Justice Grove said, "I must say my difficulty is not removed. I do not wish at all to dissent in a case where it is pure form, almost a clerical matter." But in the end he gave way, taking the view that, where the jury referred the facts to the court, it was not necessary for the jury to agree formally upon a "finding" or "verdict" at all; the long-winded conditional verdict did not in fact matter. This view was accepted by Lord Coleridge, who explained the position as follows: "The facts they have found, and the court is to give Judgment upon the facts they have so found. It is not a question of verdict at all." So the theory adopted was that in a case where a "special verdict" was found, there was in fact no verdict in the sense of a final determination of guilt or innocence by the jury at all. That particular stage in a criminal trial when the jury decided on guilt or innocence was completely left out. This theory was to cause difficulty later in the proceedings. Of course, the alternative—an agreed-upon conditional verdict—was little more than a formalized recognition of the impropriety of omitting a vital stage in a criminal trial. In either eventuality, the reality was that the judges usurped the jurymen's right to adjudge finally on guilt or innocence. In the end, Lord Coleridge too must have had second thoughts; in the version of the special verdict he read out before giving judgment, he included at the end a conditional finding further amending what had been inserted into the record, thus preserving in theory at least the principle that juries give verdicts, not judges.

But this was simply cooking the books: the jury had never agreed to it, and he knew that.

These were in the nature of preliminary skirmishes, and it was now Sir Henry James's turn to argue that the men were in law guilty of murder. Essentially his contention was that, apart from the obscure story of the seven English sailors from St. Christopher (which involved no reported legal decision), there was no authority or precedent in favor of the claim that an innocent person could be lawfully killed by another to save the latter's life. He submitted that "except in cases of legal process [i.e., legal execution or the like] or actual warfare, where a person took the life of another it could only be justified on the ground of self-defence." The judges consulted and indicated that they had a strong impression that the crime of murder had indeed been committed; at this stage there was no need for the attorney general to continue his argument. Lord Coleridge then called on Arthur Collins to present his contrary argument for the prisoners, "to see if he can remove the very strong impression at present upon our minds." He was asked to confine his argument to murder—either the killing of Richard Parker was murder or no crime at all. The possibility that it might be manslaughter was peremptorily ruled out and excised from the record, without being discussed at all. Yet in principle it could well have been ruled that the circumstances partially exonerated the accused, reducing any crime to manslaughter.

Arthur Collins had two principal arguments. One concerned jurisdiction. At the Exeter trial there had been some obscurity as to the basis of the right to try the men in England at all. Collins seems to have thought it critical for the prosecution to show that the offense had been committed on a British ship or in a dinghy belonging to such a ship. With the amendments to the special verdict now removed, for all the jury had found, the killing might have been on a Chinese ship. The judges were hostile—surely it was clear from the verdict that this was an English yacht and the dinghy her dinghy? So the point was not viewed sympathetically; to have accepted it would have been the end of the case. At this point in the argument neither Collins nor anyone else appears to have realized that, under Section 267 of the Merchant Shipping Act of 1854, English courts were given jurisdiction over crimes, wherever committed, by seamen employed on British ships at the time of the offense or shortly before; so the argument was completely ill-informed. Before judgment was given this had been discovered, and the section was eventually quoted by Lord Coleridge to justify the assumption of jurisdiction.

Collins's other contention was that English law did recognize a defense of "necessity" that applied to such a case and justified or excused the killing of Richard Parker. It was with this contention that the court was primarily concerned and for which the case is remembered by lawyers. On the legal authorities and arguments relating to "necessity" there is a very considerable literature; and the two cases that have squarely confronted the issue in relation to homicide, *U.S. v. Holmes* (1842) and *Regina v. Dudley and Stephens,* will no doubt continue to generate legal controversy for some time to come. The problems involved are often discussed by reference to hypothetical examples, the best known being Cicero's predicament of the two drowning men and the plank adequate to support only one. Another stock example is that of the mountaineer who cuts the rope holding a companion and thus saves his own life; after the disaster on the first ascent of the Matterhorn it was even said, quite unfairly, that this had happened. And a letter to the press by one "H.W.L." in 1884 (I have not traced the newspaper in which it appeared) claims that in 1843 a naturalist, Professor James Wilson, heard when visiting St. Kilda that a local had indeed cut a rope in classic fashion to save his life when catching gulls on the cliffs of that island; the letter is quoted in the *American Law Review*. Less well known is the story of the Russian master and servant riding a sledge and pursued by wolves. Their horses were cut loose one by one to satisfy the pack, until only one remained, and the insatiable creatures began to gain on the sledge. The master's altruistic suicide, his ejection of the servant in order to increase speed, the servant's ejection in order that the wolves might be delayed by eating him, the servant's killing plus ejection to save him from a more horrible death, etc.—all these possible courses of action are elaborately analyzed with the use of the casuist's doctrine of double effect by a Roman Catholic writer (R. F. Clarke) in the *Month* in 1885. The theoretical problems involved and the arguments offered are complicated still further by the existence of cases of homicide where it had been contended, and sometimes accepted, that "duress" may provide a defense: that is to say, homicide may be no crime if the killer has been threatened with death or some other grave consequence, if he does not kill or participate in the killing of a third party. A person "forced" to kill by threats is obviously in a somewhat similar position to one "forced" to kill by circumstances. A full discussion of the legal arguments lies outside the scope of this book, but it might be said that the analysis of the issues involved by Arthur Collins and the judges who participated in the argument were not particularly sophisticated. One fundamental reason was their failure to separate clearly and analyze the different bases on which the claim to a defense of necessity can in principle be advanced.

The first and most radical thesis is that in desperate conditions, such as those confronting Dudley and Stephens, men are reduced by circumstances to a state in which it is incongruous to think of laws applying at all. They are in a state of nature, where there are no legal rights, duties, or crimes. A dramatic presentation of this thesis was put forward by David Brown in defending Alexander William Holmes:

> This case, in order to embrace all its horrible relations, ought to be decided in a long boat, hundreds of leagues from the shore, loaded to the very gunwale, with forty-two half naked victims with provisions only sufficient to prolong the agonies of famine and of thirst. . . . Decided at such a tribunal, nature, intuition, would at once pronounce a verdict not only of acquittal but of commendation.

A slightly different way of putting the same idea is embodied in the saying "Necessity knows no law." Laws exist to regulate social arrangements in normal conditions, not in wholly abnormal conditions when society breaks down. Arthur Collins toyed with this approach, but he never formulated the idea involved at all clearly. The judges seem to have been quite incapable of grasping it, as is clear from this exchange:

Mr. Justice Denman:	Why was it more necessary to kill the boy than to kill one of the others. . . .
Baron Huddleston:	And if the boy had killed the captain in self-defence he would have been justified.
Mr. Collins:	Certainly.
Baron Huddleston:	Then how could it be lawful for the captain to kill him?
Mr. Collins:	It was necessary that one should be killed to save the rest.

If of course there is no law or, to put the same theory differently, if only the law of necessity exists, then questions of who is legally entitled to do what make no sense. The "state of nature" theory of necessity can be developed and supported in various different ways. Holmes's counsel, for example, made much of the absurdity and cruelty of a court attempting in normal comfortable retrospect to say what should or should not have been done in terrible conditions. The state of nature theory was also used there to support the argument that in the longboat the sailors owed no particular social or legal duty as sailors to the passengers: "But if the whole company were reduced to a state of nature, then the sailors were bound to no duty, not mutual, to the passengers . . . the sailor was no longer a sailor, but a drowning man." Baldwin, the judge in that case, accepted this thesis in principle, though he left it to the jury to say whether it applied on the facts. "Where, indeed, a case does arise, enhanced by this "law of necessity" the penal laws pass over such a case in silence; for law is made to meet but the ordinary exigencies of life."

The idea that extreme circumstances place men outside the ambit of the law is not always clearly separated from a rather different legal notion, that of jurisdiction. Survival cases, tending as they do to arise on the frontiers, may be geographically outside the jurisdiction of the court and for this technical reason beyond the reach of the law. This point is illustrated by the exoneration of Lieutenant Greely for the shooting of Private Henry; many cases of extremity may never have been considered appropriate for legal proceedings because of difficulties over jurisdiction in this technical sense. Indeed until the passing of the Merchant Shipping Act of 1854, it was by no means clear that killings in open boats at sea after shipwreck were within the jurisdiction of the English courts; what went on at sea was in this way outside the law. The idea that legal obligations were entirely dissolved on shipwreck was also encouraged by the old doctrine of maritime law, whereby, once a ship was lost at sea, all contractual obligations between seamen and ship-owner and all authority by officers over their men were dissolved.

The second possible basis for a defense of necessity is that in desperate conditions the actions of men are not truly voluntary; hence individuals who act under the pressures of extreme circumstances are not responsible for that they never choose to do. Where a charge of crime requires proof of a deliberate act (in murder, killing with malice aforethought), no such proof can be had. This thesis was advanced rather weakly by Collins, with little success:

Mr. Collins:	The prisoners have acted under necessity, and were forced to the act without their will.
Mr. Justice Denman:	They intended to kill the boy?
Mr. Collins:	Yes, but they were forced to it by necessity.

It is easy to see Collins's difficulty here. Throughout the case the deliberate quality of Dudley's act had been emphasized, and the same was true in *U.S. v. Holmes.* The facts of the two cases did not help to make this approach plausible. Common sense would perhaps suggest that responsibility can, however, be looked at as a matter of degree—perhaps Dudley and Stephens were not *fully* responsible. Collins made no attempt to argue this, nor did he attempt to argue that the men were temporarily in such an abnormal state of mind that truly free choice was excluded. Presumably he thought that such arguments were bound to be rejected by the court. At this time, the law governing mental abnormality did not embody any idea of *diminished* responsibility, as it now does; responsibility was an all-or-nothing idea. And, for reasons that have been explained, it was probably agreed that the defense of insanity (even temporary) could not possibly apply. There was at the time a curious medical label for partial derangement through starvation, "bulimia," but the concept was never mentioned in any of the arguments presented in court.

A third theoretical basis for a defense of necessity is more positive in form. In desperate conditions that present a choice between two grim alternatives, it is right to take any action, including killing, that will benefit the majority. It is better that some rather than all should die; any other principle simply condemns individuals to total inaction. This approach relies on the notion of general utility—the greatest happiness of the greatest number—and Dudley and Stephens were utilitarians, as their own account of the tragedy made clear; those with dependents and a chance to live must be preferred to a dying boy with none. Since men can adapt their actions only to what they expect to happen, not on what does in fact happen (for then it is too late), a utilitarian theory of necessity must be based on what the individuals foresee. This was appreciated in *U.S. v. Holmes* by Holmes's counsel, who ridiculed the prosecutor's contrary thesis. "They ask us to wait until the boat has sunk. We may, then, make an effort to prevent her from sinking. They tell us to wait till all are drowned. We may, then, make endeavours to save a part." Arthur Collins, like Holmes's counsel, of course put this utilitarian theory forward, but the judges seem to have found great difficulty with it. They could not see how a utilitarian theory could decide *which* individual should be killed for the benefit of the others, given the assumption of human equality. Dudley and Stephens thought that utility required the selection of those without wives and children dependent on them. The American court was not so worried by this problem of selection and thought that, in the absence of any other criteria, the selection should be by lot. This, as counsel put it, was "the law of the sea." The English judges did not like this way out of the impasse; the whole point of the prosecution was to reject the barbarous practices of seamen. Baron Huddleston himself thought the idea verged on the blasphemous, involving God in choosing the victim. But in the Queen's Bench division this solution never received a proper discussion, in part because Collins himself did not argue in its favor. This comes out in the following exchange:

> Mr. Baron Huddleston said the judge in [Holmes's] case went on the ground that lots had been cast, which he called an "appeal to Providence."
> Mr. Collins: The decision cannot be supported on that ground. . . .

Arthur Collins was not at all anxious to argue for the casting of lots since, according to the received version of the facts, none had been cast by his clients. So he was hardly likely to argue that lot casting exonerated them. Hence nobody in the case was prepared to argue seriously in favor of the custom of the sea.

The fourth possible theoretical basis for a defense of necessity differs from the others in treating desperate circumstances as merely an excuse for wrongdoing, not a justification, acceptable (if at all) because of a recognition of the frailty of human nature. This too was offered to the court by Collins at a number of points in his argument, for example, when he said, "The force of hunger was irresistible" and "This appears to come to this, that in any case natural necessity is an excuse—that is, that an absolute imminent necessity for the preservation of life is an excuse on the ground of natural necessity." This concedes that the killing is inherently wrong and cannot be *justified*. But, the argument goes, the actor should be nevertheless *excused* because he was placed by circumstances in a situation in which he found it very difficult or impossible to resist temptation. The judges in the case of Dudley and Stephens saw the problem in precisely this way: this was their preferred analysis. But the predominant view of English judges, then and now, is that it is just when temptations are strongest and the difficulties of self-control most acute that the law should reinforce the individual conscience with its threat of punishment. Hence there has always been a deep reluctance to treat temptations, however extreme, as anything more than factors that may in some cases mitigate punishment or entitle an accused to mercy, but not exempt him from conviction. In a murder case the court could not reduce the punishment; there could be only a death sentence. But the home secretary could advise the Queen to exercise the prerogative of mercy and reprieve or pardon. So the logic of the court's attitude was that necessity in capital cases was relevant to mercy only, never to conviction: a matter for the Home Office, not the courts.

The legal arguments in the case turned partly on commonsense suggestions as to what the law ought reasonably to be and partly upon an analysis of the legal authorities. Apart from the obscure St. Christopher case and the American case of *U.S. v. Holmes,* attention was focused on the few references to necessity by legal text writers—Henry de Bracton, Sir Francis Bacon, Sir Mathew Hale, Sir William Hawkins, Sir William Blackstone, Sir Michael Foster, Sir Edward East. But these and other stray references did not amount to very much, and realistically the position was as stated by Sir James Fitzjames Stephen in his *History of the Criminal Law of England,* published only the previous year, when he described the subject as "so vague that, if cases raising the question should ever occur the judges would practically be able to lay down any rule which they considered expedient." The defense of necessity had indeed been considered by a number of official bodies in the nineteenth century, though this was not brought out in argument. In 1839 in the Fourth Report of the Criminal Law Commissioners, their Digest of the Law (Article 39) had included a defense of necessity to homicide: so too did the digest published with the Seventh Report (1843), by Article 29. However, in 1846 the Commission on the Criminal Law in its second report favored leaving questions of necessity to royal mercy (see Article 19), following the India Law Commissioners' view. James Fitzjames Stephen's Homicide Law Amendment Bill of 1874 embodied a defense of necessity, which he defended before a select committee against criticisms from the senior judges, Baron Bramwell and Mr. Justice Blackburn. Stephens had changed his mind by 1884. But when the matter was considered by the criminal law commissioners (1878–79) who were concerned with a proposal to codify English criminal law, they had sat on the fence and came up with no concrete proposal; Stephen, the chief advocate of codification, had been one of the commissioners. His own solution, insofar as he offered one, was that such matters were best left unregulated to juries to settle, but this technique had been ruled out by Huddleston's devious bypassing of the jury. Stephen's solution was essentially that adopted in *U.S. v.*

Holmes, though nobody had the intelligence to point this out; it was perhaps too late. In any event, if the custom of the sea was to be declared bad *as a matter of law,* this solution was impossible.

At the conclusion of Collins's argument, and without calling on the attorney general to reply, the judges withdrew for a few moments to consult privately. They then returned into court, and Lord Coleridge announced, "We are all of opinion that the conviction should be affirmed: but we will put our reasons in writing and give them on Saturday next. Can you tell me what course you propose to invite us to take on affirming the conviction?" There having yet been no conviction, this announcement was confused indeed, and when the attorney general returned to court, a long discussion developed as to what should happen next. The attorney general thought that the correct procedure was "to ask your Lordships in this Court to pronounce judgment." Mr. Justice Denman was unclear as to what "judgement" here meant: "To pronounce judgement on the question of guilty or not guilty?" His puzzle arose because normally "judgment" meant judgment (i.e., sentence) of death; this sounded more like a verdict. But the attorney general meant by the term both what was normally called "judgment" and "sentence"—in this case, death. Collins's claim that the proceedings would end up with the judges usurping the function of the jury had now come to be vindicated, and the terminological confusion reflected this. As to the procedure, Baron Huddleston thought that the old practice had been for the judges in London to give their opinion on the point of law and send the case back to the assize court for sentence accordingly. He therefore anticipated the final stages taking place at Bodmin assizes in the spring of 1885. And, although the question carrying out the sentence was no doubt thought to be academic only, it too was raised—where should Dudley and Stephens be killed and by whom? There existed no national hanging service; executions were locally organized. Sir Henry James eventually managed to convince the lord chief justice and his colleagues that they, as the court that convicted the men, should pass sentence upon them—hence sentence of death should be pronounced in the Queen's Bench division in London, not back in Cornwall some months later.

Mr. Justice Denman then raised another problem. In an ordinary trial in a capital case, once the jury gave a verdict of guilty, the prisoner was always asked whether he could put forward any reason why judgment (i.e., sentence) of death should not be pronounced; if he did raise an objection, he was said to "move in arrest of judgment." An old case, *Rex v. Oneby* (1727), indicated that earlier, when the judges of the Court of King's Bench ruled against a prisoner on a special verdict, the prisoner was given four days to prepare, if he wished, such a motion in arrest of judgment. The court thought it only right to give Collins his four days to prepare his motion, though it was conceded that he had already given the court his reasons for saying that judgment should not be given against Dudley and Stephens, and was unlikely to think of anything new to add over the weekend. So the court now changed its mind and decided to record its formal decision at once that the men were guilty, not waiting until Saturday. Sentence would be passed on the next Tuesday; this gave Collins his four days. But Lord Coleridge could not bring himself to call the decision thus given at once a *verdict;* he knew verdicts were what juries gave. So he adopted the subterfuge of calling it a "judgement" (what judges gave). "We do not want, Mr. Collins, to shut you out from anything, and we will give our formal judgement now and we will give our reasons accompanied by the sentence on Tuesday next. That will give you 4 days to think of anything else." The consequence of this linguistic double thinking was another absurdity. The wretched Collins had four days to move in arrest of a judgment, but the formal judgment had already been given. As Lord Coleridge remarked sadly in the course of the unsavory manipulation of the procedures, "it is very difficult when we get into these technical things."

At the conclusion of the proceedings, Lord Coleridge ordered that Dudley and Stephens, who had sat no doubt bemused and alarmed when the arrangements for killing them had been under discussion, be removed to Holloway Prison. Today this is a women's prison, but in 1884 of its 741 cells most were used for men. It was selected, as Lord Coleridge explained, because "as far as there is a difference between prisons [it] is the most comfortable prison for them." Indeed it possessed central heating and separate modern toilets. Arthur Collins protested ineffectually against the legality of an order to imprison his clients when their only legal obligation was to surrender to their bail at Bodmin. His clients were now "convicted" murderers and could hardly remain at large on bail.

On the following Tuesday, December 9, Dudley and Stephens were brought back to court to hear Lord Coleridge deliver the reasons of the divisional court of Queen's Bench and pronounce sentence of death—an event bound to cause some consternation, for no death sentence had been pronounced in the Court of Queen's Bench since the case of Dr. Cameron in 1753, an incidence of treason arising out of the 1745 rebellion. Furthermore, as a court, this venerable institution no longer existed. Lord Coleridge's statement of the court's reasons needs to be read in full, though its rhetorical moral tone is easy to exemplify from such a passage as this:

> To preserve one's life is generally speaking a duty, but it may be the plainest and the highest duty to sacrifice it. War is full of instances in which it is a man's duty not to live, but to die. The duty, in case of shipwreck, of a captain to his crew, of the crew to the passengers, of soldiers to women and children, as in the noble case of the *Birkenhead;* these duties impose on men the moral necessity, not of the preservation, but of the sacrifice of their lives for others, from which in no country, least of all, it is to be hoped, in England, will men ever shrink, as indeed, they have not shrunk.

Essentially, his argument was this: to concede that the situation that confronted Dudley and Stephens provided them with an excuse for crime upon the ground of necessity would be to admit extreme temptation as exonerating individuals from criminal liability and bring about an absolute divorce between law and morality, which here forbade the killing of the innocent boy. The reasoning reflects a view of the judicial function according to which the duty of the judges is to lay down morally correct standards of behavior, even if they are standards that are hard to follow: "It must not be supposed that in refusing to admit temptation to be an excuse for crime it is forgotten how terrible the temptation was, how awful the suffering: how hard in such trials to keep the judgment straight and the conduct pure. We are often compelled to set up standards we cannot reach ourselves, and to lay down rules which we could not ourselves satisfy." This view of the judicial function in society, though not extinct, is no longer widely received, and this is one of the reasons why modern critics have found the opinion, expressed in a style appropriate to a sermon, pompous. We no longer believe in a hortatory function of legal opinions. The other reason why the opinion fails to convince is that Lord Coleridge never really dealt with the argument, poorly presented by Collins, that in extreme and desperate conditions, when there is only a choice between some or all dying, the proper course of action is to take steps to ensure that at least some survive. The utilitarian theory of balancing respective advantages and disadvantages was rejected in favor of the absolute sanctity of human life.

The opinion therefore presented the seafaring community with an exhortation to noble and self-sacrificial behavior or a recipe for total inactivity in the face of a crisis.

When Lord Coleridge had concluded the reading of his opinion, Tom Dudley and Edwin Stephens were called to stand and told, "You have been convicted of murder. What have you to say why the Court should not give you judgment to die?" This was presumably Arthur Collins's chance to move in arrest of judgment, but he had by now given up. Tom Dudley himself, presumably appalled by this grim invocation, said in a low voice that he threw himself on the mercy of the court. Lord Coleridge, caught between the demands of traditional ritualism and common humanity, compromised and without donning the black cap, passed sentence in these terms:

> You have been convicted of the crime of wilful murder, though you have been recommended by the jury most earnestly to the mercy of the Crown; a recommendation in which, as I understand, my learned brother who tried you concurs, and in which we all unanimously concur. It is my duty, however, as the organ of the Court, to pronounce on you the sentence of the law, and that sentence is that to the crime of which you have been convicted, you be taken to the prison where you came, and that, on a day appointed for the purpose of your execution you be there hanged by the neck until you be dead.

He was in fact required by an act of parliament to pass sentence of death formally, even if a pardon were inevitable. And on this less than cheerful note the prisoners were removed back to Holloway.

Although his clients had now been condemned to death, Arthur Collins's responsibility to them was not over. He could still have initiated proceedings by a little-used procedure known as a writ of error in order to have the proceedings declared a nullity, as had been done in Bradlaugh's case in 1878 and Orton's in 1881, the only recent instances. A modest amount of homework would have revealed that the court had been improperly constituted, and the *Law Journal* of December 13 claimed, without being specific, that "there is a technical question of procedure upon which many lawyers are sanguine of success." But this journal also indicated that the case was "over so far as lawyers are concerned" and that "the prisoners do not desire ever to have the appearance of being captious. They have from the beginning told their story frankly, and now they wish to know what is to be done with them as quickly as possible." Collins may have felt, with some justice, that from the outset his clients were bound to be convicted of murder and realized that the official enthusiasm for a formal decision against them, embodied in a great leading case, made the outcome quite inevitable. Furthermore, whereas a technical question of jurisdiction or a defense of necessity would free his clients completely, a technical ruling that the court was wrongly constituted would only lead to a retrial and further suffering for his clients. He may have felt sincerely that the best he could do for them was to cooperate with the somewhat shady procedures employed and rely on judicial support for a free pardon; indeed a bargain may have been struck. In effect he knew he was participating in a sort of charade and acted accordingly in the best interests of his clients. A more sinister explanation for his apparent weakness would be that he was then seeking official preferment, which he achieved when he was knighted and appointed chief justice of Madras the following year.

Tom Dudley and Edwin Stephens had now formally been adjudged guilty of deliberate murder, a decision that Dudley at least never accepted as just; they were legally condemned men. But it had been assumed throughout that they would promptly be pardoned. The London solicitors who represented them as agents for the Falmouth partnership of Fox and Tilly were Irvine and Hodges of 79 Mark Lane, and on December 4, that is, immediately on the judgment in the Queen's Bench division, they consigned to the Home Office a massive engrossed petition—"The Humble Petition of Thomas Dudley late Master and Edward [*sic*] Stephens late Mate of the Yacht 'Mignonette.' " Though signed by both men, neither in fact had a chance to read this old-world document, which simply set out the special verdict, requested a pardon, and concluded in solemn form with the time-honored conclusion: "And your Petitioners as in the strictest gratitude and duty bound shall ever pray etc." It was presumably prepared in advance in the hope that a death sentence would never have actually to be pronounced and its submission regarded by those who prepared it as form only. The document was received by the Home Office on Friday, December 5. Sir Adolphus Liddell minuted that, although there were precedents for a pardon before sentence was passed, it was not appropriate in this case; the matter should be deferred until sentence was passed or until the lord chief justice had been consulted. No doubt the reason for going through with the formal death sentence was to dramatize the condemnation of the custom of the sea. Hence it was that sentence of death was passed on the two men before any decision was taken or announced as to a pardon. The sentence was a cruel if essential formality, but no more; indeed the two men expected to be released immediately. But nothing happened, though the *Times* assured its readers on the morning following the death sentence that "the proceedings were, however, little more than formal. The Court earnestly recommended the prisoners to mercy, and no doubt a pardon will be granted by the Crown." But on December 11, the authorities were still silent as to what was to become of them. On the afternoon of December 9, after Dudley and Stephens had been returned to Holloway, the governor, Lt. Col. Everard Milman, had in fact told them that the home secretary had advised the Queen to respite the sentence of death, so they at least knew that they would not be executed soon. The *Times* later reported that "the prisoners, although the intelligence did not altogether come to them in the shape of a surprise, were evidently much relieved and pleased at the tidings." But to their puzzlement they were still not released, and behind the scenes the home secretary had issued instructions through Mr. Murdoch at the Home Office to the governor: "The prisoners are to be kept in Prison where they are at present, and not to be removed, or placed in the condemned cell, or anything of the kind, in short . . . they are to remain for the present absolutely *in statu quo*. . . ." For its part, meanwhile, the press reported a touching and possibly relevant incident. A mural tablet had been offered by Mr. John F. Haskins to Captain Mathews, foster father of Richard Parker; the idea of a tablet was changed to a tombstone, to be placed over the graves of Richard's mother and father in Pear Tree Churchyard, Itchen Ferry. I have not been able to establish any connection between Haskins and the Parker family. Haskins was an engineer and a member of the Institution of Mechanical Engineers, with an office in the City of London at 114a Queen Victoria Street. Edith Parker may have worked for him as a domestic, but this is a guess only. The stone was to read,

> Sacred to the memory of Richard Parker, aged seventeen years, who died at sea after nineteen days dreadful suffering in an open boat in the tropics, having been shipwrecked on the yacht Mignonette.
> Though he slay me yet will I trust him.
>
> Job XIII 15.

To this was added, at the instance of Richard Parker's elder brother, "Lord, lay not this sin to their charge.—Acts VII 60." It must have seemed to many that, if Richard's brother could pardon them, surely the Crown could. But the weekend came, and still nothing had been announced from the Home Office. Something appeared to be going wrong. On December 13, the Saturday the *Spectator* published a leading article dealing with the case, saying it was expected they would be pardoned. But for the first time the propriety of this was questioned:

> If they are, the case will have great interest to the mining community, a few of whom are every year exposed to the most frightful hunger and thirst, and indeed certainly die of them. It has hitherto been their habit to die quietly, and, as much evidence goes, in deep submission to the will of the Almighty; but henceforth they will have an alternative. They have only to kill the weakest amongst them, and eat him, and they will have the heartfelt sympathy of two thirds of the community. They will be legally liable to death, but that is only a form.

The ruling that the sailors were murderers appeared to be having an effect on the public attitude toward them—this indeed was the whole function of the legal decision. Opinion was moving against them.

At this time the prerogative of mercy was formally exercised by the Queen, but on the advice of the home secretary of the day, who was at this time Sir William Harcourt. That at least was the strict constitutional position established since the accession of the youthful Victoria, who was regarded as an unsuitable audience for the squalid details of capital cases. Since those days Queen Victoria had grown up a lot, and although the constitutional position remained the same, given her character, the reality was somewhat different.

The power to pardon under the prerogative of mercy was one of the mechanisms whereby the scale of infliction of capital punishment was reduced to tolerable proportions. In 1884 in strict law death was the only sanction for the crime of murder, and if all murderers had been hanged, the number of executions would have been alarming. During this period there were a very considerable number of murders, or killings that could be so categorized. Thus the coroner's returns for 1884 recorded no fewer than 192 victims of murder. Police returns, based on somewhat different principles, produced slightly lower but still large figures for the crime: in 1884, 170. Nothing like this number of prisoners were convicted of murder, much less sentenced to death. Many involved maternal killing of children under the age of one year: the mother would be convicted only of concealment of birth or manslaughter. This result was achieved either by prosecutorial discretion or by the refusal of juries to convict of murder if the full offense was charged. In other cases juries might acquit altogether (acquittal rates, calculated in some uncertain way, ran at about 22%) or, by convicting of manslaughter, give the judge the power either to impose the maximum sentence, imprisonment for life, or some lesser term. Through these and other mechanisms the number of death sentences actually pronounced was relatively small. The annual figure varied considerably; in 1884 it rose to the unusually high figure of 40, though the following year the number dropped back to a more normal 25. The number actually executed was reduced still further through the operation of the prerogative of mercy. Thus only 15 people were executed in 1884. The majority of those reprieved were given life sentences instead, but a small number were transferred to Broadmoor as criminal lunatics. Very occasionally other courses of action were adopted; thus there was one free pardon in 1884, and in two cases a sentence of 10 years' penal servitude was substituted, one in 1880 and one in 1883. In 1879, one capital sentence was commuted merely to a term of one year's imprisonment at hard labor; this was probably the pathetic case of Emma Wade, a 19-year-old servant girl who had poisoned herself and her illegitimate baby with Battles Vermin Killer. She recovered, but the baby died. Life sentences at this time involved serving 20 years in prison.

The home secretary did not of course act arbitrarily in advising the Queen on pardons and reprieves. He consulted the trial judge, took into account any recommendation of mercy from the jury, and thereafter acted in accordance with the accepted practice of the department, advised by his officials. From the accounts published in the annual *Judicial Statistics,* it is clear that many cases fell into recognized categories—the convicted person was a woman discovered to be pregnant; the death was an accident incidental to an illegal abortion; there were indications of delusions, imbecility, or insanity; the individual had been severely provoked. The decision to recommend a pardon was taken by the home secretary in person in problematic cases but by the officials if the case fell into a standard category.

Sir William Harcourt himself had quite definite and firm views about capital punishment. In a debate in 1878, he had explained that personally he favored its abolition, but in his official capacity he recognized that public opinion was not yet ready for this; in this complex sense, he "firmly believed in capital punishment." In January 1882 he had introduced to the cabinet a bill to create degrees of murder, retaining only capital punishment for a first degree crime, where there was a deliberate intention to kill; the English definition of murder at the time went well beyond this. In those types of murder where no such intent could be proved there would be penal servitude for life or a shorter term. This bill was not, however, proceeded with; apparently the judges opposed it. Earlier, in a debate in June of 1881 on a capital punishment (abolition) bill, Harcourt explained further the function and practice of the home secretary in advising the sovereign on the exercise of the prerogative of mercy. Where the jury recommended mercy, the capital sentence was, he said, *never* executed; such cases were straightforward. The principal function of the home secretary, as he saw it, was to differentiate between deliberate killings, where capital punishment was appropriate, and other killings, where it was not. The prerogative of mercy served to draw a distinction that in his view could well be built into the law but in fact was not. He had attempted to have the distinction enacted and gave up only because of strong judicial feeling that the framing of an appropriate law presented insuperable drafting difficulties. At this period it was more or less a constitutional convention that criminal law was a matter for the judges, not for governments or parliament.

Given such views, the case of Dudley and Stephens presented a serious problem to Sir William. Capital punishment was quite out of the question, but this was a clear case of deliberate killing and one that the judges had solemnly declared to be murder. It was not the function of the home secretary, in his view, to act as a court of appeal from the judges on question of law. If they ruled the crime to be deliberate and unjustifiable murder, they were to be taken seriously; consequently the sentence should be commuted to one of life imprisonment. Any further leniency would make a mockery of the judges' ruling.

Sir William's firm attitude may have been strengthened by his unfortunate brushes with Queen Victoria over the prerogative of mercy. She thought he was much too soft, particularly to those who killed their wives. "Men," she once pointed out acidly, "are lenient to criminals who murder their wives." Relations between the Queen and her home secretary reached a particularly low point over John Richmond, a 19-year-old laborer who had been convicted in 1881 at Durham assizes of murdering his wife with a poker; they lived apart and he had sought her out, quarreled, and then killed her. The Queen thought he should be hanged; her home secretary did not. Over this dispute Harcourt had even threatened to resign. The Queen gave way in the end, and peace was temporarily restored. But in June 1884 trouble burst out again over Emily (or Mary) Wilcox, a 31-year-old mother from Somerset who had killed her two-year-old illegitimate child. The Queen could see no reason for mercy, but Harcourt replied to her so effectively that she was for once actually put on the defensive, replying that his letter "gives her the impression that Sir William Harcourt thinks she wishes to be harsh and cruel." Again the Queen was prevailed upon to sign the conditional pardon, though with bad grace, consigning the wretched Emily Wilcox to imprisonment for life. Given these persistent disagreements, one would have expected the Queen to express strong views as to the treatment of Dudley and Stephens. But at the time she was wholly preoccupied with the fate of her idol General Gordon, and there is no evidence that she took any interest in the matter. But Sir William's earlier troubles with her may have strengthened his resolve to appear as a firm upholder of the law. The case was indeed a tricky one.

Of all departments of state, the Home Office seems always to have had more than its fair share of tricky problems to handle. In early December, when a decision had to be taken over Dudley and Stephens, the officials there can only have just got over the anxiety caused by the celebrated "Home Office Baby." A still-born infant had been posted to the Home Office, labelled "perishable," by an eccentric parson, the Rev. J. Mirehouse, rector of Colsterworth, who was in dispute with the home secretary over the closure of a burial ground and decided to make his point dramatically. Arriving on Sunday, November 2, the corpse gave the duty clerk a bad shock, and it was only later in the month that the matter was concluded by an opinion from the ecclesiastical lawyer, G. F. Phillimore, that posting babies to the Home Office was not an ecclesiastical offense for which the rector could be disciplined. About the first week in December, the weary officials turned their attention to the next problem—the case of the *Mignonette*—and the home secretary took the advice of the law officers. Part of the correspondence between Sir William Harcourt and the law officers (Sir Henry James and Sir Farrer Herschell) has been published, and other material survives in the Harcourt papers in the Bodleian Library. Sir Henry James had always been in favor of prosecuting Dudley and Stephens. An undated letter of his (probably of September) to Harcourt reads,

> When I was in London recently I paid a visit to Stephenson [the treasury solicitor] laid up with lumbago. I told him I thought the Mignonette people ought to be properly prosecuted—they certainly ought to be convicted for if the principle of these proceedings be admitted as correct and justifiable I shall decline for the future to sit near any man with a large appetite.

But the letter continued, "When convicted you can let them off." In December further discussion took place, and a long letter from Sir Henry, dated December 5, shows that Harcourt then had a life sentence in mind. Sir Henry argued against this: "If you announce a commutation to penal servitude for life or even to any other term you will never be able to maintain such a decision and you will have to give way." Sir Henry thought that the men had been almost insane, "in a state of comparative phrensy quite upsetting the ordinary balance of the mind." He also argued that if Arthur Collins had "sought to obtain a verdict of manslaughter the Jury would certainly have found the verdict and no judge would have inflicted more than three months' imprisonment." The solicitor general, Farrer Herschell, agreed.

Sir William set out his own views in reply in a long letter dictated to his son Lewis (a close friend of Sir Henry James), who was then acting as his private secretary. It read in some ways like an academic essay.

> If ever there was a case which required cool reflection and a firm mind it is a question like this that belongs to the most difficult problems of distributive justice. It is exactly to withstand an erroneous and perverted sentiment in such matters that we are placed in situations of painful responsibility. Everyone knows that the vulgar view of this subject at first was that the men had committed no crime.
>
> You and I accepted our several shares in the prosecution because we were convinced the men were guilty of murder. Murder you say *in* law, but the law declares that to be murder which has no moral justification or excuse. . . . The judgment of the Court in this case pronounces that to slay an innocent and unoffending person to save one's own life is not a justification or excuse, and it is therefore upon moral and ethical grounds, not upon technical grounds, that the law repels the loose and dangerous ideas floating about in the vulgar mind that such acts are venial or indeed anything short of the highest crime known to the law.

He also argued that, if he were to arrange a free pardon, "I should pronounce it an innocent act and deserving of no punishment. If I were to do that I should condemn the law and say I believe that it has arrived at an unjust conclusion." In a passage prophetic of problems that have arisen in modern times over the defense of duress, he added, "If to kill an innocent person to save your own life is an act deserving of pardon, by what right can a Fenian assassin be punished who kills, because the lot has fallen upon him to do the murder and if he does not execute it he knows his own life will be forfeited[?]" His letter continued to suggest by way of compromise a respite during the Queen's pleasure, so that "such measure of punishment may be finally awarded as may be deemed appropriate." In his journal Lewis Harcourt gives a full account of the further development of the controversy. On December 8 he had a long talk with his father, in which he argued strongly for a short sentence only. "He quite agreed that they should not go unpunished but took my view that it would be very mischievous to excite sympathy with them by the infliction of a long term of imprisonment." Lewis argued in favor of six months, and while he was away shooting at Woodcote, Sir William gave way. On December 12 it was decided that the sentence be commuted to six months' imprisonment, not at hard labor, to be dated from December 4, the date of judgment against them, not sentence. Lewis Harcourt noted, "This is very satisfactory as it is just the length of imprisonment for which I made such a fight, but I shall look with anxiety at the criticisms in the papers on it for if it goes off badly I shall be told that it was all my fault." But on his father's return on December 15, Sir William said kindly, "Well, I hope you are satisfied with the result of the Mignonette sentence. All the papers seem to approve." As we shall see, this was not quite accurate.

As far as Dudley and Stephens were concerned, the news, given to them on Saturday, December 13 by the governor, came as "a painful surprise." Phillipa Dudley, who had seen her husband the day before, said that "her husband did not ever dream that any punishment would be inflicted." He had expected to be home with his family in Sutton by Sunday; she added that all their savings had been consumed in the costs of the defense. There was talk in the press of further moves being taken to secure her husband's early release. Dudley and Stephens were at once deprived of the privileges they had previously enjoyed as "first class misdemeanants": visits, their own food, their own clothes, free exercise, and association with each other. The only concession was that their hair was not ritually cropped. This last was not on the instructions of the Home Office and must have been an act of kindness either by the governor or the prison doctor. Separately confined in 13-by-7-foot cells, but not wholly isolated as they would have been in more rigorous prisons, they began to serve their sentences for the murder of Richard Parker, and as a legal event, the case of the *Mignonette* was now concluded. Simultaneously Madame Tussaud's exhibition was reorganized to include what was described as an excellent waxwork portrait model of Captain Dudley, though whether he achieved the peculiar distinction of the Chamber of Horrors is not clear. The *Weekly Dispatch* commented, "Among the latest additions, which, with questionable taste to say the least, have been added . . . are models, of Captain Dudley, and Mrs. Gibbons. More acceptable are models of Mr. Irving and Miss Terry as Hamlet and Ophelia." Mrs. Gibbons, who had murdered her husband, certainly was placed in the Chamber, though she too was reprieved.

The judges had now solemnly pronounced the action of Dudley and Stephens to have been premeditated murder; their Queen, on the advice of her home secretary, had pardoned them on December 15 on condition that they served six months' imprisonment, not at hard labor. It was now time for the organs of public opinion to take stock of the whole affair, to consider how it had been handled, and what if anything, had been achieved.

Among the professional journals there had been reservations about the procedures followed, but the *Law Times* of December 13 expressed the general mood of satisfaction. The common law itself had come out well, and so had its lord chief justice: "The judgement of Lord Coleridge in the *Mignonette* case is universally recognised as having been perfect in its way. It consisted of a lucid exposition of the law and an eloquent statement of the code of morality which should govern the conduct of men whose lives are in peril, which he proved is in harmony with the prescription of the common law." Sir James Fitzjames Stephen, whose views had been relied upon by the defense, let it be known publicly that he entirely agreed with the judicial opinion of his senior colleagues, lest any crack in the judicial fabric weaken the authority of the decision. This was reported in the *Times* after the paper had been officially informed. The only sustained technical criticism of the judges' decision was published in the *National Review* and was the work of Sir George Sherston Baker, Bart.; it was he who had located and drawn attention to the seventeenth-century story of the seven sailors of St. Christopher in Tulpius's *Observationem medicarum*. Sir George was a barrister and legal writer, and his publications included works on international law and an edition of Archbold's *Practice of the Court of Quarter Sessions,* then a standard text. His argument was ingenious. Jurisdiction over incidents on the high seas had originally rested with the Court of Admiralty, which applied not the common law of England but a body of law of an international character based upon ideas derived from Roman law, or "civil" law, as it is technically called. This body of law incorporated maritime and mercantile custom. A series of acts of parliament, originating with one of 1536 and continued with acts of 1799; 1834; and 1844, had transferred the power to try criminal cases arising on the high seas from the Court of Admiralty, which no longer existed, to the common law judges. But, Baker argued, this transfer of jurisdiction did not alter the fact that the appropriate law to be applied was "civil" (i.e., Roman) law, not common law. While conceding that under the latter necessity was no defense, he argued that in civil law it was, citing as civil law authorities Leonardus Lessius's *De iustitia et iure* (1606), Juan de Lugo's *Disputationum de iustitia et iure* (1670), and Samuel von Pufendorf's *De officio hominis et civis iuxta legem naturalem* (1673) to support his argument. This, he argued, was the explanation of the exoneration of the sailors of St. Christopher—the colonial court had correctly applied civil law. Indeed Chief Justice Mansfield had explicitly ruled in *Regina v. Depardo* (1807) that the Admiralty applied civil law and maritime customs; and Baker, warming to his theme, contended that

> it might not be impossible to establish that the practice which has sometimes prevailed of casting lots for the purpose of saving some lives at sea to the prejudice of other lives, whether by granting them places in a boat, or by sacrificing others for their food, may be some old maritime custom, one of the *consuetudines marinae* spoken of by Lord Mansfield. Everard Otto, a commentator on the passage of Pufendorf, says: "Therefore the judgement of the lot will be necessary, as in the history of Jonah." That the appeal to the lot was a maritime custom at the time of the prophet Jonah appears from what is narrated in the Book of Jonah (Ch. 1 v. 7) when the prophet was going from Joppa to Tarshish. Joppa being on the Syrian coast and comparatively close to Rhodes, this maritime custom might very possibly be of Rhodian origin. This, if certain, would be a very curious fact, since the Rhodian sea laws are part of Admiralty law.

It is difficult to say what, if anything, the Queen's Bench would have made of this argument, if Collins had presented it. Somewhat similar points arose in *Regina v. Keyn* in 1877, and the majority decision in that case, though not directly to the point, would not have encouraged others to advance such a startling thesis, which would, I suspect, have been rejected.

But in general the national press welcomed both the theoretical decision of the judges and the practical solution adopted by Sir William Harcourt. Thus the *Saturday Review,* agreeing with the judges, described the notion that it was legitimate to draw lots in such circumstances as a "blasphemous absurdity" and the act of the two men as "a very base and wicked act." Lord Coleridge's opinion, the paper continued, "is in every respect worthy of his high office and of this serious occasion. In gravity, in dignity, and in subdued eloquence, it could not well be surpassed." On the legal principles involved, the leader writer was equally enthusiastic: "The Court . . . was really driven back to the elementary considerations on which all civilised systems of jurisprudence profess to be founded. To protect the rights of the weak when confronted by the violence of the strong, is one of the objects for which all law exists." It was "impossible to measure the consequences which might have followed" if any other decision had been given. Conceding the terrible sufferings of the men, the leader concluded, "but the depositories of power must hold fast to principles without which the earth would indeed be full of darkness and cruel habitations."

The *Times* took the same line, even deploring the "mawkish sympathy" shown to the men, though approving the pardon. But the leader writer addressed a warning to the seamen of England that, now the legal position was clear, future cannibals could expect no such clemency. Whether this message reached the forecastles of the merchant marine or was much discussed on the futtock shrouds one doubts.

The Roman Catholic *Month* discussed the decision as a question of moral theology and welcomed both the judges' ruling and the sentence of imprisonment: "If the men had been set free at once, the perverted moral sense of some of their fellow countrymen would have made heroes of them. If they had had a long term of imprisonment they would have had just reason to complain of being treated with undue severity." The decision vindicated the science of casuistry—this was a situation in which the distinction between right and wrong, though absolute, was "the distinction of a hair's breadth, one which mere commonsense and the judgement of the untrained moralist are quite unable to discern." The writer understandably did not explain how the unfortunate Tom Dudley—not a qualified casuist—was supposed to tell the difference in mid-ocean.

The *Spectator* took a particularly strong line in welcoming the decision. "The conviction that such murders are justified by the law of self-defence, and are not, therefore, illegal, is so general amongst seafaring men, and has so infected naval literature, that a solemn judgement to the contrary, pronounced by more than one judge, has become indispensable." The journal had held to this view consistently, and on December 13 another leader had, as we have seen, attacked the general expectation that the men would receive a free pardon. The *Spectator,* however, seemed satisfied with the short prison sentence.

The *Standard* adopted a more questioning attitude. Originally it had been hostile to Dudley and Stephens, arguing that it was "impossible to justify such revolting acts; even wild beasts will often die rather than eat their own species." By the time of the trial it had come around to urging the grant of an unconditional pardon, and by December 15, when it was all over, a note of cynicism had even crept in: "It is difficult not to see something farcical in the solemn trial at Assizes, the parade of learning and research in the arguments of counsel on the special verdict, and the grim formality of the sentence of death actually passed by a Court of five judges, when everyone knew that the result arrived at was a foregone conclusion from the very first. To say it was 'arranged' would be to use a wrong expression. . . ." But the paper took comfort in the argument that the value of the decision lay not in its practical utility as a guide to conduct that would seriously affect starving seamen but in the awful perils inherent in any other ruling: "Once let any system of jurisprudence accept the pleas of necessity, and Society would drift back into a 'struggle for existence' almost as brutal as that which goes on in a South American forest."

Lurking behind this odd reasoning, first set out in a letter by "Another Barrister" in the *Daily Telegraph* on September 12, 1884, lies a conviction that the common law should reject Darwinism as an appropriate principle for human social behavior, a curious echo of the controversies to which *The Origin of the Species* had given rise: human beings must be viewed as standing outside the brute creation. It will be recalled that a September 13 editorial in *Lake's Falmouth Packet* quoted Darwin's principle in the sailors' support, and the same argument had been advanced by their lawyer, Harry Tilley. In a leader on December 15, specially devoted to the home secretary's decision, the *Standard* approved it:

> It is far better in the interests of morality that DUDLEY and STEPHENS should spend the next six months in prison than that they should at once return to their homes to be presented with subscriptions and treated almost as heroes. They are men deeply to be pitied, scarcely to be censured, and with strong claims to be forgiven; but it must be remembered that they have already been forgiven much, and that if the distinction between right and wrong is to be preserved by the Law, it will not do for morality to regard temptation as an excuse for crime.

The *Daily Telegraph,* though expecting a free pardon, did not protest the home secretary's decision. But in a leader on December 10 it too became somewhat cynical about the proceedings: "From beginning to end of this trial of the Mignonette survivors there has been an air of unreality pervading the whole business." The actual passing of the death sentence, which could have been avoided by the grant of a conditional pardon in good time, was deplored; and the leader writer (who thought the yacht sank in the Pacific) waxed eloquent on the inability of judges to appreciate the sufferings of the men: "It is a trial of the judicial temper, if lunch be too late, and for dinner not only to be delayed, but altogether withheld, would involve a departure from composure, which would make BRACTON and HALE very untimely. What if breakfast, lunch, dinner and supper, too, were to be denied for a whole day, for two days, for even a week?" But it was left to letter writers to bring out more explicitly the apparent absurdity involved in the outcome of the whole affair. One Geo. Shea, in a letter to the *Standard* published on December 16, argued that the practical result of the whole affair would be nil. Presented with the choice between death by starvation or six months' imprisonment, "castaway seamen will eat and be eaten as before." He went on, "Of course if the castaways should be so unspeakably blessed as to have got Lord Coleridge's beautiful judgement by heart before putting to sea, the noble sentiments there expressed would go a long way to encourage them to die like Judges and Christians. But what reasonable hope can we entertain that the ordinary run of common seamen will put to sea so fortified?" No doubt he was right in supposing that common seamen did not read the law reports—

many of them, like Richard Parker himself, could indeed read nothing at all—but in fact the story of the *Mignonette* did pass into the traditional tales of the sea, and to this day oral versions of the story are current, no doubt adulterated by elements derived from written accounts, particularly in the West Country, in Southampton, and in Tollesbury. One such version (which I was told by Mrs. Vivienne Parker, whose father-in-law, the late Dan Parker, was a cousin of Richard) was not what the judges had hoped. For the family tradition was that the men were only tried because they cheated in not drawing lots; had they followed the approved maritime practice, all would have been well. It is today impossible to re-create with any confidence the form in which stories circulated in the late nineteenth century, but this fragment of evidence perhaps indicates that maritime tradition was to some degree proof against the activities of Lord Coleridge and his companions.

Perhaps the best evidence of contemporary folklore developed out of the case is to be found in ballads. Of three that I have been able to trace, one (written by F. Morgans of Greenwich) reflected the official view; Ned Brooks was the hero of the story, and Dudley and Stephens, by implication, the villains:

There sailed upon the ocean
The bonny "Mignonette"
Where came the storm in motion
As high the billows met.

Then sad the crew! she going
As came a dreadful gust;
The sailors thence were rowing,
Their ship no longer trust.

For days and nights they drifted,
Upon the stormy sea;
Where hunger e'er insisted
On crime!—that was to be.

But up there rose one only,
Hard fare he'd often seen
Whose heart did plead so lonely,
In that wide sorrow's mien.

"Good skipper" use him truly,
For he is ill and sad
"Hush! Hush!" he cried, then cruelly

He kill'd the little lad.

And as the night drew darker
Upon that ocean wild,
There dead lay Richard Parker,
Thro hunger, they defiled.

In vain was all imploring!
But justice paid the debt;
Tho' lost where seas were roaring
The boy and "Mignonette."

A second, published by T. Brooks of Bristol and set to the tune of "Dream Faces," simply reflected the maritime world's sympathy and the certainty that the men would both be freely pardoned. It was obviously written before the six-month's sentence was announced and after the judicial decision:

The captain and mate of the yacht, Mignonette
By troubles so long these poor men were beset,
Tried by a jury and five judges as well,
What they have suffered it is hard to tell,
They have been condemned and sent back to gaol,
And quickly respited they need not bewail,
The Queen in her mercy can soon set them free,
And so end this terrible tale of the sea.

[Chorus]

They were tried, condemned, and respited as well,
What they have suffered no tongue can tell,
The Queen's gracious pardon will set them free,
And end this terrible tale of the sea.

On the seventeenth of June when crossing the line,
The weather till then had been calm and fine,
It began to blow hard and the furious waves
Threatened each moment to send them to their graves
Day after day they were tossed on the sea,
Every hour they thought their last it would be,
At last a great wave upon them was bourne
The little ship foundered and quickly was gone.

Alone on the ocean, three men and a boy,
The weather seemed fated their lives to destroy,
A few preserved turnips was all they could save,
Not one drop of water had they on the wave,

For long days and nights no help to be seen,
No friendly ship passing near them had been,
Parched with thirst and starving as well,
A sad wretched story they have lived to tell.

The poor boy lay dying in the bottom of the boat,
A few boards was all that could keep them afloat,
They had all been starving they had no food at all,
Such suffering the stoutest heart would appal,
At last they resolved the poor boy must die,
For this dreadful task the captain drew nigh,
He stabbed and killed him with a small pocket knife,
They drank human blood to preserve their own life.

They were rescued at last by a ship passing by,
In a few hours more they must have been doomed to die,
They came home to England and did confess
They took the boy's life to allay their distress,
At the Exeter Assizes the jury could not then
Find in their hearts to convict the poor men,
So before all the judges they have been tried,
And sentence of death upon them did decide.

But England would never allow them to die
On the gallows for murder, so pardon is nigh,
They've complied with the law by the sentence they give,
And the Queen by her pardon allows;
We hope our brave sailors who travel by the sea,
May never endure sufferings like these,
Pity these poor men I'm sure we all do,
Captain Dudley and all the Mignonette crew.

The third, which may come from Falmouth itself, was compiled before the final decision was taken and again reflects sympathy rather than condemnation. It was to be sung to the mournful air of "Driven from Home" and has already been quoted.

We may guess from these ballads, and from the distortions in the oral tradition that survive (I have even corresponded with one informant who collated the story of the *Francis Spaight* (1836) with the *Mignonette* (1884), and this in 1981) that by the time the case of *Regina v. Dudley and Stephens* reached the forecastles of the last of the sailing barques the opinion of the Queen's Bench division had been extensively edited, perhaps to the point of near conformity to the old traditions of the sea. As long as one drew lots, all would be well.

As a question of law the status of the defense of necessity was virtually settled in 1884; only in very recent times have the waters been muddied a little by decisions dealing with the related question of duress as a defense against a charge of murder. Nearer the date of the case of the *Mignonette* itself, its legal effect can be seen in the extraordinary story of the *Lady Douglas* in 1887. Here Captain James Cocks, First Mate Edwin Evans, Second Mate James Gleaves, and Ordinary Seaman John Webster were convicted before Sir James Fitzjames Stephen for the murder of Hassim, their fellow sailor. He was a Malay, one of three shipped from prison in western Australia after a mutiny, presumably without their consent. One tried to stab Evans and was immediately put ashore; Hassim and another remained. The ship sailed undermanned from Gascoigne on January 11; Able Seaman Charles Goodlif Hunt, who sailed with her, was suspected of having been involved with the mutineers. On February 21 Hassim disappeared and was assumed to have fallen overboard. He was in fact still on board, in hiding, and on March 3 he was located in the forepeak, low down in the ship where the coals were stored. He announced that he wished to die; emerged briefly; and then retired again, having added the cook's knife to his own. It was dangerous to approach him, so the hatch was battened down to confine him; nevertheless he succeeded in escaping from time to time and roamed the ship at night—on one occasion he cut up his shipmate Karl Christiansen's blankets, or was believed to have done so. Since one other seaman, Charles Hunt, was also at large and probably insane, one cannot be sure. Christiansen had been taking no chances and was not asleep in his usual bunk; the crew lived in terror of unexpected incidents. Later Hassim again emerged and was placed in irons, but he succeeded in slipping them on April 21 and returned again to his fortress in the forepeak, armed both with knives and, the crew believed, matches, an even more alarming weapon. Terrified of a Malay who was thought to have run amok, the crew agreed with the captain that if he could not be secured "by fair means" he must be shot, and all but Hunt signed a statement in the ship's log to this effect. They feared that Hunt was in league with Hassim and that the Malay might fire the ship, a possibility intensely feared by sailors, with excellent reason. On April 23 he was shot in the foot by the first mate and then in the side by the second mate; at the captain's suggestion, he was then hauled out of the forepeak by grappling his leg irons. According to the cook's evidence at the trial, "he appeared to be conscious and looked wild about him—he did not speak . . . when we saw the condition he was in we all agreed that he was so badly wounded the best way was to kill him outright." Webster then shot him in the head with the captain's revolver. All this was dutifully reported to the British consul at Le Havre, and the Board of Trade and Home Office were informed; no attempt whatever at concealment took place. At the trial the men were separately represented by counsel; the well-known Horace Avory, who subsequently became a fearsome criminal judge, appeared for the second mate, James Gleaves. Avory contended that the men had acted in defense of themselves and the ship, as did counsel for the captain. Evans's counsel, one Mr. Geoghegan, alone claimed that the men "were compelled by absolute necessity and by the law of self-preservation to do the act." Clearly the case could have been viewed as raising the same theoretical question as that of the *Mignonette,* though the facts also indicated an obvious distinction—there was some evidence that Hassim might have attacked his fellow sailors or set the ship on fire, so that his existence, unlike that of Richard Parker, could have been viewed as a potential danger. But the facts could not be converted into a leading case of necessity; that question had been legally concluded by the case of the *Mignonette.* Fitzjames Stephen summed up strongly against the sailors but conceded that they themselves thought their action was both morally and legally justified. The jury convicted them of murder, adding a rider handed in on a slip of paper. It survives in the Public Records: "We strongly recommend them to mercy. Because we believe what they did they did in Ignorance of the law. And we wish our recommendation to receive consideration, your lordship most merciful [*sic*]." All were sentenced to death, and the Home Office file, which contains their petition, reveals yet again the curious gap in mutual understanding between seamen and the law, in this respect strikingly reminiscent of the case of the *Mignonette:*

> Your petitioner Cocks quite admits the grave responsibility which rests upon him, but he says now, as he has all along, that he acted in a full belief that the death of the Malay was absolutely necessary to the security of the ship and the crew, and that it was in that belief that he was put to death. As a matter of fact he was regarded as a dangerous madman armed with a deadly weapon, possessed with the idea that the death of a Christian at his hand would ensure his entrance into paradise and consequently quite indifferent to his own life as long as he could take that of another.

The Home Office communicated with Fitzjames Stephen, who had only a limited sympathy with the men, though he agreed with the recommendation of mercy. "I consider that the prisoners especially the Captain deserve to be punished substantially and indeed with some severity for their cowardice and brutality. They might easily and with no serious risk have secured Hassim without killing him or desperately wounding him." It was the final shooting of the wounded Hassim that particularly shocked the judge. "This is the part of their conduct which seems to me most blamable." On shipboard, perhaps far from medical aid, "easing the passing" of one certain to die may have appeared rather less heinous. In the event, the captain's sentence was commuted to five years' penal servitude, Gleaves and Evans to 18 months' hard labor, and Webster (who was only 21) to 12 months; this was in line with the views of the officials in the Board of Trade, where Thomas Gray opined, "As to the man being a Malay, we all know they are dangerous as this man was, but as a rule colored men are more amenable to discipline than whites." There was no immediate outburst of public sympathy, though the treatment of the men, lenient by the standards of the time for a case of perfectly deliberate killing, can only be explained as reflecting an awareness by officialdom that, in spite of their protestations, a profound gulf separated the cold and comfortable moral rationality of the law from the brutal conditions at sea, in which a decision had been taken in an undermanned ship terrorized for some two months, of whose sailors two were probably insane and the rest superstitiously fearful of Malays, to whom they attributed strange and dangerous homicidal skills. Indeed the following year, in March, two petitions for further clemency were organized and presented to the home secretary. One had been signed by 4,500 individuals from "all classes in society"—the signatories included the marquis of Carmarthen and, of all people, Sir Edward Bates. The other was signed by some 1,700 mariners. The appeal was even supported by Sir Edward Clarke, the solicitor general, but as far as I have been able to discover, the Home Office remained unmoved. The attitude of the mariners also illustrates the survival, long into the era of rank and authority, of recourse to the general council of all the ship's complement, and the belief that in the little kingdom of a sailing barque a decision taken by such a council legitimated any action taken in consequence.

In the common law world, no other maritime case involving killing to ensure survival has ever come to court. There was indeed another very suspicious incident in the same year as the case of the

Mignonette, involving an American pilot vessel, the *Turley.* On Monday, November 24, four men from this vessel set out in an 18-foot skiff to put a pilot, William Marshall, and a cook, Thomas Bunting, on the S.S. *Pennsylvania,* which they did; while rowing back in heavy seas and thick weather to the *Turley,* they lost contact. There were now three men in the skiff—Pilot Marshall Bertrand (the grandson of Pilot Marshall), Alfred Swanson (Scandinavian in origin), and Andreas Hansen (Norwegian). Only two of them, Bertrand and Hansen, survived to be rescued on November 26 by the schooner *Emma F. Angel* (Captain George Tripp), and they landed on November 27 at Lewes, Delaware. The two Scandinavians were apprentices, Hansen being 16 years of age. The survivors made no secret of the fact that they had eaten their companion and thrown his body overboard just before they were rescued. According to the account that they gave to a reporter on the day they landed, "all Monday, Monday night and Tuesday they drifted aimlessly about, suffering the extremes of hunger, thirst and cold." The two apprentices became delirious, and on Tuesday evening Swanson attacked Bertrand with his knife, saying that he would kill him and drink his blood; he was, however, too weak to carry out this threat. "Exhausted by his long fast, and clad in his icy garments, as in a coat of mail, he fell shrieking and gasping across the thwarts at Bertrand's feet. In a few minutes he was dead. The clouds had passed away, the moon had risen, and its beams fell upon the contorted features of the dead sailor, upon whose face the freezing spray quickly formed a film of ice." Next morning, at Bertrand's suggestion, they started to eat him, the arrangements described in terms reminiscent of a Gothic novel. A reported interview the next day added more detail of their ordeal, including an account of the failure of an unnamed ship to rescue them on Tuesday, its captain calling out to them, "By ——— I hope you'll sink before sunset." Bertrand now said that both the apprentices were preparing to kill him, that Swanson might have died on Monday and that Hansen took the initiative in eating him soon after he died. Both men became evasive when asked why the body was thrown overboard, and a report in the *New York Times* suggested that Swanson might well have died in a fight. This suspicious case was known in England—indeed there is a reference to it in the Home Office file on the case of the *Mignonette.* There is no way of determining whether Swanson was murdered or not. I have notes of several other suspicious cases. For example, one cannot but wonder by what means the survivors of the *Lady Frances* prolonged life in a waterless ship's boat off the North African coast. Their story, or as much of it as they thought prudent to tell, appeared in the *Times* in October 1885, and it included an account of the steward calling for a knife and the captain, maddened with thirst, setting out to walk across the water to the coast. Again, there was a man named Petersen, the single survivor of the barque *Ellen,* which foundered on July 12, 1891, off the east coast of Australia: he lived by some expedient for nine days without water, while his three companions in the boat did not.

In the common law world, the last nineteenth-century instance of a frank admission of cannibalism after a shipwreck took place in 1889 and involved an American crew. While on a voyage from Baltimore to Rio de Janeiro, the S.S. *Earnmoor* (Captain Richard J. Gray) foundered in a hurricane on September 5, and of her complement of 33, eight survived in the single boat that got away, to be rescued on September 25 by the schooner *Mosquito* of Salem, under Captain Johnson, some 300 miles off Cape Hatteras. Of these men one, John Johnston, died of drowning during or immediately after the rescue, the black cook, Edward Jackson, having risked his life in an attempt to save him. The remaining seven, all in a mordant condition, were H. W. Stone, second officer; Thomas Meldrum, second engineer; Carl Crane (or Graner) and August Forster (or Koster), firemen; William Wright and William Davis (or Dewitsch), cooks; and one seaman, Ludwig Loder. The *Mosquito* landed them at Nassau on September 30, and in due course they reached New York on October 19 on the S.S. *Santiago*. News of the loss of the *Earnmoor* and the rescue appeared in the world's press on October 4, but it was not until October 25, when Carl Crane and Ludwig Loder talked to the press in Baltimore, that suspicions as to how they had survived in an unprovisioned boat for 20 days were confirmed.

For the first 15 days they lived on seaweed, a flying fish, and some small sea birds. Eleven vessels passed them by, one, a British barque, deliberately; or so they believed. On the sixteenth day Davis, one of the cooks, attacked Loder with a knife, wounding him on the cheek; he had been encouraged to do so by one August Plagge (or Flager), a fireman, who, with Davis and others at one end of the boat had decided to kill and eat him. Loder thought he had been selected on culinary grounds "as, I suppose, being pretty fat, I looked inviting." The attack was repulsed, and that night Plagge jumped overboard and drowned. Next day William Robinson died in his sleep, and the other cook, William Wright, was ordered to prepare the body for eating in accordance with the proper tradition of the sea. He did so, and full details of the process were published in the London *Times* and *Standard,* as well as in America. The same fate overtook Edward (or Thomas) Hunt on the nineteenth day. One cannot but suspect that these deaths may not have been natural. By 1889 maritime candor may well have been tempered by caution. As far as I have been able to tell, no legal proceedings were ever taken against the survivors. No doubt an exhaustive search would reveal other suspicious stories of survival at sea, including perhaps incidents during the Second World War.

Outside the common law world two classic cases of the custom of the sea occurred after the date of the case of the *Mignonette,* both involving Norwegian sailing vessels. In the declining years of sail the ownership of many sailing barques passed into the hands of Scandinavian ship-owners, and the last real home of the trading barques was indeed the Finnish Aland Islands. Here Gustav Erikson (known affectionately to his crews, according to Eric Newby, as "Ploddy Erikson") maintained a fleet until the outbreak of the Second World War, making possible the writing of Newby's classic *The Last Grain Race.*

The sailing barque *Thekla* had been built in 1876 by J. McFee of Courtenay Bay, St. Johns, New Brunswick, for P. G. Carvill and Co. of Liverpool, who named her *Erin's Gem.* She had various Liverpool owners—in 1879 William M. Simpson, in 1887 G. W. Roberts, and later E. F. and W. Roberts. Although no photograph of this vessel has been traced, she was probably very similar to *Erin's Isle,* built in the following year in the same yard. A photograph published by F. W. Wallace in *Wooden Ships and Iron Men* shows the latter carrying skysails above her royals on all three masts; so *Thekla* probably at least began life as a tall ship. She sailed under the British flag with Captain L. Hall until 1888, when she was sold to Gustav C. Hansen of Tønsberg, who renamed her *Thekla* after the Christian saint of that name. In 1892, on December 1, she set out from Philadelphia to Le Havre carrying petroleum in casks, and on December 22 she became waterlogged after springing a leak in a storm. In an attempt to lighten her, the mast and a yard were cut away, but this made matters worse, as the hatches were damaged in the process; shortly afterward, the wheel was smashed. Of the crew of 19, Captain Math Hansen, the officers, and a number of seamen got away in one of the ship's boats, and they were never heard of again. Nine or so seamen remained clinging to the masts and rigging and were soon reduced in number as men were swept off; at last only four remained.

They sheltered, if that is the word, in the foretop. The crew of the *Thekla* consisted of Swedes, Norwegians, and one Dutchman, called Fritz, who came from near Rotterdam and had joined the ship in Philadelphia. His other name may have been Hannens. He was one of the four left alive. The other survivors were Kristian Hjalmar Jakobsen, aged 23, from Kristiansund and Ole Andersen, aged 21, from Tjømø, both Norwegians; and Alexander S. Johansson, aged 26, from Fiskebakkilen in Sweden. They possessed neither food nor water, except what they could catch from rainfall. On January 7, 1893, the three Scandinavians were rescued in a very weak condition by the Danish schooner *Herman* of Skelskør, under Captain J. C. Andersen, some miles from Azores Flores. The legless and headless remains of Fritz were hanging on board the derelict vessel. Four other sailing vessels had previously passed them by, either failing to see the hulk of the *Thekla* or ignoring it. They were landed at Cuxhaven on January 29, and Johannsen, who was ill with a gangrenous leg caused by frostbite, was placed in a hospital there. The burgomaster of Cuxhaven, Dr. Mönckeberg, made arrangements for their arrest after the Norwegian and Swedish vice-consul had investigated the matter and learned the basic facts. He took the view that, since the death occurred on a Norwegian ship on the high seas, it fell within Norwegian jurisdiction. On February 3 he informed the consulate in Hamburg, and the Hamburg police became involved. On February 20 the Norwegian government instituted proceedings, under a treaty of 1878, for their extradition to Kristiana (now Oslo) to face a judicial inquiry. The request for extradition was first investigated in Hamburg, a hearing taking place on February 11 before a presiding assessor, Judge Siewers, assisted by a merchant, Edward August Eriksen, and an engineer, Karl Paus; and their extradition was ordered. They reached Kristiana on March 15, and between March 17 and 22 a formal hearing took place in the municipal court; Public Prosecutor Vogt appeared for the state, and Doctors P. E. Winge and H. Holm appeared as medical experts. The procedure followed performed something of the same function as the preliminary hearing before the magistrates in the case of the *Mignonette;* on the basis of the investigation, a decision would be taken as to whether the men should be placed on trial or not.

The story that emerged is fully set out in a report by the public prosecutor:

> The other four sought refuge in the rigging and remained there for many days. . . . The days that passed are described by them as hor-

> rible. They had nothing to eat and nothing to drink but seawater, which they drank from time to time—and in addition they suffered from frost and cold. They grew weaker day by day, and their thirst was particularly unbearable. On January 4th, i.e. 13 days after the 22nd of December, they began to discuss whether one of them would have to sacrifice himself in order if possible to save the others. Kristian Jakobsen says that this had also been mentioned one or perhaps two days previously. They now agreed that it should be decided by lottery which of them would have to sacrifice his life for the others. There had been no bad feeling or hostility among any of them; their mutual relationship had all the time been good. The method of the lottery was that Kristian Jakobsen tore four strips, three shorter and one longer, off a towel which Alexander Johansson had had round his head, and the agreement was that he who drew the longest strip should die, and that he should offer no resistance. The Dutchman drew the longest strip, but when Alexander Johansson demanded that the lots should be drawn again—neither he nor the others have been able to establish the reason for this demand—this was done, and the lot again fell on the Dutchman, whose only comment was that after the result of the lottery there was nothing else for it but that he should die.

And so the Dutchman was stabbed by Johansson and consumed, and true to tradition, the account records that "previously Kristian Jakobsen and Alexander Johansson had cut the head off the body with a knife and an axe because it was so dreadful to look at, and the former had also cut off the hands which were thrown into the sea."

After rescue "they were in an extremely weak condition. Alexander Johansson's feet were so bad that he could not walk at all, and the two others could barely stagger forward with support. The former was also quite out of his mind, a condition which lasted for several days. Ole Andersen also took a day or so to collect himself." All insisted that the lots had been fairly drawn but offered no explanation of the oddity of treating the longest lot as fatal. The two medical experts (who were resident physicians at the Kristiana Insane Asylum and at the Rikshospital) then gave their opinion in writing: "The instinct of the accused to quench their thirst must have been so strong that the large majority of people in a similar circumstance certainly would not have been able to resist it, but would have sought any kind of expedient at all. The experts regard it as certain that the accused have undergone much more than enough suffering to disturb the balance of their minds." They concluded, "We assume: 1) that the above-mentioned accused were in an extreme state of hunger at the time of the action with which they are charged, and that they probably would have died within a short time if they had not had recourse to the above-mentioned desperate action, and 2) that none of them was already out of his mind at that time." On March 23 the public prosecutor held a conference with the head of the Department of Justice and Police, Mr. Qvam, and ordered that the men be released from custody. The formal decision that no further proceedings should be instituted against them was taken by the King on the advice of the royal cabinet on April 15. The public prosecutor, under paragraph 91 of the Law of Criminal Procedure, gave a reasoned explanation of his decision to release the men.

> To the best of my knowledge, no sentences have ever been carried out against people who under circumstances similar to those described here have committed the same misdeed as the accused. In other countries, particularly in England, proceedings have apparently been instituted against the culprits on certain occasions, but the sentences awarded in those cases have been waived by a pardon.
>
> Everyone will presumably also agree that the accused in the present case could not be punished if they were prosecuted for a breach of the criminal law ch. 14 s. 2, cf. s. 1 and found guilty. It can thus be taken for granted that Your Majesty in that case would pardon them their punishment. But in that case, prosecution alone would be a matter of form, and since s. 85, last sentence, of the criminal law admits the dropping of charges under particularly mitigating circumstances, it is my opinion that in the present case one should avail oneself of that permission. I therefore humbly recommend that no charges be raised against the sailors Kristian Hjalmar Jakobsen, Ole Andersen, and Alexander Johansson on account of the homicide committed by them on the wreck of the "Thekla" in the Atlantic on the 4th of January 1893.

Minister Qvam agreed, and so did the cabinet. So, unlike the case of the *Mignonette,* the *Thekla* never became a lawyer's case.

This solution appears to have satisfied public opinion, and a ballad by Jacob Andersen, written and distributed before the judicial inquiry, assumed that they might expect to be mercifully treated. After they were released on March 23 one of them, Johansson, true to the ballad tradition, announced that he would go to sea no more. They were penniless; the police gave them a small sum to tide them over, and the Mission to Seamen appealed for money for them. Collecting boxes were placed in two shops and in the seaman's reading room, and they moved into the home of a Mr. Nielsen, owner of the Casino Dance Hall. This provoked some moralizing criticism; they might be subject to temptations that would have been avoided if they had been accommodated at the Seaman's Mission. There was also fear that they might make a profit out of the whole affair—presumably by appearing as cannibals. It turned out that the men preferred to stay with Mr. Nielsen rather than go to the mission and had been taken there by the police, who had a low view of sailors in general and these in particular. But the press was generally on their side, and a contemporary comment pointed out that this recourse to a lottery "shows more clearly that in them we are confronted not with unscrupulous criminal natures but with well brought up individuals with a clear sense of justice. They acted as highly socially conscious people, devoted to comradeship, among them equal regard and equal rights apply as the most natural thing in the world." Pointing out that the stronger had not killed the weaker, the leader continued, "We may conclude how unaffected these people are by amongst other things the theory, known in England as the 'struggle for life,' according to which the right of the stronger [*Sterkeres Ret*] is exalted to law [*Retten*], to the Regulation of the human as of the animal world." In Oslo, as in London, Darwinism as the basis of a legal code was thought inappropriate. As persons, the survivors of the *Thekla* then vanish from history, though at the time their story was celebrated in a ballad. But they were to have a strange, more permanent memorial. In May 1902 there passed into law the Norwegian Penal Code, which was largely the work of one Bernhard Getz (1850–1901), chairman of the Penal Code Commission of 1885. The code as enacted was based on a draft of 1896, and the case of the *Thekla* and its three survivors therefore arose while this draft was being prepared. The incident is consequently referred to in the prelegislative documents, which adopted a utilitarian solution to the problem: necessity could be a defense if it produced a balance of advantage. A note mentions the case itself.

> In a case that occurred a couple of years ago on a Norwegian ship (Thekla) no charges were ever brought, and this seemed to win general approval. Nor does the decision conflict with the demand for proportion. When in all human probability the death of both the person killed and of the others would have taken place in the course of some few hours if the killing had not taken place, the injury done—the shortening by some hours of one individual's death struggle—certainly appears insignificant in relation to the good obtained: the rescue of all the others.

This utilitarian approach won the day and was built into Section 47 of the code of 1902, a permanent legal memorial to the sufferings of the survivors of the barque *Thekla*.

The last classic enactment of the custom of the sea has, to a historian, an unsatisfactory outcome. The wooden three-masted sailing barque *Drot* (1,198 tons gross and 185 feet overall) was another vessel that had passed into Norwegian ownership. She had been built by Lemont and Robinson in Bath, Maine, in 1874; Alfred Lemont owned her, and she first sailed under Captain Henry C. Tarbox, bearing the name *Almira Robinson*. In 1883 she was sold to E. Berentsen of Stavanger, who rechristened her *Drot*—in old Norse the name means "king" or "leader," and Berentsen had previously used the name for another vessel that had come to an unfortunate end, destroyed in an earthquake in the harbor of Pabillon de Pica. A painting of her as *Drot* survives. He would perhaps have been better advised to abandon so ill-omened a name, but for many years *Drot* sailed the high seas under Captain Jonas Sorensen without disaster, visiting the East Indies, China, Australia, and the east and west coasts of South America. She then became engaged in the petroleum trade between Philadelphia and France and, as she aged, worked in the lumber trade from Pensacola, Florida, to Britain. On August 2 or 3, 1899, she sailed with a cargo of lumber from Ship Island off Pascagoula, Mississippi, bound for Buenos Aires, and foundered in a hurricane off the Florida Straits on August 11. She carried a crew of 17, of whom the captain and eight sailors were lost with the ship. The remainder of the crew, including the first mate, escaped on a raft, which was formed of wreckage from part of the poop deck and deck house. This soon broke in two. One part had the first mate and one seaman; the mate jumped overboard, and the other sailor, Oscar Niklason, was rescued by the German steamship *Catania* on 20 August and landed at Baltimore. The other part had six men aboard, and they possessed a fishing line. A contemporary report, based on conversations with the survivors, tells how

> there was nothing to drink. The fishing line thrown out from the raft brought back good returns, and the raw fish, wriggling in life, were devoured viciously by the starving demons. No sweet delicacy could have been a finer morsel. The raw meat with the scales and slime still on it, was eaten, and then a deeper thirst touched the men to make their agony all the worse. Lips were parched and throats were burning. A piece of ice would have been more precious than a mountain of

> diamonds. It was while in this condition that one of the men was standing near the edge of the raft fishing. His line was thrown out: a fish nibbled and then took the hook in the head. He jerked at the line. In an instant the man had gone mad. His companion saw the strange, fierce look on his face, and then heard his cry as the fish was lifted from the sea: "I'm saved," he screamed, and the next moment he jumped as high as his weak condition would allow; and fell over into the deep, still holding the line and screamed "I am saved" until he went below and was lost forever.

The five survivors now had no means of securing food or drink (for fish can provide a considerable amount of fluid). And so

> it was not long after this crazy act that another member showed signs of death in his face. He was going out fast. His hands and feet got cold and clammy: his companions all the while feeling for his heart: a knife was raised all the while to strike his breast at the signal word. His heart beats became fewer. With life ebbing slowly but surely away the knife was plunged into his heart, and the blood trickled out to be drunk by the half-famished, thirsty mortals by his side. While the fearful feast was in progress another member began to drop away; he was dying fast, his head fell back and his eyes were closed. Like birds after fresher prey the man-eaters rushed to the second victim, stabbed him, and sucked the milk-warm blood as it oozed from the great slash about his heart. The last of his blood was gone. The sight and taste of it had made the men mad. They refused the dead flesh, after tasting it sparingly, and then in the wild desire for more and warmer blood, they cast lots for a victim.

There were by now three men alive—Mauritz Andersen, a 23-year-old Swede; Goodmund Thomassen (also recorded as Goodman and Thomas), a 17-year-old boy sailor from Stavanger; and Max Hoffman, a 35-year-old Austrian. Predictably, Hoffman lost the lottery. One account claims that no details of the lottery could be recalled; another suggested that the best nautical practice had been followed, as embodied in *La Courte Paille,* straws being used. Yet another was that six sticks were used; this places the incident earlier. Hoffman, again in conformity with tradition, accepted his fate and bared his breast. He was stabbed in the heart (one account claims he was first stunned); his heart was torn out and his blood drunk. The two survivors were rescued on Thursday August 31, some 260 miles from Charleston, South Carolina, by the English steamship *Woodruff* under Captain Milburn; at some point they had apparently agreed to draw lots among themselves. At the time of the rescue Andersen (physically the strongest) was variously described as engaged in eating Hoffman or in feeding pieces of him to the sharks that swarmed around the raft; Thomassen had been severely bitten by him. The scene was a remarkable one: "The sharks were still fighting for their prey and had to be driven off when small boats were sent out from the Woodruff and the two men put aboard. There were signs of the ghoulish feast. . . . And when the two crazed demons were lifted aboard the *Woodruff* the big ship pulled away from the scene of suffering and death and left the sharks playing about the raft, still making great lunges to reach the remnants of the German's body." They were landed at Charleston on September 2 and placed in the city hospital there under the care of Dr. Johnson Buist, where Thomassen began to recover on a diet of beef tea and dry crackers; Andersen, however, remained ill and mentally disturbed, and both were in a very serious physical condition, being severely ulcerated. The vice-consul in Charleston who handled consular business for Sweden and Norway was one C. O. Witte, a Hanoverian, and it happened that he also acted for the German Empire. He communicated the facts to New York, and on September 22, while the men were still in the hospital, he secured warrants from U.S. Commissioner Smith for their arrest on a charge of murder with a view to securing their extradition. In order not to distress them, they were not told they were being kept under guard in the hospital by a U.S. deputy marshal. The legality of their action was of course much discussed, and the Charleston *News and Courier* devoted a leader to the subject, under the headline "Murder or Necessity":

> The law in such cases is doubtless as infinitely vague and contradictory as it is in many others, but we have been informed that the taking of a human life in such circumstances and under the conditions in which Andersen and Thomas were placed has been held not to be murder. It has been decided, it is said, that in view of the fact that self-preservation is the highest law, a number of men may agree together that one must be sacrificed for the other—that they may, in other words, cast lots for a victim; and so long as the selection is accomplished impartially and without Fraud in the eye of the law, they, those who profit by it, have not gone beyond the bounds within which a man may take any course which promises to preserve his own life. While there is more than a semblance of logic in such a contention, we are not entirely satisfied that its principles have found universal acceptance by the Courts, and we would be grateful to learn what the best au-

> thorities say on the subject. There is no doubt, of course, that the heroism of the sailors would have awakened universal admiration had they withstood the pangs of hunger and thirst, and have died together rather than resort to the horrible expedient by which the lives of two of them were saved. The nobility of such a course would have been beyond dispute, but the question raised is not as to their heroism, but as to their legal right to have obeyed the animal instinct in them—an instinct whetted to the keenest edge by sufferings which the most vivid imagination can realize but imperfectly. The incomplete record now before us lends a certain dignity to the unfortunate German who was the victim of the necessities of his comrades. He joined with them in the compact that contemplated the sacrifice of one of the party, but, having lost in the fateful game in which he engaged, he seems to have abided loyally by the decision which chance rendered. It is said that he bared his breast that the knife might more readily reach a fatal spot. It would doubtless have been both cowardly and contemptible had he struggled and fought for his life after agreeing with his comrades to forfeit it if fortune were against him, but there is many a man who would have done so, and he deserves the meagre credit which good faith and courage, in trying circumstances, command.

Thus Hoffman became, like Ned Brooks, the hero of the story.

Thomassen and Andersen were apparently never extradited. The Stavanger papers had announced the arrest and planned extradition in late September, and this caused some local concern. But on December 2 it was reported that this was unlikely to happen. An official of the Department of Justice was quoted as saying,

> some time ago there was a question which came to the office of the Public Prosecutor as to whether the two sailors from *Drot* who, after long sufferings, had been guilty of cannibalism, should be ordered to be sent home. To this the Department of Justice answered that any such move would not take place for the time being. On the other hand it was added that the Swedish Norwegian Consul should question them when they have fully recovered. The final decision as to what shall be done shall then be taken about the unhappy sailors. However, if in this interrogation no other evidence comes to light . . . they will not be prosecuted. We also have precedents in the *Thekla* affair . . . these unfortunate sailors have suffered enough.

This attitude apparently satisfied the public, and the absence of any record of extradition proceedings suggests that the matter was dropped. Precisely what happened to the sailors I have not been able to discover, in spite of efforts on my behalf by archivists in America and Scandinavia and help from Mr. T. R. Waring, grandson of Consul Witte. Oscar Niklason certainly recovered, but I am told by Mr. Arne B. Andersen, director of the Stavanger Maritime Museum, that one of the sailors—presumably Andersen—never did recover his sanity. One can but hope that Thomassen, the ship's boy, came home in the end, being more fortunate than his counterpart of the *Mignonette*.

10
Aftermath

God bless all poor seamen their children and wives,
In trying to get their bread how they venture their lives,
So now to conclude what I've mentioned is right,
God protect all poor seamen by day and by night.

—"Ballad of the *Essex*"

The case to which the sufferings of the crew of the *Mignonette* gave rise enjoys an assured legal immortality, and the conflict between the old custom of the sea and the comfortable morality of the common law is unlikely ever to arise again. So much has changed in the last century both socially and technologically that it has even come to be forgotten that such a conflict once existed. And as for the unfortunate individuals who featured in the world of nineteenth-century cannibalism—boys like Patrick O'Brien and men like Timothy Gorman and James Archer—in the main all memory of them has passed away, a fact in itself surprising in view of the continuing macabre fascination excited by both murder and cannibalism today. Of all the nineteenth-century cannibals, only Alferd Packer achieved and still retains heroic stature. We left Alferd, the Colorado Man-Eater, or "the great American Anthropophaginian," as he was then called, in the Gunnison County Jail, serving the community as a tourist attraction. His fame spread through the 1884 publication of *Tales of the Colorado Pioneers* by Alice Polk Hill, which contained a long account of him. In all probability folk ballads were sung about him, though only a possible single stanza has been traced in oral tradition by Olive Woolley Burt, a collector of such ballads in America: this has already been quoted at the start of an earlier chapter. Alferd occupied himself in making horsehair watch chains and other curiosities and realized a handsome income from their sale to tourists. He grew his hair long and, according to the *Denver Republican*, "satisfied the most sanguine hopes of the visitors who expected to see a strange creature when calling upon him." In October 1884 the murderer Al Garvey, whose conviction had been marred by the same legal flaw as Alferd Packer's, was set free by the Colorado supreme court. It had been decided in Garvey's case that, although his conviction for murder was invalid, he could be retried for manslaughter instead. Judge Elliot thought a retrial of someone so obviously guilty was rather a waste of time, so he dispensed with this tedious formality and simply sentenced Garvey to eight years' imprisonment. The supreme court thought this improper and ordered a retrial, but it subsequently set him free under the Colorado Habeas Corpus Act, which imposed a time limit on criminal proceedings that had clearly been exceeded. Although precisely the same criticism could be made about the proceedings against Packer, no such indulgence was granted him, though the point was raised on his behalf in a petition to the supreme court filed on December 4, 1885, and again in 1886. There could be no respectable justification for this treatment, though the court argued that the delay was all Alferd's fault. So it was ruled by the supreme court in *Packer v. The People* (1885) that Alferd was still liable to retrial for manslaughter. This too was curious because of the legal principle of double jeopardy. But the supreme court adopted a Gilbertian view of the situation—though Packer had been sentenced to death for murdering Israel Swan, and invitations to the hanging had actually been sent out, he was never *legally* at risk, since the whole performance had been invalid from the start. It can hardly have seemed like that at the time. And so, after further long delay, Alferd was eventually brought to trial in 1886, charged with the manslaughter of all five of his companions, including Israel Swan, for whose murder he had been tried three years before; and to all these charges he pleaded not guilty. The judge was not Judge Gerry, author of the celebrated homily in 1883, but Judge William Harrison; and all five charges were consolidated and tried before a single jury at one trial, which began on August 2, 1886. No transcript survives, but press reports make it possible to reconstruct most of what happened. The evidence against Packer was much the same as at the first trial, and Packer himself gave evidence for some eight hours (another account says five). He was the star; all accounts confirm his wild and incoherent manner. The *Denver Daily News* describes him "standing in his shirt-sleeves, waving his mutilated hand and haranguing the jury in broken sentences. He wouldn't use the maps furnished by the State in pointing out the route he took, but made maps of his own on the floor with volumes of law reports, chairs, etc. He frequently cursed his enemies in very plain words and refused to be governed by his counsel. Replying once to a remonstration on their part, he said 'You shut up. I'm on the stand now.' " The *Rocky Mountain News* had it that "no pen could do justice to a report of Packer's statement" and added, "When he approached that period of his history wherein the narration of the killing should come in, he repeatedly dodged away from it as if dreading to give its horrid details (as no doubt he did) and finally cut that portion of his tail [*sic*] short." Essentially, he claimed to have acted in self-defense; it was eat or be eaten. But the jury did not believe him, and he was convicted of voluntary manslaughter. Judge Harrison let him speak before sentence was passed, and Alferd took the opportunity to address both the jury and the people of Gunnison, adopting his curious practice of referring to himself frequently in the third person: "I do not want the Gunnison people to think that I hold any malice toward them. They have been good to me during the last three years I have been here in jail. And I do not want them to think that Packer harbors anything against them for Packer had a fair and impartial trial here in Gunnison." While claiming innocence, he sagely admitted the weight of the evidence against him and said he expected a sentence of 40 years in prison. This Judge Harrison obligingly gave him, eight years on each count, to run consecutively, and Packer hung his head, murmuring, "Forty years." It was at the time the longest term ever imposed by an American judge. The *Pueblo Times* reported the sentence frivolously under the headline "Packer's Portion." The outcome gave general satisfaction, and the *Rocky Mountain News* of August 5 reported it with the headlines "The Cannibal Convicted—Alferd Packer the Murderer of Five Men on whose Flesh he Feasted Guilty of Manslaughter—One of the Most Horrible and Revolting Cases in the Annals of Criminal Literature. . . ." The "San Juan Ghoul" was now to be sent to serve out his time in Cañon City Penitentiary, but before he left (indeed, while the trial was still in progress) he was interviewed in his cage at Gunnison by the *Denver Daily News*. The reporter, "after receiving instructions as to the number of kicks I was to give the door when I wanted to get out," discussed the whole business with Alferd, who again maintained his innocence and became highly excitable when talking of his treatment by the press: "He walks rapidly up and down his cell; his eyes flash, his whole frame trembles and his hands open and shut convulsively." But in the penitentiary he became a model prisoner, and in the remarkably relaxed regime to which he was subjected there—free visiting, for example—he grew flowers and made belts and watch fobs, which he sold. From time to time accounts of his life reached the press, as in this note in the *Denver Daily News* of January 2, 1890: "Packer, the San Juan maneater, is plodding along serving out a sentence of forty years. He attends mostly to the lawns and flowers." Within the prison, sympathy for him began to develop. But outside it was different, and the *Denver Times* in 1892 recorded that in Lake City, near the site of the original incident, a skull with a bullet hole was exhibited in the *Lake City Times* newspaper office as that of one of his victims, and people there were still angry that he "got off."

Although when sentenced Alferd said that he expected to die in prison and regarded himself as dead to the world, he continued to attempt to secure his release and became both an indefatigable litigant and a persistent petitioner for a pardon, though he could not always rely on professional help. In December 1886 an appeal was lodged, but this was dismissed for want of prosecution in January 1889. In March 1893, when eight years of the sentence (less remission) had been served, habeas corpus proceedings were taken to challenge the legality of the imposition of successive sentences; the proceedings, which were unsuccessful, are reported in the *Colorado Law Reports* of 1893. In 1898 a writ of error was brought on a number of grounds, including the delay in bringing the case to trial. This again failed, as did another attempt in 1899. In all, Packer's case reached the Supreme Court of Colorado on five occasions, always without success. Numerous efforts were also made to secure him a pardon, and the controversy that these generated also helped to keep the story alive. Alferd also came back into the limelight in 1893. Circulating at the time were rumors that Packer was "a dangerous lunatic, with an unnatural lust for human flesh, determined to whet his appetite on any piece of a man's anatomy on which he could fasten his teeth. . . ." It was said by one paper that he had declared his intention of "eating his way out of jail" and that he was refusing prison food; only "chops a la genus homo" would suit him. For this reason, or more simply because the warden of the prison wanted an opinion as to whether Packer ought to be moved to a hospital, a medical commission was appointed to examine him, and the proceedings were published. It is clear that by 1893 his epilepsy had become very much worse; the prison physician reported that the attacks were "becoming more frequent and violent and the other effects on his mind lasting longer." A prison officer said he had several fits each day. Then, in a dramatic scene, Packer himself appeared before the commissioners:

> Quick footsteps were heard outside, the screen door was thrown open, and Warden McLister entered with a tall, slender, stoop-shouldered man in convict garb. On the breast of his coat were the figures "1389" marked in indelible ink.
>
> "Gentlemen," said the Warden, "this is Mr. Packer."
>
> "How are you, Mr. Packer?" "Take a seat, Mr. Packer," the doctors said. . . . "How are you feeling?"
>
> "Pretty lively" was the response.

Packer told them his story, that he had acted in self-defense, and the doctors at least were convinced: " 'I believe you, Mr. Packer,' said Dr. Thombs. 'And I too,' added Dr. Grissom. They all shook hands. 'You may believe it or not, gentlemen,' answered Packer, 'but it is the truth.' 'Come, Packer,' said the Warden, and the two men left the room."

Shortly afterward a reporter for the *Denver Republican* interviewed him and recorded his whole story, beginning with his childhood, and Packer indeed had a mild fit when telling it. All this appeared in the paper, the first really good publicity Alferd had yet received from the press. Public opinion at last began to move in his favor. Late in 1899 his case was taken up by a formidable Virginia journalist, Mrs. Leonil Rose O'Bryan, who wrote in the *Denver Post* under the name "Polly Pry." The *Denver Post* was at the time under the editorship of Harry H. Tammen and Frederick J. Bonfils, and it established a reputation for lively and sensational journalism. Through the paper "Polly Pry" ran a spirited campaign for a pardon. She opened it by claiming that a pardon for Packer had been refused because Otto Mears, who had given false evidence against him, had persuaded the governor not to release him for fear of Packer's revenge. The style employed has come to be familiar; it was then new:

> Governor Thomas has refused to parole Alferd Packer.
>
> Do you know why?
>
> I do. I am going to tell you.

> Do you know what it is to be afraid—to tremble at a shadow—to see things in the dark—to lie awake and listen to things you can neither see nor here [*sic*]—things born of your own evil conscience—to remember a wrong you have done and the payment you must make—do you know the feeling?
>
> No, of course you don't.
>
> But this man, the good friend of Colorado's distinguished Governor, he knows.

By 1899 Otto Mears had become a prominent Colorado citizen, and such an attack was bound to attract enormous attention; later in the article Polly Pry described him as "a little old man with a shrewd face and a shifty eye, a trader who always has a new scheme and who never gets the worst of a bargain." Packer himself was quoted as saying, "I am an old man and I want the privilege of spending my days outside a prison cell. I am innocent of the hideous crime with which I am charged—I do not ask for revenge." A lively press controversy followed, the *Lake City Times* arguing for Packer's guilt, the *Denver Post* for his innocence. On January 8, 1901, Polly Pry continued her campaign by publishing a list of all those who in fact had been pardoned by Governor Thomas, under the headline "Polly Pry passes in Review the Troop of Ravishers whom Kind Hearted Governor Thomas has seen fit to Parole." She also gave an account of the prison warden's view of Alferd—"Packer is the soul of generosity." Apparently Alferd, who was paid a small military pension of $25 a month, was accustomed to lend or give away money to other prisoners. Petitions for Packer were organized and widely supported.

In the course of this campaign, a local attorney was engaged to represent Alferd. His name was William W. Anderson, but he was known as "Plug Hat Anderson" or "The Inveterate Peanut Eater." He visited Packer in prison and obtained some $25 from him, allegedly to help with expenses. Polly Pry thought this was fraudulent, and they quarreled. On the morning of Saturday, January 13, Plug Hat Anderson visited Messrs Tammen and Bonfils at their *Denver Post* office; it was known as "The Bucket of Blood" and normally contained a sawn-off shotgun as standard office equipment. According to the best-known account of the discussion, it was not marked by much civility:

> "Sir," said Anderson, "I'm a Missourian and a man of culture." Tammen shouted: "You're not a man at all. You're a low-down son of a bitch! And a robber to boot!"

Thus provoked, Plug Hat shot them both, and had not Polly Pry concealed Tammen under her skirt and seized the Smith and Wesson revolver, both would have been killed. The trial of Plug Hat for assault with intent to murder in April 1900 was inconclusive (he was in fact retried twice and eventually acquitted in spite of the evidence). But it brought Alferd into public view, since he appeared as a witness and was even allowed a grand tour of Denver City, unmanacled. The following January Governor Thomas granted Alferd Packer parole, subject to a number of conditions, including a condition of abstinence from intoxicating liquors; Thomas was up for election and may have been currying popular favor. It is also said that Alferd gave his word to the governor not to be exhibited as a cannibal (as Brooks was), apparently a recurrent fear in the minds of those who dispense mercy to man-eaters. He had served just under 18 years of his 40-year sentence when he came out of the penitentiary at 10:00 in the morning on January 10, 1901.

Alferd was now well on his way to making the transition from villain to hero, and his progress was assisted by the *Denver Post,* which published an appropriate ode by W. A. Simmons, which concluded,

> Life to me has been a burden
> Oh—how bitter was the bowl
> And you say that he has signed it?
> That I'm going on parole?
>
> Tell the Post I'll ever bless it;
> Tell my loyal friends for me
> That an angel came and found me,
> Swung the door and set me free!

The angel herself, Polly Pry, wrote ecstatically (if tactlessly) about the "old man suffering from an incurable malady, doomed to a speedy death" and described the original incident back in 1874 yet again: "Months later high on a cruel plateau, 10,000 feet above the sea . . . under a pitiless sky, in a scene of awful cold and desolation, four gave up their lives to a madman's fury and two fought as wild beasts fight—and later, after many weeks one came, a vacant minded wreck, and fell on the threshold of a house in the agency. And this one was Packer." She pleaded for fair play for him now, arguing that "it is a recognised lawful act on the high seas." She had not studied *Regina v. Dudley and Stephens.*

Packer's new-found popularity was no doubt connected with the fact that a nostalgia had begun to develop over the early heroic days of the West, a nostalgia that has of course since then flourished mightily. In reality, if one may judge from the advertisements in early Western newspapers, the old timers were not a particularly prepossessing crowd, being principally worried about constipation, impotence, venereal disease, and, to a lesser extent, hernias (their womenfolk were plainly troubled by unwanted pregnancies, nonetheless). But that was not how it had come to seem. Men like Alferd G. Packer had an irresistible romantic air—Alferd had, after all, roughed it in the early days before there was a State of Colorado, had known Chief Ouray (who died in 1880), and heard the Ute braves "a-yellin' and a-whoopin' "; they didn't do it much any more, having last risen in bloody if belated revolution in 1879, when they impaled Indian Agent Nathan Mecker on a stake. It turned out that Alferd had even been a scout for General Custer, though he prudently avoided being present at Little Big Horn. Polly reported with typical carelessness about the facts "his career as a scout in that wonderful campaign when Custer and his immortal band met their heroic death." A few years after his release in 1904, Alferd was run to earth by a reporter in Sheridan, near Fort Logan, where he lived in a small shack with vines trailing over it. It was simply and appropriately furnished with a bed, a chair, and a stove. There Alferd played out the unique part of a mountain man—his only possible rival, Liver-eating Johnson, had died in 1900 and was not from Colorado. Alferd, coming up to his sixty-second birthday, was in a philosophical mood: "I have some rabbits and chickens here on my little place, and they form my society, aside from a few of the children." Though officially barred from alcohol, Packer admitted having become drunk on whisky on one occasion, as befitted an old mountain man, when he had been refused the right to vote. He "couldn't see why he should be deprived of this right of citizenship and he turned to whisky to allay his disappointment." He had developed a keen interest in politics, but whether appropriately as a Republican, is unrecorded. Commenting on his drinking habits, Alferd conceded that "I do take a drink whenever I feel like it though, but so long as I behave myself I don't see it's anybody's business but my own." He corresponded regularly with the warden of the Cañon City Penitentiary, who would write back, "You're all right Packer. Just keep it up." Whether this exhortation was intended as an encouragement to orthodox gastronomic habits is obscure. The reporter himself fell under the spell and wrote, "Alferd Packer is really a relic of the days when the State of Colorado was not. He is a mountaineer, plain and simple. City streets and crowds bewilder him . . . he spends a part of any year in the mountains, and these are his happiest days." And so he lived on, feeding candy to the children and telling them tales of the old days, and for form's sake doing a little prospecting for copper up in Deer Creek Canyon. He died there on April 23 or 24, 1907; according to a contemporary press report, his death was appropriately dramatic: "He seemed possessed of superhuman strength . . . he barked and snapped like a dog. During his rational moments Packer continually repeats that he was innocent of the crime charged against him." He was buried at Littleton with military honors as a Civil War veteran; as an old man he claimed indeed to have fought in two engagements. Very shortly before his death, he made a last approach by letter to the governor for a pardon, declaring, "I am dying and I am innocent of the crime." This final appeal was ignored. Whether Alferd was, as he claimed, wholly innocent of murder (he admitted cannibalism) and had acted in self-defense only, or whether he had in fact murdered his companions for gain or food, is a complex question with which this book is not concerned. There is, however, one other possibility, which is that Alferd himself never actually knew what had happened out there in the wilderness, having been reduced by the combined effects of his long-standing epileptic condition (coupled possibly with the effects of lead poisoning) and by privation almost to automatism. His own retelling of his experiences in 1893 was punctuated by a fit, of which he was quite unaware: "Here Packer suddenly stopped, riveted his eye on the floor, and sat rigid, lost in thought apparently. There was a furrow of anxiety in his forehead, which deepened until with a start he gave himself a shuddering shake and without a word of explanation continued his story." His story was dreamlike in quality: "There I was alone in the middle of my dead companions, and I had killed one of them. It must have been then that I began to get leery." He "slept" for long periods and otherwise felt "ecstatically happy." He "sang joyous songs and shouted forth pleasant remarks." He must have been at the scene of the killing "two or three months," an impossible estimate. "After a while there came moments when I had lucid intervals and occasionally I caught myself wondering why I was there and why I laughed and shouted." Eventually he was overtaken by a frenzy to get away, and he left, carrying fire in a coffee pot; how long he stayed near Dead Man's Gulch he did not know. His condition could well have been aggravated by starvation and cold (he tended to have fits at night—that is, some time after he had taken food), and his lying may have been in part an attempt to explain his confused memory of the ordeal.

Since then the legend of Alferd Packer has flourished continuously, and today thousands of pilgrims visit his grave annually, which is carefully protected by a thick bed of concrete. Accounts of his exploits appeared in early histories and reminiscences of life in the territory (for example, in Frank Hall's four-volume *History of the State of Colorado* [1891]) and became even more widely known through the publication in 1933 of Gene Fowler's *Timberline,* a best-selling account of Bonfils, Tammen, and the heroic early days of the *Denver Post.* Since then, there have been two full and serious books on the trials of Alferd—Paul H. Gantt's *Case of Alferd Packer, the Man-Eater* (1952), and Ervan F. Kushner's *Alferd G. Packer: Cannibal! Victim?* (1980)—and very many slighter contributions, some serious, others less so. His story has particularly fascinated the Denver Posse of the Westerners, one of whose members, Robert W. ("Red") Fenwick, opened his study of the story thus: "The strange fearsome figure limped down out of the mountains. . . . Long, black, matted hair clung to the back of his neck like soiled mattress stuffing. His dark eyes burned in deep-set sockets. . . . He looked like a man who had walked through hell, barefooted, without a canteen." This was illustrated with portraits of "the ghoul" by H. Ray Baker. Today the Packer bibliography is massive, and scarcely a year passes without a new contribution; in the course of the years Alferd has moved from being a hero to becoming an essentially comic figure. The Packer literary corpus thus includes such items as *Alferd Packer's Wilderness Cookbook* by James E. Banks; and when the late Fred and Jo Mazzulla published *Al Packer: A Colorado Cannibal* in 1969, a limited number of specially bound copies were available at $50 each, bound, it was rumored, in skin.

Yet more bizarre homage has been paid to the story. In 1903, there was a reenactment of the original incident, organized by a local photographer, in which Alferd himself was persuaded to take part; a photograph of this survives, showing Alferd looking disapproving. August 1, 1928, saw the unveiling near Lake City of a memorial to the five men who died in Dead Man's Gulch. It was presented by the Ladies Union Aid Society of Lake City, and the proceedings, which opened with the singing of "America," concluded with "a magnificent fish fry with all trimmings." The site, incidentally, changed hands in 1976 under the name of "Massacre Site," advertised as "excellent unimproved 1.48 acres adjoining Colorado Highway 149 near Lake City. . . . First Time offered, Interesting History. Quiet Five Plot Cemetery (occupied) included. Price $5,000." In 1958, the seventy-fifth anniversary of the second trial was celebrated in Lake City by a performance of a melodrama entitled *They Wuz Et* in the original courtroom; moved to the Bent Elbow, a saloon in Silverton, it ran for some time with success under a different title. Packer reached the screen in *The Legend of Alfred Packer* (1979), a film which won no Oscars, based on a script by Professor Burton Raffel and directed by Jim Roberson. The cast included a pederastic hermit, and Packer was played by Patrick Day, a Chicago actor. The longest speech given him consisted of musings on the Civil War, perceptively reflecting the philosophic aspect of Alferd's character: "Bodies rollin', people screamin', too much blood, too much killin'." Possibly more successful was the ritual absolution of Alferd, conducted in September 1940 by Bishop Frank H. Rice of the Liberal Church, Littleton, Alferd's sins being transferred to a goat by the name of Angelica, borrowed for the ceremony. An extract from the absolution prayer captures the air of this homely if theologically odd occasion:

> O kind and merciful Father, who looketh down upon this scene knowing full well that we are met here today to transact certain Holy Business which probably should have been transacted many a year ago, give us thy blessing: Here in the cemetery of Littleton, Colorado, lies whatever remains of the body of one Alfred Packer. Since no man knows where his soul may be, this spot will do as well as any other for the observance of this Holy and Divine Ritual. And we beseech thee, O Heavenly Father, to spread the ample mantle of thine incredible goodness over the departed souls of the five men who were eaten by Alfred Packer, so that it might never be said that Your compassion favored those whose major sins brought to them a surpassing amount of attention. . . .
>
> Here [*sic*] now, what comforting words were spake by Jehovah, who frequently did entreat his chosen people to kill and eat one another. In Leviticus, 26th chapter, 29th verse, the Bible sayeth "Ye shall eat the flesh of your sons, and the flesh of your daughters shall ye eat." And again in Deuteronomy, 28th chapter, 53rd to 57th verses, doth it say, "And thou shalt eat the fruit of thine own body, the flesh of thy sons and daughters." Again in Jeremiah and in Ezekiel doth the One God proclaim his espousal of cannibalism. Therefore, Alfred Packer, we won't hold that against you. . . .

In the 1950s an attempt was made by the Republican party to have set up in the capitol building a gold memorial plaque in honor of Alferd, the consumer of Democrats. It failed, after a debate on a motion that began, "Whereas it is fitting and proper that citizens who have made substantial and lasting contributions to the welfare of this great State should be suitably remembered by this Honourable Assembly. . . ." The latest incident in Alferd's rise to fame has been the attempt by Judge Ervan F. Kushner to secure a posthumous pardon for him; this treats him more kindly as a human victim of man's injustice, neither hero, villain, nor comic turn. The petition, dated July 7, 1980, was based on the judge's book, quite the most thorough and scholarly study yet made: sadly, it was rejected by Governor Richard D. Lamm in March 1981; the *Rocky Mountain News,* under the headline "Lamm Nips Packer Pardon" reports how the governor admitted that Alferd had had "a raw deal." He perpetrated even worse puns on July 7, 1982, when unveiling Tom Miller's bust of Alferd at the state capitol ("I have little appetite to appear before you today"). No doubt the matter will not rest there. For in the state of Colorado, Alferd remains a significant figure, honored by the Packer Club and celebrated annually on Packer Day, April 10. What is probably his Colt is in the State Museum in Denver, and in Boulder you can apparently eat at the Alferd E. Packer Grill in the University Memorial Center. In its present form, this grill dates back to 1968 and was the brainchild of a student leader, Paul Danish; at its launching, a raw hamburger was thrown at the wall, where it stuck for some minutes. The cult of Alferd Packer is even spreading; they now celebrate Packer Day in at least one college in Ohio, a state with which he had, as far as I know, not the least connection. Collectors can acquire suitably inscribed T-shirts. If you go to the waxwork museum in Denver, you can see a figure—which does not look remotely like the real Alferd—kneeling before a flickering fire, surrounded by polystyrene snow and the bones of his supposed victims. And if you press the adjacent button *firmly,* as the instructions recommend, you can even hear the wind howling down Slumgullion Pass onto Dead Man's Gulch, as it did in 1874, and reflect on the need for cannibals to choose both their original context and their subsequent literary history with real care if they are to achieve a fitting immortality.

For nothing of the kind happened to the survivors of the *Mignonette,* whose subsequent history I have attempted to re-create with only limited success. Indeed, once Dudley and Stephens, as prisoners 5331 and 5332, had been taken back to Holloway Prison to serve their sentence there under the supervision of Governor Everard S. Milman, the general public and the press soon forgot about them. Apart from Dudley's apparently short appearance at Madame Tussaud's, they vanished from public view and public notice, and as far as I have been able to discover the English press did not report their release from prison or anything of their later life. Ned Brooks did remain in the public view for a short while, for he apparently succumbed to the temptation to appear for money in amusement shows. Here the source of information is Phillipa Dudley, who recounted of her husband that, "although managers of Public Places of Amusement have offered him large sums of money to induce him to exhibit himself, he has refused. The publicity and misery of the Tragedy have been too painful for human endurance." In the same letter (which was written on February 19, 1885, to one Ellis Lever) she wrote bitterly of Brooks "that the bravest and most honest should suffer, must seem *hard;* when *one, too cowardly* to do, was *not* too *scrupulous* to share, yet could be permitted to go unpunished, and then make a market out of the misery of his companions." In what shows Brooks appeared I have been unable to discover.

As far as Dudley himself was concerned, committal to prison must have been additionally painful because of his domestic problems. At the time of the hearing in London his daughter Winifred, then aged three, was so seriously ill with "congestion of the lungs" that there were doubts as to whether she would survive; Dudley had been acting as night nurse for his daughter. Under the prison regulations of the time, Dudley, no longer a first-class misdemeanant, could receive only one letter and one visit every three months, even from his family. He would also have been to a considerable degree isolated from Stephens and other prisoners, though unlike many prisoners of this period he was not held under the "separate" or "silent" system.

There is some reason to believe that Stephens was particularly seriously affected by the sentence. Physically he had suffered more than Dudley, and it appears from the Home Office file that he wrote no fewer than 23 letters to the Home Office from prison, in contrast to Dudley's single petition; this may indicate a distressed state of mind. The custodians of the Public Records in apparently some fit of misguided tidiness have deliberately destroyed 22 of these, so it is impossible to be sure.

But if the world in general soon began to forget its sympathy for the survivors of the *Mignonette,* some few individuals did not.

One A. Paul, a solicitor, wrote to say that the captain and mate ought never to have been brought to trial and should now be freed as temporarily insane: "These men when it was said they committed murder . . . were labouring under temporary insanity and I venture to say if such a plea had been put forward it would have been sustained." The mayor, magistrates, corporation, and inhabitants of Falmouth organized a petition for a free pardon; and this document, dated December 30, 1884, was sent to the Home Secretary; the new mayor, Richard Carter, signed it, as did his predecessor, Mr. Henry Liddicoat, now an alderman. Most of the signatures have been detached and destroyed, again depriving historians of evidence. Included with the petition was a separate communication from John Burton: "Respected Sir William. May I ask the favour of your sympathies for Dudley and Stephens. Trusting yourself and Lady Harcourt are well. P.S. I might here add that I am the person who stood bail for Dudley, Stephens and Brooks here." This slightly familiar approach was explained by a booklet (also enclosed) about The Old Curiosity Shop, which revealed that Sir William had himself visited Falmouth and the shop in April 1882 and taken a sailing trip out to the Manacles Reef. Another petition, organized in Plymouth by Mr. John B. Harvey, arrived in January, with 19 pages of signatures, 18 now sadly destroyed. The first two to sign were James Elsan, workingman; and Peter Masters, master mariner; the latter came from Oreston, where the Dudleys had lived. There was also one from Penzance, organized by a town councillor, Thomas Rossiter, and signed by the mayor, corporation, and many inhabitants of the town. I have not established any direct connection between Penzance and Dudley or Stephens, but the Julian family may have had connections there as well as in Plymouth. Tollesbury's petition arrived on January 30. It appears to have been organized jointly by the Rev. J. C. Battersby, the Anglican parson of Tollesbury and Mersea from 1857 to 1900, and the Rev. W. M. Anstye, who presided over the rival Congregational church from 1863 to 1893. This document emphasized Dudley's blameless life and his terrible ordeal. It also made the point that medical evidence was never called at his trial at Exeter, though available, and related as an additional argument the information that further incarceration would exclude him from the chance of taking over a business offered him by a relative in the colonies. It may be that other public petitions have been lost or destroyed, for it is surprising to find nothing from Southampton.

Dudley himself submitted a long petition in his own hand, which he signed on January 24. What follows is an extract from this lengthy document.

> I beg to call your attention what our terrible sufferings while in our 15 feet boat for 24 days. The only food we had for the first 11 or 12 days was one half pound of Turnips and say at the most three pounds of raw Turtle each and you may say next to no water only our own urin to drink day after day and for the next 8 days not any food whatever and two days of which not one drop of water can any one on shore judge the state of our bodys and what must our poor brain and mind have been when that awful impulse came to put the poor lad out of his misry for he was dying at the time the salt water killed him and the terrible deed was done for the sake of something to eat and exist upon that ghastly food it makes my blood run cold to think about it now and would to God I had died in the boat I should have saved the pain from those belonging to me whatever. I can assure you I shall never forget the sight of my two unfortunate companions over that gastly meal we all was like mad wolfs who should get the most and for men fathers of children to commit such a deed we could not have our right reason and it cannot be expected we had, straining our eyes day and night over the horizon looking for help what mortal tongue can tell our sufferings but our owen about the 15th day when lots was spoke about we all was about the same in bodly health—Brooks must admit that I offered my life did the lot fall to me and I was quite prepared to die and have God for my witness but no one else would hear of it but it was not to be done until the last passable momant and I feel sure had we not that awful food to exist upon not a soul would have lived untill we were rescued but as I have said I wished I had died rather than to have pain cast on those who are dear to me or had let the poor lad died we should not have had many hours to wait I am sure.

Dudley went on to describe the horror of his rearrest: "We were allowed to return to our happy homes then to live extra well to get up our bodly strength for three months—But then comes the pain again that recalls all the terrible past it makes my sad affar doubly hard to bare. . . ." He then made a number of requests: first, a free pardon "and let me return to my happy home and get my living honistly as I have done at sea since I was not ten years old. . . ." If this was rejected, he asked second that his sentence be dated from the day of the trial at Exeter. Third, he asked for a relaxation of prison regulations so that he could communicate with his wife. Fourth, he asked to be allowed "one good meal daily namely the Hospital dinner that I was supplied with at first for a few days," or a meal at his own expense.

Edwin Stephens also submitted a short petition on February 13, asking for a remission of the remainder of his sentence and for permission to communicate with his family at more frequent intervals: this document adds nothing to the account of the shipwreck.

The most curious of all these attempts to secure more favorable treatment consisted of a letter from Miss Alice Maud Lever of Culceth Hall, Bowdon, Cheshire, dated January 2. She was the sister of a wealthy philanthropist, Ellis Lever (1833–1911), who had been born the youngest son of one James Lever, a working collier. Ellis Lever rose in the world through his own efforts and became a very successful businessman, devoting his spare time and money to good causes—particularly parks, museums, picture galleries, and the relief of unemployed cotton workers. His sister, who appears to have taken the initiative in involving him in this particular good work, wrote, "While we are met together as families to enjoy the festivities of the Christmas Season it is very distressing to think of the poor fellows Dudley and Stephens who are undergoing a term of six months' imprisonment and to learn that the families of these men are in poverty." She enclosed a draft of £50 for the Home Office to send to their families as a New Year's gift and asked also that they be given a free pardon. Enclosed was a press cutting from the *Manchester Courier* of December 27, recounting the case of the *Turley,* headed "Another." The money constituted a problem. Sir William took the view that it should be returned to her and the addresses of the families withheld, "as I do not wish to encourage presents of this kind"; the whole point of the sentence was to prevent any public displays of sympathy. An official, probably E. Ruggles-Brise, suggested she be given the address of Mr. Arthur Glennie of 15 Devonshire Street, Portland Place, who was in charge of the defense fund, which apparently held a surplus for families. The draft was returned, carefully registered. A consequence of this initiative was that contact was established between the Levers and Phillipa Dudley, and in February Ellis Lever sent a petition to Queen Victoria herself via the Home Office, where it arrived on February 24, accompanied by a long letter to Lever from Phillipa Dudley, dated February 19, 1885. This set out an account of the whole affair and extolled the virtues of her husband: "Without wishing to speak slightingly of his fellow sufferers, but in justice to my husband, his wonderful forethought, bravery and unselfishness were very prominent." In it she also mentioned their plan to emigrate: "Now he is eager to leave England as soon as possible: we trust soon to settle our affairs and make a fresh start in Australia." Ellis Lever had also apparently actually met Phillipa Dudley, and the petition stressed the proposed voluntary transportation of Dudley: "Prior even to his unfortunate start in the yacht 'Mignonette' and as indeed a main motive for the voyage, certain kinsfolk in Sydney had made Captain Dudley the offer of a promising interest in a ship chandlery business in that city." It was essential that he take up this offer soon. Included with the petition was a photograph of Phillipa Dudley, now unhappily missing, though the family possesses what may be the original.

In response to these various requests for a free pardon or for remission of the residue of the sentence, the home secretary remained firm: he regarded the sentence as settled and unalterable. There exists his note of March 2 to Queen Victoria dealing with the petition: "This is a melancholy case but the sentence is a light one and cannot be altered." The note responded to a minute by one of the officials, probably Sir Adolphus Liddell, which was more sympathetic: "It is said he will go with his wife to Australia as soon as released. His wife's letter, giving an account of her anxieties, is very pathetic." Although the petition was formally submitted to Queen Victoria on March 10, there is no evidence that she took any particular interest in it, and it was formally rejected. Sir William was more sympathetic about family visits; in response to Dudley's petition, he wrote, "I am however inclined to give rather greater indulgence in respect of communications with his family." He did not in fact know what the regulations were, but, on being told of the restriction to one visit (no more than two visitors, and a maximum time of 20 minutes) and one letter every three months, he instructed that Dudley should have a letter and visit each fortnight, and Stephens later received the same privileges. Special food was not permitted, no doubt on the ground that if the prison doctor thought it necessary on medical grounds, it would be provided in any event. Sir William had also taken a fairly unsympathetic line over the replacement of Dudley and Stephens's Board of Trade certificates as master and mate, respectively; the certificates had gone down with the *Mignonette*. They applied for replacements—or at least Stephens did by a letter on November 8 (no letter from Dudley survives)—but the board thought their replacement then might encourage Stephens to break bail by signing on for a foreign voyage: it was easy for sailors to vanish.

The Home Office was consulted, and Sir William minuted, "I think the certificates ought not to be replaced until the Court has decided whether these men were guilty of murder." And so the matter rested until they had completed their sentence.

They were eventually released from Holloway on May 20, 1885, exactly a year and a day after the voyage of the *Mignonette* began; and they returned to their homes, Dudley to 1 Myrtle Road and Stephens to 73 Northumberland Avenue. On May 22, both wrote to the Board of Trade again requesting the replacement of the lost certificates, Stephens writing on black-edged mourning paper, perhaps because of the recent death of Thomas Ridley Stephens, probably an uncle, or perhaps as a token of respect for Richard Parker. Their requests were granted without further reference to the Home Office. The two sailors could now both return to their profession of the sea.

Of the three survivors of the *Mignonette,* least of all is known about the later career of Ned Brooks. Since he was not a certified officer, the Board of Trade records do not provide any simple way of establishing details of his later career as a seaman; it would only be reconstructed at quite disproportionate effort in the dispersed surviving crew lists of merchant vessels. He continued to base himself in Southampton, and local tradition maintains that he worked as a rigger in Fay's Yard and as a yacht hand. He may also have worked on Union Line vessels to the Cape, as he had done in the past. A curious account of him in 1906 survives. The late Daniel Benjamin Parker (1891–1971), whose father, Ben, had been mate of the Kaiser's yacht *Meteor* and a cousin of Richard, worked as a boy and young man as a yachtsman and in 1906 was working on a 50-foot cutter, *Una,* which set out across the Solent to collect a load of oak knees to be used in boat construction by Harry Stevens, who ran Stevens's Boat Yard. In 1963, he was persuaded to write an account of his meeting with Brooks on this voyage:

> I was to assist Teddy Brooks with a load of oak knees to be picked up there. After picking up our cargo we sailed home in a South West gale with rain. Brooks lost his sou'wester so used a bucket—a very sensible precaution. I was huddled up under the weather bulwark close to where Brooks was sterring. He looked quite a sight in his bucket with a long dark beard. The conversation was general on things that were in sight and then he asked if I was related to Dick Parker who

> was eaten after the Mignonette was lost. Dick Parker was my second cousin—my father's cousin. He then related the story to me.

Brooks went on to tell that lots were drawn but faked. After this macabre meeting the bearded and bucketed Brooks fades away again. Tradition has it that at one point he even lived in Itchen Ferry itself at Smith's Quay next door to Albert ("Curly") Bedford (1884–1979), whose father-in-law was Dan ("Bucky Eye") Parker (1860–1940), second mate of the Kaiser's *Meteor* and another cousin of Richard's. "Curly" Bedford used to tell how Brooks, in drink, would cry out at night that he "didn't do it." Brooks lived on in Southampton and died on July 22, 1919, of a heart attack at the age of 73; he was then in the parish infirmary, and his death was reported by his widow, of 105 Bevois Street, in Northam, Southampton. He had married Sarah Anne Cox on October 13, 1891, in St. Mary's; she was then a widow and the daughter of a seaman who bore the unusual name of Samuel Gumb. At the time of their marriage, both were living at 4 St. Mary's Buildings, where, one suspects, Ned Brooks was the lodger. There appear to have been no children of this marriage, and the fact that there was no will or grant of letters of administration suggests that Brooks, like so many seamen, died poor. Exhaustive attempts have been made to locate an earlier marriage, but without success; I suspect that Brooks's wife of 1884 was a myth, the wife in every port of maritime tradition. He was the longest lived of the three survivors and died almost exactly a quarter of a century after the day Richard was killed.

Edwin Stephens also continued for some time to live in Southampton, first at 73 Northumberland Avenue and later, in 1887, nearby in a marginally larger house at 6 Oxford Avenue. From the Board of Trade records, it appears that he undertook no voyages in 1885, but in 1886 he sailed as master on the *Madeline,* a yacht owned by George Drover of Cowes; and on the *Sareca,* a steam yacht sold to the Egyptian government. He was discharged in Alexandria. He returned there on the *Varda,* which again was sold in Alexandria. His maritime career is then again interrupted for some six years. One of the traditional stories about him is that he worked again on Red Funnel Line vessels, as his father had done, but checks of crew lists and the records of Lloyd's and the Board of Trade do not confirm this; I suspect that tradition has confused his career before 1884 with what happened later. The company may, of course, have given him a shore job, but its records for the period were destroyed in the last war. In August 1893 he went to sea again in command of *Lavinia* on the North Atlantic run, and the following year he sailed to South America on *Mary Low.* Again there is a gap, and then in 1898 he sailed for the last time on the steamship *Jourcoing* (Captain Pearse), as mate at £1.17s.6d. a week. His last voyage took him to Sardinia from London, departing on March 15 and returning to Portsmouth on May 12. Tradition has it that Stephens never recovered fully from his ordeal and became unbalanced and melancholic, given to drink. Again, there is no direct evidence, but the decline of his career as a mariner is consistent with this. In 1890 he is no longer listed as a master mariner at his home in Oxford Avenue, and a Mrs. E. Stephens, perhaps his wife, is recorded at 48 York Street, Northam: it is possible the family had broken up, though on his last voyage he was allotting wages to dependents. At that time he was living at 7 Mayville Road in Leytonstone, a suburb of east London, though whether as owner, tenant, or lodger is impossible to tell. Stephens died on June 25, 1914, at 22 Thomas Street, Hull, at the age of 66; he may have had a number of relatives in Hull, for there were two master mariners, Fred Stephens (b. 1871) and William Henry Stephens (b. 1870) listed in Lloyd's records as coming from the city. His son, Charles G. Stephens, lived in Hull at 51 Laburnum Avenue, Garden Village, and was with him when he died. Presumably he looked after his father in his declining years. Like Ned Brooks, he left no will, and letters of administration were not taken out. He died a poor man.

Tom Dudley's subsequent career was shorter than that of either of his shipmates and in one sense more tragic. He had, as we have seen, been considering emigration when he undertook the command of *Mignonette.* His conviction and official stigmatization as a murderer no doubt reinforced the arguments for starting a new life with his family in the colonies. For however sympathetically the yachting fraternity felt toward him at the time of his trial, he would no longer find it easy to obtain employment as a sailing master. The job involved an element of the gentleman's gentleman, and nobody was likely to engage him in that capacity after what contemporaries would have described as his singular experiences; he had to make a new start. He was not the only reprieved murderer (technically his position) to take such a decision in 1885; for it was the same year in which Constance Kent emerged on July 18 from Fulham convict prison where she had completed 20 years' penal servitude for the murder of her 5-year-old half-brother, a celebrated crime committed in 1860 out of jealousy of her stepmother, to which she had confessed five years later. Perhaps the most remarkable of all Victorian criminals, Constance Kent, unlike Tom Dudley, accepted her own guilt and prudently changed her name to Ruth Emilie Kaye before sailing. Characteristically, Tom Dudley did not; he was in his own eyes morally innocent, with nothing to conceal. His prospects in Australia were promising. In addition to other possible relatives, he had an aunt, Mrs. R. W. Pettigrew, who ran a business as a tent maker at 38 York Street, Sydney. The business also involved trade in yacht chandlery, a growing trade, for Sydney was developing as a yachting center. It may well be that Mrs. Pettigrew was widowed and elderly and needed assistance.

The Dudleys emigrated in 1885; their ship was the Orient Line's steamship *Austral,* well known for having sunk in Sydney Harbour on her maiden voyage through inattention to stability during coaling. Raised and refitted, she left Gravesend on Wednesday, August 19, under Captain Charlton, calling at Plymouth (where the Dudleys probably embarked) on August 21. As *Austral* set out on the long voyage *Mignonette* had attempted a year earlier, the yachts *Irex* and *Marguerite* were competing at the Royal Portsmouth Regatta, though whether Ned Brooks and Daniel Parker were involved in the proceedings I do not know, though Brooks was understandably not a member of the crew of *Irex,* on which Richard's cousin was second mate; Daniel, Richard's brother, was probably still on *Marguerite. Austral* called at Naples and then sailed on through the Suez Canal, reaching Sydney in the afternoon of October 5. With the Dudleys and their three children traveled one of Phillipa's sisters—either Jenny or Elizabeth Julian. The other sister later joined them; both were schoolteachers.

In Sydney, Tom Dudley continued to use his own name, and there is no evidence that the tragedy in which he had been involved impeded him in any way. By 1889, if not before, he was established as a tent and tarpaulin maker at 221 Clarence Street, which runs parallel to the waterfront of Darling Harbour behind the wharfage. This business was no doubt combined with sail making and yacht chandlery. He may for a short time have had a residential address in Fig Street, and there is directory evidence of his living in 1886 in Toogood Street in the inner suburb of Macdonaldtown. It was then a good middle-class area.

According to stories told to Donald McCormick, life for Tom Dudley was eased for him by Jack Want, who had also visited him in prison in England and helped the family to emigrate. Given the contemporary regulations that severely restricted visits, the visit is highly improbable, and we know that Tom Dudley's main wish was to see his family. The move to Sydney was basically a family matter, though it is quite possible that Jack Want assisted him on arrival; I have found no direct evidence of this. If he did so, it was perhaps by placing yachting business in Tom's way. Life in Sydney for Tom Dudley was also enlivened by the arrival there, so Donald McCormick records, of Otilia Ribeiro. We last met her in Madeira after her near drowning and her blow on the head from Richard Parker. She had traveled via Luanda and Goa, dressed as a man, and on arrival descended on Dudley, who was originally, McCormick incorrectly has it, anxious to conceal his identity: this was some time in 1887 or so. This transvestite girl possessed, as her imaginative chronicler maintains, "remarkable initiative for an orphan flower girl," and in her travels certainly conforms to the standard maritime yarn of the ship's boy who proves, on closer inspection, to be the ship's girl. A well-known ballad on this theme is "The Female Cabin Boy":

It is of a pretty female, as you shall understand
She had a mind for roving unto a foreign land,
Attired in sailor's clothing she boldly did appear,
And engaged with the captain to serve him for one year.

She engaged with the captain as cabin boy to be,
The wind it was in favour, so they soon put out to sea,
The captain's lady being on board, who seem'd it to enjoy,
So glad the captain had engag'd the handsome cabin boy.

So nimble was that pretty maid, and done her duty well,
But mark what follow'd, often the thing itself will tell,
The captain with that pretty maid did ofttimes kiss and toy,
For he soon found out the secret of the female cabin boy.

Her cheeks appear'd like roses, and with her side locks curl'd
The sailors ofttimes smil'd and said, he looks just like a girl,
By eating captains biscuit, her colour did destroy,
And the waist did swell of pretty Nell, the handsome cabin boy.

As through the Bay of Biscay their gallant ship did plough,
One night amongst the sailors there was a pretty row,
They bundled from their hammocks, it did their rest destroy,
And they swore about the groaning of the handsome cabin boy.

O doctor, O doctor, the cabin boy did cry,
The sailors swore by all was good the cabin boy would die;
The doctor ran with all his might and smiling at the fun,
For to think a sailor lad should have a daughter or son.

The sailors when they heard the joke, they all began to stare,
The child belong'd to none of them they solemnly did swear,
The lady to the captain said, my dear I wish you joy,
For its either you or I betray'd the handsome cabin boy.

So they all took up a bumper, and drank success to trade,
And likewise to the cabin boy, though neither man nor maid.
And if the waves should rise again the sailors to destroy,
Why we then must ship some sailors like the handsome cabin boy.

According to McCormick, Otilia and Dudley also appear to have had some premature familiarity with psychoanalytic theory, and Dudley was deeply guilt ridden over the death of Richard Parker. In the end of McCormick's version, their bizarre adventures culminate in a symbolic reenactment of the voyage of the *Mignonette,* in which Otilia masquerades as "Ricardo Parker," and they sail off together up, inevitably, the Great Barrier Reef, the aim being, as they put it today, to "let it all hang out." In the course of this trip, Dudley soliloquizes as follows:

> Half in mockery, half in masochistic frenzy, Dudley's mind wandered like a nightmare of fantasy in which he saw himself slashing a morsel of flesh from his buttocks. While Otilia slept he bandaged his self-imposed wound tightly with the canvas he had removed from her breasts, then lowered his buttocks over the side of the boat so that the salt water would check the bleeding. And then, in the tiny galley, he would cook this morsel and present it to her when she woke. Buttocks, and beans, he laughed to himself. Yes, that would be the supreme sacrifice, the one act which would obliterate his crime and make her realise how much he thought of her.

Prudently, however, Dudley did not practice this Freudian *haute cuisine,* and those who wish to follow the tale in detail must turn to *Blood on the Sea* for further details, in what the author concedes to be an imaginative reconstruction.

I have been unable to locate Otilia Ribeiro (alias "Ricardo Parker," alias "Jack Straw") in any of her haunts. Ribeiro is a common surname and also a place name north of Funchal. Nor have I found any confirmation of McCormick's picture of Tom Dudley as a man in moral decline, visiting "some of the low taverns around Sydney," smoking opium (never, we are reassured, more than 10 pipes a night) and—this with some overtones—taking up with an aboriginal woman, not to mention concealing his identity and making illicit trips with Otilia on the sailing vessel *Sanctuary*. All this seems wholly out of character, and where it can be tested (as over concealment of identity) is demonstrably incorrect. It is hard to believe that a successful business could have been built up by such a caricature of a human being.

His business, conducted under the name of T. R. Dudley and Co., came to be established at numbers 47, 49, and 51 Sussex Street, occupying the first floor over three shops near the junction with Erskine Street. The business prospered, and Dudley became a large-scale contractor for sails, tarpaulins, and tents. He also dealt in flags and was well known in yachting circles as a yacht rigger and outfitter. The yachting business appears to have been centered upon a boathouse and slip near the bridge over the Parramatta River, then known as the Parramatta Bridge and now replaced by Gladesville Bridge. This slip would be south of Five Dock Point. Eventually, many years later, according to one of my informants, it came to be used by the sea cadets and may be still identifiable; it probably lay to the north of what is now Drummoyne Park by what is now The Esplanade. Close to it, only some 50 yards or so away, was the family home. At the time, the area was not built up, and it was somewhat separated from any other houses; its location is variously given as on Cambridge or Bridge Street or Road; to judge from a map, it may be that Cambridge Road (Street) was also called Bridge Street. Local council records note that Dudley owned Lots 14 and 15 on North Road, and this suggests a house between North Road (now Victoria Place) and Cambridge Street. At Drummoyne, Dudley fitted out yachts, dealt in chandlery, and may have built yachts—he advertised as a yacht builder in 1890. His business premises in Sussex Street also had residential accommodation attached. By 1900, the business employed some 40 men and women. His foreman was Charles Kingswall, and he also employed a book-keeper, William Weatherill; a sail maker, James Channon; a general handyman, Archibald Macdonald; and numerous others. His family too had grown, three more children being born to Phillipa after the family emigrated. One, a boy, died young or in infancy; two girls, Elizabeth Eulalia and Charlotte, were to survive him. Whether Tom Dudley continued to captain yachts after he emigrated is a matter on which traditions are contradictory; it may be that in Sydney evidence survives that would establish the truth. There is a tradition and slight documentary support for one visit home to England between 1885 and 1900, but I have been unable to confirm this.

In that year, however, disaster struck the family yet again. From the province of Yunnan in China, and ultimately from its reservoir in Central Asia, bubonic plague reached Hong Kong in May of 1894, and in the following years of the third pandemic, which killed 13 million people, it was carried by ships to all the major seaports of the world. How precisely it reached Australia was never firmly established, but it almost certainly came from Noumea on the S.S. *Rockton*—the first case may have occurred in Adelaide, where a sailor by the name of Appstan, who had deserted his ship, the *Formosa* of New York, died on January 12, 1900; but the diagnosis was dubious. About the same time, the disease reached Sydney. The first sign of its presence was that rats were seen dying in large numbers around the wharves of the Union Shipping Company and Huddart Parker and Co., and it soon became established in the squalid rat-infested area around Darling Harbour. Never having encountered plague before, the rats would possess no resistance, and a very high proportion of their population was bound to die until an equilibrium was established or the disease died out through failure to establish one. There its presence was soon recognized by Dr. Ashburton Thompson, president of the Board of Health, who had anticipated the epidemic, though it was not until February that he managed to culture the bacillus *Pasteurella pestis* from a dead rat. The first suspected human case was that of Arthur H. Payne, who worked at Dawes Point for the Central Wharf Company, and by January 26, he and some 11 contacts were in quarantine; the presence of the disease among human beings in the city was publicly confirmed. Arthur Payne in fact recovered, and at first the disease appeared to have been contained, though Dr. Thompson assumed from the outset that an epidemic would occur until the rat population itself was drastically reduced by the disease or by sanitary action. By 1900 it was becoming established that plague was a disease of rats transmitted occasionally to humans by rat fleas, though earlier theories still had some support. Dr. Thompson's meticulous reports of the epidemic contributed to confirming the newer theories.

Dudley's business premises in Sussex Street lay at the back of the wharves of Darling Harbour, on the first floor, where there was a water closet. This was connected to sea level by a drain pipe that was defective and accessible to rats; one morning in February he had in fact removed the corpses of five recently dead rats from the water closet. From fleas deprived of their preferred host he contracted plague, a classic example of the mode of transmission of the disease, becoming ill on Saturday, February 17, at Sussex Street, where he and some of his large household commonly spent the night. After remaining there for two days, he was moved to his home in Cambridge Street, Drummoyne. In the course of his illness he was attended by three doctors. The local medical profession was aware of the danger of plague, but Dudley's case presented difficulties of diagnosis. He had recently fallen against a plank and injured his lower abdomen; internal rupture and peritonitis was suspected, though apart from a general fever there were no indications of peritonitis; two of the doctors were consultants called in to assist in diagnosis. His illness was not thought dangerous, but he died unexpectedly in the afternoon of Thursday, February 22, at the age of 46. This mercifully sudden death aroused a suspicion confirmed by laboratory examination at 3:30 P.M. of specimens of his glands by a Dr. Frank Tidswell. There was then no doubt that Dudley had died of a particularly virulent form of the disease. Between then and July, when the city was at last declared free, some 303 cases were identified, and 103 persons died, a low mortality rate of 34%. Tom Dudley, the first victim, was soon followed by John Makins, who died in quarantine on February 27. As could well be expected, the death of Dudley from bubonic plague caused very considerable alarm in Sydney; no disease causes comparable public terror. It was fully reported in the press, though an early report in the local *Balmain Observer* withheld his name to spare the family. However, later reports give his name and other details, but no report I have seen connected him with the tragedy of the *Mignonette,* a little more than 15 years earlier. This, I suspect, was deliberate reticence, rather than ignorance, in a society where there still existed a certain sensitivity about "criminal" ancestry, however irrational that might have been.

As soon as the cause of death was established, at about 4:45 P.M., the police without warning isolated Dudley's business premises and home, and all those who had recent contact with him were taken off into quarantine at the station on the North Head of Sydney Harbour. From Sussex Street there were four so quarantined. Two were employees; the others were young Phillipa (called in the press Phillis) Dudley, now aged 20, and a Mr. Arthur Gibbs Wilson, who was 22. He was described as a friend of the family: he later married Phillipa and ran his own yacht chandler's business. From the Dudleys' home in Drummoyne 13 individuals were taken away. They were Mrs. Phillipa Dudley and two other children, Winifred and Julian. Winifred was now 19 and married, as Mrs. Ludgate, her husband a tailor and the son of a sea captain from Kent; Julian, who was to take over the business, was 17. Also quarantined was a Mrs. Haskins; before her marriage, she had been Jenny Julian, Tom Dudley's sister-in-law; it is tempting to suspect some connection with John Ferguson Haskins, who paid for the memorial to Richard Parker, but I have found no evidence of this. The others included Mr. Erakwa Bush, a Japanese seaman, who had arrived with the yacht *Jess,* which was to be cleaned; the owner's son, 11-year-old James Cox, was on board too. Then there were some who had called to express their sympathy at Captain Dudley's death, for he was a greatly respected man, and others whose presence was unexplained—including, enigmatically, a Mrs. Parker and Alexander J. Parker, both aged 32 and presumably married to each other. Alexander worked as a clerk in the Railway Department and did not normally live with the Dudleys. Was he, one cannot but wonder, some relative of Richard's whom the Dudleys, as an act of atonement, had befriended? There was also Peter Gorman—surely not from Limerick? Later, other contacts were traced and quarantined, including Frederick Louis Richards, a haberdasher, and Miss Maggie Beattie, aged 18, who the press announced had nursed Dudley in his last illness. This last enraged Dudley's widow, who telegraphed indignantly from the North Head Quarantine Station that she had herself nursed him. Maggie Beattie came from Sussex Street and presumably worked for Dudley as a seamstress: there are overtones of strong motives for the widow's anger, and the incident could be interpreted as evidence of an improper relationship. I find this most implausible. In the family the tradition exists that Dudley met his death through his involvement in charitable work for those less fortunate than himself. Though strictly not correct, this could be a confused reference to work with "unfortunates"—could Maggie Beattie perhaps have been such a person whom Dudley tried to redeem? It would have fitted his known character more closely.

With friends and family gone, Dudley's body lay alone in the guarded house, and the Drummoyne council that formally considered the matter at a meeting on Tuesday, February 27, was to protest later that the health authorities left it there with untended pet animals for two days; given the fear of plague, it may have been difficult to find anyone to enter the house. On Monday the premises were fumigated, under the supervision of Dr. Armstrong, and at some point arrangements were set in hand for Dudley's burial, which apparently took place on Saturday, February 24, under the supervision of a Dr. Pickburn. Whatever indignities he had inflicted on the remains of the unfortunate Richard Parker were now to be matched by Drs. Thompson and Pickburn's men. Wrapped in sheets soaked in disinfectant, and placed in a coffin itself wrapped in a disinfected sail, the body was removed by launch down the Parramatta River and out to the Quarantine Station on the North Head, where an exceptionally deep grave had been dug to receive it. Finally, for the sake of precaution, a hole was bored in the coffin lid, and it was filled with "a very strong disinfectant." Contemporary evidence shows that Dr. Thompson favored sulphuric acid or perchloride of mercury, and I assume it was the former that was employed. What sad scenes, if any, took place at the graveside—for the family was not there—is not recorded, but there is something appropriate in the last resting place of Captain Tom Riley Dudley in grave Number 48, wrapped in a sail, situated on a steep slope and looking out to sea southward across the gateway of Sydney Harbour toward the South Head. He lies there still, but Mr. Walker of the Quarantine Station has told me that the grave stone that was placed over his last resting place has long since crumbled and become illegible.

If the death and burial of poor Tom Dudley at the height of the panic generated by the most dreaded of all human diseases has about it something of the inevitability of Greek tragedy, there remains his real memorial in the family that he and Phillipa established in the new world in the face of such misfortune. None of those quarantined in 1900 contracted plague. Phillipa was to survive her husband by more than a quarter of a century, dying at Chatswood after a short illness in 1928 at the age of 86. Her two youngest daughters (who both married) had predeceased her. The three children who had come out from England in 1885 were all still alive and married, and Julian took over the business of T. R. Dudley and Company, which remained in the control of the family until around 1946; it was finally put into liquidation in about 1978. There are those who can remember the green-painted weatherboarded premises in Sussex Street, with "Captain T. R. Dudley" writ large on the exterior, and the smart horses that Julian drove to his business. He was apparently a somewhat flamboyant individual, who inherited his father's love of the sea. I have been able to trace quite a number of descendants and more distant relatives both in Australia and England, some of whom have kindly helped in this attempt to re-create the story of the *Mi-*

gnonette and those who sailed in her, as far as they are able. No private papers appear to survive—some once did, but their owner died recently, and they now seem to be lost. The family in Australia have one photograph of "Grandad Dudley"—it was once one of a stereoscopic pair, and the self-same picture was printed in 1884 in the *Pictorial World*. They also have a very handsome pair of portraits of Tom and Phillipa, probably painted in the 1890s, and a photograph of Phillipa with her two eldest children, taken about 1882. Such traditions of Tom Dudley's character as have been passed down tally with what else is known of him—at a time when sea captains were so often hard and even brutal men, he was kindly and respected by all. However, there is a curious absence in family tradition of anecdotes about him, as if the family in a sense preferred to know nothing very specific about him. The distorted ritual processes whereby he was labeled a criminal seem even more inappropriate today than many found them back in 1884. Understandably, of course, the story of Tom Dudley's trial and dramatic death has been preserved with some disquiet. One relative has told me how she was told "by my mother when I had reached an age she thought appropriate to understand the ghastly story"; she explained further that many thought his death to be a retribution for that awful voyage. It must indeed easily have seemed so. Another version of the story that has passed down through the family reflects the persistence of the maritime tradition: lots were drawn, as they ought to have been. This too no doubt originates in unease. Understandably, some have found the story one that is better forgotten, but of this there is no possibility. I can only hope that this fuller explanation of the historical background to the tragedy of the *Mignonette* may at least help to make brave Tom Riley Dudley a more understandable human being.

Of the *Mignonette* herself, her keel and ballast presumably lie intact on the bed of the South Atlantic, where she foundered. She must at some time have been photographed, but the extensive attempts I have made to locate a photograph have failed. There is a possibility that similar yachts by Aldhous survive either in commission or as hulks. *Peregrine* (1873), a 27-ton yawl, could be one; I have been told it or its hulk could be lying in Wootton Creek on the Isle of Wight. The yawl *Dusmarie,* built in 1884 and originally named *Daisy,* is still in commission but has been extensively reconstructed in modern times. Neither have been traced. All we now have are drawings by Tom Dudley and, indirectly, by Edwin Stephens, together with an indistinct photograph of a model of her hull, last known to exist in the 1920s. Of the dinghy, too, nothing appears to have survived. In Falmouth the tradition is that it was burned at some uncertain date on the instructions of Jack Want. This is what maritime tradition requires—an ill-omened vessel should be consigned to the fire; and in very recent years, an English lifeboat that had killed its crew was ritually burned on the shore. Another tradition is that it was exhibited for gain in fairs, and this is probably true, for a contemporary source (the vicar of Brightlingsea) recorded its sale in August 1885 to an Exmouth man for the very considerable sum of £50. A photograph of it on show in the Royal Polytechnic Hall at Falmouth was made into a postcard, and one specimen survives in the Falmouth Public Library. It clearly shows the damaged port side. A photograph—probably this one—was presented to Albert Aldhous, who had built this remarkable vessel. The oarlocks of the dinghy, as we have seen, are missing, and so is the penknife that Dudley wanted as a keepsake. It never became an exhibit at the trial, and the police force no longer exists in whose custody it was kept. Nor is it, or any other relic of the affair, to be found in the possession of Madame Tussaud's. It may still survive in some macabre collection. Dudley's chronometer certificate with his last letter to Phillipa must surely have been treasured, but I have not located it, either. The name *Mignonette,* which some might have thought ill omened, remained popular; Lloyd's yacht register of 1889 notes two yachts of the name and no fewer than six *Mignon*s; later the name was even used by the Royal Navy, though not happily.

The *Moctezuma* also is no more; indeed hardly any of the old sailing barques have survived. Vast sums are expended on the preservation of undistinguished "historic" buildings, but ships are left to rot. She was sold in 1886 to D. Davidson of Farsund, Norway, partly rebuilt, and renamed *Alliance.* On her first voyage for her new owners from Hamburg to Savannah she was engaged in another last-minute rescue, picking up, after half an hour in the sea, a sailor named Theis Salvesen, who was unable to swim; he later became the director of the Norwegian Federation of Ship-Owners. Later, in 1894, the *Alliance* was sold to G. J. Jensen of Farsund. Her good fortune eventually ran out, for in November 1902, on a voyage as a collier from the Tyne to Sannesund under Captain H. Isaksen, she sprang a leak, and her pumps became choked with small coals. She was abandoned in a sinking condition. At least two paintings of her exist, and a photograph taken in 1895 shows her under tow, leaving or entering her home port. Of the vessels connected with this story, the longest survivor of all was the *Lord Elgin*, on which Stephens had served the Red Funnel Line as mate. Built in 1876, she survived as the last working, cargo-carrying paddle steamer in Britain and, under Captain Joe Sowley, sailed on her last voyage to the breakers on May 13, 1955.

No contemporary photographs of Stephens or Brooks have been traced. A poor drawing of Dudley in the *Illustrated Police News* is recognizably authentic and no doubt based on a photograph; it shows a lean, emaciated man. The *Pictorial World* also published a set of drawings produced at the time of the trial, as well as a full trial scene. The quality of all the drawings is poor; they include, however, the only picture of Ned Brooks and quite an entertaining depiction of the bullying Baron Huddleston, with the perceptive caption "His Lordship informs the Jury of *his* intentions." Edwin Stephens is portrayed there and in drawings in the *Illustrated London News* and *Graphic.* Richard Parker's likeness has been wholly lost, but a photograph exists of his elder brother, William ("Flop"), whom he resembled; it was taken when William was an old man, probably between 1930 and 1935. "Flop" as a younger man sailed on the Kaiser's *Meteor,* and it may be possible to identify him on photographs of the crew of the yacht, one of which I possess, but I have not been able to do so with any confidence.

At Falmouth, it is still possible to visit many of the places involved and re-create a little of the scene at the landing and committal of the survivors of the *Mignonette*. The elegant customs house where they made their depositions is still there, much as it was in 1884, though the Long Room you enter today is not quite the same. The counter is modern, but if you look beyond it you can see at the back of the room to the right the counter as it was then, on which Mr. Tressider recorded their depositions, and in front of which Dudley re-enacted the scene and was arrested by Sergeant Laverty. Mr. Tressider's modest home at 23 Dunstaville Terrace has also survived, as has the home of Pilot Collins at 10 Norfolk Road. You can even stay at Robert Gandy Cheesman's villa in Melville Road, once called "Morvah," then "The Morvah Hotel," and now "The Collingbourne Hotel." The Old Curiosity Shop at 27 Market Street is no more, but the premises survive as "Flair" and A. B. Harvey and Sons. The legal firm of Wilson L. Fox and H. Tilly is also gone, though the remote successors to the practice, Messrs I. F. M. Hine, continue to practice law from Barclay's Bank Chambers. The police station at 33 Market Street where the three men were detained has been demolished, but the old courtroom where they came before the borough magistrates survives as the Old Town Hall, little altered. It has had a chequered history since 1884, being used in the mid-1970s as a Mormon Temple. When I visited Falmouth recently, it was in use as an antique shop by Mr. Michael Cater (it has since changed hands), and you could walk down the passageway opposite to the ruins of Barracks Opie Quay, where they landed. By some fortunate accident of planning, it is even still possible to leave Falmouth, as Dudley and Stephens did, by train along the single track line completed in 1865. Of the old maritime world of Falmouth, there are many reminders—the Fox family, of whom Robert Fox as German vice-consul was involved in our case in 1884, still operate the firm of G. C. Fox and Co., Shipping Agents, from their eighteenth-century premises at 48 Arwenack Street, as they have since 1762. But the great days of the port are now over, and a visit there has a sadness to it.

In Exeter, you can still visit the castle and see the courtroom where Dudley and Stephens stood trial, but the interior has been modernized in outstanding bad taste and now looks rather like a coffee bar. When I visited it, the police officer on duty, Sergeant Macdonald, knew all about Dudley and Stephens, having studied the case as part of his professional training. Further to the east, the next port of call is Southampton. Parts of Northam remain little changed since 1884, but Fay's Yard has gone. It was taken over by Camper and Nicholson in 1912, and they too have now left. Vanished as well is the County Tavern, where Ned Brooks lived when on shore and no doubt entertained his cronies in the bar with tales of the voyage of the *Mignonette*. Edwin Stephens's modest little terrace house is still intact, near a particularly magnificent Victorian public house that, one hopes, he visited. His later home at 6 Oxford Avenue is also still in existence, and the Red Funnel Line, for which he and his father worked, still operates as it did then, though the old paddle steamers they knew have now all gone. You cross the Itchen River today on the new suspension bridge, which replaced the floating bridge that, in its turn, destroyed the livelihood of the ferrymen of Itchen Ferry. When the new bridge was opened, a suggestion was made that it be called "Parker Bridge," but the idea did not catch on. Near its foot and along the waterfront there still remain a few cottages from the lower part of the village; and it was here that the Parkers, the Cozenses, the Jurds, the Mathewses, and the Diapers lived. The Yacht Tavern, where the yachtsmen of Itchen gathered, is still there as their memorial. Up Sea Road from Smith's Quay you come to Pear Tree Green, on which old Chick Parker once played cricket; the original pear tree has gone, but a replacement was planted in 1951. The little church is unchanged, and in the graveyard on the side near the school where Richard failed to be educated is his memorial. It is now rather cracked and discolored and no longer upright as it once was; it is near the stone of Sarah Parker, Richard's aunt, who died in 1898. The stone was damaged some years ago by a falling tree, and in the early 1970s it was lying broken: The Rev. Wincott tells me that parishioners with no connection with the Parker family paid for it to be set up again, and it is still located over the unmarked graves of Richard's father and mother. Photographs of it before it was damaged show it in a remarkably clean condition, and there is a persistent tradition (though one that Mr. Wincott does not accept) that it was kept in good order through a discreet arrangement made by Dudley's family. A Mrs. Smith, variously said to have carried out this task and to have paid for the preservation of the stone, has not been traced: a report in the *Echo* places the restoration as taking place in March 1974 or a little earlier. It is not the only curious stone there. Though in a brief visit I have not located it, there existed there a stone with the following epitaph to a sailor:

> My sails are split, my mainmast gone,
> My soul is fled the deck,
> Now, underneath the cold grey stone
> My body lies, a wreck,
> Yet still the promise stands secure,
> It shall refitted be
> And sail the seas of endless bliss
> To all eternity

One can hope for no less for Richard Parker.

In Brightlingsea, where the yacht *Mignonette* was built, the story is well known, partly through local tradition and partly through the writings of L. W. Southern; but like Tollesbury, where it began, Brightlingsea has no memorial to the affair. As a child, Tom Dudley's home was in Head Street, Tollesbury, but is no longer identifiable; I have also been told that at one time he lived in a cottage near the school, but this has now been demolished. Down on the saltings, yachts are still repaired and laid up, but the demand for winter mud berths has declined in the age of fiberglass, and in consequence many of the berths are now empty, while some contain the hulks of vessels that must date from the days of the *Mignonette* herself. But the oysters and the work which went with them appear to have now gone, and as a center for professional yachtsmen Tollesbury is not what it was. And the Dudleys' house in Sutton at 1 Myrtle Road no longer exists; it was pulled down in about 1965, and on the site now stands part of the Manor Park School, where the successors of the children Phillipa Dudley once taught receive their early education; Phillipa's earlier school at Oreston is still there. Otherwise Myrtle Road is not very much changed, though Tom Dudley is long forgotten. Culcheth Hall, where in the Christmas season of 1884 Alice and Ellis Lever pondered the unhappiness of the separated Dudley family, still exists, now being used as a girls school, founded in 1891 after the Levers had ceased to live at Bowdon.

But in Tollesbury, Falmouth, and Southampton, the story of the *Mignonette* still survives in tradition, especially in the families of those connected with it. In Tollesbury, the link is preserved through the Frost family, particularly through surviving relatives of William and Jim Frost, who were to have sailed aboard her. Jim Frost, who died only relatively recently, was a well-known barge skipper; William Frost owned a number of sailing barges and, among other business ventures, ran a coal business: you can still see his faded sign. Somewhat hostile to the British political system, he made a point of flying the American flag on his vessels, and in the same unpatriotic spirit he even called his home "Roosevelt" after Teddy. In Falmouth too the story is well remembered, though with the passage of time the facts have become somewhat confused. It is, for example, said that Dudley, Stephens, and Brooks were themselves Cornishmen. This myth will become more prevalent perhaps since the publication in 1980 by Mr. David Mudd, the local M.P., of *Home Along Falmouth and Penryn,* in which it is said that Thomas Dudley came from Falmouth itself. A circumstance that may have encouraged the belief that the story of the *Mignonette* involved Falmouth men is that Captain Dan Parker, master of the Falmouth ocean-going tug *Turmoil,* was related to the Parker family of Itchen Ferry, though his relation to Richard must have been very distant. Dan Parker died in 1955 (there is a memorial in Bitterne Church, Southampton); he became a national figure when involved in an attempt to rescue the crippled American vessel *Flying Enterprise* in 1952. When I visited Falmouth recently, Mr. Cheesman's successor, Mr. B. Cornwall, knew all about the great scene that had taken place nearly a century earlier in the customs house, and nearby in the basement of the International Stores

Mr. Minton took me through the sides of bacon and the mounds of butter to an old wall close to the street front, on the site of the Old Fal Café, which stood there in the 1960s. Striking a massive piece of masonry, he told me that it concealed the cell in which Dudley, Stephens, and Brooks had been incarcerated in September 1884; he looked into it during building operations in 1967. The tradition he recorded may well be correct historically, though another account places their cell in the basement of the modern Woolworth's; no doubt further research might settle the point.

In Southampton, traditions connected with the *Mignonette* are largely associated with the Parker family, many members of which know traditional stories of the affair, as well, of course, as having read about it in the press. Whereas there appear to be no surviving relatives preserving links with Ned Brooks or Edwin Stephens (as far as I have been able to discover), the Parkers have preserved their contacts both with the locality and with the tragedy of 1884. It appears that of Richard's brothers, only William ("Flop"), twice married, had children, one of whom, W. S. Parker (1892–1973) was contacted by Donald McCormick when the latter was preparing his book. One of William's children was called Edith, presumably after Richard's younger sister Edith. The family tradition is that young sister Edith was educated, unlike most of the family in the late nineteenth century. One version is that her education was financed by money discreetly provided by Dudley. This could be a reference to the use to which the surplus in the defense fund was put. All other traces of Edith have vanished. Three grandchildren of "Flop" Parker are still in Southampton; and one, Mr. E. J. Parker, now a builder, told me how his Aunt Edith used to request the local paper, the *Echo,* not to print stories of the *Mignonette,* as they were very distressing to her father. When I visited Mr. Parker, I was pleased to hear that, in true Parker fashion, he had always wanted to go to sea. His yacht, *Latonia,* which he personally built, was by his house; he had not thought it appropriate to revive the name *Mignonette.* Other more distant relatives of Richard also preserve memories of the affair, such as Mr. Ivor Bedford. His father, Albert "Curly" Bedford (1884–1979), married a daughter of Daniel Parker (1865–1944) and Sarah Parker; Daniel's father was Richard's uncle. "Curly" Bedford told his son the story of Ned Brooks crying out at night when he lived at Smith's Quay. Another relative is Mr. Keith Parker, whose mother, Mrs. Vivienne R. Parker, recalls the story that the men were only tried at all because they cheated in not drawing lots.

Since 1884, there have been many accounts of the story of the *Mignonette* in books, periodicals, and newspapers; few have added any real information, and most have been grossly inaccurate. The only full study of the story is *Blood on the Sea,* in which a considerable amount of reliable information is mingled with myth and imaginative reconstruction, so that it is hard to tell where history ends and myth begins. All lawyers know of the case, though only from the law reports, and there has been extended discussion in professional literature of the principal legal point involved—the defense of necessity—but virtually nothing has appeared on the other legal questions raised by the strange legal procedures involved, apart from a short article in the *Chicago Law Review* by Michael G. Mallin, inspired by Professor Norval Morris. In modern times, dramatists have turned their attention to the story, which on its face has certain features reminiscent of a classic tragedy. *The Mignonette* by Arthur Britten was published as a drama for schools in 1973, and Keith Parker at one time worked on a play dealing with the fate of his distant relative; but this, unfortunately, has never been completed. *The Ballad of the Mignonette* (also given the title *A Case of Necessity?*) by Jean Bernard-Williams, Nick Girdler, Graham Sinclair, and Eve Thomas was produced in the Salisbury Playhouse in 1975, and in Southampton in 1977 and 1979. The BBC has related the tale, and a version dramatized by David Edwards as *The Broken Flower* was transmitted by Radio Southampton in July 1974. Mr. Don E. Good of the Southampton *Echo,* who wrote two very informative articles on the case some years ago, indicated in conversation with me his belief in the inherently dramatic character of the story, which he saw as involving a conflict between the principle of survival and self-preservation on the one hand, inculcated at the time as a virtue, and on the other hand the nobler principle of self-sacrifice. No full-scale dramatic presentation is known to have taken place, and one of the most curious features of the case of the *Mignonette* is that Dudley and Stephens have never captured the public imagination as human individuals, much less as comic figures of myth; they have lived on merely as actors in a theoretical legal debate. In this they differ strikingly from such Victorian and Edwardian English immortals as Dr. Palmer or the sinister, much-married bath attendant, George Joseph Smith. Perhaps the explanation is that they could never be regarded as *genuine* criminals at all, while at the same time their intensely honorable characters and their frailty in the face of awful temptation hardly qualified them as saints, either. Society likes its folk heroes to be one thing or the other.

Appendix A
The Special Verdict

NOTE: The text as printed here is taken from the law reports and represents the final official version. It includes the additions struck out by order of the Queen's Bench on December 4; these are printed in italics. The names of the prisoners, one incorrect, were not in the original text either. The conclusion, printed here also in italics, was not in the text as drafted by Huddleston, read out to the jurors, and copied by James Read in the assize minute book. The original conclusion is given at the end; so also is the more elaborate version read out at the commencement of the argument on December 4 in London.

> That on July 5, 1884, the prisoners, Thomas Dudley and Edward [*sic*] Stephens, with one Brooks, all able-bodied English seamen, and the deceased also an English boy, between seventeen and eighteen years of age, the crew of an English yacht, *a registered English vessel,* were cast away in a storm on the high seas 1600 miles from the Cape of Good Hope, and were compelled to put into an open boat *belonging to the said yacht.* That in this boat they had no supply of water and no supply of food, except two 1 lb. tins of turnips, and for three days they had nothing else to subsist upon. That on the fourth day they caught a small turtle, upon which they subsisted for a few days, and

this was the only food they had up to the twentieth day when the act now in question was committed. That on the twelfth day the remains of the turtle were entirely consumed, and for the next eight days they had nothing to eat. That they had no fresh water, except such rain as they from time to time caught in their oilskin capes. That the boat was drifting on the ocean, and was probably more than 1000 miles away from land. That on the eighteenth day, when they had been seven days without food and five without water, the prisoners spoke to Brooks as to what should be done if no succour came, and suggested that some one should be sacrificed to save the rest, but Brooks dissented, and the boy, to whom they were understood to refer, was not consulted. That on the 24th of July, the day before the act now in question, the prisoner Dudley proposed to Stephens and Brooks that lots should be cast who should be put to death to save the rest, but Brooks refused to consent, and it was not put to the boy, and in point of fact there was no drawing of lots. That on that day the prisoners spoke of their having families, and suggested it would be better to kill the boy that their lives should be saved, and Dudley proposed that if there was no vessel in sight by the morrow morning the boy should be killed. The next day, the 25th of July, no vessel appearing, Dudley told Brooks that he had better go and have a sleep, and made signs to Stephens and Brooks that the boy had better be killed. The prisoner Stephens agreed to the act, but Brooks dissented from it. That the boy was then lying at the bottom of the boat quite helpless, and extremely weakened by famine and by drinking sea water, and unable to make any resistance, nor did he ever assent to his being killed. The prisoner Dudley offered a prayer asking for forgiveness for them all if either of them should be tempted to commit a rash act, and that their souls might be saved. That Dudley, with the assent of Stephens, went to the boy, and telling him that his time was come, put a knife into his throat and killed him then and there; that the three men fed upon the body and blood of the boy for four days; that on the fourth day after the act had been committed the boat was picked up by a passing vessel, and the prisoners were rescued, still alive, but in the lowest state of prostration. That they were carried to the port of Falmouth, and committed for trial at Exeter. That if the men had not fed upon the body of the boy, they would probably not have survived to be so picked up and rescued, but would within the four days have died of famine. That the boy, being in a much weaker condition, was likely to have died before them. That at the time of the act in question there was no sail in sight, nor any reasonable prospect of relief. That under these circumstances there appeared to the prisoners every probability that unless they then fed or very soon fed upon the boy or one of themselves they would die of starvation.

> That there was no appreciable chance of saving life except by killing some one for the others to eat. That assuming any necessity to kill anybody, there was no greater necessity for killing the boy than any of the other three men. *But whether upon the whole matter by the jurors found the killing of Richard Parker by Dudley and Stephens be felony and murder the jurors are ignorant, and pray the advice of the Court thereupon, and if upon the whole matter the Court shall be of opinion that the killing of Richard Parker be felony and murder, then the jurors say that Dudley and Stephens were each guilty of felony and murder as alleged in the indictment.*

The original conclusion, as recorded by James Read, read,

> But whether upon the whole matter the prisoners were and are guilty of murder the Jury are ignorant and refer to the court.

The shorthand transcript confirms that exactly this version was read to the jury.

The form of the conclusion as revised and read out at the start of the proceedings in London is again different from the version published in the law reports (which would have been approved by Lord Coleridge) and is as follows:

> And if upon the whole matter aforesaid by the said Jurors in form aforesaid found the Court shall be of opinion that the killing of the said Richard Parker in manner aforesaid done and committed be felony and murder then the said Jurors on their said oath say that the said Thomas Dudley and Edwin Stephens are each guilty of the felony and murder aforesaid in manner and form as in and by the Indictment aforesaid above specified is against them alleged. And if upon the whole matter . . .

The text in the same form sets out the possibility of manslaughter, with an appropriate finding, and then goes on:

> [If] the court shall be of opinion that the aforesaid killing of the said Richard Parker be neither felony and murder nor felony and manslaughter then the said jurors on their oath say that the said Thomas Dudley and Edwin Stephens are not guilty of the premises in the indictment.

Appendix B The Explanatory Note in the Law Reports, Dated 1885

In this case, which is reported ante, p. 273, it has been thought desirable to add the following statement to prevent any misconception of the effect of the case as a precedent with regard to the practice to be pursued upon a special verdict in criminal cases. Though, as stated in the report, the assizes had been adjourned until the 4th of December, the day on which the case was argued, the argument was heard by the judges, not as commissioners of assize, but as judges of the Queen's Bench Division of the High Court of Justice. Prior to the argument Sir H. James, A.G. applied that the record should be brought into Court by the clerk of indictments of the Western Circuit. This was done, and the Court directed that it should be filed. It was filed accordingly, and the argument proceeded.

A.P.S.

[A.P.S. was Arthur P. Stone, the law reporter.]

Appendix C
Ballads Illustrating the Custom of the Sea

"A Copy of Verses Written on the Lamentable Shipwreck of the Brig George, Capt. M'Alpen. Which sailed from Quebec in America, for Greenock in Scotland, in September 1822."
(Text from a copy in the Cornwall County Record Office, DDX 106/29)

Attend ye British landsmen
  And listen unto me,
While unto you I do relate
  The dangers of the sea;
The 12th day of September
  From Quebec we did sail,
Bound for the port of Greenock
  With a sweet and pleasant gale.
Landsmen all, pray pity me,
  While toss'd upon the raging sea.
With timber we were laden,
  Our vessel was well stor'd
Nine seamen and 3 passengers,
  Were all the hands on board;

Till the 6th day of October;
  We plough'd the raging main,
In hopes that we should soon arrive
  In Scotland once again.
Yet fortune prov'd unkind to us,
  All on that fatal day,
A storm arose and soon did wash
  Three of our hands away.
Until the setting of the sun
  Did foaming billows rise.
The waves did lift their lofty heads,
  To meet the lowering skies.
Then thro' the dark and hazy night
  Fresh sorrows did revive,
To save us from a watery grave,
  Each seaman bold did strive.
Unto the pumps all hands were call'd
  Our efforts were in vain,
And men and stores were wash'd away
  Into the raging main.
At six o'clock next morning,
  Most shocking to relate,
One female only was on board,
  Hard was her helpless fate;
The little infant at her breast,
  The husband tried to save,
Though soon was forc'd to yield it up,
  Unto the briny waves.
The storm that burst upon our heads
  Was dreadful to behold,
Our mainsail then we did let down
  To shield us from the cold;
With uplift hands to heav'n above,
  We utter'd many a prayer,
In our distress relief we sought,
  But no relief was near.
Six days and nights with all our might
  We brav'd the foaming tide,
The seventh day in the morning,
  The wretched female died;
Yet still the howling tempest
  Upon our heads did burst,

At length we drank the female's blood
  to quench our raging thirst.
Her wretched husband was compel'd
  Her precious blood to taste,
But for the whole ship's company,
  The same did not long last;
Her body then they did dissect,
  Most dreadful for to view
And serv'd it out in pieces,
  Amongst the whole ship's crew.
Eleven days more we did survive,
  Upon this horrid food,
With nothing to supply our wants,
  Save human flesh and blood.
When five more of the wretched crew
  Had then resign'd their breath,
With raging thirst and hunger
  Slept in the arms of death.
Full twenty one days longer
  Our perils did survive,
Eating our dead companions
  We kept ourselves alive.
The captain and a seaman bold
  Their lives did yet retain,
They were all that now surviv'd
  To brave the foaming main.
For 30 and 8 days and nights,
  We on the wreck did lie,
Until brave Captain Hudson
  Our peril did espy.
He sent to our assistance,
  And kindly lent a hand,
But quickly we were wreck'd again
  Off the coast of Cumberland,
Yet heav'n all bounteous proved,
  Soon bade our sorrows cease,
The ship broke her chain cable
  And caused a kind release.
Unto the main we bade adieu,
  Where foaming billows rose,
In safety we at length arriv'd
  Upon our native shore.

"The Shipwreck of the Essex"
(From a copy in the Cornwall County Record Office, DDX 106/32)

On the 19th of December, believe what I say,
It is of a dreadful ship-wreck that happened at sea,
Its concerning the Essex an American ship,
She was struck by a large whale and sunk in the deep.

As we were crossing the ocean so wide,
It was under our ice bow a large whale we espied,
Before we had power our ship for to back,
We were struck by a whale and compleatly a wreck.

Just under the ship's head the whale made a blow,
Stove the ship's bow in pieces, in the water did flow
The sea through the cabin window began to fly,
Which made all the ship's crew to sigh and to cry.

Our ship laid on her beam-end 'twas a sorrowful sight,
We cut away her main mast and soon brought her upright,
We cut away her fore-mast and her mizen also,
Likewise the rigging over board it did go.

Our boats were stove in pieces excepting two,
In the midst of our trouble not knowing what to do,
Says the captain to his ship's crew we must do the best we can
For life is precious to every man.

We launched our two boats and in them we went,
For to float on the ocean it was our intent,
We seen some fresh water and biscuit for to crack,
For 3 days and 3 nights we remained by the wreck.

Expecting in sight some ship would appear,
But to our misfortune no ship did draw near,
The captain and ship's crew for mercy did cry,
There was nothing but the ocean, and above, the black sky.

It was early next morning some land did appear,
It was Ducy island and for it we did steer,
We steer'd for the island and safe got on shore,
We never expected to leave it any more.

We ranged through, no food could we get,
Confined their a long time, nothing for to eat.
Till we all cast lots to see who should die,
Which made our ship's crew for sorrow to cry.

Then lots were drawn one man was to die,
For his wife and poor children most bitterly did cry,
To kill him says the captain or take away his breath,
But to starve with hunger is a deplorable death.

Then his messmates they killed him and cut off his head,
And all the ship's crew from the body did feed,
And at eight different times lots amongst them were drawn,
For to keep them from starving that's the way they went on.

What men there were left in a small boat they went,
To steer for their continent it was their intent,
To steer for the main land it was the design,
The captain & boy they both stayed behind.

As they were floating on the ocean so wide,
It was by good Providence some ships they espied,
It was a South Seaman towards them did steer,
And took them aboard it as soon you shall hear.

They took them on board and behaved to them well,
O where is your captain pray to us now tell,
We left him on Ducy island in trouble to repine.
The captain and the cabin boy they both stayed behind.

We steer'd for Ducy island and fired a gun,
The captain and cabin boy from the wood they soon came,
That very same morning they cast lots who should die,
But it happened to fall on the poor cabin boy.

God bless all poor seamen their children and wives,
In trying to get their bread how they venture their lives,
So now to conclude what I've mentioned is right,
God protect all poor seamen by day and by night.

"Driven from Home"

Out in this cold world, out in the street
Asking a penny of each one I meet,
Shoe-less I wander about thro' the day,
Wearing my young life in sorrow away;
No one to help me, no one to love,
No one to pity me, none to caress,
Fatherless, motherless sadly I roam,
A child of misfortune, I'm driven from home.

No one to help me, No one to bless,
No one to pity me, None to caress;
Fatherless, motherless, sadly I roam,
Nursed by my poverty, driven from home.

(The music for this ballad follows).

"You Seamen Bold" or "The Ship in Distress"
(Numerous versions exist; this comes from J. Ashton, *Real Sailors Songs,* 1891)

Ye sailors bold that plough the Ocean,
  see dangers landsmen never know,
Some gain glory and promotion,
  no tongue can tell what we undergo.
Through dismal storms, and heat of battle,
  there's no back door to run away;
Where thundering cannons they do rattle,
  mark well what happ'ned the other day.

A merchant ship, under Divers, captain,
  long time had been bound to sea,
The weather being so uncertain,
  we were drove to great extremity!
Nothing was left these poor souls to cherish,
  for the want of food most feeble grown,
Poor fellows, they were almost perish'd,
  nothing was left but skin and bone.

Their cats and dogs, O, they did eat them,
  their hunger for to ease, we hear,
And in the midst of all their sorrow,
  Captain and men had equal share;
But now a scant has come upon us,
  a dismal tale, most certainly,
Poor fellows they stood in torture,
  Casting lots to see who should die.

Now the lot it fell on one poor fellow,
  Whose family was very great,
Which did the more increase his sorrow,
  for to repent it was too late:
I'm free to die, but, messmate brothers,
  unto the top mast head straightway,
See if you can a sail discover,
  whilst I unto the Lord do pray.

I think I spy a sail to windward,
  come bearing down for some relief,
These very words when I did hear,
  O, they did quickly banish grief.
Captain and men, in one connection,
  all sorts of food denied us not,
And by this great and friendly action,
  safe into Lisbon harbour got.

"Le Petit Navire"

Il était un petit navire,
Il était un petit navire,
Qui n'avait jamais navigué
Qui n'avait jamais navigué.

Au bout de cinq à six semaines
Le vivres vinrent à manquer

On fit tirer la courte paille,
Pour savoir qui serait mangé

Le sort tomba sur le plus jeune;
En sauce blanche il fut mangé.

Il monta sur le mât de hune
Et vit la mer de tous côtés

"O Sainte Vierge, O ma patronne,
Préservez-moi de ce danger."

(The music for this ballad follows.)

"Dream Faces" by W. M. Hutchison
(Reproduced by permission of Leonard, Gould and Bolttler, Music Publishers. The music for this song is still in print and may be obtained from Messrs. Leonard, Gould, and Bolttler, 24 Boreham Road, London N.22.)

The shadows lie across the dim old room,
The firelight glows and fades into the gloom,
While mem'ry sails to childhood's distant shore,
And dreams, and dreams, of days that are no more.

Sweet dreamland faces, passing to and fro, . . .
Bring back to mem'ry days of long ago. . .
Murmuring gently thro' a mist of pain, . . .
"Hope on, dear loved one, we shall meet again!" . . .

Once more I see across the distant years
A face, long gone with all its smiles and tears,
Once more I press a tender loving hand,
And, with my darling, 'neath the old oak stand.

Sweet dreamland faces, etc.

But all I loved are gone,
And I alone in life,
To wait, and wait, and wait, . . .
Till Death shall end the strife;

Until once more I join
The hearts that loved me best,
Where the wicked cease from troubling,
And the weary are at rest! . . .

Sweet dreamland faces, passing to and fro, . . .
Bring back to mem'ry days of long ago. . .
Murmuring gently still the old refrain. . .
"Hope on, dear loved one, we shall meet again. . .
we shall meet, shall meet again! . . .

"The Sorrowful Loss of Lives and Casting the Lots On Board the Francis Spritt. From Limerick to St. Johns North America."
(Text from a copy in the National Library of Ireland)

You landsmen all on you I call and gallant seamen too,
Till I relate the hardships great we lately have went through,
From Liverpool in the Francis Spritt for St Johns we did sail,
On the 20th of November last with a sweet and pleasant gale

We had 18 hands on board besides our captain too,
The first 10 days we sailed the sea right fair the wind it blew
On the third day of December a storm began to rise,
The welling seas tossed mountains high & dismal was the skies

It was some hundred miles away on her beam end she lay,
Our fore and main mast instantly we had to cut away,
And when our mast fell over board she soon did rise again
In angle [*sic*] deep in water till daylight we did remain.

And when the daylight did appear we viewed our awful state,
Eight of our hands were drowned and Griffin our first mate
Down below we could not go where our fresh water lay,
And as for meat we had none to eat for all was washed away.

All we got saved from the wreck was three bottles of port wine
When we got weak we then did take a small drop at a time
We had no fresh water for to drink but what fell from the sky
Not one dry spot was to be got where we could sit or lie

In this awful situation we lay there for ten days,
The craving grasp of hunger on us began to seize,
We cried to the Almighty to save us in distress
The harships that we suffered brother seamen you may guess

There was four youths among our crew most comely to be seen
Growing in the prime of life their age was scarce nineteen,

Come let the four boys now cast lots the captain he did cry
They have no wives to lament their lives 1 of the 4 must die

While the lot they were preparing those four youthful boys,
Kept gazing on each other with salt tears in their eyes,
Over young O'Brien's eyes a bandage they did tie
The first lot was called upon O'Brien you are to die.

O'Brien says to his comrades you'll let my mother know,
The cruel death I underwent when you to Ireland go,
John Gordon he was called upon to bleed him in the veins,
He tried the blood from him to take but not one drop there came.

Oh, cruel captain he did say this work will never do,
Gorman you must cut his throat or else you'll suffer too,
The trembling cook he took the knife which him sore confound,
He cut his throat we drank the blood as it flowed from the wound

Early the next morning as day light did appear,
The American Ship "Ignora" in haste she did draw near,
It was providence sent her that way for to preserve our lives,
We have got once more to Erin's shore to our children and our wives.

Appendix D
Joseph Conrad and the Case of the *Euxine*

Conrad's *Falk: A Reminiscence,* first published in 1903 and set in Bangkok, which he visited in 1888, tells the horror story of a ship's master who survived in the traditional cannibal manner but without the drawing of lots. N. Sherry in *Conrad's Eastern World* (Cambridge, 1966) investigates Conrad's experiences in the East and their relation to his writings and discusses, among other matters, both Conrad's relationships with Henry Ellis, the choleric Master Attendant at Singapore, and the possible "sources" for the story of Captain Falk. Ellis, who found Conrad his first command, the *Otago,* appears in the autobiographical *Shadow Line* under his own name and in *Falk, Lord Jim,* and *The End of the Tether.* Conrad visited Singapore on three occasions, the first time in 1883 after his ship, the *Palestine,* had sunk in much the same way as the *Euxine.* At the Sailor's Home (which Peter Archer of the *Euxine* would have visited again in 1883) he must surely have heard the story of the *Euxine,* but *Falk* has no obvious connections with it. It is even conceivable that Conrad met Archer, but this is a mere possibility.

Bibliographical Notes

This book has not been encumbered with footnotes, but scholars wishing to check specific points are welcome to write or inspect the collection of materials that I now hold. The list of sources given is not exhaustive, and much material traced has of course not been used in this book, to avoid excessive length.

Extensive efforts have been made to locate any family papers surviving in the Dudley family, but with little success. Papers did once exist in the hands of Mr. William R. (or G.) Gridley of 9 Whiterock Street, Southwick, Sussex; he was Dudley's nephew, and the papers were apparently lent to Donald McCormick (who also writes under the name of Richard Deacon) in 1961 or thereabouts. Although relatives in England have been located, these papers seem now to be lost. Numerous relatives in Australia have also been located, but their generous efforts to find documentary material have not been successful. Attempts to locate relatives of Stephens and Brooks have failed. Numerous members of the Parker family have helped me in my inquiries, in particular about the alternative account of the death of Richard.

A massive body of maritime records of both ships and individuals exists in the Public Record Office and dispersed among the National

Maritime Museum, local record offices, and the Memorial Library in Newfoundland, all of which have helped me generously. Anyone intending to use this material should first consult C. T. and M. J. Watts, "Unravelling Merchant Seamen's Records," *Genealogists Magazine* 19 (1979): 313; and N. Cox, "Sources for Maritime History (II)—The Records of the Registrar General of Shipping and Seamen," *Maritime History* 2 (1972): 168. The National Maritime Museum holds application forms for certificates of competence (used principally to establish Dudley's and Stephens's early careers) and a MS index to shipwrecks. The Guildhall Library holds the Lloyd's Maritime Collection, which includes captains' registers (see MS 18567, 8, 9) recording maritime careers from Board of Trade records in a more convenient form. Movements of vessels can be traced through Lloyd's List (MS index in the National Maritime Museum and Guildhall) and particulars of vessels in *The Mercantile Navy List* (published annually), in *Lloyd's Register* and *Yacht Register,* and *Hunt's Yacht List.* I have not attempted to track down extensive material on all the ships, incidents, and individuals mentioned in the book. The following list indicates areas explored fairly fully.

Archival Material

A. Public Record Office, London
(legal records held in Chancery Lane, other records at Kew)

1. Relevant to the case of the *Mignonette*

HO 144/141 A 36934, HO 34/52 (the basic Home Office file)
KB 6/6 (2) (contains Dudley's draft letters)
IND 6687/2 (index to KB 12/155)
KB 12/155 (the indictment and special verdict)
CUST 31/244 (correspondence with Falmouth; permission required to consult)
CUST 67/11 (correspondence with Falmouth; permission required to consult)
BT 108/14 (registration particulars)
BT 109/204 (sale of *Mignonette* to Thomas Hall)
ASSI 21/71 (the minute book of the assizes)
MT9/257/M9658 85 (Board of Trade file)
DPP 4/17 (a complete transcript of the trial and subsequent legal argument in London)
BT 122 (contains records of service of certificated officers)

NOTE: treasury solicitor's papers on the case were probably destroyed in the last war: I am grateful to the treasury solicitor for looking into the possibility that they might survive. Apart from the material transferred to the P.R.O., the director of public prosecutions today holds no other documents on the case. The Board of Trade records have been searched for a possible apprenticeship of Dudley, without success. Brooks's apprenticeship will have been recorded, but I have not checked it. Dudley's voyages up to 1878 have been traced from his certificate application and incomplete ships' papers dispersed among the P.R.O. (BT 99), the National Maritime Museum, local records offices, and the Memorial Library in Newfoundland. His later voyages are recorded in the Board of Trade records and in a letter in the Home Office file by Phillipa Dudley. His certificate was 04729, renewed as 014939; Stephens's were 91234, 04475, and 014741 (see BT 122).

2. Relevant to the case of the *Francis Spaight* and Timothy Gorman's career

BT 107/74, 75, 371, 385, 391 (registration particulars)
BT 108/208, 210
BT 98/338, 365, 687, 986, 1277, 1633, 1927, 2905, 3405, 5137, 5489 (ships' papers)
BT 112/25 (seamen's register)
BT 115/5, 9 (masters' register)
BT 124/5, 15 (masters' records)
BT 125/25 (masters' records)
BT 150/15, 16, 17 (apprenticeships)
Timothy Gorman's application for a certificate as master mariner dated January 24, 1851, is in the National Maritime Museum (Cert. No. 40380 of February 19, 1851); his certificate was renewed as 72541 on August 15, 1859
The eventual fate of the *Francis Spaight* is recorded in the *Illustrated London News*

3. Relevant to the case of the *Euxine*

MT9/101/M257/75 (the basic Board of Trade file)
MT9/112/M13696/75 (problems of dispersed witnesses)
CO 273/76 and 80 (Colonial Office correspondence)
HO 34/35 (Home Office out letters)
BT 122/63, 71 (James Archer's voyages)
MT9/532/M6421/95 (problems of dispersed witnesses in a case in 1895)

BT 99/90 (ships' papers)
James Archer's certificate was 92215, renewed as 0535; his later voyages were traced through Lloyd's captains' register in the Guildhall MSS; no other material on this case appears to survive with treasury solicitor or in the Home Office.

4. Relevant to the case of the *Lady Douglas* (*Regina v. Cocks and others*)

HO 144/199 A 47204 B/43 (Home Office file)

5. Relevant to the case of the *Cospatrick*

MT 9/1011/M257 (the basic file)
MT 9/99 (the report of the inquiry: contains depositions)
CO 273/76, 79, 80 (Colonial Office correspondence)

6. Relevant to the case of the *William Brown*

FO 27/634 (contains depositions, press accounts, and correspondence)

7. Census material for Tollesbury, Brightlingsea, and Itchen Ferry

RG 9/1091 (Tollesbury 1861)
RG 10/1675, 1689 (Tollesbury and Brightlingsea 1871)
RG 10/1196 (Itchen Ferry 1871)
RG 11/1778 (Tollesbury 1881)
RG 11/1217 (Itchen Ferry 1881)
RG 11/1206 (Southampton 1881)

B. Riksarkivet, Oslo

Relevant to the case of the *Thekla*

Report of the Proceedings of the Royal Cabinet, April 15, 1893, Item No. 671

C. Staatsarchiv, Hamburg

Relevant to the case of the *Thekla*

Senat (Cl. VI Nr. 10 Vol. 3b. Fasc. 14 Inv. 7c) "File concerning the extradition of the Swedish/Norwegian seamen . . . of the vessel Thekla in 1893"

Newspapers

(These have been consulted mainly in the British Library Collection at Colindale)

1. Relevant to the case of the *Mignonette,* September–December 1884

Colchester Chronicle
Colchester Mercury & Essex Express
Collection of press cuttings in the Mitchell Library, Sydney, N.S.W. (gift of J. H. Want)
Collection of press cuttings held by the Royal Sydney Yacht Squadron (from the *Sydney Mail*)
Devon Evening Express
Essex Standard
Essex Telegraph
Exeter and Plymouth Gazette
Falmouth News Slip
Falmouth and Penryn Weekly Times
Graphic
Hampshire Advertiser
L'Illustration
Illustrated London News (contains illustrative material)
Lakes Falmouth Packet and Cornwall Advertiser
Morning Post
New York Times
Pall Mall Gazette
Penny Illustrated Newspaper
Pictorial News (contains illustrative material)
Police News (contains illustrative material)
Police Guardian
Royal Cornwall Gazette
Southampton Observer and Winchester News
Standard
Southampton Times and Hampshire Express
Spectator
Sutton Herald
Times

2. *The Medusa*

Times, September 17, 1816

3. The *Brig George*

Sydney Gazette, November 13, 1823

4. The *Elizabeth Rashleigh*

Plymouth Journal, January 17, 1835

5. The *Home*

    Limerick Star and Evening Post, January 8, 1836
    Cornubian, January 28, 1836
    Times, January 6, 1836

6. The *Hannah*

    Times, September 19, 1836

7. The *Earl Kellie*

    Cornubian, January 28, 1836
    Times, January 19, 1836

8. The *Caledonia*

    Bristol Gazette, November 23, 1837
    Bristol Mercury, November 25, 1837

9. The *Francis Spaight* (and Timothy Gorman)

    Limerick Times, January 11 and 28; February 1, 1836
    Limerick Star and Evening Post, January 12, 1836
    Cornwall Royal Gazette, January 6 and 15, 1836
    West Briton and Cornwall Advertiser, January 8, 1836
    Cornubian, January 7, 1836
    Falmouth Packet and Cornish Herald, January 6, 1836
    Times, June 22, 1836; January 3, 1859 (and see Annual Register, 1836, pp. 74ff.)
    Irish Independent, February 3, 1916 (the story of Miss Ada Crehan)

10. The *William Brown*

    Times, May 15, 17, 18, and 20; June 16, 1841
    New York Herald, October 11 and 18, 1841; April 15, 23, 24, and 25, 1842
    Philadelphia Public Ledger, June 29, 1841; April 23 and 25, 1847

11. The *Blake*

    Times, April 24, 1856

12. The schooner *Leader*

    Times, June 22, 1865

13. The *Jane Loudon*

    Times, February 26, 1866

14. The *European*

    Times, December 8, 10, 12, 14, 21, and 22, 1871

15. The *Cospatrick*

    Standard, January 5, 1875

16. The *Euxine*

    Times, December 22 and 29, 1874; April 6 and 28, 1875
    Singapore Daily Times, November 12, 13, and 17, 1874; January 7, 8, 16, 23, 28; February 1, 2, 3, and 12; March 29; April 19, 1875
    Straits Observer, November 14 and 15, 1874; February 1; April 22, 1875
    Daily Recorder, July 12, 1875

17. The *Sallie M. Steelman* (or *Stedman*)

    New York Times, February 12 and 13; March 2 and 3, 1878

18. The *Princess Alice*

    Times, September 4, 1878, et. seq.

19. The *Turley*

    New York Times, November 28 and 29, 1884

20. The *Lady Frances*

    Times, October 23, 1885

21. The *St. Pierre*

    Times, October 19, 1887

22. The *Zoo Battesta*

    Times, January 7, 1888

23. The *Lady Douglas*

    Times, March 10, 1888

24. The *Earnmoor*

    New York Times, October 4, 20, 22, and 26, 1889
    Times, October 26, 1889
    Standard, October 26, 1889

25. The *Arethusa*

    Times, January 9 and 29, 1890

26. The *Thekla*

Times, February 1, 1893
Norges Handel-og Sjøfartstidende, March 17, 18, 21, 23, and 24, 1893

27. The *Drot*

Times, September 4 and 25, 1899
New York Tribune, September 3 and 22, 1899
News and Courier, Charleston, September 4 and 23, 1899
Collection of press cuttings from the Stavanger Maritime Museum

28. Dudley in Australia

Sydney Mail, March 3 and 17, 1900
Sydney Morning Herald, February 24, 26, and 28; March 1, 1900
Sydney Daily Telegraph, January 15, 25, 26, and 27, 1900; February 2, 22, 24, 26, 27, and 28, 1900; March 3, 5, and 6, 1900
Balmain Observer, February 24; March 3, 1900

29. The Greely (Lady Franklin Bay) Expedition

New York Times, February 19, 1883; September 7, 8, and 12, 1884; August 12, 13, 14, 15, and 18, 1920
Times, July 18; August 13, 14, 15, 16, 19, and 29, 1884

30. The Case of Alfred Packer

Harper's Weekly, October 17, 1874
Gunnison Daily Review Press, December 5, 1883
New York Times, April 14, 1883
Denver Tribune Republican, October 31, 1885
Pueblo Times, August 4, 1886
Rocky Mountain News, August 4, 5, and 6, 1886
Lake City World, August 14, 1886
New York Times, August 7, 1886
Denver Post, January 3, 8, and 14, 1900; January 9 and 10, 1901; November 13, 1904
Collection of press cuttings of various dates in the Miscellaneous MSS of the Colorado Historical Society (see esp. the Howe and Dawson Scrapbooks)

Ballads

1. Connected with the case of the *Mignonette*

"Fearful Sufferings at Sea, Lad Killed and Eaten"
Air—"Driven from Home" This has two printer's devices, an eagle and a falcon, but no printer's name. My photocopy comes from Dr. Patrick

Marnham, who thinks it came from Falmouth. No original copy has been traced.

"Richard Parker of the Ship *Mignonette*" by F. Morgans, Greenwich. Printed by Dixon, Printer, 52 Church Street, Greenwich. British Lib. 1874 e 4, "A Collection of Topical Songs."

"The Terrible Tale of the Sea"
Air—"Dream Faces." T. Brooks, Song Publisher, 56 Green Ann Street, St. Jude's, Bristol. This appeared in pamphlet form with a prose account of the incident, and ballads of the execution of Joseph Laycock and the murder of the child Mary Cooper in Middlesborough. From the John Johnson Collection, Bodleian Library.

A poem or ballad was composed by Charles Harrison of Magdalene Street, Southampton, in 1884; it has not been identified.

Donald McCormick, when writing his book, communicated with Mr. Allan E. Bax of Prudential Buildings, 39 Martin Place, Sydney, who possessed a pamphlet that I have not been able to locate but is described as follows:

> *THE TERRIBLE TALE OF THE SEA*. Being a narrative of the awful sufferings at sea of the shipwrecked crew of the yacht Mignonette in verse. By G. Winchester. Printed and published by A. White & Co., 62 and 64 Wilton Street, Finsbury, London E.C.

2. Other ballad material

This has come principally from the British Library (cataloged under "Collection"), the Cornwall and Devon county record offices, and the Dublin Public Library. The ballad of the *Betsey,* lost on September 27, 1821, is from the British Library (1981 f. 13; see also 1880 c. 20 Vol. II, No. 592). The *New York Trader* is in British Library 11621 h. 11, Vol. 7, f. 79. Broadsheets related to the *Frances Mary* and *Caledonia* are in the British Library 1880 c. 20 Vol. 2, and concerning the former also in the county record office at Truro. Of the two ballads of the *Francis Spaight,* "The Sorrowful Loss of Life and Casting of Lots on Board the Francis Spritt" is in the National Library of Ireland, and "The Sorrowful Fate of O'Brien" is from James W. Healy, *Irish Ballads and Songs of the Sea* (Cork, 1967). Ballads dealing with the case of the *Sallie L. Stedman* and the *Thekla* have been located for me by Dr. Henningsen, director of the Danish Maritime Museum at Helsingør, and by the Stavanger Museum. Information on W. M. Thackeray's "Little Billie" or "The Three Sailors of Bristol City" is in G. N. Ray, *The Letters and Papers of W. M. Thackeray*

(Oxford, 1945), vol. 2; and in W. M. Thackeray, *Ballads and Verses* (London, 1904).

See also

Ashton, J. *Real Sailors' Songs*. London, 1891.

Bratton, J. S. *The Victorian Popular Ballad*. London, 1975.

Entwhistle, W. J. *European Balladry*. Oxford, 1939.

Hugill, S. *Shanties of the Seven Seas*. London, 1961.

———. *Shanties and Sailors' Songs*. London, 1969.

Kennedy, P. *Folksongs of Britain and Ireland*. London, 1975.

Neuburg, V. E. *Popular Literature*. London, 1977.

Sharp, C., and Karpeles, M. *Cecil Sharp's Collection of English Folk Songs*. Oxford, 1973.

Smith, L. A. *Music of the Waters*. London, 1888.

Wolf, D. F. J., and Hoffman, D. C. *Romances viejos castellanos: Primavera y Flor de Romanceros*. 13 vols. Madrid, 1896–1908.

Other Manuscript Material

The Colorado Historical Society holds a copy of the transcript of the first trial of Alferd Packer and an extensive collection of miscellaneous material, including statements about the case by J. D. Martin and Nathaniel Hunter (interviewed in 1923) and Carol Clark. Much of this is used by Judge Kushner in his recent book and was earlier used by Gannt.

Of the home secretaries involved there is much material in the Harcourt Papers, now in the Bodleian, but nothing relevant exists in the Cross Papers (Brit. Lib. Add. MSS 51271 and 51274).

Law Reports and Legal Texts

1. The *William Brown*

U.S. v. Holmes (1842) 1 Wallace Junior 1, 26 Fed. Cas. 360.

2. Alferd Packer

Packer v. The People (1885) 8 Colorado Law Reports 361

Packer v. The People (1893) 18 Colorado Law Reports 525

Packer v. The People (1899) 26 Colorado Law Reports 306

McAllister, H., "Mr. Justice Campbell's Contribution to the Law of Colorado," *Rocky Mountain Law Review* 5 (1932): 4

3. The Case of the *Mignonette*

Regina v. Dudley and Stephens (1884) 14 Q.B.D. 273, (1885) 560, 1 Times Law Reports, 29, 118; other law reports add nothing

Mallin, Michael G. "In Warm Blood: Some Historical and Procedural

Aspects of Regina v. Dudley and Stephens," *University of Chicago Law Review* 34 (1967): 377

Williams, G. "A Commentary on *R. v. Dudley and Stephens,*" *Cambrian Law Review* 8 (1977): 94

Fuller, L. "The Case of the Speluncian Explorers," *Harvard Law Review* 62 (1948): 616

4. The Case of the *William Douglas*

Regina v. Cocks, Gleaves, Evans and Webster (1887) Central Criminal Court Cases Vol. 106, p. 222, No. 718

5. Special Verdicts in General

Rex v. Pedley (1782) Leach Crown Cases 242
Rex v. Oneby (1727) 2 Ld. Raymond 1485
Mackally's Case (1612) 9 Co. Rep. 65b
Hazel's Case (1785) Leach Crown Cases 368
Regina v. Jameson and others (1896)

(No attempt has been made to compile a general bibliographical guide to the legal literature on the defense of necessity. In English law a convenient starting point would be J. C. Smith and B. Hogan's *Criminal Law* and P. R. Glazebrook's article in *Cambridge Law Journal* 30 [1972]: 87.)

Official Reports

Most of these are conveniently available reprinted in the Irish Universities Press Series of British Parliamentary Papers, *Shipping Safety,* vols. 1–9. The principal reports are

Select Committee Appointed to Inquire into the Causes of Shipwrecks 1826 (567) Vol. XVII

Report from the Select Committee on Shipwrecks of Timber Ships 1839 (333) Vol. IX

First and Second Reports from the Select Committee on Shipwrecks 1843 (549) (581) Vol. IX

Preliminary Report from the Royal Commission on Unseaworthy Ships 1873 [c. 853] Vol. XXXVI, [c. 853-1] Vol. XXXVI

Final Report of the Royal Commission on Unseaworthy Ships 1874 [c. 1027-1] VOl. XXXIV

Report of a Select Committee on Transportation, 1832, App. I. 56.

Report of the Outbreak of Plague at Sydney 1900, by the Medical Officer of Health (J. A. Thompson) (Sydney, 1900)

Books and Other General Publications Consulted

Abel, W. *The Safe Sea.* Liverpool, 1932.

Adams, W. H. D. *Great Shipwrecks: A Record of Perils and Disasters at Sea, 1544–1877.* London 1877.

A. F. S. "Sea Drama That Caused a Sensation." *Southern Daily Echo,* December 22, 1934.

Alexander, M. *Mrs. Fraser on the Fatal Shore.* New York, 1971.

Andenaes, J. *The General Part of the Criminal Law of Norway.* South Hackensack, N.J., 1965.

The Annual Register (various dates)

Arens, W. *The Man Eating Myth.* New York, 1979.

Ashley, F. W. *My Sixty Years of Law.* London, 1936.

Athearn, R. G. *The Coloradans.* Albuquerque, 1976.

Baker, Sir G. S. "The Judgement in the Mignonette Case." *National Review* 4 (1884–85): 702.

Bates, M. *A Quick History of Lake City.* Colorado Springs, 1973.

Bernhard-Williams, J.; Girdler, N.; Sinclair, G.; and Thomas, E. "The Ballad of the *Mignonette.*" Typescript, 1975.

Bertrand, K. J. *Americans in Antarctica, 1775–1948.* New York, 1971.

Bisset, J. *Sail Ho!* London, 1961.

Blair, C. *Survive.* New York, 1973.

Bourgogne, Sergeant. *Memoirs of Sergeant Bourgogne, 1812–1813.* New York, 1958.

Britten, A. *The "Mignonette."* London, 1973.

Burt, O. W. *American Murder Ballads and Their Stories.* New York, 1958.

Clarke, M. A. H. *For the Term of His Natural Life.* London, 1952.

Clarke, R. F. " 'The Mignonette' Case as a Question of Moral Theology," *Month* 53 (1885): 17.

Cleland, R. C. *A History of California: The American Period.* New York, 1922.

Constable's Miscellany of Original and Selected Publications. Vol. 89, *Shipwrecks and Disasters at Sea.* London 1883.

Cooper, W. ["Vanderdecken"]. *Yachts and Yachting.* London, 1873.

———. *The Yacht Sailor.* London, 1862.

Dalzell, J. G. *Shipwrecks and Disasters at Sea.* Edinburgh, 1812.

Dannevig, B. *Faksunds Sjøfarthistorie.* Farsund, 1967.

Darling, H. T. ["Taffrail"]. *Sea Escapes and Adventures.* London, 1927.

Dean, J. *A Narrative of the Sufferings, Preservation and Deliverance of Capt. John Dean and Company.* London, 1710.

The Denver Westerners Brand Book (Annual Publication of the Denver Posse of the Westerners). Articles by Raymond Colwell (1950), Fred Mazzula (1964), Wilson Rockwell (1968), Dr. Benjamin Draper (1971), Edward V. Dunklee (1946), and Inez Hunt (1971).

Disher, M. L. *Blood and Thunder.* London, 1949.
Dorset, P. F. *The New Eldorado: The Story of Colorado's Gold and Silver Rushes.* London, 1970.
Dunn, R. S. *Sugar and Slaves.* London, 1973.
Dunstan, B. *The Book of Falmouth and Penryn.* Falmouth, 1975.
Eitner, L. *Géricault's "Raft of the Medusa."* London, 1972.
Elliot, B. *Marcus Clarke.* Oxford, 1958.
Encyclopaedia Brittanica, 13th ed.
Eyries, M. *Histoire des naufrages.* Paris, 1859.
Fenwick, R. W. *Alfred Packer: The True Story of Colorado's Man-Eater.* Denver, 1963.
The Field. London, various dates.
Fowler, G. *Timber Line: A Story of Bonfils and Tammen.* Reprinted New York, 1947.
Frank Lesley's Illustrated Newspaper. August 23, 1884.
Fritz, P. S. *Colorado: The Centennial State.* New York, 1941.
Gantt, P. *The Case of Alfred Packer, the Man Eater.* Denver, 1952.
Gardiner, A. G. *Life of Sir William G. G. V. Harcourt.* London, 1923.
Gee, M. B. *Captain Fraser's Voyages, 1865–1892.* London, 1979.
Gibbins, R., ed. *Narratives of the Wreck of the Whale Ship Essex.* London, 1935.
Good, D. "Cannibalism on the High Seas." *Southern Echo,* September 2, 1977.
Gray, T. *Fifty Years of Legislation in Relation to the Shipping Trade.* London, 1887.
Great Shipwrecks during Queen Victoria's Reign. Liverpool, 1887. (Brit. Lib. Shelfmark 8807 b 43).
Gribble,L. "The Captain Ate the Cabin Boy." *True Detective,* October 1972.
Hafen, L. R. *Colorado and Its People.* New York, 1948.,
Hall, F. *History of the State of Colorado.* 4 vols. Chicago, 1889–95.
Hamilton, F. *The Changing Face of Limerick.* Limerick, 1977.
Hardy, Uncle [William Senior]. *Notable Shipwrecks.* London, 1873.
Hirst, F. *The Conquest of Plague.* Oxford, 1953.
Holmes, R. C. "Murder at Sea." *American Neptune* (1956), p. 180.
Houghton, E. P. D. *The Expedition of the Donner Party.* Chicago, 1911.
Hughes, J. S. *Unfair Comment.* London, 1951.
Hunt, R. D. *California and the Californians,* Vol. 3 of 4 vols. Chicago, 1930.
Hunt's Yacht List. London, various dates.
Hunt's Yachting Magazine. London, various dates from 1852.
Illustrated London News. September 20, 1884.
Kushner, E. F. *Alferd Packer: Cannibal! Victim?* Frederick, Colorado, 1977.
———. *Otto Mears: His Life and Times: With Notes on the Alferd Packer Case.* Frederick, Colorado, 1979.

Langham, C. *A True Account of the Voyage of the Nottingham Galley*. London, 1711.

Layson, J. F. *Memorable Shipwrecks and Seafaring Adventures of the Nineteenth Century*. London, 1884.

Leather, J. *The Northseamen*. Lavenham, 1971.

———. *The Salty Shore*. Lavenham, 1979.

Lee, E. C. R. *Safety and Survival at Sea*. London, 1980.

Lindsay, W. S. *A History of Merchant Shipping and Ancient Commerce, 1874–1876*. 4 vols. London, 1874–76.

MacDonagh, O. *A Pattern of Government Growth, 1800–1860*. London, 1961.

McGlashan, C. F. *History of the Donner Party*. 3d ed. San Francisco, 1880.

Mariners Mirror 8 (1922): 52.

Marnham, P. "Cannibalism on the High Seas." *Daily Telegraph Magazine*, September 17, 1971.

Masters, D. *S.O.S.* London, 1933.

Mazzulla, F. and J. *Al Packer: A Colorado Cannibal*. Denver, 1968.

Memorial and Biographical History of Northern California. Chicago, 1891.

Mudd, D. *The Falmouth Packets*. Bodmin, England, 1978

———. *Home Along Falmouth and Penryn*. Bodmin, 1980.

Murray, D. L. *Internal Memorandum on Shipwrecks*. London, 1849.

Murton, W. *Reminiscences*. N.p., n.d.

———. *Wreck Inquiries, the Law and Practice Relating to*. London, 1884.

Nicholson, J. *Traditionary Tales Connected with the South of Scotland*. N.p., 1843.

O'Connor, G. W. *The First Hundred Years: The Southampton, Isle of Wight and South of England Royal Mail Steam Packet Company Ltd*. Southampton, 1962.

Paine, R. D. *Lost Ships and Lonely Seas*. New York, 1921.

Parkhurst, P. G. *Ships of Peace*. New Malden, England, 1962.

Peters, G. H. *The Plimsoll Line*. London, 1875.

Pigney, J. *For Fear We Shall Perish*. New York, 1961.

Plimsoll, S. *Our Seamen*. London, 1873.

Poe, E. A. *The Narrative of Arthur Gordon Pym*. New York and London, 1838.

Pritchard, E. "Death in the Tropics." *Hampshire: The County Magazine*, June 1962.

Read, P. P. *Alive*. New York, 1974.

Reports of the Commission on Indian Affairs. Reports of 1873 from Los Pinos by C. A. Adams and of 1874 and 1875 by H. F. Bond.

Rogers, S. *Tales of the Fore-and-Aft*. London, 1935.

Russell, W. C. *The Death Ship*. London, 1888.

Savigny, J. B. H., and Corréard, A. *Naufrage de la frégate "La Méduse" faisant partie de l'expédition du Sénégal en 1816*. Paris, 1817.

Shyllon, F. O. *Black Slaves in Britain*. London, 1974.

Simpson, W. J. R. *A Treatise on Plague*. London, 1905.
Southern, L. W. *Stories of the Colne*. 1949.
Sprod, T. D. *Alexander Pearce of Macquarie Harbour*. Hobart, Tasmania, 1977.
Stackpole, E. A. *The Loss of the "Essex."* Nantucket, Massachusetts, 1977.
Stewart, G. R. *Ordeal by Hunger*. New York, 1936.
Tannahill, R. *Flesh and Blood: A History of the Cannibal Complex*. New York, 1975.
Taylor, B. *Cruelly Murdered*. London, 1979.
Thomas, L. *The Wreck of the "Dumaru."* New York, 1930.
Thornton, J. D. *Plough and Sail*. Tollesbury, England, 1977.
Thornton, J. Q. *The Californian Tragedy*. 1849; reprint ed. Oakland, California, 1945.
Thorp, R. W. *Crow Killer: The Saga of Liver-eating Johnson*. Bloomington, Indiana, 1958.
Thurston, G. *The Great Thames Disaster*. London, 1965.
Todd, R. H. *Abandoned: The Story of the Greely Expedition, 1881–1884*. New York, Toronto, and London, 1961.
Trial of Alexander William Holmes. Pamphlet. Philadelphia, 1842.
Villeneuve, R. *Histoire du cannibalisme*. Paris, 1965.

Individuals Consulted

Mr. J. W. Adams of the University of Kent, Canterbury, Kent
Mr. John Alderson of the Devon and Cornwall Constabulary, Exeter, Devon
Mr. Peter G. Ashton, librarian of the *Southern Evening Echo*, Southampton, Hampshire
Mrs. F. Banday of Newton Stewart, Wigtownshire, Scotland
Mr. Ivor Bedford of Southampton, Hampshire
Mr. W. J. Bibby of Tollesbury, Essex
Mr. S. Blakstad of Stavanger, Norway
Mr. L. Borge-Andersen of the University of Oslo, Norway
Professor Anders Bratholm of the University of Oslo, Norway
Mrs. Jackam Brown of London
Mr. T. Cadogan of Cork, County Cork, Eire
Mr. Michael Cater of Falmouth, Cornwall
Lady Pauline Chapman, archivist of Madame Tussaud's Ltd., London
Mrs. V. R. Chapman of Colchester, Essex
Mr. D. B. Clement of Exeter, Devon
Mr. Vernon Cole of Southampton, Hampshire
Mr. B. Cornwall of Falmouth, Cornwall
Professor P. Davison of the University of Kent, Canterbury, Kent
Mr. Charles Dean of Sydney, Australia
Mr. R. Derbyshire of Heversham, Cumbria, England
Captain C. C. H. Diaper of Southampton, Hampshire

Dr. Horace Dobbs and Mrs. Wendy Dobbs of North Ferriby, North Humberside, England
Dr. D. E. Dudley of Colchester, Essex
Mr. W. Dumbleton of St. Ives, Cornwall
Mrs. Ruth Dunstan of Falmouth, Cornwall
Mr. C. L. Fox of G. C. Fox & Co., Falmouth, Cornwall
Mr. J. R. Frost of Tollesbury, Essex
Mr. Raymond Frost of Tollesbury, Essex
Mr. Vic Gammon of Ringmer, Sussex
H.M. Consul C. E. A. Garton of Funchal, Madeira, Portugal
Mr. Nicholas P. Girdler of the Southampton Drama Centre, Southampton, Hampshire
Mr. S. Glynn of the University of Kent, Canterbury, Kent
Dr. D. E. Good of the *Southern Evening Echo,* Southampton, Hampshire
Mr. R. Greentree of Drummoyne, New South Wales, Australia
Mr. Gordon A. Gregory of George's Hall, New South Wales, Australia
Mr. Maurice Harbor of Truro, Cornwall
Mr. Keith L. Hayden of Sydney, Australia
Mr. J. W. Healy of Cork, County Cork, Eire
The Rt. Hon. Edward Heath, M.P., of London
Dr. Henning Henningson of the Danish Maritime Museum, Helsingor, Denmark
Professor R. F. V. Heuston of Trinity College, Dublin
Mr. J. Dyson Heydon of Sydney, Australia
Pastor B. G. Higginbottam of Drummoyne, New South Wales, Australia
I. F. M. Hine, Solicitors, of Falmouth, Cornwall
Mr. W. Howarth of the University College of Wales, Aberystwyth
Mr. A. Hurst of Brighton, Sussex
Professor Dennis J. Hutchinson of the University of Chicago
Dr. W. Louis G. James of the University of Kent, Canterbury, Kent
Miss M. Jeffs of Sydney, Australia
Mr. Eric P. Johnson of Southampton, Hampshire
Miss Ruth Jones of Falmouth, Cornwall
Mr. H. J. Kent of Marazion, Cornwall
Mrs. D. Kershaw of Southampton, Hampshire
Judge Ervan F. Kushner of Boca Raton, Florida
Professor J. H. Langbein of the University of Chicago
Mr. R. J. Larn of Carlyon Bay, Cornwall
Mr. T. Larsson-Fedde of Farsund, Norway
Mr. John Leather of Ivinghoe, Essex
Mrs. Phillipa Legg of Tamworth, New South Wales, Australia
Mrs. B. Lester of Southampton, Hampshire
Dr. S. F. Lutman of the University of Kent, Canterbury, Kent
Mr. W. McCartney of Newton Stewart, Wigtownshire, Scotland

Mr. Donald McCormick of Beckenham, Kent
Noel and Carol Machin of Marshside, Kent
Mr. Minton of Falmouth, Cornwall
Professor Norval Morris of the University of Chicago
Mr. Victor E. Neuberg of the North London Polytechnic, London
Captain A. Nichols of Southampton, Hampshire
Mr. Peter Nicholson of Gosport, Hampshire
Dr. S. C. O'Mahony of Limerick, County Limerick, Eire
Dr. Rowton Old of Hayle, Cornwall
Mr. Osborne of Falmouth, Cornwall
Mr. K. J. Palmer of Sydney, Australia
Mr. R. Palmer of Birmingham, England
Mr. Douglas S. Parker of Southampton, Hampshire
Mr. E. J. C. Parker of Southampton, Hampshire
Mrs. Edith Parker of Southampton, Hampshire
Mrs. J. E. Parker of Southampton, Hampshire
Mr. Keith Parker of Southampton, Hampshire
Mr. Peter D. Parker of Colchester, Essex
Mr. R. T. Parker of Southampton, Hampshire
Mrs. V. R. Parker of Southampton, Hampshire
Mr. R. H. Parsons of Magill, S. Australia
Mr. D. Payne of Falmouth, Cornwall
Mr. E. H. Payne of Great Missenden, Buckinghamshire
Mr. William Pook of Mylor Bridge, Cornwall
Messrs Pretty and Ellis, Auctioneers, of Great Missenden, Buckinghamshire
Mr. Oliver Price of the Royal Cornwall Polytechnic Society, Falmouth, Cornwall
Mr. Adrian B. Rance of the Tudor House Museum, Southampton, Hampshire
Mrs. H. Reed of Tamworth, New South Wales, Australia
The Rev. R. S. J. Roberts of the Missions to Seamen, Southampton, Hampshire
Professor Michael Roe of the University of Tasmania, Hobart, Tasmania
The Rev. David Rydings of Great Missenden, Buckinghamshire
Professor Alec Samuels of Southampton University, Hampshire
Mr. J. D. Sandercock of Oreston, Devon
Professor A. G. L. Shaw of Monash University, Victoria, Australia
Mr. A. W. Smith of Southampton, Hampshire
Dr. E. A. Stackpole of Nantucket, Massachusetts
The Rev. M. R. C. Swindlehurst of Brightlingsea, Essex
Miss S. D. Thomson, Archivist of Southampton, Hampshire
Miss A. Thornhill of Limerick, County Limerick, Eire
The Rev. J. D. Thornton of Kelvedon, Essex
Dr. P. T. van der Merwe of the National Maritime Museum, London

Mr. Richard Want of Sydney, Australia
Mr. T. R. Waring of the *News and Courier,* Charleston, South Carolina
Mrs. Weaver of Penzance, Cornwall
Mr. Stephen White of the University College, Cardiff, Wales
Messrs Wildy and Sons Ltd. of London
Mrs. D. Williams of Randwick, New South Wales, Australia
Mrs. L. Wilson of Page, Australia Commonwealth Territory, Australia
The Rev. S. C. Wincott of Southampton, Hampshire
Miss Sheila H. Edwards of the Bodleian Library, Oxford

For Translations I am indebted to the following:
Mrs. Helle Bilton of Oslo
Mr. Peter Bilton of Oslo
Mrs. E. Elphi Corbett of Canterbury, Kent
Miss Lise Opdahl of Canterbury, Kent
Mr. Richard Scase and Mrs. Anita Scase of Canterbury, Kent

Institutions Consulted

The Altonaer Museum, Hamburg, West Germany
The Altringham Local History Library, Altringham, Cheshire
Messrs Beken, Photographers, of Cowes, Isle of Wight
The Bergen Maritime Museum, Bergen, Norway
The Berkshire County Library, Reading, Berkshire
The Brick Store Museum of Kennebunk, Maine
The British Historical Society of Portugal, Lisbon
The Buckinghamshire Record Office, Aylesbury, Buckinghamshire
The Central Library of Manchester, Lancashire
The Charleston Library Society, Charleston, South Carolina
The Cheshire County Record Office and Museums Service, Chester, England
The City Museum of Plymouth, Devon
The Colorado Historical Society, Denver, Colorado
The Cork County Library, Cork, Eire
The Cornwall County Record Office, Truro, Cornwall
The County Library, Avon, England
The County Museum and Art Gallery of Truro, Cornwall
H.M. Customs of Falmouth, Cornwall
The Danish Maritime Museum of Helsingør, Denmark
The Denver Public Library, Denver, Colorado
The Devon and Cornwall Constabulary, Exeter, Devon
The Devon County Record Office, Exeter, Devon
The Director of Public Prosecution's Office, London
The Drummoyne Municipal Council, Drummoyne, New South Wales, Australia

The Edinburgh University Library, Edinburgh
The English Folk Dance and Song Society, London
The Essex County Record Office, Colchester, Essex
The Falmouth Public Library, Falmouth, Cornwall
The Falmouth School of Art, Falmouth, Cornwall
The Federal Archives and Records Center, East Point, Georgia
The Federal Archives, Washington, D.C.
The Fort Collins Museum, Fort Collins, Colorado
The Free Library of Philadelphia, Pennsylvania
The Guildhall Library (Lloyd's Insurance Records), London
The Hampshire Record Office, Winchester, Hampshire
The Hereford and Worcester Record Office, Hereford
The Historical Society of Pennsylvania, Philadelphia, Pennsylvania
Holloway Prison, London
The Home Office, London
The Humanities Research Center of the University of Texas, Austin, Texas
The Institution of Civil Engineers, London
The Institution of Mechanical Engineers, London
The Isle of Wight Steam Packet Company Ltd., of Southampton, Hampshire
The Kodak Museum, Wealdstone, Harrow, Middlesex
Lake's Falmouth Packet, Falmouth, Cornwall
The Library of the University of Sheffield, Sheffield, South Yorkshire
The Limerick City Library, Limerick, Eire
Lloyd's Shipping Information Service of London
Madame Tussaud's Ltd., of London
The Maine Historical Society, Bath, Maine
The Maine Maritime Museum, Bath, Maine
The Marine Society, London
The Maritime History Group of Memorial University, St. John's, Newfoundland
The Maryland Historical Study, Baltimore, Maryland
The Massachusetts Historical Society, Boston, Massachusetts
The Mercantile Marine Service Association, Wallasey, Merseyside, England
The Metropolitan Police Force Crime Museum, London
The Middle Temple Library, London
The Missions to Seamen, Southampton, Hampshire
The Mitchell Library of Sydney, Australia
The Nantucket Historical Association, Nantucket, Massachusetts
The National Archives and Records, Washington, D.C.
The National Maritime Museum, Greenwich, London
The National Union of Seamen, London
The Norwegian Maritime Museum of Oslo
The Norwegian State Archives, Oslo

The Old Gaffers' Association, Falashiels, Selkirkshire, Scotland
The Peninsular and Oriental Line, London
The Oslo Police Department, Oslo
The Portsmouth City Record Office, Portsmouth, Hampshire
The Quarantine Station of Sydney, Australia
The Rozelle Hospital, New South Wales, Australia
The Royal Archives, Windsor, Berkshire
The Royal Cornwall Polytechnic Society of Falmouth, Falmouth, Cornwall
The Royal Institution Museum of Truro, Truro, Cornwall
The Royal Ministry of Foreign Affairs, Oslo
The Royal Norwegian Archives, Oslo
The Royal Sydney Yacht Squadron, Sydney, Australia
The Sandefjord Maritime Museum, Sandefjord, Norway
The South Carolina Historical Society, Charleston, South Carolina
The Southampton City Record Office, Southampton, Hampshire
The Southampton Master Mariners Association, Southampton, Hampshire
The *Southern Evening Echo,* Southampton, Hampshire
The State Archives of Hamburg, Hamburg, West Germany
The Stavanger Maritime Museum, Stavanger, Norway
The Treasury Solicitor's Department, London
The Tudor House Museum, Southampton, Hampshire
The Union Castle Mail Steamship Co. Ltd. of London
The Waxworks Museum of Denver, Denver, Colorado
The West Virginia Historical Society, Charleston, West Virginia

Index